MT. ANGEL ABBEY

A Centennial History of the Benedictine Community and its Library

1882 - 1982

MT. ANGEL ABBEY

A Centennial History of the Benedictine Community and its Library 1882 - 1982

By Lawrence J. McCrank

SR Scholarly Resources Inc.
Wilmington, Delaware

First published 1983
Printed in the United States of America

Scholarly Resources Inc.
104 Greenhill Avenue
Wilmington, DE 19805

Library of Congress Cataloging in Publication Data

McCrank, Lawrence J.
Mt. Angel Abbey.

Bibliography: p.
Includes index.
1. Mt. Angel Abbey (Saint Benedict, Or.)
2. Mt. Angel Priory (Saint Benedict, Or.)
3. Mt. Angel Abbey (Saint Benedict, Or.). Library.
I. Title.
BX2525.S225M37 1983 255'.1'00979537 83-10536
ISBN 0-8420-2212-0

CONTENTS

PREFACE

In fall 1975 a colleague, Robert Pallatino, a calligrapher and member of the studio arts faculty at Reed College in Portland, Oregon, invited me to go to Mt. Angel Abbey to see some medieval manuscripts. He was planning a field trip for a class and knew about my interests through a mutual friend, Charles Holden, who shared our regard for monasticism. I was then teaching a specially dedicated course in Western mystical literature to the Trappist juniorate at Our Lady of Guadalupe Abbey in nearby Lafayette. Our planned visit coordinated with the field trip did not work out, but the invitation piqued my interest in Mt. Angel so that a separate visit was arranged. Expecting to see just a few leaves as exempla of medieval handwriting, I was surprised to discover a wealth of research materials, a jewel of a library, and rare books scattered about in boxes, crates, makeshift shelving, and on skids. The monks were in the process of cleaning out the abbey attic and old stack areas to move the rare books into the new library building. I browsed through the material and was intrigued by the possibility of working through an unprocessed cache of potentially unique, rare items. In that basic curiosity was born a project which lasted for nearly six years.

Although my work for Mt. Angel Abbey was at first merely an attempt to bring the rare books and manuscript codices under minimal bibliographic control, the project became more—a case study in cost-effective cataloguing procedures by using computers to aid research and verification work. In addition, the inquiry into the Mt. Angel library became for me a fascinating historical study about a little-known subject (one deserving more research on other houses): the continuing monastic tradition of library development in Western Civilization and its role in contemporary monasticism and spirituality. It soon became clear that the catalogue would be enhanced by a history of the Mt. Angel community and library, an analysis of the collection, and the reprinting of Sir Richard Southern's address at the dedication of the new building. In order to make the project more feasible and affordable, the format of the proposed book was divided into two: a history in paperback and the catalogue in microfiche.

During the half decade of part-time work on this, I made many friends and incurred several debts for which I must express my sincere gratitude. Not least among these were members of the Benedictine community who have invested valuable time and effort of their own in coming to my assistance. My thanks to the whole community for its traditional Benedictine hospitality is expressed especially to Abbot Anselm Galvin, who approved the project's inception, and Bonaventure Zerr, the current abbot whom I first met in his capacity of coordinating acquisitions for the library. Fr. Albert Bauman, publicity director, helped with prepublication promotion of the book and proofing of the narrative chapters. Fr. Luke Eberle likewise proofed portions of the history and provided valuable comments. The staff of the Mt. Angel library provided much needed service. Of all those who encouraged and supported me, I must especially thank Fr. Martin Pollard, OSB, Mt. Angel's rare book librarian, whose range of experience, breadth of learning, and boundless energy are truly amazing.

The Collins Foundation of Oregon initiated the project with a pilot grant and furthered its ultimate aims by giving Mt. Angel a second grant for the conservation and restoration of the rare books. Out of this came a small but necessary subvention for the inclusion of the photographs found between Parts I and II of this volume. The University of Maryland's College of Library and Information Services, where I then was Assistant Professor, provided funds for half-time graduate assistants for three years. Research and travel grants were also forthcoming from the UMCP Faculty Research Board and the University's Division of Human and Community Resources. My thanks to the staff of the UMCP Computer Center are detailed in the preface to the microfiche catalogue.

As an historian trained traditionally, but with added training in library and information science, I began this project as a neophyte in data processing and the design of an automated information storage and retrieval system. There were times of desperation when I felt that my novitiate would never end, and once I wished aloud that I could expand my second-area graduate degree, the MLS, into a Ph.D. in order to cope better with the problems I encountered. My wife, Ruth, retorted jokingly that any court in the land should accept the endurance of a husband getting a second doctorate as grounds for divorce! So the project also became my informal, non-degree educational program. Indeed, I fear that it was an ordeal no less demanding of her support, as I was seemingly forever on the computer terminal in our home, engrossed in piles of printout or archival documentation, or lost in my rare books and manuscripts. That our marriage endures is testimony to her tolerance and love. My daughters, Kirstin and Jaime, also deserve credit for their cooperation and understanding; as teenage girls, they made the ultimate sacrifice of letting me tie up our telephone lines for hours on end while talking to the University of Maryland's UNIVAC computer some twenty miles away.

Last, let me congratulate the Benedictines of Mt. Angel Abbey on the centennial celebrations. I hope that they find this a fitting contribution to their community's centenary, and that it helps them serve the larger community of scholars by making their history and valuable rare book and manuscript collections more available.

Lawrence J. McCrank, Head
Department of Rare Books and Special Collections
Indiana State University
June 1983

AUTHOR'S NOTE

The volume grew out of a project to catalogue the rare books and manuscripts of Mount Angel Abbey. Because of this origin, certain compromises were made between style and format common in cataloguing standards and those dictated by writing manuals and especially the house style of the publisher, namely *A Manual of Style*, 12th ed. (University of Chicago, 1972). Moreover, other changes were made to use computerized text processing to greater advantage than merely mechanizing a manual procedure. The *Manual* is for manual processing and does not accommodate either the creative capacity of computerized photocomposition or its limitations. Furthermore, certain conventions in such manuals contradict accepted usage and style in other contexts; in this case, the preference toward secular forms had to be altered to accommodate Catholic usage, especially in titles. Despite such compromises, internal consistency was an overriding goal.

Changes most notable are preferences toward standardized abbreviations. Abbreviated titles (Fr. for Father, Bp. for Bishop, Abp. for Archbishop, etc.) are most common, but Abbot spelled out is preferred to ABT in Part I, because of its confusion with the German 'Abt'. Likewise, symbols are used (% for example) in preference to spelling these out, since such conventions are used in condensation of data for cataloguing. Also, to avoid double references, citations for notes are placed within parentheses rather than suprascripted; these then are placed as close as possible to any text references to the document, rather than at the end of extended quotes. Numbers are usually given in figures rather than characters in order to utilize the global search abilities of computer processing.

The Rare Book and Manuscript Collection of the Mt. Angel Abbey Library: A Catalogue and Index is available on microfiche from Scholarly Resources Inc.

I.
MOUNT ANGEL ABBEY, 1882–1982: A CENTENNIAL HISTORY OF A BENEDICTINE COMMUNITY

Introduction: The Lineage

Mount Angel Abbey takes its Anglicized name from its motherhouse, Engelberg, in Switzerland, and is heir to a monastic tradition and lineage reaching back into medieval history to a point where folklore, mythology, and substantiated fact are indistinguishable. During the eighth century one of the famed Celtic wandering monks from Ireland, Saint Fintan, ventured to Rome on a pilgrimage which brought him into contact with the Benedictine reform emanating from Monte Cassino. He left Italy to return to the primitive north-central part of Europe where so many other insular missioners were engaged in evangelization and the foundation of monasteries as pockets of Christian culture amidst Germanic paganism. These foundations eventually played a crucial role in the cultural evolution of Europe; they were intimately associated with the Carolingian reform and the so-called twelfth-century Renaissance.

Fintan's part in this drama is less well known than the activities of some of his contemporaries. It is said in tradition that he carried with him a copy of the Rule of St. Benedict and a relic of St. Blasien from his sojourn in Italy. Around these and himself, he attracted a group of hermits who formed a nuclear monastic community which about 778 A.D. became Rheinau abbey in modern Switzerland. More than a century later, in 945, monks from this abbey founded another house in the Black Forest; it was dedicated to St. Blasien. In turn, a colony of monks from there in 1027 founded still another abbey, Muri; and monks from Muri subsequently founded Engelberg, the mother of Mt. Angel Abbey in the New World and which, in line, has had children of her own. Indeed, the lineage can be traced like the ancestral litanies of the Old Testament which tell who begot whom in memonic chant. Like all families, this monastic lineage passed along sets of customs and traditions which can be discerned in the monastic life of Mt. Angel Abbey and its associates in the American Swiss Congregation of Benedictines. Like all families, the current community takes pride in its genealogy and family history.

Engelberg's foundation dates by tradition to 1082 when Conrad von Seldenüren from Zurich decided to endow a monastic community with property along Lake Lucerne. It was not until 1120, however, that monks under Blessed Adelhelm from the abbey of Muri formed the first resident community, with Conrad as one of its confreres, and which was subsequently augmented by recruits from St. Blasien. Adelhelm served as prior from 1120 to 1124 when he was recognized as abbot by the Holy See. Pope Calixtus II took the newly constituted abbey under the protection of St. Peter on April 5, 1124, and shortly thereafter on December 28 of the same year, the emperor Henry V extended his royal protection to Engelberg. The settlement was not along the lake, but instead in an isolated valley under the shadow of Mt. Titlis, the highest peak in the central Alps. The reasons for the relocation are not documented, but rather than for reasons of natural defense, legend attributes the move to divine intervention. An angel supposedly warned Conrad to seek a more secluded site and when an exploration party reached a mountain empass at the end of a valley, it appeared again to direct the founder to a foothill which was appropriately called "Angel's Mountain". Hence the name Engelberg for this foundation and the famed white angel of Engelberg's shield which also appears on the town's coat-of-arms, the monastery's insignia, and a popular emblem sewn on the jackets of Alpine skiers to this day.

The history of Engelberg from the twelfth century onward is sporadically well documented, and at other times there are few extand records. No critical history of this important house has been written (1). The archives of Engelberg are intact, however, and therein the foundation of Mt. Angel Abbey is well documented (2). Likewise, in Engelberg's history are the traditions which influenced the American daughterhouse.

The first buildings at Engelberg were destroyed by fire in 1200. A larger complex was built thereafter, and this too was ravaged by fire in 1306. Fortunately much of its library and archives survived, bearing witness to the scriptorium which flourished there under Abbot Frowin of St. Blasien (1147-73); over forty manuscript codices exist from this early period of production. Likewise, the archival series which began after rebuilding in 1200, continue to the present. Local folk followed the monks to the highland valley, especially as the reputation of this monastery spread. A small village, today with a population of about 1500, grew in front of the abbey's main gate. In 1149 the monks established the parish of Engelberg and in the centuries afterward extended their seigneurial authority over both the village and the surrounding territory. The abbots ruled as the valley's temporal lords until 1789. Its territorial rights, extensive patronage system, work in education and scholarship, and development of an impressive physical complex, are remarkable given the relatively modest size of the abbey's community. Much of its land was leased or was held by tenants, and the monks concentrated their attention on parish and educational work while maintaining by themselves a farm of small proportion compared with their lands. The abbey underwent significant changes after the Reformation and in the era leading to the French Revolution, most notably in declining numbers of monks and restrictions on its former rights. Its lands were encroached upon; the village became more self-governing; and the abbey itself was partially destroyed in 1729 by a disastrous fire. Hence, the eighteenth century was largely one of restoration and conservation. The community thrived into the next century, but the monastery as a major corporation had diminished status and power in temporal affairs.

The nineteenth century, with its liberal and anticlerical revolutions following the Napoleonic settlements, was particularly disruptive for the Church throughout Europe. The secularization of welfare and educational institutions was especially chaotic, and monastic foundations left unscathed by the French Revolution and its aftermath, were in continuous jeopardy. The German south, predominantly Catholic, was also suspicious of the Prussian-instigated unification movement and the new state's attitude toward the Church with the rise of nationalism. Monasteries in particular faced the instability of both the rising national and declining local governments in constant fear of suppression beyond the preliminary restrictions on their enterprises and the expropriations of their properties. Such fear was the primary motive most often attributed to Engelberg's exploration of America for suitable sites in case the community were forced into exile. Although the Swiss government took no official stance against monasteries within their borders, largely because the religious preferences of the people were so mixed and balanced, those cantons which swung to the far left during an age of extreme political vacillation often confiscated church property in order to limit the traditional territorial rights of the larger houses. This was motivated partially by religious polarization, but also the necessity of forming a tax base for their own regimes. Moreover, the relative indifference of lay Catholics afforded monasteries little protection against the state. Consequently, the cantons began to secularize the school systems as well as appropriate coveted lands, thus curbing the educational activities of the Benedictines. Some liberal regimes suppressed a few monasteries totally, forcing their abandonment and closure, while others took more indirect measures to reduce the influence of religious institutions in the traditionally Catholic, German-speaking south from Austria through Bavaria and Switzerland. A civil war broke out on November 4, 1847. The Protestant majority led by Augustine Keller in the Federal Diet thereafter began repressive measures as anticlericalism became even more intense. Sankt Gallen, a landmark in Swiss cultural history, had been suppressed in 1805, as were the houses of Pfäiffers in 1836, Muri in 1841, Fischinger in 1848, Rheinau in 1861, and Maria Stein would be in 1874. The monks of Muri and Maria Stein fled and lived communally in exile, while others found shelter in neighboring houses as consolidation occurred. The monks of Muri sought refuge at Sarnen, but also took over an Augustinian priory at Gries in Tyrol.

Engelberg was, therefore, not without ample reason to seek alternatives to its deteriorating predicament when Abbot Anselm Villiger of Stans (d. 1901) assumed the abbatial office in 1866 (3). Moreover, the monastery's splendid isolation in an Alpine valley was being eroded, if not by government interference, then by the skiers and tourists who after the 1880s discovered the area's slopes, local scenery, and the hospitality of the villagers as Engelberg became a resort town. Nor was Engelberg alone in looking to the New World for a solution to its problems. The famous abbey of Maria Einsiedeln in 1854 had sent a colony of monks to America for similar reasons, largely for a home in exile; this resulted in the establishment of a famous daughterhouse, St. Meinrad's archabbey, after its educational activities in 1852 were severely restricted. Although Einsiedeln thereafter was inexplicably passive about St. Meinrad's welfare, except to protect its own interests and reputation, the motherhouse had ample reason to foster a home away from home, an asylum in case of dire need. Abbot Heinrich IV Schmid von Baar of Einsiedeln wrote of the bishop of Vincennes, Indiana, in 1854: "Ever since our first expedition our adversaries have uttered cries of alarm, saying that we wanted to remove our personnel and goods from our country in order to tranport them beyond the ocean" (4).

American churchmen, inheriting a tradition of both a secular and regular clergy, lacked the latter and were sympathetic to the continuance of Western monasticism. When the archbishop of Oregon, Charles J. Seghers, visited Rome in 1884 he made a pilgrimage to the premiere shrine of Benedictinism, the abbey of Monte Cassino which had just been confiscated by the new Italian government. On February 1 the prelate in an open letter to his flock expressed his feelings thus (5):

> ...that mountain, I need not tell you, is the cradle of the Benedictine order, and, as the world is becoming more and more prejudiced against monastic institutions, I resolved to give the good Fathers of Monte Cassino a tangible proof of the profound esteem I have for the 'Regular' portion of Christ's army, and of the earnestness with which I protest, as far as in my power, against the ingratitude Christian nations nowadays show to the monks.

Moreover, after 1850 German immigration to the United States was increasing. German workers were welcomed by American industry in preference to other immigrant labor, but rural German families were more interested in opportunities to own their own land and to continue farming in the West. German immigration to the United States increased dramatically after the Civil War; in 1866-67 the count at the New York immigration office alone skyrocketed from 50,000 to 117,500 in one year's time (6). In the 1870s German-American newspapers widely publicized land opportunities for Germans in the Old World as well as those having recently settled in the eastern and midwestern states (7). Because of the increasingly difficult political situation of German Catholics, after 1850 35% of German immigrants to America were Catholic. Moreover, many of these new German immigrants moved through German-settled areas along the eastern seaboard, predominantly Protestant as these areas were, and thereby extended the so-called German belt across the Midwest and from there to the Northwest via the Oregon trails leading out of Missouri (8). It was not accidental, therefore, that German-speaking monastic communities, indifferent if not adverse to nationalism and the growing rigidity of national boundaries, considered immigration as a possible solution to their problems at home. Both St. Vincent's archabbey in Latrobe, Pennsylvania, America's first Cassinese-Benedictine foundation, and St. Meinrad in Indiana, the earliest Swiss-Benedictine house, were partially motivated by the prevailing conditions in Europe. Colonization was a viable means of anticipating their worst fears. Another letter from Einsiedeln, dated June 12, 1873, offered further justification for concern (9):

> ...things have moved forward with frightening rapidity in our afflicted Europe, and particularly in Switzerland.... The outcry against the monasteries is becoming more violent. And it is no longer a matter of greed for the property of the monasteries that motivates these people. They are now determined to drive the Roman Church from Switzerland and they see in the monasteries a bulwark of strength for the Church. And what is more natural than that they should have our monastery especially in mind. What will the newly-elected government do? Unless God and the Blessed Mother protect us miraculously, they will certainly forbid the taking of novices, if indeed they do not decree, as everyone here fears, the complete suppression of the abbeys.

His confrere in America thought similarly, as indicated in correspondence back to Einsiedeln on June 30, 1873: "All around here [at St. Meinrad's]—and people say the same in New York—it is said that only a miracle can save the monasteries in Switzerland from suppression". The same monk wrote to Engelberg on September 3 of that year: "I feel as though a sword were suspended over the monasteries of Switzerland. Everything should be done to reach the heat of the people so that there, at least, we can find shelter when savage forces drive us from our homes" (10). Despite this critical situation and pervasive sense of urgency, the abbot of Einsiedeln was overly cautious, hesitant, and refused a total commitment to support an American foundation as a secure refuge outside of Switzerland. There was grave, emotional reluctance to contemplate leaving the homeland. Consequently, Einsiedeln's relationship with St. Meinrad's founders was undecided, fickle even, and not altogether rational. Whereas Metten Abbey and Boniface Wimmer deliberately founded a full-scale monastery at Latrobe, Abbot Heinrich IV of Einsiedeln had in mind a mission house of smaller scale, as an extension of the Swiss motherhouse rather than a true daughterhouse which could mature to full independence. The stature achieved by St. Meinrad in many ways was less the creation of Einsiedeln as of Abbot Martin Marty and historical circumstance rather than design.

In correspondence during 1881 between Engelbergians in the Old World and those sent to explore the New, came this observation from America (11):

> I do not know what the conditions are now in Europe. I see only from the papers that the [political] weather on the other side of the high mountaans [i.e., north of the Alps, or news from the other side of the Rockies] is not to be trusted. In the event that the worst should happen, the Swiss monasteries as well as those in other countries will be half or entirely ruined. Should this happen, what God forbids, I would know that for my confreres at least, at the present time, no better, no more acceptable and suitable location for a monastery exists than... [the American West, here referring specifically to a possible site in California].

These were the words of the founder of Mt. Angel Abbey.

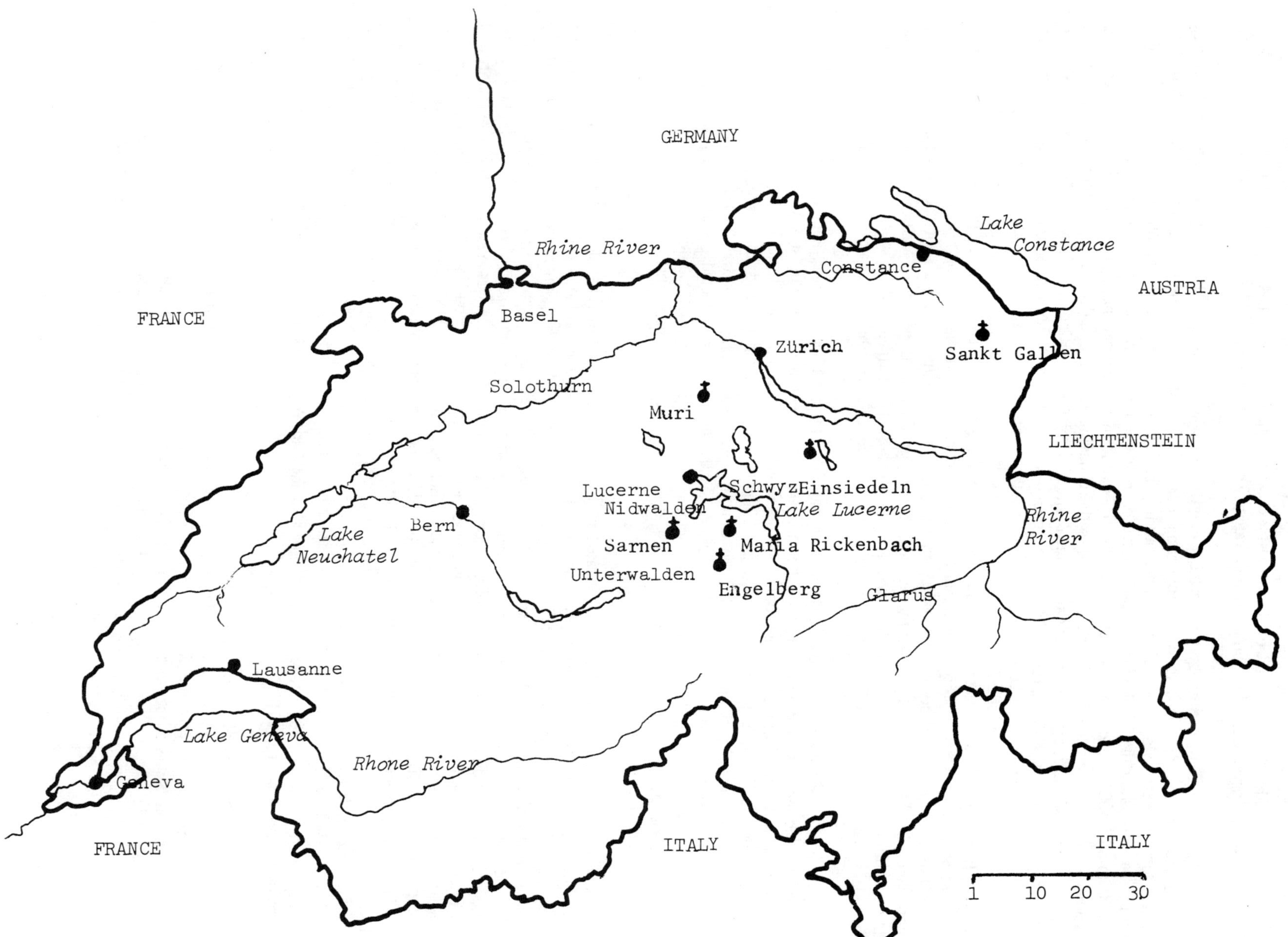

Fig. 1. Switzerland's cluster of Benedictine monasteries.

Antecedents and Precedents, 1865-80

Mt. Angel was not the first American foundation from Engelberg; rather the first colony settled in Missouri as part of the German movement West. North of the town of St. Joseph, in the northwestern corner of the state, the mission Church was just being organized into a diocese proper under the archiepiscopal jurisdiction of St. Louis. Catholicism in this area had not flourished before, except in the pockets of Irish settlement brought about by the recruitment of cheap labor from the East to build railroads. Catholicism was established more formally only with the wave of German Catholic immigrants after the Civil War. St. Joseph's first bishop, John J. Hogan, had earlier in his career as a frontier missionary been arrested in 1865 for daring to preach in public at Chillicothe, Missouri, only three years before his appointment in 1868 to the new see (12). Thereafter anti-Catholicism became lesss/public, certainly unofficial, except that Catholicism was associated still with the newcomers, Euroop's poor farmers and laborers who spoke broken English or none at all. Although the Catholic population was increasing significantly circa 1870, the clergy was not. The diocesan ordinary was desperate to attract religious to the area and thereby support his meager band of diocesan priests, many of whom still traveled from parish to parish as circuit preachers did a century before in the eastern states. The diocese may have became a canonical reality in 1868, but it took longer to turn the paperwork into social and cultural reality. When the prelate traveled to Europe to attend the Vatican Council of 1870, therefore, he eagerly publicized the central plains to be an opportune mission field.

One of Bp. Hogan's life-long associates, Rev. James Powers, had also entertained the notion of a religious foundation in northwestern Missouri, possible by the Cistercians from Mount Mallery Abbey in his native Ireland (13). This house had already in 1857 founded a priory, New Mallery, near Dubuque, Iowa. Because of the lasting effects of the 1845-46 potato famine, and the reception promised by many Irish in the American clergy, it was even contemplated transfering the entire community to the United States. In that case, if the priory became the abbey, a new priory might have been placed elsewhere. However, the White Monks declined Fr. Power's overtures and never left Ireland *en toto*. Consequently, later in 1865, Powers approached Abbot Boniface Wimmer of St. Vincent's abbey on the same subject. Apparently from later reports in 1874, the abbot responded positively enough, but the archbishop of St. Louis failed to take any initiative. The Benedictines themselves were unable to press the issue because of their own problems at home (14). Upon his return from Rome, Bp. Hogan continued similar tactics and pleaded with St. Meinrad for at least one or two extra men to care for those parishes whose members now were predominantly German-speaking immigrants. Some of his once Irish parishes were Germanized within only a couple of years, causing even more stress on his overtaxed Irish priests. At first the overture was to take on a parish such as that at Conception junction where Fr. Powers labored, but then on November 8, 1872, the prelate offered the abbot a 160-acre tract near St. Joseph and a house, together appraised at $50,000, which was promised to the diocese by a wealthy Irishman who had earned his fortune during the boom created by the railroad some years earlier. As the bishop explained, "I must get a religious community at once, or very soon, to further the pious intentions of the donors that greater good may be done" (15). The idea was to get a seminary started which could help the bishop with his shortage of trained manpower.

Abbot Martin Marty was slow to respond to this second overture, mainly because he too faced a shortage of trained religious, his own house was not entirely in order, and Einsiedeln was not forthcoming with the kind of support he expected and needed. Indeed, Abbot Marty had been ordered at one point by Einsiedeln to disband the American community if St. Meinrad could not survive on its own. Einsiedeln gambled on conditions in Europe improving, and ultimately got its prayed-for miracle; it was never suppressed (16). In any case, such delay meant that the opportunity was missed because the bishop soon thereafter gave the land to the Holy Cross Fathers of Notre Dame in South Bend, Indiana (17).

The overture did have indirect consequences, however, because Abbot Martin feverishly worked for St. Meinrad's independence despite criticism for departing from European norms, and he championed the cause of the Benedictine missionary work in America (18). When he learned that Abbot Anselm Villiger (1825-1901, elected in 1866) was seriously thinking about a New World foundation in case the worst should happen to Engelberg, he contacted an old classmate from Einsiedeln, Fr. Frowin Conrad, now a monk of Engelberg, and encouraged him to contemplate the prospect of an American foundation. Abbot Martin's letter of January 17, 1872, displays his zeal, in contrast to any thought of abandoning St. Meinrad (19):

> Benedictine monasteries are needed in America more than anywhere else in the world. But where will they come from? Who will found them... individuals and communities that do not multiply themselves are dead. Therefore we should press forward with a united effort....
>
> The simplest approach to such a foundation, it seems to me, would be for Engelberg to send one or two priests to St. Meinrad's as soon as possible so they might begin to familiarize themselves with the language, the country, the people, and the customs, and in the meantime they could be looking from there for a suitable place to make a foundation.

In November of that year, Abbot Martin informed Abbot Anselm about the option in St. Joseph, thinking that the property was still available. The latter, perhaps reacting to the turn of events like his colleague in Einsiedeln with a 'wait-and-see' attitude, on June 25, 1872, declined the offer. Thereafter Martin focused his attention on Fr. Frowin, who in turn convinced the abbot that the possibility should at least be explored (20):

> "It seems to me," wrote Martin again to Frowin, "that the monasteries of Europe are like a forest where the trees are so thick that they no longer have room to grow. If a few of them were to be weeded out, those remaining would have the light and air to expand and to grow to their full stature".

Marty thought Engelberg should send a scout to America, and specifically to St. Joseph. His third letter to Frowin of December 15, 1872, arrived at the opportune moment during another crisis in the unpredictable politics of the Swiss cantons. Fr. Frowin was able to convince the abbot to consider an American refuge, and the matter was presented to the chapter. Abbot Anselm commented about the St. Joseph option in his diary: "Since I have been thinking for a number of years about making a Benedictine foundation from Engelberg in America, this invitation is most welcome. I shall recommend it in the most favorable manner to the chapter for a decision (21)".

The chapter approved the venture and Frowin Conrad volunteered to undertake it. Fr. Frowin was a slight man, small frame and stature, who had been born on November 2, 1833 in Auu, Canton Aargau, in a family of twelve children (five of the eleven boys became priests, four of which were Benedictines). He had gone to a Jesuit gymnasium, had studied theology at Einsiedeln after his noviciate and then another six years at Engelberg. He became a professor in Engelberg's school, served as the pastor of Engelberg's village parish, and then became additionally spiritual director for the nuns of Maria Rickenbach (22). His travel companion, by Abbot Anselm's order, was to be Adelhelm Odermatt (1844-1920), the future founder of Mt. Angel (23). The latter was born on December 10, 1844 at Ennetmoos near Stans, Nidwalden, along Lake Lucerne. When he entered Engelberg on September 29, 1865, he changed his name from Karl to Adelhelm in memory of Engelberg's first abbot. He was ordained by Bp. Greith at the cathedral church of Sankt Gallen, and thereafter he taught as a professor at Engelberg and served with Frowin as the assistant pastor of the village's parish. Fr. Frowin had some reservations about his younger associate, but did not protest the abbot's decision. The two prepared for their journey, an adventure into unknown trials in the New World, knowing nothing about what they should expect except whatever had been conveyed in Abbot Martin's letters.

For reasons unknown, Abbot Martin was not informed about the chapter's positive decision until Frowin and Adelhelm on May 8, 1873, left for America. Even at Engelberg the mission was kept secret. Abbot Anselm's diary entry for April 27, 1873, attests that Engelberg's parishioners learned about the monks' departure only that Sunday during Frowin's last sermon: "We had to keep the project completely secret until the day of their departure" (24). Later Frowin remarked that, as at Einsiedeln before, the monks feared local officials who might react adversely if they suspected the abbey of transfering personnel and possessions abroad. He reflected one year later in his diary for September 3, 1873 (25):

> I feel as if a sword were suspended over all the monasteries of Switzerland. Everything should be done to reach the heart of the people so that there, at least, we can find shelter when savage forces drive us from our homes.

He, as did others, expected the eventual suppression of Engelberg Abbey, and of Einsiedeln as well.

The pair traveled with a student, Joseph Widmer (who became Brother Meinrad), to Havre where they boarded the ship *Ville de Paris* and embarked for New York. They arrived in the United States on May 20, 1873 (26). There, in a pattern now well set by monks traveling to American daughterhouses, they secured help with local arrangements from the Benziger brothers, the Catholic publishers. The three Engelbergians traveled to St. Vincent's in Latrobe where Abbot Boniface Wimmer waited to greet them, and then onward to St. Meinrad. Meanwhile, the latter's prior, Fr. Fintan Mundweiler, went to St. Joseph to arrange for a substitute for the now unavailable land near the town (27). There Fr. Powers helped by offering $1000 from his family's savings and by securing the deed to a 260-acre farm owned by one of his parishoners in Nodaway County, some fifty miles east of St. Joseph. The site was inspected by the prior, and was described to Abbot Martin as prime farmland with wooded creek beds, adequate water supply, and soft black loam soil over two feet deep which could be plowed easily (28). Adjacent prairie land could be purchased then for $5.00 per acre, and the more developed farmland was selling for $15-20 an acre. Fr. Fintan remained as temporary pastor at Weston while tending arrangements for the Engelbergians. As Fr. Adelhelm was to remark much later, in a letter of May 2, 1920 to Abbot Athanasius Schmitt, "Prior Fintan Mundweiller had warmed our nest in Conception and Maryville" (29). Fr. Powers suggested that the monks take over the parish as well, since he was near retirement. Meanwhile, Frowin and Adelhelm studied English at St. Meinrad's and were tutored by Abbot Martin himself in basic management, and Fr. Frowin was given some practical experience with parishes at Henryville and in Indianapolis.

Frowin Conrad recorded in his diary, which he continued until his death in 1923, the foundation of Conception Abbey; its early history has been studied in detail by Fr. Edward E. Malone, OSB, of Mt. Michael Abbey, whose account is largely followed here. Frowin's diary can be supplemented by that of Abbot Anselm in Engelberg's archives, and Conception Abbey's archives have remained intact far better than documentation for Mt. Angel. Frowin, Adelhelm, and a new candidate from Zug, Carl Henggeler, left Indiana on September 15, 1873, traveled to St. Louis, then onto St. Joseph to meet Bp. Hogan, and finally to the largest of the parishes in Nodaway County at Maryville (30). There a hundred Catholic families awaited their new pastors. Despite severe reservations about assuming extensive parish obligations, Frowin agreed out of a sense of obligation to the bishop, to assume for an indefinite time some of the parishes and mission work of the struggling diocese.

Conception was fourteen miles away from Maryville. Originally a small colony from Reading, Pennsylvania, it had now attracted enough settlers to boast of a population of about 500 souls. The Catholics there were served by a small chapel built immediately after the Civil War, and since then Fr. Powers had been pastor. The monks, who agreed to take over both parishes, built their priory adjacent to the Conception church in accord with the land grant and endowment from Fr. Powers. While construction was ongoing, the first novices were boarded at Maryville. The new wood frame building was blessed on December 8, 1873, but even this invocation of God's help seemed unable to speed the finishing work. Construction came to a halt during harvest season when nobody could spare time to volunteer labor for the building, and winter hampered further work. On Christmas 1873, ready or not, the small community gathered together for the fist time to recite the Divine Office in the new church (31). By the New Year of 1874, the monastery was functioning; it, like the parish before, was dedicated to the B.V. Mary of the Immaculate Conception, hence 'Conception' for short.

One reason for studying the early foundation of Conception Abbey is that the spread of the Benedictines westward was traumatic and problematic, characterized by discord rather than close harmony, and the new communities had some difficulty defining their own character in this American frontier. Obviously, the Old World Benedictines thought that they could merely extend themselves into the New World and duplicate their way of life, without due consideration of the hardships facing the colonists and the constraints of frontier living. Just as America was a satelite of Europe and part of Western Civilization, but with unique cultural patterns created by the new mix and the geographical disassociation from the homeland, the American Benedictine foundations, although part of the larger world of Christianity and Benedictine monasticism, still sought some individual identity of their own. Abbot Anselm, following the example set by Einsiedeln in regard to St. Meinrad, envisioned at first a mission house and was initially cautious about any commitment to a full-fledged monastic foundation. Frowin, appointed Conception's first superior, was influenced by Abbot Martin and began thinking in terms of a monastery with some autonomy, both by design and necessity. Despite his training at Engelberg and experience at St. Meinrad, his model was St. Martin of Beuron and its controversial reforms. Beuron, in addition to returning to more ascetical life styles, also avoided parish work except as a means to an end. Extended commitments to parishes, it was argued, eroded communal life. Fr. Adelhelm, on the other hand, despite his comparatively minor parish experience, thought like Abbot Martin that parish service to the German-speaking Catholics was natural, indeed a primary obligation of a monastery in the New World, in keeping with the intention of Mettin in founding St. Vincent's, the persuasion of St. Meinrad's abbot, and the example set by Engelberg. Two incompatible approaches to monastic life and Benedictinism were at play in the foundation of Conception. The only real common point of consensus in interpreting the Rule and developing a communal life style, was in regard to Conception's subservience to Engelberg. Yet Engelberg herself was not at first the mother for which one might have wished, largely bel se of the example of Einsiedeln. The first novices at Conception, who entered the community on December 31, 1873 and began their noviciate on January 1, 1874, were required to sign a rather stark, stringent agreement protecting the mother abbey from any legal or even moral obligations toward them, but nevertheless placing them under "loyalty and obedience" to Engelberg. The contract stipulates (32):

> 1. After having passed through the required period of probation the undersigned will be accepted as a member of the Benedictine monastery at Conception, and if he then conducts himself properly, he is assured of the necessary support and care by the monastery, *as long as the monastery itself is self-supporting, by the fruits of its own industry and the gifts which are given to it* [italics mine].
>
> 2. For this reason, the candidate so accepted promises by means of an oral promise or contract, loyalty and obedience to the monastery and makes the simple vows of a Religious which will bind him as long as the monastery exists and as long as he remains a member of that monastery.
>
> 3. After this agreement has been signed, the one so accepted may not leave the monastery of his own volition, but he may be dismissed by the incumbent superior, or may be sent away by him should the srsd cdidate prove disobedient, stubborn or immoral, or should he act in any way that might discredit the monastery.
>
> 4. But if the one thus accepted should become incapacitated through no fault of his own, either through sickness or bodily injury, then he cannot be dismissed for this reason alone; on the contrary, he will be in this case entitled to receive support and care from the monastery which was founded with his help.
>
> 5. *If the monastery because of unforeseen misfortune should cease to exist, or should no longer be able to support its members,* or should the said candidate be dismissed for any of the reasons mentioned above, *then it is expressly agreed that the one thus dismissed must consider the education, the board and lodging, the care and the clothing which he received while he was living in the monastery and until the time of his departure as full compensation for his work and he may not claim any further recompense.*
>
> 6. It is further stipulated that should such a candidate be promoted to Major Orders, this must be done only *sub titulo missionis* and with the previous consent of the diocesan bishop and under the condition that if the one so ordained should later on be dismissed by the supedior of the monastery, or if the monastery should cease to exist, the one so dismissed is to be considered suspended and is forbidden to say Mass, or to perform any other priestly functions, until such time as he has provided with a sufficient patrimony, according to the requirements of canon law.

This Latin document was signed on December 31, 1873; the novices thereby insured Engelberg protection against future claims should Conception fail, and if disbanded, it protected the monk-priests from being conscripted into diocesan service without due provision on the ordinary's part. The contract may seem harsh today, but was seen as necessary given the distance between the motherhouse and its daughter, when discipline could not be administered directly. It was modeled after the statutes of St. Meinrad as issued by Einsiedeln's abbot in 1853, and was in part motivated by troubles in Indiana when imprudent decisions were made about admitting unworthy candidates. Conception's novices thereafter, until 1881, signed another document attesting the paranoia of the motherhouse:

> The undersigned testify herewith that once having made the profession of religious vows in the monastery of the Immaculate Conception of the Blessed Virgin Mary, *they will never make any legal or material claims for support upon the motherhouse at Engelberg, Switzerland.*

Significantly, there is in the archival records no similar contractual statement of the motherhouse's obligations, nor is a reciprocal relationship defined in the *Instructions for the Superior of a Mission House to be Founded* which was disseminated via St. Meinrad's (33). The colonists therefore were taking more risk upon themselves than was the corporation they represented. It is natural therefore, that the American monks often resented interference from Europe and that they grew more independent than the motherhouses wanted. From the latter's perspective, they often were like rebellious children entering adolescence when autonomy is sought; as all parents know, such growth and development strains any familial relationship. This is generally what happened repeatedly in the relationships between the European abbeys and their American foundations. Before *de iure* independence was granted, *de facto* independence was a reality. Meanwhile a superior was always placed in the position of supplicant, asking for whatever resources the foundling needed. In this regard, Frowin learned quickly from Abbot Martin that if one had to beg, to do it well. Both administrators tended to prevail upon the abbot's generosity, and neither minimized requests. Perhaps they even asked for more than they expected to receive, like modern administrators who present idealized asking budgets, suppress a working budget for the absolute minimal for survival, and realistically expect to get something between these extremes. Despite these stringent measures, Engelberg was coaxed by its daughterhouse into the role of a caring mother, moreso than Einsiedeln ever was with St. Meinrad; and by the time Mt. Angel was founded, she was even more relaxed and liberal, and Engelberg supported the latter at considerable expense even to her own welfare. In a very significant way, the trial of raising the first child, which may have been too strict, made the second child's life easier as the parent relaxed with the tasks and expenses of good upbringing. Mt. Angel, therefore, received attention and consideration not previously shown to Conception, nor known to the monks at St. Meinrad.

Soon after the monastic settlement at Conception, plans were made to bring a contingent of Benedictine sisters to Missouri to complement the work of the fathers, especially by developing an undergraduate academy modeled after the German gymnasium as a support to the seminary which the monks were expected to develop. It was natural for Prior Frowin to turn to his consuors at Maria Rickenbach where he had served as spiritual director. Maria Rickenbach was a relatively new foundation, not really well enough established to provide for a mission house on the American prairies. Its history went back only to 1853 when two nuns, Gertrude Leupi from Wikon in Canton Lucerne, and Vincentia Gretner (d. 1862) of Cham in Canton Zug, formed a Society of Divine Providence to care for children orphaned by the Sonderbund War, and to introduce the rite of Perpetual Adoration at a popular shrine site dedicated to the Virgin—hence, Maria Rickenbach (34). In forming their splinter community from the mainstream of Swiss Benedictinism, they secured the help, spiritual and material, of the then Prior Anselm Villiger of Engelberg who continued helping them as abbot. The two houses have maintained close ties ever since.

The convent was organized in 1862 when its first buildings were finished on August 28. The small community began to flourish with the help of several neighboring religious houses, but the general political situation which threatened well-established monasteries like Einsiedeln and Engelberg must have seemed even more fearsome to a fledgling foundation. The sisters, therefore, shared the same motivation of Abbot Anselm in considering an American foundation. They thus reacted positively to a request in 1873 from Prior Frowin for a satelite community to open a school in Maryville where the prior assured them that "they would win the love of both Catholics and Protestants...". (35). Mother Gertrude responded immediately, and on January 16, 1874, Frowin learned the good news and that Anselm hoped to send two more priests as well. The nuns came, the additional men from Engelberg did not (36).

The sisters were accompanied by George Keel, a business associate of the Benziger Publishing house, who had to go to New York. They traveled the usual route from Zurich to Havre, to New York, then alone to St. Meinrad's, onto St. Louis, St. Joseph, and finally on September 5, 1874 arrived at Maryville. They were joined by a Benedictine nun from Immaculate Conception convent in Ferdinand IN, who could help with their English. The nuns were placed under the governance of Mother Anselma Felber, OSB, and were carefully chosen for their stamina and health, in ages from 23 to 35, and because of skills they possessed such as teaching, needlework, dressmaking, and cooking. They had to adjust to their new life on the prairie which was in stark contrast to their old home. Sister Beatrix Rengli, who recorded the trip in a journal, remarked silently to herself: "...the place is exposed to every wind that blows. ...the winter proper has not yet begun. Still, I have already come closer to freezing to death here than I ever did in the depth of winter at Maria Rickenbach" (37).

The nuns moved into the rectory with Fr. Adelhelm, who was described by them as a "little thin man". This cohabitational arrangement, necessary until a convent proper could be built, was a matter of no little concern to Fr. Frowin who dreaded some sort of scandal. It took a year to get the school started; indeed, it took that long for the sisters to learn enough English to do so, and for two of them to earn their Missouri state teaching certificates. On Wednesday, September 1, 1875, the school opened its doors to all children, Catholic and non-Catholic "who possessed good morals" for the nominal tuition of $1.00/month in advance (38). Later that fall two of the nuns were transferred from Maryville to Conception to open a second school. Still later, in 1879, they took over another, the so-called "Wild Cat" school or St. Mary's, and began an orphanage which was finally transferred to the diocese at St. Joseph. They also established a women's academy for higher education which ran until 1934. Moreover, their teaching activities were drawn to the Dakotas where they worked with the Indian missions. Colonies of nuns established an independent convent at Jonesboro, Arkansas, and in 1908 they began a far-flung mission at Chewelah, Washington state, which was ultimately closed in 1928 (39). The willingness of these nuns to support the Catholic education system in the western states became well-known, so that it was not long before they were asked to help the church in the Oregon territory.

The monks at Conception secured initial help from Bp. Hogan and Fr. Powers. The core estate of 260 acres had a 20-acre addition by purchase, but the monastery was put on firm financial footing only when an original settler, Joseph Clever, sold his farm to the Benedictines for $5.00. He did this in return for an old-age pension of $500 a year for himself and his wife, or $300 a year for one of them alone, guaranteed by the monastery. Such an arrangement appears similar to the medieval confraternal system which provided for old-age or "social security". Thereafter other donations or similar token sales allowed the monks to expand their farming activity and develop income sources through lease arrangements. Four of the wealthiest landowners in the area each gave 80 acres, and Nicholas Felix "sold" his 560-acre farm for $1.00. Additional land was bought for $5-6/acre, so that by 1879 Conception owned more than 1807 acres! The monastic estate was to grow beyond the 2000 acre mark by the turn of the century (40). At the same time that the monastic farm was being developed, the construction of a permanent monastery was undertaken; its cornerstone was laid on May 13, 1879 (41). Thereafter Frowin moved the site slightly off Clever's land to the present location. A new cornerstone was laid on April 6, 1880, and the first wing of the new monastery was blessed on June 11, 1881 by Bp. Hogan. The foundation looked secure.

It was when the monastery was beginning to feel assured of its stability that, after the initial developmental and collegial phase, problems began to appear as a standardized monastic life was being refined. There were, of course, the ever-present human issues of compatibility and personality, but also more serious philosophical notions about the character of Conception. The sisters had as many such difficulties as the fathers, but the problems always seemed, at least to the prior, to coalesce around Fr. Adelhelm and his circle at Maryville in opposition to Frowin's administration at Conception. The situation was described as follows by the historian of Conception Abbey, Fr. Malone (42):

> Here at the very beginning of these foundations may be discerned the divergence of personalities, aims and objectives which was to have a profound effect on the development not only of Conception Abbey but also to result in the founding of Mount Angel Abbey, th Congregation of Perpetual Adoration, and the Congregation of St. Gertrude. First of all, it soon became evident in the handling of the Sisters from Switzerland that the personalities of Fr. Frowin and Fr. Adelhelm were almost exactly opposites. Fr. Frowin, as he is described both by those who knew him at Engelberg and at Conception, was a firm, ascetical man, severe with himself even more than he was with others, business-like and determined to keep power centralized in his own hands. He was,... not primarily a missionary but rather a monastic founder completely dedicated to the ideal of creating a monastic institution fashioned after the model of Beuron. Fr. Adelhelm was almost diametrically opposed to Fr. Frowin in all these things. In his manner he was vivacious, energetic, restless and possessed of an overpowering drive for the care of the German Catholics who had come to America and whom he felt were suffering great spiritual neglect. He had a pixie-like sense of humor and, above all, had little sympathy with the introduction of a Beuronese type of monasticism at Conception in preference to the traditions and customs of Engelberg.

Malone adds:

> Fr. Adelhelm's letters to Maria Rickenbach form quite a contrast to Fr. Frowin. Fr. Frowin's are always grave, serious and deeply spiritual. Adelhelm's, while always deeply respectful, sparkle with sly sallies and he cajoles the Sisters with a boylike enthusiasm that makes his letters a living expression of his colorful personality. He assures Mother Gertrude that she need not worry about whether she learns to speak French and English well since the Holy Spirit understands both languages, and of course still understands German!

After what Malone calls a period of collegiality until 1875, the rift between the two monks turned into an insurmountable chasm. There is no evidence that the two men ever formed a close working relationship, say nothing of genuine friendship. Moreover, from 1874 onward, Adelhelm was involved more with his pastoral work at Maryville than with the establishment of Conception priory, and he extended his services voluntarily outside Maryville to surrounding villages in northwestern Missouri. While at Maryville, the monk-pastor earned a reputation for extraordinary zeal and energy, ability to make friends even among the non-Catholics, dedication and perseverance. Bp. Hogan remarked later that in seven years Adelhelm converted one of the worst parishes in the archdiocese into one of the best, and the mother-superior of St. Gertrude's convent could not but help admire him, and to note how the parishioners adopted him as "our" Fr. Adelhelm (43). That admiration was not always shared by Prior Frowin, partially because from his perspective Conception priory subsidized the Maryville parish too much. Nevertheless, when Adelhelm informed Frowin that he would not join Conception, the latter regarded the message as "sad news" but not a surprise. He expected as much by then, and did not press the issue. It is not clear, however, that the prior understood just how strongly Adelhelm felt about the kind of communal life which was developing at Conception. As early as September 17, 1876, Adelhelm told Abbot Anselm, as recorded in the latter's diary, "I feel more at home in this sin-and-vice ridden city [Maryville] than I do at Conception" (44). That statement, of course, can be read two ways; either it reflects poorly on Adelhelm who had grown too accustomed to his secular position so as to feel comfortable with sin and vice, or it maligns Frowin for developing a communal lifestyle no better than secular society.

The "bitterness" as Frowin himself refers to the friction between the two monks from then until 1880 when greater distance between them would heal some of the wounds from this period. Their problems were exacerbated by the arrival of two other personalities from the Old World in 1875 (45). Frater Othmar was from St. Boniface in Munich who had spent two years at Beuron, but who did not share Frowin's enthusiasm for the latter house. The other was Frowin's own brother, Fr. Ignatius from Einsiedeln, recruited after Abbot Anselm failed to send the two additional priests promised in 1874. Othmar was disliked by Frowin from the onset, both for his open distaste of Beuron but also criticism of Placidus Wolter, the abbot of Maredsous and former mentor of Frowin at Beuron. Frowin came under the latter's influence during his stopover in 1873, and thereafter he deferred to his Beuronese confreres on numerous occasions for detailed advice (46). In 1888, when reflecting retrospectively on his interpretation of monastic life and Abbot Maurus Wolter, the brother of Placidus, he admitted to the latter (47):

> I have had nothing but the most profound veneration for your monastery [Beuron]. There I believed I had discovered for the first time the meaning of Benedictinism; and when I was sent by my abbot to make a foundation in the New World, Beuron became my ideal. If that ideal has fallen far short of the mark here [at Conception], I would attribute this to my own deficiencies.... Beuron can be justly said to be the boast and the hope of our holy order.

Such a leaning toward the strict reform-orientation of Beuron seemed to many like a betrayal of Engelberg. Fr. Ignatius sided with Adelhelm in his condemnation of Frowin's leadership in defining Conception's corporate personality. That was an unexpected blow to Frowin who then reacted even more adversely toward Adelhelm for undue influence over his brother and in turn, being uncritical in accepting the influence of Othmar. Frowin thought that Abbot Anselm had given him clear authority to maneuver as he saw fit, even though the latter had wanted him to retain "as much as possible from Engelberg's usages" (48). When reports reached Anselm that Conception was not turning into a "New Engelberg" as anticipated, the Abbot began slowly to tighten control over Frowin. That too worsened the situation at Conception, because he felt that Adelhelm and others were back-biting in reporting directly to Abbot Anselm. However, so long as Adelhelm remained subject to Engelberg directly, there was little Frowin could do about it. In fact, Adelhelm's correspondence to his abbot was privileged and private, and Frowin was never informed precisely what charges were made. Abbot Anselm's diary and the extant letters reveal that Adelhelm's complaints went beyond the general to the very specific, and that with reports from Ignatius, there was a crescendo of complaints building into the impression that something was radically wrong at Conception. The first complaint appears in Anselm's diary entry for April 15, 1875, where Adelhelm's words are paraphrased (49):

> ...the prior at Conception is altogether too niggardly with regard to food and allows it to be cooked only in water without proper stock and seasoning. He meddles too much in the kitchen affairs and even regulates minutely how much butter the Brothers use. The Fathers and Brothers, all of whom must study and work hard and who are also burdened with heavy manual labor in the fields, need and deserve a much better fare. He should not be so eager to copy Beuron and should rather stick to the customs of Engelberg.

As such complaints begin to mount, Abbot Anselm began to urge Frowin to follow Engelberg's customs more and more imitatively, and finally applied the maximum pressure of threatening deposition of the prior. Even to this day, Adelhelm is suspected by the monks of Conception Abbey of having been disloyal to Frowin, if not outrightly disobedient (50). He was certainly thought of as a ring leader by Frowin, operating sort of a Fifth-column movement within the community which threatened its unity and harmony, and Frowin's own reflections in his diary suggest that the prior assumed that Adelhelm would have his job if the abbot did decide on a change of administration for Conception.

The dissensions within the community were forced to a crisis point by Abbot Anselm who for three years tolerated deviations by Frowin from the norm of Engelberg practices, but who could no longer ignore the complaints of Adelhelm, Ignatius and Othmar. At home there was an adverse reaction to Beuron as well, as Ignatius had earlier informed Frowin. Moreover, another Engelbergian, Nicholas Frey, now joined the opposition to Frowin's reform-mindedness. Finally, in reaction to a long description of Conception and its problems by Fr. Ignatius, which is paraphrased in the abbot's diary in over 3000 words, Anselm reflected upon the reasons for this internal chaos when outwardly things were going well for the foundation. Either God was testing the young community, or "the hand of Satan" was active there setting "one man against the other to strangle every good seed as soon as it is planted or at least to hamper its growth" (51). Or, there was insufficient self-sacrifice and humility in the venture. In accord with the latter speculation, Abbot Anselm provided his own lesson in humility in a scourging letter of November 8, 1876 to Prior Frowin which has been described as a veritable "bomb" (52). He ordered the wholescale remodeling of monastic life at Conception in compliance with the standards and practices at Engelberg, specifically the eradication of influence from both Beuron and St. Meinrad. He scolded (53):

> ...I was firmly convinced that you were going there [to America] to found a new Engelberg—new in spirit, holy and edifying in its customs and practices.... I had hopes that the mother abbey would be revived and rejuvenated by the accomplishments of her daughterhouse...
>
> You need not have been ashamed of Engelberg, an abbey which has been under the special protection of the Queen of the Angels for over 800 years. Under that unmistakable and undeniable protection, Engelberg has withstood the ravages of the centuries, the storms and vicissitudes of the times. Like a fragile ship she has been safely guided through the reefs and breakers.

Then he lashed out at Beuron, describing the customs of this house as "affected, untried and Frenchy, and which have no reputable past or tradition!" Or again, the Beuronese customs are condemned as inappropriate, "because their whole system is so vague, immature, fluctuating, changeable, and contrary to the oldest and most venerated traditions of the Order". He expressly forbade following the Beuronese constitution, and added: "If you do not do that [observe the Swiss Benedictine Congregation's constitution] I shall replace you as Prior with Fr. Adelhelm".

The connection between this letter and Adelhelm's complaints, not only the last letter of Ignatius, is undeniable since the abbot even paraphrased some of Adelhelm's words in order to make his case against Frowin. The abbot protected Ignatius from any recrimmination from Frowin by giving the former a free hand as pastor of Conception, and Frowin was ordered to direct all of his attention to the internal affairs of the monastery. Frowin nearly resigned because of this strong reprimand. His diary shows that he was hurt emotionally, frustrated, and thought that he had been misrepresented to the abbot. In true humility, he had the abbot's letter read aloud to the chapter for all to hear, and he announced simply that Conception would comply; he began then instituting the required changes by singing the Office according to the Swiss usage adopted from Sankt Gallen. Fr. Malone adroitly summarized the situation (54): "Abbot Anselm and the chapter at Engelberg wanted a 'New Engelberg' in America and... Frowin wanted 'Another Beuron in America', [but] what resulted was neither of these, but rather a rejuvenated Engelberg based on vigorous but tempered reforms of Abbot Maurus Wolter".

The counterreform at Conception priory might have ended all internal problems had the personalities involved been more compatible and less forceful. Damage had been done to the monks' sense of community. One possible solution was to allow a split and to formalize what had already occurred by making a second foundation. Frowinnontemplated this option.

> This evening the thought came to me that this might be a hint on the part of God that I ask the abbot to allow me to withdraw and seek a new place for a foundation. Fr. Adelhelm could very well take my place here. Then I could begin a new foundation with full freedom to introduce what I feel would be best of the order. ...may this cross which has been sent to me be my salvation...

He had thought similarly earlier, but that Adelhelm might be asked to move on and make a new foundation. Abbot Anselm's diary for August 1, 1875, relates that Adelhelm knew about such a possibility, since it quotes part of a letter from the latter: "...but young upstart that I am, I do not feel qualified to found a monastery. But if it should ever happen that in holy obedience I should be called upon to make such a foundation, I would found nothing but a 'New Engelberg'" (56). Indeed, Prior Frowin thought that Adelhelm had already founded a quasi-autonomous mixed community at Maryville, working there as he did with Fr. Ignatius and as the dominant influence over the Benedictine sisters. The mother-superior of St. Gertrude's wrote to Anselm that Adelhelm made twice the number of converts as did the cathedral church at St. Joseph, and was unsparing in her praise (57). Yet, Frowin's diary reveals no jealousy over this, but simply concern and realization that the community could not forever have two leaders. Sooner or later, one of them would have to leave; if Frowin were to step down, he would leave; if he remained the superior, Adelhelm would have to leave by choice or under orders.

From 1876 to 1878 the situation at Conception remained an uneasy truce and one of Adelhelm's deference to Frowin's authority as prior, but the underlying antagonism had not really been solved with Fr. Frowin's conformity to Abbot Anselm's directives. Fr. Ignatius in May 1878 left Maryville for St. Joseph to become pastor of its cathedral, mainly at Bp. Hogan's request. Ignatius was subsequently in 1892 chosen to lead the new community at New Subiaco priory and was eventually elected its abbot; he remained there until his death. Fr. Frowin kept his office as prior and

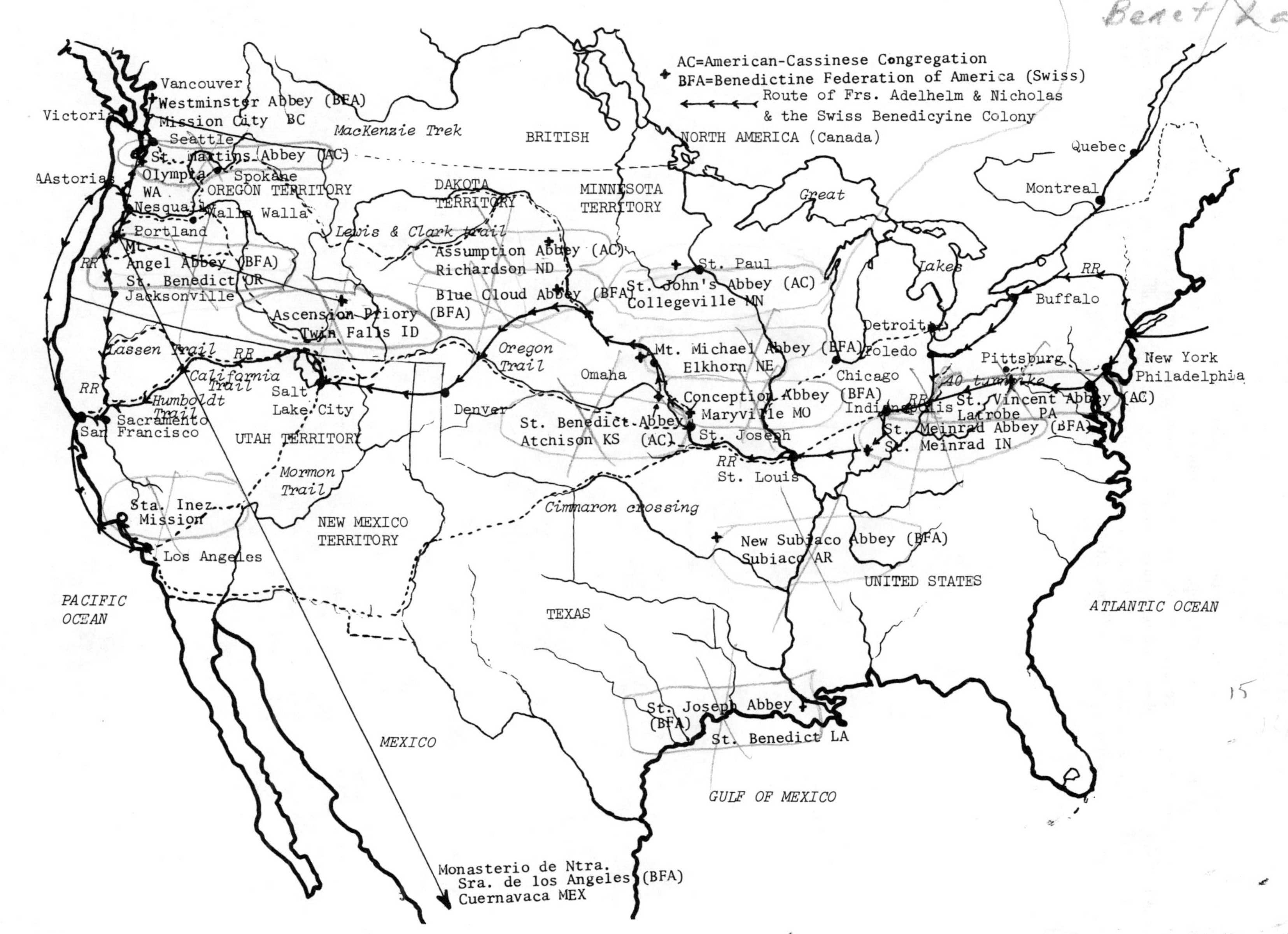

Fig. 2. The Swiss-Benedictines in America, 1854-1882 and after. Note the routes traveled by Frs. Adelehelm & Nicholas in 1882 and the relations between houses.

worked for abbatial status for Conception. Papal approval for the noviciate was accorded on April 30, 1876, and Bp. Hogan backed Frowin's efforts for Conception's independence. Abbot Anselm's interfffrence in November 1876 would, no doubt, have encouraged Frowin to seek autonomy for his house. Nevertheless, he proceeded cautiously in order to get Engelberg's cooperation. In a letter of December 1, 1876, Abbot Anselm in a conciliatory frame of mind restored Frowin's sphere of authority and descretion in adopting whatever "you consider most useful for an American monastery.... (58)". Consequently, the abbot approved Bp. Hogan's petition of August 2, 1878 to Pope Leo XIII to recognize Conception as an independent abbey. The Sacred Congregation approved the petition and renamed the foundation to "New Engelberg Abbey" at Conception, Missouri (59). The act was official on April 15, 1881. So long as he lived, Frowin Conrad continued to serve as an extention of Engelberg's authority in the Swiss-American Congregation, and to promote the spread of Benedictinism to the West Coast.

The Foundation, 1880-82

During the summer of 1880 Adelhelm must have written to Abbot Anselm of Engelberg requesting permission to explore the feasibility of still another foundation in America. Later that year, on November 27, Abbot Frowin wrote to Abbot Anselm alluding to previous correspondence, Adelhelm's disaffection with New Engelberg and desire to "make another beginning," and requested Engelberg's reaction and possible funding for exploring another site (60). The same letter reports that one of Adelhelm's colleagues from Engelberg, Fr. Nicholas Frey (b. 1841), was equally dissatisfied with the situation at Conceepion, even though other missioners from Switzerland were at the same time transferring their stability to their new home (61). Fr. Nicholas during 1880 had expressed his discontent directly to his superior, and provided ample reason when describing his lodging at Maryville where "the wind would whistle around the bed all night, leaving ice instead of water in the wash basin". On April 5, 1881, he was critical not only of the long, severe winters, but also of the extremes in temperature to intense summer heat and poor water (62).

Adelhelm apparently considered Maryville as a plausible site, where his parishoners offered a base of support up to $800 a year in pledges, but this was really too close to Conception Abbey (63). Abbot Frowin was displeased with Adelhelm's correspondence to Engelberg, perhaps mistrusting the latter's motives and because of sensitivity that criticism of Conception put his own administration in bad light. At first he would not sanction an attempt to found a second daughterhouse (64):

> I am glad if Engelberg is successful in anything Fr. Adelhelm starts, but the time for a new foundation has not yet come. Maryville is too close to Conception. You would blame me later if I recommended it. In the wealthy East it might work if two institutions were in the same neighborhood, but not in the destitute West since in America monasteries have no endowment. The charge has been made against us that we are even too close to Atchison [St. Benedict's, a Cassinese Benedictine foundation], although we are in another State, another diocese, and some 60 miles away. At best, Maryville might become a priory dependent on Conception.

Fr. Adelhelm, of course, as Frowin reminded Abbot Anselm, was not under Conception's discipline but Engelberg's. Abbot Anselm, who had recommended Adelhelm to Bp. Hogan, was responsive to the idea of another house, but the bishop was reserved about the plausibility of a second foundation in his diocese (65). He was unsure about any split which might hamper the development of a seminary for the diocese. Moreover, he was unsure of Adelhelm's intentions and authority to act without Frowin's approval. The American bishops had not had that much experience in dealing with the regular clergy. Consequently he inquired of Frowin:

> Now it is proper and very necessary for me to ask if this proceeding of Fr. Adelhelm's is according to obedience, and if it has your sanction and the sanction of the Abbot of Engelberg; as otherwise I do not think that I would be governing my diocese according to God's Holy Will by permitting the disintegration of a religious order, the scattered members of which, as not having a blessing from God, could not bless anything or keep themselves in holiness.

> As this is a grave matter and requiring prudence, I forbid you to name it to anyone else except to the abbot of Engelberg whom I require you to consult. If Fr. Adelhelm is to go, it will be edifying for all to know that he goes to open another house where it is needed for the honor and glory of God, the good of religion, through obedience to his superiors, and with the approval of the bishop.

In this letter of November 27, 1880, as related by Abbot Frowin in correspondence of December 17, 1880, the prelate asked that he be advised about such negotiations and any issues "especially when your rights or interests are concerned" in support of his commitment to Conception Abbey, which would be compromised in the case of a second monastery in his jurisdiction. Moreover, he seems to have rebuked Adelhelm in one instance, according to Abbot Frowin, saying "Maryville is out of the question. P. Adelhelm should first pay his debts there" (66).

Fr. Adelhelm could be very persuasive and personally charming. No doubt he was very convincing when he expressed his attachment to Engelberg and his desire to found a true New Engelberg or "einem haus nach Engelbergschnitt," as a refuge in America if not for the Swiss monks themselves, at least for their ideals and customs (67). Abbot Anselm's diary entry for July 23, 1881, confirms that Adelhelm earlier, in a letter of January 11, 1881, had been commissioned to look for a second site (68):

> Following receipt of this information (that Conception had been made an independent abbey), I learned that on the opinion of the bishop, Fr. Adelhelm will probably not become a member. I have therefore written to the bishop of St. Joseph just recently that I would recommend that Fr. Adelhelm and Fr. Nicholas make a new foundation.

Frowin remained skeptical about such an undertaking, and in particular of Adelhelm's ability to direct it or to make such a foundation genuinely monastic (69);

> Today I celebrated in the Cathedral of St. Joseph with the assistance of the Rt. Rev. Bp. and my brothers, a requiem with the office for the repose of the soul of our departed mother. On this occasion I consulted with the Rt. Rev. Bp., as well as with Fr. Adelehlm and Fr. Nikolas about their refusal to join us, togethhe with the reasons for it and the consequences. Both of these Fathers are religious subjects of the abbot of Engelberg. As pastors they are subjects of the bishop, to whom Fr. Adelhelm has submitted a report in writing.... They no longer have any connection with Conception except that I have allowed them to have Fr. Anselm as an assistant.
>
> Fr. Adelhelm has allowed his worldly spirit to grow and he no longer even wears the capuche. This division among us has not made a good impression on the bishop. This whole affair has caused me great grief, but it all came about without my knowledge. I do not believe that if the bishop were in possession of the facts he would have so easily given permission for this private enterprise. But unfortunately, a decision has been reached with giving me time to make my views known. My talks with Fr. Nicholas have convinced me that our views of religious life are so far apart that we could never agree. Fr. Adelhelm, it seems to me, paints too rosy a picture of the prospects for a new foundation.

Before April 5 Adelhelm was already soliciting funds for an exploratory journey west, and despite reservations Abbot Frowin on May 11 agreed to let Adelhelm have any surplus parish revenues which might be collected (70). Why this support and decision to extend themselves further? Fr. Nicholas in a letter of August 15, 1881 to Abbot Anselm explains, as does subsequent correspondence from Adelhelm, that foremost in their minds was the continued fear that Ennglberg's entire community would soon be exiled to the New World. The situation at Conception must have seemed very foreign to Abbot Anselm and his Swiss confreres; Missouri was never described in his diary or in the ongoing correspondence as an ideal home away from home. It is doubtful that Anselm ever sanctioned the second foundation for its own sake or for Engelberg's good, but rather to bring about a resolution to the disquiet at Conception Abbey.

The search for an alternative site beyond Missouri was already far flung by spring 1881, since these frontier monks were then referring to an offer of land for a possible monastery in California, described later as an opportunity which Engelberg should not "let slip out of its hands" (71). While considering other sites than in Missouri, Adelhelm's attention was also drawn to Oregon by letters from a homesteader, a Mr. Olwell, who had been a parishoner at Maryville and who had followed the Oregon Trail to resettle at Central Point near Jacksonville in the highlands between the California and Oregon valley lands. Olwell's descriptions of Oregon led Adelhelm to describe it, sight unseen, in a letter of January 26, 1881 to Abbot Anselm, as "a sort of Paradise, if one can speak of such a thing on earth".

Both the Pacific Northwest and parts of California were relatively primitive and unsettled at this time, and available land was still a viable lure for westward expansion of the American populace. Dr. John McLaughlin's mill town at the Willamette Falls, Oregon City, was further upstream than where after 1846 the most intensive settlement had occurred. After 1849 when territorial status became official, Oregon underwent extensive colonization, mainly along the Columbia and Willamette rivers. The latter valley was just being cleared, allowing for better farmsteads away from the river's flood plain. In 1850 the Oregon territory had only 13,294 inhabitants, but the census of 1860 recorded a spectacular increase to 52,465 and within another decade Oregon after statehood (1859) would swell to 90,923 residents (72). The first Catholics in the mid-valley were fur traders rather than farmers, mainly associated with the Hudson Bay Company's operations out of its factory at Fort Vancouver on the Columbia River. Portland was a growing town, but the first significant settlement had been at Oregon City where portage had to be made around the Willamette Falls in order to go upstream, south into the fertile and rich valley. The settlements along the Willamette River from Oregon City southward were known collectively as French Prairie, extending south as far as modern Salem. In contrast to the latter name, which denotes a New England Protestant settlement, the main French settlements were at St. Louis, St. Paul (1845), and Champoeg (or Newellsville) (73). Salem was a boom town of 1139 by 1870. Marion County in 1850 had 2749 people, 7088 in 1860, and 9965 in 1870; it was still very rural, but the area around Salem itself was being populated rapidly by native-born Americans, mostly from New England. In 1870 only a tenth of Marion County was settled by foreign immigrants. Of the 916 "foreigners" counted in that census, there were 193 German, 37 French, 27 Chinese, and 19 Swiss. The French-German-Swiss Catholic families lived mostly in the northern reaches of the county, in the farmland of the so-called Salem Plains, an extension of the French Prairie, or in the foothills of the Cascades. Separating them from Salem was swampland called various names, most frequently Lake Labish. The first Catholic church was a crude log cabin built in 1836 at St. Paul, but the first Mass was not celebrated there until 1838 with the arrival of missionaries from Montreal, Francis Norbert Blanchet and his cohort, Modeste Dimers. At the former's instigation, the Holy See prematurely created the archdiocese of Oregon on July 24, 1846 with Blanchet as the first archbishop (until 1880). He brought in 21 missionaries from Europe and began to develop the Church, but the territory was vast; the metropolitanate stretched from the Rockies to the coast, from the northern California boundary to yet undefined boundaries to the north (the 49th parallel was not recognized as an ecclesiastical boundary until much later). Because of the enormous territory, there was always a shortage of Catholic secular clergy. After 1862 when Abp. Blanchet moved the episcopal residence to Portland (the see was officially transferred only in 1928) from Oregon City, the prelate tried on several occasions to entice missionary and religious orders to come to the Pacific Northwest.

The retired archbishop on January 12, 1881 at the instigation of Fr. Brouillier wrote to Abbot Edelbroch of St. John's Abbey in Minnesota to secure help from the Benedictines for the missions throughout Washington and Oregon. The Catholics had tried to establish a missionary diocese in the eastern foothills with a see at Walla Walla, but this attempt failed and in the wake of the Whitman massacre there, the Catholic effort was concentrated south in Oregon. The Catholics also ran schools in the foothills of the Cascades in the valley and along the coastal range. One of these was at Grand Ronde reservation in western Oregon (as distinct from the Umatilla Reservation on the Grande Ronde River in northeastern Oregon). The Jesuits from Spokane dominated the Catholic mission work in the Great Columbia basin and Oregon desert east of the mountains. At Grand Ronde in the west was an Indian school, but there was continued difficulty in staffing it. The Minnesota Benedictines had already undertaken mission work with the Dakota Sioux and Chippewa, and the Swiss Benedictines from Conception and St. Gertrudes would serve in the South Dakota Indian missions as well (74). As a result of Blanchet's appeal to St. Johns for teachers, on April 7, 1881 prioress Scholastica and four Benedictine nuns from Mount St. Joseph's convent in Crookston, Minnesota (along the Pembina ox cart trails going north along the Red River Valley to Canada), undertook an exploratory journey to the Oregon archdiocese. They were met by Blanchet's younger successor, Abp. Charles John Seghers (1880-84), and a fellow priest, who on horseback accompanied the wagon carrying the sisters into the wild highlands of the Grand Ronde. The party then returned to Portland, and the nuns ultimately agreed to take over the Indian school. Abp. Seghers later returned to scout the land adjacent to the Indian reservation for an appropriate site for a Benedictine monastery to provide backup for the nuns' mission. He apparently also contacted St. Vincent's Archabbey in Pennsylvania as well as St. John's to stimulate interest in his mission field.

While this was transpiring, overtures were also extended to the Swiss Benedictines at Conception Abbey. A letter of Fr. Nicholas to Abbot Anselm on May 15, 1881, infers that in exploring an alternative to Conception Abbey, he and Fr. Adelhelm had already been in contact with the archbishop of Oregon. Whomever, Blanchet or Seghers, the prelate had promised the monks their choice of sites within his jurisdiction, but apparently said nothing about the ongoing negotiations with the Cassinese Benedictines. This overture, coupled with Mr. Olwell's descriptions and the almost mythographical legend spreading about Oregon, aroused the monks interest in the far West more than just exploring the adjacent states.

Fr. Adelhelm planned to depart May 24, 1881 on the trek westward, but by the time of their departure, their itinerary was far from a direct route. Fr. Malone reacted thus to their reports (75):

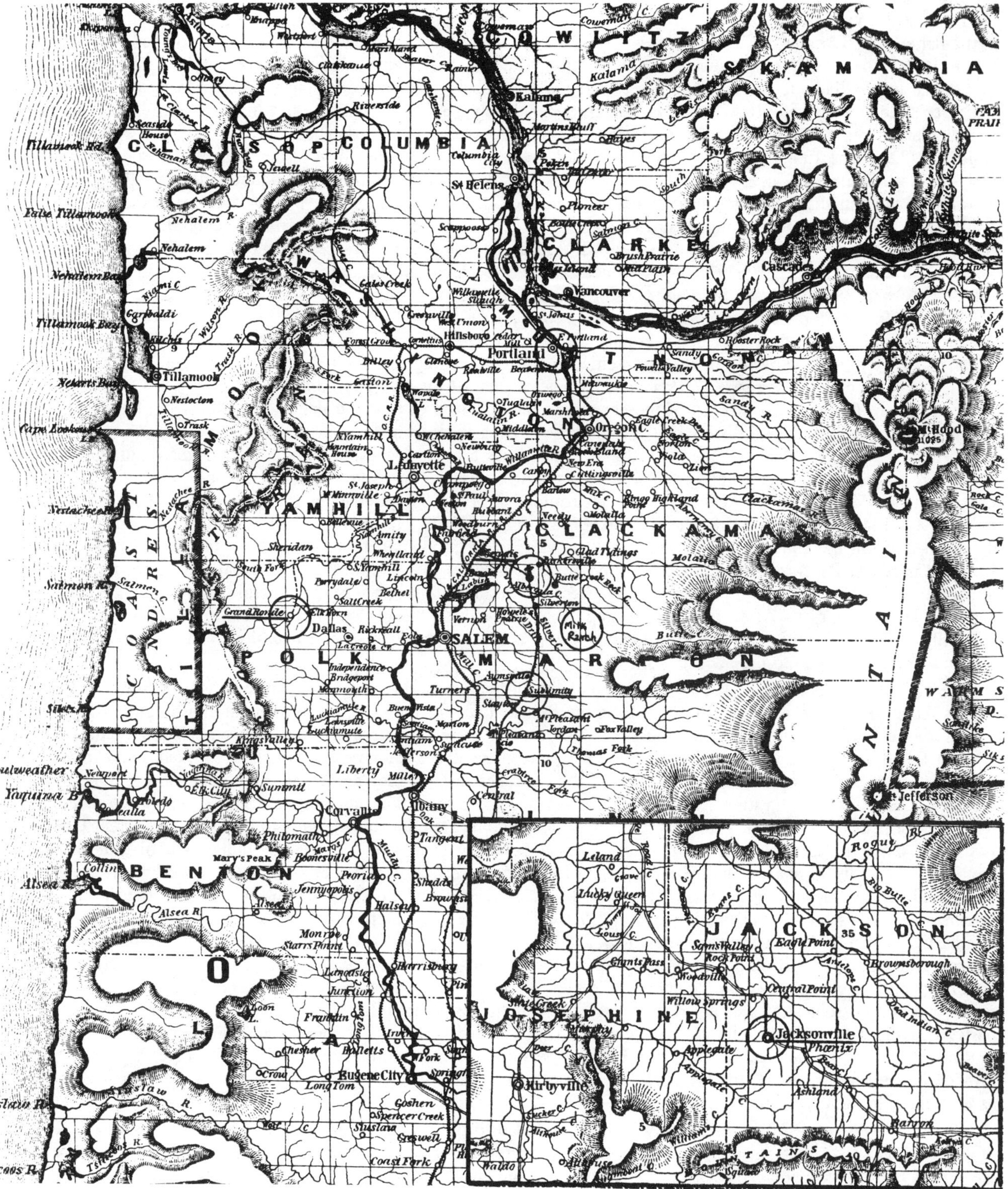

Fig. 3. The Willamette Valley, Oregon, 1878-1886. Note the location of Mt. Angel at Fillmore OR, its first parishes, the Milk Ranch, and the importance of the second north-south railway. Insert: Jacksonville OR in the south. J.K. Gill Map. Co., Ptld. OR, 1878; courtesy of Library of Congress Geography & Map Div.

> Both Fr. Adelhelm and Fr. Nicholas left detailed accounts of their experiences during their search for a location for a new foundation. Fr. Adelhelm's bears the stamp of his colorful and complex personality. He manages to give the impression of a mild ecclesiastical boomer, but at the same time the deep dedication and inexhaustible energy of the dedicated missionary are clearly discernible. He is always enthusiastic Swiss and the nostalgic Engelberger. Mountains attract him, especially if they havve¡a few proper glaciers as did those he saw in Colorado—barren mountains without grass or timber are not really proper mountains at all for any self-respecting Swiss. There is always a bit of the land speculator in Fr. Adelhelm, a trait that was to reach alarming proportions later on in his life. Although he is doubtful about the usefulness of the land offered him in California as a suitable place for a foundation, he kennels this offer safely in the back of his mind for future reference. This land, he thinks, ought to be obtained, perhaps as an endowment for the foundation he plans to make somewhere or possibly as an endowment for Engelberg. Throughout the report there runs a visionary optimism, half-serious, half-facetious, but never any doubt as to the eventual success of the venture he was undertaking.

Their trip deserves detailed description. It was, after all, an exploratory venture. On June 1 the pair left their confreres at Conception Abbey and, after a rousing sendoff from Maryville on June 4, Fathers Adelhelm and Nicholas "shook the Missouri dust from their shoes," left Missouri and traveled to Omaha, Nebraska. They were apparently supplied not by Conception Abbey, but by the Maryville parish. Indeed, Fr. Frowin remarked in his diary that after their departure, the assistant and now new pastor, Fr. Anselm, had to come to the abbey to get the vestments and altar pieces he needed to celebrate Pentecost. "Fr. Adelhelm seems to have left very little behind, but then perhaps he will need these things (76). Once in Omaha the pair stayed with Bp. James O'Connor (1885-90), who tried to persuade them to try Montana with its "valleys even more beautiful than those in Switzerland...," if a suitable site were not identified on the West Coast (77). From there they traveled north into the Dakotas where they met briefly with Abbot Fintan Mundweiller of St. Meinrad's, and his predecessor Abbot Martin Marty who after 1879 was the Apostolic Vicar for the Dakota territory. They were inspecting the mission schools maintained by the Benedictines for the Plain's Indians, especially among the Sioux in that bleak period of their history following the legendary but singular triumph in 1876 at the Little Big Horn. Afterwards the Engelbergians journied to Denver, Colorado, to pursue an earlier invitation (alluded to by Frowin in his letter of December 17, 1880 to Anselm) from its bishop, Joseph P. Machebeuf. Denver, as Adelhelm described it, was "a tastefully built city which cannot be matched in elegance by the cities of the East" (78). The climate is pleasant and the city is framed by a spectacular range of mountains, and here and there a glacier can be seen! But they are mountains of barren rock and for the most part there is no timber; and unfortunately most of the valleys are not suitable for farming... much too high for farmers or students (79). He obviously never envisioned his monks as cowboys! The stay there was unfruitful. Abbot Anselm had written an introduction for Adelhelm and Nicholas on February 17, 1881, but the distance and poor mail system allowed too much time to lapse; the bishop had gone to Rome without knowing about the arrival of the monks (80). Colorado had been envisioned as delightful for its mountains, but upon inspection the monks thought it too harsh for wheat farming which Adelhelm thought was the surest way for a Benedictine foundation to become self-supporting. In a letter of August 15, 1881, Adelhelm explained his reaction (81):

> In Colorado where Fr. Nicholas and myself at your wish and that of Bp. Machebeuf. ...looked around, I saw very little to attract us. The country through which the train carried us looks dry and sandy, and sparsly populated. The Bp. had not yet returned from his trip to Europe, being absent for more than a year. The poor man is not bedded on roses we are told. The Vicar General seems to be a person with whom one is glad to have nothing to do.

According to Abbot Anselm's diary, the pair "investigated Colorado from one end to the other," but in addition to the land itself, the monks were put off by their experience in Denver (82). After their disappointing encounter with the bishop's vicar general, an ex-Trappist whom Adelhelm thought "could not stand the smell of religious," the Swiss monks went on to Utah, Nevada, and ultimately California. By now Adelhelm wanted to have a look at all possible sites. His never-ending enthusiasm is depicted in such remarks as "The future of this country lies in the West". And again, on leaving Colorado, "we had better go west—to paradise" (83).

These monk-scouts traveled next to Pueblo, then Salt Lake City where the Mormons offered little encouragement for a Catholic monastery, and through Nevada toward Adelhelm's real goal, California (84). "It took us 36 hours to pass through this wilderness,...". he said, referring to Utah and Nevada. Adelhelm had a mixed reaction to his first glimpse of California; it was not what he had envisioned (85).

> To the travelor coming down from the Sierra-Nevada, California gives an odd impression. In

> winter everything is green with flowers everywhere, while in summer the mountains and valleys, with trees excepted, look yellow and scorched by the heat. Yet, it is claimed that on this soil are raised the best wheat and the best fruits in all of the union.

In reaction to Sacramento, he exclaimed: "It is a beautiful city with a marvelous climate and a majestic setting—but it is hot in the summer, and vice versa. Very much like Missouri...".

> It is not without reason that California is called a paradise. It is a most fruitful land in every sense of the word. Farther inland the climate is even better since near the coast there is much humidity and fog. Toward the evening and whenever one is exposed to the wind, one can comfortably stand an overcoat even on the warmest days. But we hardy Swiss get along very well without one, and we prefer this crisp weather to the heat which prevails almost everywhere else. And we are convinced that all good Engelbergers could easily adjust to this climate. It is consistently mild without any extremes. And farther south in Santa Barbara the weather is even milder and more consistent, and this the year around,...

The monks were drawn to California by Abp. Alemany of San Francisco who had a 36,000 acre federal grant in the Santa Inéz Valley in Santa Barbara County. It was subsequently described by Adelhelm as a 16 x 4 mile spread between Sta. Inéz and San Rafael, inland about fifteen miles from the ocean. Two-fifths of the grant were shared with the diocese of Monterey-Los Angeles, but a portion of the northern three-fifths was tentatively offered to the Benedictines if they could supply two fathers and three or four brothers "who would have to teach the Indians how to work..., [then] they could do well there" (86). Unfortunately observed Adelhelm, "the archibishop himself is stingier with his land" than Bp. Mora would be (87). After Adelhelm and Nicholas left Sacramento and visited San Francisco, they were sent to inspect the land itself, some 35 miles north of Santa Barbara. There was already a Christian Brothers "college" there, isolated and poor, which was really more of an orphanage. Abp. Alemany had brought the Brothers to San Francisco and Oakland in the 1870s. The Santa Inéz mission had been entrusted to the McMahan brothers, Justin and Bettelin, in the summer of 1879. They cared for about 30 boys from the city and provided the Christian Brothers from St. Mary's College with a summer retreat site. Adelhelm misunderstood their situation entirely in calling the mission a college. It has been described by historians of the Christian Brothers more accurately as merely an "inexpensive boarding school" (88). Adelhelm unjustly ridiculed its "sacred halls" and described it as nothing more than a shack filled with forty unruly youngsters: "the exterior of these young gentlemen is about as attractive as that of a lazzerome [a Neapolitan bum!]; one is dirtier and more ragged than the other" (89). In his letter of August 15, 1881, he explained further:

> You can understand such a condition, when you consider that between the college and the next shoemaker or tailor there lie forty English miles. Such conditions, naturally, are not making the work of the school brothers attractive, the more so, because it is not in their line of business to do farm work.

Adelhelm knew little about the Christian Brothers' pioneer work in the Napa Valley! Whatever their motives for abandoning the mission school, the Brothers did show the monks most of the valley. The school itself was obviously not what the prelate had in mind for his rural flock; nor did it impress the monks. Adelhelm's impression of the land itself, was more positive. In a letter sometimes misattributed to Nicholas, Adelhelm provided a detailed description to Abbot Anselm (90). Apart from his impression that the college was "the most miserable of its kind I have ever seen," the land was described as being as good as that owned by Engelberg. In further high praise, Nicholas had told the abbot that the land held good promise for farming and orchards, and that he personally liked the ocean breeze which "makes the evenings cooler and fresher than is the case even in Engelberg". Coincidentally, the diocese being developed there by Los Angeles was called *mons angelorum* or Mountain of the Angels, which Adelhelm took to mean Engelberg rather than anything to do with the Spanish nomenclature of California. Bp. Marty had also remarked earlier in his letter of introduction to Abp. Alemany that the prelates would consequently realize that by providence the monks belonged there (91). In any case, Abbot Anselm's diary may actually have been recalling Adelhelm's impression, since the latter wrote about seeing "luxurient wheatfields, places where grapes, oranges, apples, and pears are successfully cultivated,... [and] springs, wells supplying plentiful water," in apparent contradiction to his derogatory remarks about the Christian Brothers' shortcomings as farmers. He also recalled visiting the ruins of an old Franciscan mission house which still had its church standing: "In the right hands, it could be restored to a nice church". He concluded, "I believe living here [written later from Oregon] that, as the Christian Brothers told us, we would find nowhere a healthier place, and I still have this belief at this hour of writing [August 15, 1881]" (92). In self-contradiction, he later alluded to his "misgivings" about the Sta. Inéz Valley which might "prove groundless". He was certainly impressed with the valley's isolation, since he repeated the image of how far away were the nearest shoemakers and tailors! Yet Adelhelm had assurance that such isolation would not remain if this site were chosen for a Benedictine monastery. "A few families already declared," he informed Abbot Anselm, "their intention to settle near us. A flour mill owner wants to come to our place to have for his children the chance of obtaining a religious education. The same man promised to donate $1000 towards the establishment". The prospects were indeed enticing.

In order to secure land in the Sta. Inéz valley, consent was needed from Bp. Francis Mora of Los Angeles. Communications were hardly effective; the Benedictine scouts traveled to Los Angeles to discuss the matter personally, only to discover that he too was in Rome. They enjoyed the hospitality of the Spanish vicar-general there, and jokingly remarked to Abbot Anselm in subsequent correspondence: "Such courteous bowing never has been given to us anyplace,or by anybody!" Adelhelm wrote to the bishop urging him to visit Abbot Anselm in Engelberg and to discuss the deal directly with his superior, and at the same time Nicholas wrote to the abbot preparing him for the possible visit. The latter advised Anselm about how much the Spanish-American churchmen loved music and that old-fashioned Benedictine hospitality for the prelate should include a concert or two: "The Spaniards here in this country value music very highly, so pile on the music when the Bp. comes. For each beautiful piece he hears in Engelberg, he will certainly add another acre to his land donation" (93). Adelhelm knew too well: "It will all depend on the bishops, on the terms with which they invite us, and the places and the help which they promise to give us". Anselm could not try this tactic, however, since the bishop was never entertained at Engelberg.

Nothing came of this flirtation with the California prelates, despite prolonged negotiations. Abp. Alemany decided against making a grant to the Order from only the San Francisco shares. Apparently the diocese was planning to sell large sections of the land grant for prices ranging from $3 to $9.00 per acre in order to reduce the central administration's debt which stood, so Adelhelm overheard, at $300,000 or as he reckoned, about 1.5 million francs. The archbishop controlled only 21,600 acres directly, so that even at the highest price, the sale could not liquidate this debt. He may not, therefore, have been able to offer the Benedictines a very sizable tract, or if they were seriously interested perhaps hoped that the Order would be a possible buyer. In any case, he was prepared to match Bp. Mora's offer, if only that offer were known. Adelhelm speculated that even if their monastery were not built there, that they could retain whatever grant were forthcoming. He and Nicholas estimated that a 640-acre grant of good farmland could yield a harvest then valued at $8-10,000 a year. Consequently, the land was worth keeping as an investment if not for the immediate foundation. Moreover, Fr. Nicholas was impressed especially with the California prospect to develop great potential in the future. He was worried about the summer aridity, and apparently neither realized the irrigation potential of the Sta. Inéz River. Yet, they hoped for a sizable tract as a gift, without the necessity of purchase, and if Bp. Mora came through with a donation the two monks speculated that the total estate could be as large as 1000 acres (94). While waiting for word from Los Angeles, Abp. Alemany rethought the situation and asked that the Benedictines themselves act as his brokers; that is, he would provide a nuclear estate as a gift, and the monks would devest the rest of the land for the prelate while earning a commission for their services which would in turn let them buy additional land to augment the donation. Adelhelm did not like the idea; he referred to it as "a string attached to his offer," but he identified a Swiss-German from Baden near Aargau who was already working in the bishop's service as a land agent. In case a donation came through and the monks did not want to enter into the real estate business, which they assuredly did not, he would agree to act as the broker for a 5% commission. Hence Adelhelm had an arrangement in mind should the monks have had to act as salesmen in order to get their land. In any case, the affair suddenly became complicated (according to Fr. Nicholas, at the instigation of the bishop's chancellor) and a bargain could not be struck immediately without Bp. Mora's presence, so meanwhile Adelhelm decided that there was time to investigate the invitation from the archbishop of Oregon (95).

The two monks left San Francisco on July 26 aboard the steamer Columbia and arrived in Portland on August 3, 1881. They found Abp. Seghers busy with preparations for a forthcoming diocesan synod, swamped by demands of new Catholic families coming into the Willamette Valley, and still very interested in a Benedictine foundation in Oregon (96). He had so few parish clergy that he asked the monks to temporarily relieve the pastor of Jacksonville, the influential Francis X. Blanchet, so that the latter could attend the synod to be convened on August 10. The favor, coaxed the archbishop, would be an ideal way to explore western Oregon. So they left Portland on August 5 by train as far as Roseburg, and then by stagecoach to Jacksonville where they arrived late, on August 14. Fr. Nicholas vividly described the experience and travel conditions in Oregon at the time (97):

> Half the way we could travel by train, then for 19 hours we were packed into a clumsy, extremely massive mail coach with six horses; we began the craziest trip I have ever made. The feelings that are aroused in one's backside by this reckless speeding up hill and down dale may, of course, not be described here! Sometimes one actually had to protect one's skull from being crushed, a fate which my new straw hat did not escape!

Despite the hardships of travel, the trip south through the Willamette Valley was, as the archbishop argued, valuable for surveying the countryside. As their diaries and accounts attest, the Swiss monks were favorably impressed with the snowcapped Cascade mountain range, the forested terrain, and the way the valley was protected as well to the west by the coastal range. After coming from California, they were especially impressed by the greenery, those "magnificent forests and abundance of fruit trees such as I have never yet found anywhere else". Their destination, however, was above the valley in the highlands separating California from Oregon, between the Willamette and Sacramento River watersheds. Jacksonville lay in the Rogue River country, which Adelhelm called variously the "Spitzbuben flusstal," and the "Schelmenfluss" or "Schelmenflussthal". It was tucked into a small valley which reminded the monks of home much more than did the semi-arid hills of California. According to the census of 1870, Jackson County had 3721 people, of whom 1582 were native born. Of the 1057 "foreigners" or immigrants, the largest number were Chinese, but there were also 144 German families and 25 from Switzerland.

They found Jacksonville "situated in an extraordinarily fertile and really beautiful valley.... The Catholics and even the Protestants there showed us more than a little joy at our arrival, and they are continuously urging us to respond to the valley's deeply felt need for a Catholic school for boys". Fr. Nicholas continued his report to Abbot Anselm, that four nuns were already working with the girls, and that one parishioner offered the monks $200 and others pledged $500 contributions, if they chose to settle there. Thus Nicholas concluded, "I believe that we would easily be in a position to buy a fine big piece of property with house and barn, and would not have to worry about firewood and provisions, for both are available in abundance" (98). The total pledged came to nearly $2000, and the monks had time in Jacksonville to become acquainted with the townspeople, so they felt comfortable about settling there. Moreover, they were struck by the real need for religious to do parish and education work in this frontier. "What a great field of activity is given to religious communities in America, you know already," Adelhelm wrote to Anselm. "You could not wish for a nicer and larger field of activity for a new foundation". He continued, remembering that Mass attendance at the cathedral of San Francisco was only about 200 families: "Here in Jacksonville, the baptized Catholic Germans alone could fill the church, but only four come to church. Of the thirty French Catholics, not even three of them attend Sunday services" (99). Not only were they welcome there, but their work was clearly visible.

Six weeks later Adelhelm's trip back through the Willamette Valley made him realize that there was a host of other viable sites in the region. In a letter of October 19, which echoed his companion's earlier complaints about traveling "in a miserable carriage speeding up and down," and lauded the railroad service in the valley itself, he reflected on Jacksonville's isolation which seemed as remote, if not moreso, than the Sta. Inéz Valley was. The latter at least had mail and supply service from the ocean, but the white water of the Rogue River afforded Jacksonville no communications until such time that Oregon and California could be linked by an overland railway. Everyone hoped that time would be soon, but the time was not predictable given the difficulties and expense of constructing a highland passage.

In a letter of October 30, 1881 Adelhelm had high praise for the Willamette Valley itself; his only complaint, now that the summer dry season had passed, was how often it rained! "[It] is a charming big valley. Only it rains there in winter even more than in Jacksonville; people say, often a week long, night and day, so that some call the valley a 'frog pond.' However, that does not permit a missionary zealous for souls to be discouraged". Again at the request of the archbishop, he agreed to visit the village of Fillmore to celebrate Sunday Mass for twelve German-American Catholic families which had settled there sometime after 1849 when the area was opened by two Minnesotan Germans, a banker and a real estate agent (100). The monks found there "good hearted people who offer everything to get us [to stay]". Their host, a Swabian settler named Mathias Butsch, took him to the top of a nearby old volcanic cone from which Adelhelm could look over the Willamette Valley to the west and to the east "Howell's prairie" stretching to the Cascade foothills. It was a 400-foot butte which Adelhelm underestimated at 200 to 300 feet "with a magnificent view" with a vista of nearly a hundred miles to the north where the top of Mt. St. Helens could be seen, and with a closer panorama stretching south of majestic Mt. Hood (101). This was an old Abiqua Indian site called *Tap-a-lam-a-ho* meaning "the Mount of Communion" or more descriptively the "dwelling place of the Heavenly Spirit," which the white settlers less ceremoniously called Lone Butte Hill or Graves' Butte (102). The summit not only had some strange rock outcroppings from its formation, but also several semicircles of stones arranged to form seats for prayer-circles. Later Adelhelm inquired about their significance and was told that a land surveyor who explored the butte in 1859 likewise had his curiosity piqued; the latter inquired among the area's surviving Indians and was told that the Indians often traversed the valley north and south along the Abiqua creek which cut through Howell's prairie not too far from the outcropping. They would climb the butte to meditate and be one with nature, since to them it was hallowed ground (103). At the time of his first visit, however, Adelhelm did not realize that this sanctuary would one day be reconsecrated as a Benedictine abbey (104). Others later maintained that he made up his mind there upon the spot.

The immediate correspondence, however, reveals less about Adelhelm's interest in anthropology or Indian mythology, and more about his practical concerns. Apparently while viewing the valley, he discussed the possibility of the Benedictines coming to Fillmore. In retelling his conversation with Mr. Butsch to Abbot Anselm, he focused on the prospect of acquiring "some 320 acres of good and also poorer land, pasture, and some timber" (105).

Fig. 4. Scott's Mills, Marion Co. OR, in the 1870s, near Grave's Butte. Engraving by J.F. Whiting, land ownership survey of 1870; courtesy of the Library of Congress Geography & Map Div.

> We told the people that if they could get the five parties who own the hill (all Yankees) to donate the land to us, we would possibly start something. One of them, whom I asked, showed himself willing as regards his part.

Adelhelm thus was immediately interested in the site, although it was not immediately in reach. Instead, Adelhelm was encouraged by the German settlers to consider a more practical site near the village of Sublimity, Oregon, where on November 1, 1881, he celebrated Mass for forty to fifty families who had not seen a priest since the previous Easter. They promised him their new two-story schoolhouse for a starter, plus twenty acres of land which they all contributed to endow their rural parish. Sublimity, like Fillmore according to Adelhelm, was a viable site because it was only three miles from the railroad, and it was on high ground "so these areas are not under water as the valley generally is". This small town had been founded in 1849 by Johann Brohn and German-speaking settlers from the prairie states. Sublimity's population in 1870 stood at 726, of whom only eleven were foreigners. However, nearly all the newcomers thereafter were German-speaking immigrants from the German Belt, so that the area underwent a significant change. One settlement was even called Little Switzerland and others were "New" towns named after the old. Certainly the ability of the settlers at Sublimity to raise $2000 for their school, which they hoped would be staffed by Benedictine sisters recruited by the archbishop, was most encouraging. Matters were complicated, however, because the townsmen at Fillmore promised $2000 as well, plus two cows, should the monks settle there (106).

Adelhelm thereafter negotiated with Abp. Seghers about the administration of these two rural parishes, Fillmore and Sublimity, as a basis of support if the monks were to recommend this site to their superior in Switzerland. During their talks, the villages of Turner and Aumsville were included in these parish jurisdictions, and in addition to the "exclusively German settlements" the Abp. suggested that a third be included as well, namely the boom town of Gervais which with St. Paul, and St. Louis had been settled by French-Canadian fur trappers working for the Hudson Bay Company (41). Many of the trappers brought wives with them, or married local Indians, and settled them in the valley on permanent homesteads while the men continued trapping, widespread travel, or eventually worked in the nascent lumbering industry. Gervais was a farming community, moreso than the trade colonies along the Willamette River. However, as early as 1870 it had become a regional mercantile center, turning over $210,000 a year in business. The town itself, in expectations of a future that never materialized, was laid out on a grid-iron pattern in an era when city planning in this region was unknown. The parish of Gervais extended to the outskirts of Salem and as far north as the area served from Oregon City. Consequently, the Abp. was suggesting that the monks take over most of the old French Prairie from Oregon City to Salem and from the Willamette River to the Cascades. Gervais was bigger than either Sublimity or Fillmore, numbering about seventy-five families or about five hundred Catholics. Many, however, were Catholic in name only, the area was unevenly settled, transportation was poor except where the railroad ran, and the offer held in it as many problems as prospects for success (108).

While Adelhelm and Abp. Seghers discussed terms for a Benedictine foundation in the Willamette Valley, Fr. Nicholas visited Bp. Aegidius Jungers (d. 1895) of Vancouver, Washington, whose diocesan jurisdiction called Nesqually, was defined in 1850. It was the remnants of the aborted see at Walla Walla and the proto-see of Seattle, which was responsible for the organization of the church in Washington state. Bp. Junger was then trying to get the monks to consider sites either near Walla Walla where the Methodists had been so active, or around the Puget Sound which had no Christianity save what little the Jesuits had managed to bring to the area's small missions (109). He offered the Benedictines 640 acres if they would settle in his diocese, and he continued these overtures through 1882. Consequently Frs. Nicholas and Adelhelm after November 5 embarked on a grand excursion through Washington state, traveling up the Columbia River by barge, then along the Walla Walla River to the mission and town of the same name. They traveled overland along the Yakima and across the Cascade range to the old Cowlitz mission, then to Olympia and on to Seattle before returning to Portland by boat (110). The Puget Sound area was deemed unsuitable because it was too forested and lacked cleared farmlands; less understandable today is that the Walla Walla area was rejected for the same reason!

The offers from these American churchmen were all interesting and enticing. Fr. Ambrose Zenner, after working through Adelhelm's correspondence in Engelberg's archives during 1950-51, suspected that he was envisioning by late 1881 a string of priories along the West Coast, all dependent upon the Swiss motherhouse, all mission oriented and supported by farming and parish work with the aim of widespread Catholic evangelization (111). Certainly some letters, such as that on August 15, 1881 from Jacksonville, reflect uncertainties and contradictions. Fr. Maurus Snyder in his reminiscences claimed that Adelhelm's decision was made before the Washington tour, as if the trip were a rouse to move Abp. Seghers to action. More possible is the speculation that the prelate still wanted a Benedictine foundation in the eastern stretches of the diocese to counter the incursion of Protestantism both among the white settlers and the Indians, and to initiate an education effort in the Grande Ronde area. Perhaps he hoped for two priories, one in each part of the state and because the Swiss monks had made no promises yet, was still enlisting the aid of the Cassinese Benedictines at the same time he was courting Frs. Adelhelm and Nicholas (112).

Fr. Nicholas seems to have been less zealous and visionary than Adelhelm, and more realistic in sensing that the investment opportunities afforded by Oregon and Washington's open lands and virgin forests could be superior to the prospects in California. He did not have his colleague's bias toward wheat farming; even if he shared that view, neither could foresee the rich wheat harvests of the future from the volcanic ash soil underlying the forested hill country of Walla Walla once these were cleared, any more than they could foretell the success the Christian Brothers would have with their California vinyards. Most certainly their correspondence reveals vacillation, a faith that somehow the best choice would be made, and a hope that this choice might mean retaining several grants of land in different locations for investment purposes or for future expansion. Both monks were affected by the massive speculation which characterized the decade, and were little prepared for the competition of the Catholic bishops who all saw in Benedictine colonization a means of improving their parish and parochial education systems.

If there is any bias that surfaces in the records, it was perhaps against entering into service in the Indian mission field. The preference is clearly toward the German-speaking communities of Oregon, as opposed to the children seen in the Sta. Inéz Valley or the troublesome Indians who so frustrated the Benedictine nuns. The latter complained that at the Grand Ronde schools the Indians tended to think of the missionaries as servants, whereas the nuns thought of the Indians as their inferiors in need of civilization and conversion. They were at times unteachable, since in the view of the nuns, they lacked discipline. There was ample reason for the Swiss monks to be weary of such missionary work when it was so foreign to their own backgrounds. Moreover, there was an ample mission field among the white settlers of West as Adelhelm told Anselm more than once. Fr. Nicholas was well aware that any educational endeavor in the West would be difficult. When in California, he quoted a priest from near San Francisco in a letter to Engelberg, making a point with which he concurred: "...if there is no success in winning the youth by that extent [i.e.

Catholic schools], the Church in California must die out". The Benedictine agreed, and elaborated (113):

> It is almost unbelievable what unrestricted freedom is allowed the children of America. Even Catholic parents sometimes bring their offspring to school with their cheerful declaration that their child has to learn only what it pleases and may do whatever it wishes. Almost all those who go to public schools are being lost to the Church. The same complaint is prevalent among believing Protestants.

Similar complaints were voiced about the Indian schools, except they were worse. The common theme in their observations was that evangelization and proper Christian education in this region would take time, and therefore there was the dire need to operate from a firm foundation. The monks were convinced by late 1881 that this basis was not a school, but a multi-faceted economic enterprise consisting of farming, husbandry, lumbering, and related industries. Educational endeavors like parish work were services, not means of support.

In contrast to the Indian mission work, meritorious as the Benedictines thought that to be, the invitation to parish work among the Oregon pioneers was in harmony both with Adelhelm's predilections and the original motives for founding a refuge for Engelberg's community in America. It is not surprising therefore that the western Oregon sites were seen as more favorable than either California or Washington. Adelhelm recalled more than once numerous incidents which served to illustrate how comfortable the Swiss Benedictines would be among the German-speaking immigrants of Oregon. He described in detail his work at Fillmore, Sublimity and Gervais in order to illustrate need as well. He explained how on Christmas Eve he preached twice in three languages (English, French, and German), heard confessions from 7 to 12:00 PM, celebrated midnight Mass, preached again, and afterwards heard confessions again until 3:00 AM, took a short nap, and then on Christmas Day returned to the confessional from 6 until 8:00 AM, said another Mass which lasted until 10:30 AM, preached again, celebrated a final Mass, and at 1:30 PM, instead of collapsing, put on "street clothes" and went with friends to a local restaurant for "breakfast". Such was his stamina and incredible zest for human interaction which so contrasts with the stereotype of the retreating, recluse monk. Such service brought him $80.00 from "my sheep" to defray his personal expenses and continue his exploratory mission. He concluded by noting: "A Protestant brewer had sent a little barrel of beer as his Christmas gift" which he was finally able to savor after his twenty-hour ordeal (114).

Because of the same feelings of insecurity and persecution present at Engelberg, other German and Swiss Catholics were emigrating to the United States and were seeking homesteads in the still available lands of the Pacific Northwest. In fact, they were lured there by German-American newspapers; among the authors of such articles were settlers at Fillmore, including Adelhelm's host Mathias Butsch. The continuing trek of German-speaking settlers to Oregon, especially the Willamette Valley, made this area increasingly endearing to the Swiss monks. Their explorations at Fillmore and vicinity cannot be disassociated from this larger picture of westward migration. Back home there was an interesting attempt to settle a German commune in Oregon which became fused with the Engelberg mission. A group of about fifty disenchanted southern German and Swiss families headed by Baron von Stotzingen of Radolfzell, the noble family of the Grand Duchy of Baden, approached Abbot Anselm Villiger with a most interesting proposal to buy large tracts of land around Fillmore provided that Engelberg found a priory there. The envisioned cooperation was considered symbiotic: the embryonic monastery would be surrounded by a supportive lay community, and the laymen would be guaranteed the amenities of their religion and a European education system for their children. According to the abbot's diary, the baron had envisioned a settlement (115):

> ...with the monastery the center in every regard; it would have to be the hearth in which the flame of religion would be maintained, the spiritual focal point, but also the intellectual center by means of its school. The monastery would have to be founded first and the settlement of lay families would be grouped around it.... The families concerned would retain liberty according to a uniform plan, and with the agreement of the monastery to have colonists come and make homesteads on lands made available to them [and to hold them] in the manner of hereditary fiefs.

The baron realized that the families he had in mind were not themselves farmers, but would be investors. He hoped that they could attract farmers, invest in timberland for quick profits, and use these to develop more land for agriculture and long-range economic stability. Time was of the essence, since he had already heard about the land speculation in Oregon as well as the indiscriminate cutting of its forests (116):

> According to highly trustworthy reports from America... the forests are being devastated to such an extent that within twenty years at most a shortage of timber will definitely occur. Therefore, quite a lot of forested land would have to be purchased, and crops would be cultivated only for the needs of the settlement. Forest property does not require any especially

> expensive care and it grows, as is said, into money.

In a detailed letter to the abbot, he proposed that each family put up 5,000 marks of a total minimal investment of 25,000 marks (ca. $6000 at $.24/mark), for a total corporate investment of 250,000 marks or about $60,000. Of this, 100,000 RM (Reichmarks, or $24,000) would be deposited with Engelberg Abbey for its foundation in Oregon; the remaining 150,000 DM ($36,000) would be for land purchases. Each family was further to encumber itself and insure the financial independence of the new monastery by tithing for the next fifty years from its American-generated income.

The baron's letter clearly states the prime motivation for collaboration with Engelberg was the tense political situation in Europe which was having its influence on emigration to America and investment in the New World economy (117):

> Our prospects for the future are, as elsewhere, anything but reassuring. In regard to religion, I believe that we are still far from a satisfactory solution. On the one side we are faced with the demonic hatred of social democracy; on the other the attempt to make the Church a slave of the state. In political matters, I fear the Prussian (German) centralized state which is threatening us as the source of great disorder and conditions not to my liking. The economic situation of the medium-sized landowner is hopeless; on the one hand he is almost crushed by debts and taxes, and on the other he is without defense, being at the mercy of competition from foreign countries which produce more cheaply.

Apparently the abbot and baron met to discuss this proposal in detail, since subsequent events indicate that the two knew each other personally and that the idea of investing in forest lands in the Pacific Northwest remained alive for several years. More than the one German family now preeminently associated with the Northwest's lumber industry as the main landlord of the area's privately held forests, was interested in such investment. Fr. Adelhelm knew about these negotiations, although perhaps not in detail. The latter reacted in writing during March 1882 by contacting the baron directly, providing more details about escalating land prices, the inflationary selling price for cordwood, and the increasingly developed rail and water transportation system for logging operations. There is not evidence, however, that Adelhelm was the informed source to whom the baron had previously alluded. In any case, Adelhelm honestly advised the baron that commercially such a venture might do better in Washington than in Oregon. He was certainly interested in the proposal since it provided a means of support for the new foundation, but by that time he was more inclined toward farming as the immediate basis of support for the new community. In any case, the abbot's diary contains a cryptic annotation simply that "Nothing ever came of it!" The overture does illustrate, however, the kind of intricate negotiations undertaken while the Swiss monks were scouting in Oregon and Washington, and it places the subsequent decisions into the contexts of both political uncertainty in Europe and the rising tide of German emigration to the United States.

Meanwhile, Adelhelm continued to explore the Fillmore site. In a report of January 6, 1882 he admitted that Abp. Seghers "and other competent people" were pushing the hill site (118). It was surveyed as being one mile long and a half-mile wide; its trees measured up to four and five feet in diameter, thus insuring good building timbers; and there was also plenty of loose stone for construction. Moreover, "on St. Nicholas day a water-seeker found it [water] at two places, 52 feet deep at one and 64 feet deep at the other" (119). As always, the vista from the hilltop remained a strong lure to Fillmore.

While Fr. Adelhelm assumed responsibility for the three parishes and took up residence at Gervais from where he would serve Fillmore and Sublimity once monthly, Fr. Nicholas traveled to San Francisco to serve as a chaplain for the Christian Brothers at Sacred Heart College where he was also to improve his English. The latter post was also a decision of strategy in order to keep the California option alive (120). Exploiting all possibilities proved difficult, and matters were then complicated by a visit to Oregon from Abbot Alexius Edelbroch of St. John's Abbey in Minnesota to follow up Abp. Blanchet's earlier invitation to the Cassinese Benedictines to establish a house in Oregon and to work with the state's Indians. He and Fr. Adelhelm met at the invitation of Abp. Seghers, and by now the Swiss monk learned all about the almost simultaneous overtures to the two Congregations to establish priories in the diocese. It is not at all clear which monk reacted the worse to the double-dealing of the prelates, but Adelhelm later claimed that the abbot "went off vexed" and indignant because the Swiss Benedictines were already in Oregon. Adelhelm further related to the abbot of Engelberg that "when Abbot Alexius heard that we were stting here, he left in bad temper because, as he later told Fr. Nicholas, we had stolen the best from him" (121). Abbot Alexius saw the latter in San Francisco where he sought in vain to contact the California prelates about the Sta. Inéz lands for St. John's Abbey. Presumably Fr. Adelhelm told him about that possibility (or did Abp. Seghers?), and this suggests that the Swiss had by then settled on the Oregon site. It is never explicitly stated, but it seems that Abbot Alexius was not enthusiastic about an eastern Oregon site, isolated as it would be, but might have been interested in locating a daughterhouse in the Willamette Valley had Frs. Adelhelm and Nicholas not been there. Later Fr. Maurus Snyder in his rcollections maintained that the abbot, who had arrived in a very wet December, so disliked the aridity of the plains and the contrasting rainy season of the valley, that he used the presence of the Swiss Benedictines as an excuse to respond negatively to the archbishop. This explanation is hardly plausible, given Adelhelm's correspondence to Engelberg. Moreover, the machinations of the monks and churchmen suggest a complicated game being played, in which the stakes were considered high. Adelhelm, who seems to have been as vexed as Abbot Alexius about their competitive circumstance, also wrote to Abbot Anselm that Engelberg ought to hold onto both sites, Oregon and California, since either could provide a good setting for a Benedictine foundation (122). It was then that he indicated the rationale behind Fr. Nicholas' trip to California by hoping that his confrere "can beat him [Abbot Alexius] to the draw!"

Fr. Adelhelm was still wishing that the Sta. Inéz grants would come through, if not as the initial site, then as an investment; he referred to the option as "a good milk cow". Fr. Nicholas, however, returned to Oregon on May 9 without having accomplished either mission, learning English or securing the California lands for Engelberg. Fr. Ambrose Zenner reports that Nicholas was angered, possibly by Abp. Alemany's insistance that he take charge of a mission during his stay in San Francisco. In any case, Nicholas blamed the archbishop's chancellor for all of the difficulties, not the archbishop himself; but the Swiss monk left so abruptly that he never took leave from the prelate, and so rather undiplomatically irritated his prospective patron (123). Apparently the archbishop withdrew his offer, despite one last attempt by Fr. Adelhelm to keep him interested in the negotiations. Apart from such personality problems, the prelate's financial difficulties were still a major obstacle to any significant grant from the Sta. Inéz lands. There is no indication that he was able to respond any more favorably to Abbot Alexius. In a letter of April 10, 1882 Fr. Adelhelm finally admitted to Abbot Anselm that the California option was dead; in his words, the final reason was not one of personality conflict, but that the "conditions attached are excessively burdensome" (124). Meanwhile, Bp. Mora of Los Angeles approached the Cassinese Benedictines and in 1888 enticed monks from St. Benedict's in Atchison, Kansas, to San Diego county with an offer of fifty acres, water rights, and a $10,000 endowment from land sales (125). The two Benedictines sent there were withdrawn shortly thereafter because Abbot Innocent Wolff needed them back home when recruits were not forthcoming as promised from the eastern houses.

In view of these open-ended negotiations, opportunism, and continuing land speculation, as well as the jostling of monk against monk and bishop against bishop, some decisions had to be made. Fr. Adelhelm was not empowered to act without Abbot Anselm's directive, and the latter had to rely on somewhat contradictory and vacillating reports which were several weeks late by the time they arrived. The lag time before his replies reached the American West Coast made things even more difficult. Adelhelm certainly felt undermined by his lack of authority and inability to communicate more directly with his superior. As early as October 19, 1881, he inquired about which of them, himself or Fr. Nicholas, should act as the other's superior; he confided that their lack of title and clearly defined authority was problematic.

> More and more I feel the need to talk with you by word of mouth.... One time last winter [1880] you wrote that you wished I could see the renovated church and new organ [at Engelberg], as I too wish, but at that time I could not think of it. Perhaps now..., it might be done before a beginning is made anywhere. Around the stove [in conversation] plans for a generation could be made. Actually it should be done.

In the same letter he discussed deliberations with the local ordinaries and conversations between himself and Nicholas who thought too, that Adelhelm ought to return to Engelberg to recruit some manpower, to solicit funds, and to plan for the new foundation. Adelhelm recounted how the Abp. of Oregon had "asked us immediately, which of us was the superior". The two avoided a direct answer, but the prelate persisted and his queries made them aware that it would have been better for both to have had the line of authority clearly established. Adelhelm at first regarded Nicholas, his senior, as the superior, but the latter would not act the part without the abbot's expressed appointment. Nevertheless, Adelhelm disliked the possibility that the two monks, when acting separately, could also act independently and therefore be played against the other: "...in this country it is necessary [to have someone in charge] because of the people who otherwise like to flatter both parties, etc..... And we ourselves have experienced this". The issue was not forgotten by them or the archbishop, as Adelhelm recalled from another occasion (126):

> The people and priests are always asking questions. In this country one has to make an impression or else not undertake anything. The people make so much of titles. It seems that these make more of an impression than laudable missionary work does. The Abp. also asked me what position I hold in the American-Swiss Congregation. I told him I was a common soldier, a common monk-priest. He laughed, but was unimpressed.

He continued:

> One of us should be able to present himself everywhere and say 'I am Prior so and so,....' As long as it is merely 'Father,' the Americans are indifferent, or less, because in English every priest is called 'Father,' so again that does not make enough impression. I should have written this to you long ago, but I was ashamed that I might appear to be proposing myself, or as if I could not wait for the hour to strike from on high.... So the Abp. here wanted me to write this to you, and to ask you to make one of us two the superior. Do entirely as you think best, of course.

Certainly Adelhelm knew that they were playing in big league ecclesiastical politics in building the nascent Catholic Church in the West, and that the outcome would have long-range consequences. He does not seem, however, to have fully understood the Abp.'s probing into his status, since he was probabely unaware of the prelate's communications with the abbot of St. John's. All accounts agree that Adelhelm was personally captivated by the charismatic charm and diplomacy of Abp. Seghers who, in reality, had neither the establishment, finances, or prestige of the see, in contrast to his episcopal colleagues in California, to locate the Benedictines in his diocese. What he lacked in resources, he made up with personality, persuasion, and grace. It was, of course, the relatively primitive state of the Church in Oregon that attracted Fr. Adelhelm because the territory provided such an ideal mission field and potential for a secure foundation. However, one cannot underestimate the wiley archbishop who, while having coaxed the Cassinese Benedictines on a scouting expedition to Oregon at the same time he was persuading the Swiss monks to settle there, was responsible for some of the information relayed to Abbot Anselm by Fr. Adelhelm. Abp. Seghers, for example, told Adelhelm "True, all the priests in the Oregon diocese were happy to see Abbot Alexius leave, but they were pleased with the Swiss Benedictines and have an interest in them" (127). It was the same prelate who awhile later tried to prejudice the monks against California because it was a haven for Irish rather than Germanic Catholicism, and perhaps was responsible for Adelhelm's impression that Abbot Alexius went to California "in order to pay us back for the Oregon strike by contacting Bp. Mora about Santa Inéz". Seghers would later use the same tactic, encouraging the Swiss monks to hurry in developing the Oregon site while the diocesan ordinary was friendly to them and before an Irishman were elected to the see! Consequently, it is possible that the archbishop was responsible for pitting the Cassinese against the Swiss Benedictines in their bids for Californian land. Fr. Ambrose Zenner speculated that Adelhelm, despite his personal predilection toward Oregon, still felt California to be, if not better, certainly a competitive site. Indeed, the latter told Abbot Anselm, "We want to hold onto both" Oregon and California, and in this maneuvering certainly felt upstaged and outranked as a mere monk, or a "common soldier" as he put it, against the abbot of St. John's.

Adelhelm was finally recalled to Engelberg on February 5, 1882 by Abbot Anselm; the letter arrived by March 8, and the monk left Oregon on May 9 with Abp. Segher's written permission in response to a formal petition from Engelberg to establish a priory in Oregon. Anselm noted in his diary: "It [recalling Adelhelm to Engelberg] costs a great deal, but the thing is important and fraught with consequences". Adelhelm's reply to the recall was ecstatic, almost foolish, in admitting that he was so overwhelmed by the prospect of returning home that he kissed the letter several times. He delayed his departure only until the archbishop could arrange for someone to care for his parishes, to confer with Fr. Nicholas, and to recover fully from an attack of influenza. At the request of Bp. Jungers, Adelhelm took one last look at the Puget Sound area, before leaving Seattle by boat for San Francisco and then traveling overland to Missouri where he stopped at Maryville just long enough to recruit three nuns from the convent of St. Gertrude (Sisters Maria, Agnes, and Frances de Sales) for the Grand Ronde school and to obtain from the Mother Superior a promise to send other nuns for Gervais (128). He then left for New York from where he boarded a trans-Atlantic liner for Cherbourg, France, and road by rail from there to Engelberg—a trip lasting thirty-two days (61). After June 17 the two, Adelhelm and Anselm, met at the motherhouse and there narrowed the final choice to Fillmore, Oregon, or perhaps, should this fail, a still indefinite place in Washington. The California possibility was discarded, partially because of the anticipated competition from St. John's Abbey. However, it is in the Engelberg records that Adelhelm's reservations about California are articulated as never before, and his worst fears seem to have been stimulated by Abp. Seghers. Indeed, just before departing from Portland, the prelate, having only then returned himself from San Francisco, told the monk, as translated by Adelhelm for Anselm: "We [the Swiss Benedictines] would not be as welcome down there in California as up here because so many Irish are there and a bad spirit toward Religious priests is prevalent among them" (129). This suspected anticlericism in the state was something to which the Swiss were perhaps overly sensitive because of their own predicament at home. Both Anselm and Adelhelm therefore agreed that Oregon, with its heavy German and Swiss immigration, offered the more receptive political, if not natural, climate for a foundation. Earlier while seriously entertaining the California choice, he had written (130):

> You may have read of the astonishing growth and the remarkable success of the Catholic Church in America, but you hardly ever hear how dioceses, parishes, and churches are laboring with big debts. Neither will you have heard it said that without Catholic immigration, the Church will not hold its own ground against infidelity and hundreds of sects. Secret societies

> have become great powers.... Old people, who have seen better times in Europe, say that the people in this country are all pagans. We are facing about the same conditions as our forefathers did a thousand years ago.

Adelhelm was prone to feel not only less foreign among the German immigrants, but much safer among families of known Catholic, old-world upbringing.

Jacksonville was discredited as being too isolated; the railroad had yet to cut through the highlands between Oregon and California. By the time of the chapter hearings on June 30, 1882, Fillmore was presented as the only viable option—a selection which A. Zenner later attributed to Adelhelm's apostolic idealism without accounting for Engelberg's paranoia and Abp. Segher's political savy. Others, particularly Fr. Maurus Snyder, always Adelhelm's critic, characterized the decision as simply irresponsible since land in Oregon had to be purchased, but the California land was potentially free (131).

On July 3, 1882 the chapter completed its deliberations and approved the foundation of another New Engelberg or Mount Angel priory under Adelhelm Odermatt as prior, with a colony in addition to Fr. Nicholas Frey, consisting of Fathers Beda Horat (b. 1837), Barnabas Held (b. 1851), and Anselm Wachter (b. 1857), plus Brothers Theodule Würsch (b. 1852)(132). Br. Columban was also appointed to the mission, but later declined. A formal petition for recognition was sent to Rome, resulting in a papal bull of permission dated on July 16, 1882. Meanwhile the travel party continued to grow; it would be forty persons by the time it was ready to leave Engelberg, consisting of the prior and three priests (Beda, Barnabas, and Anselm), four choir monks (Fundman, Burre, Fuerst [b. 1868], and Maurus [Edward] Snyder himself [b. 1865]), and three crewmen or lay workers (Shilter, Kundig, and Künne). There were also five sisters (two from Maria Rickenbach and three from Sarnen) under Rev. Mother Prioress Bernadine, and four postulants. These made twenty-two; the other eighteen were monks and novices heading for Conception Abbey plus some nuns from Rickenbach heading for Clyde. The process of selection is not clear, but Abbot Anselm wrote in his diary, that Adelhelm arrived exhausted and tense, but looking splendid in his thick black beard: "His stories are interesting. He is begging hard for Fathers, Brothers, and candidates. We shall pray, ponder, and consult about how the zealous missionary can be helped" (133). The abbot had mixed feelings about the monks who decided to go with Adelhelm, as noted also in his diary: "No one can imagine what is required to begin a new foundation, no matter how unpretentious. By sending away these fathers,... I am making a great sacrifice". He was worried not only about the expenses, some 1,400 francs apiece ($1,280) for travel, but also the permanent loss to Engelberg. Fr. Barnabas had just completed an extensive education in music at considerable expense, and now his talent would be "lost to Engelberg," and Fr. Anselm was a very promising young theologian. The abbot simply concluded his thoughts with a Latin prayer: "I offer you, O God, our dear brothers, begging and pleading that you send us others no worse than these" (134).

By the time the mission was ready for departure from Engelberg, the abbot calculated the cost to exceed 10,000 francs, not counting the supplies to be sent along and shipped later. Apparently Adelhelm and the others realized how upset the abbot was, and particular for their behavior in demanding more and more from Engelberg and its abbot. He apologized for "what they had done amiss through boldness and turbulence". The abbot remarked to himself in his diary: "They are full of courage and zeal. May God and Mary accompany them!" Abbot Anselm was ultimately appeased and became cautiously optimistic about the expedition. He might have been even enthusiastic, had it not been his shoulders on which the major responsibilities rested. He was worried not only for the colony, but for the future of Engelberg which now gambled much of its limited liquid assets on this venture. Even so, it was maintained by Fr. Maurus Snyder later that several in the troupe had their way paid by their families rather than by Engelberg, or at least subsidized the abbey by as much as 1000 francs each. Many in Engelberg's community shared the abbot's reservations; the expedition never had the unanimous support of the chapter. Fr. Maurus recalled that the subprior of Engelberg, Ignatius, referred to the group as a *Vorbrecher Kolonie* or "colony of criminals," an allusion harkening back to the Middle Ages when monasteries resettled frontier sites by supplying their lay brethren with convicts whose colonization was a condition for their pardons, and recognizing that these Engelbergians had just been consigned to hard labor. Not that this was a motley lot, but their penance certainly seemed severe as they set out for the remote parts of America (135). Indeed, several like Fr. Beda and newcomers like Fr. Wehrner and Br. Adelhelm Kreuger, never survived a decade after their departure. The abbot, in one of his most pessimistic moments on September 8, wrote in his diary (136):

> What displeases me even more [than the cost of the expedition] is that they have recruited too many people to go along, among them even first and second syntaxers who are still too immature to choose their state in life. Against this latter I intervened. I do not place real confidence in this expedition because to me those who are departing are lacking necessary experience.

The party nevertheless left Engelberg on September 25, was joined at Lucerne by the nuns from Sarnen, and together they traveled to Basel, Belfort, and to Paris where they enjoyed some sightseeing (137). From Paris they traveled by rail to La Havre where they embarked on the steamship *Labrador* for New York. On October 11, 1882 the mission arrived in the United States; the monks were greeted by friends, among them the Benziger Brothers, Nicholas and Louis, the publishers who were building their business by specializing in Catholic literature. They acted as hosts for the day, showing off New York City and arranging for the next day's departure across country. The Swiss monks and nuns eagerly anticipated their coming adventure, but with no realistic sense about what to expect. Most of them could not communicate in English, they lacked perception about the distance still before them, and apart from the stories told by Fr. Adelhelm knew nothing about the Pacific Northwest. Like modern-day pilgrims, they arrived with little more than their wits, hopes, and an abiding faith.

Mount Angel Priory, 1882-1904

The Swiss colonists on October 12, 1882 left New York, boarded a train in Jersey City, and spent the next two nights and a day getting as far as Toledo, Ohio (138). After a refreshing break, they boarded another train for St. Louis where they enjoyed another stopover with German-American hosts. Then they journied to Conception Abbey and St. Gertrude's convent where the party split up according to their assignments. After a cheerful reunion, the Oregon-bound troupe left by wagon on October 17 to nearby Council Bluffs where they caught a connecting train for the overland run to California. After what was described as a tedious and slow trip, they arrived exhausted in San Francisco where Abp. Alemany greeted them, apparently with no incriminations for the lack of success in their previous negotiations. From there on, their trip was more comfortable; they took a streamer, the "Columbia," to Portland and were greeted on the docks by a delegation of diocesan priests sent by Abp. Seghers (139). The Abp. was unable to meet them immediately, but the wait in Portland gave them the opportunity to acquaint themselves with the town, the diocesan church and some of its clergy, and visit such institutions as St. Vincent's hospital. The bull of Leo XIII, dated July 16, 1882, was either presented to or left for the Abp., presumably on October 30 while in Portland and when the prelate and prior met for a public press conference. This is the date, October 30, recorded by the Benedictine Confederation of America as the priory's official foundation (140). The local press had indeed been wondering what this seemingly inundation of Catholic clergy and religious meant, and the reporters knew so little about Catholicism that they failed to distinguish between the fathers, brothers, or workmen—all were simply called priests! They managed to discern a difference between men and women, but not necessarily monks and nuns, and the initial coverage by the non-Catholic papers made no identification of these recruits as being Benedictines. Their purpose, simply explained by Abp. Seghers, was to further Catholic education in the Oregon territory.

The monks settled at Gervais where housing was available, on October 31, 1882 when their baggage finally arrived from Switzerland (141). According to Abbot Anselm's diary, thirty large pine boxes had been packed with supplies for the foundation (142):

> Beds, even the mattresses, abundant four-to-five fold clothes, linens, shoes, vestments, chalices, shoemaking tools, kitchen utensils, farm implements, a great quantity of books, devotional items, music, writings, transcripts, etc., were packed into thirty large boxes for them.

The abbot's list is hardly inclusive at this point, for other entries mention among other things, their having raided the Engelberg kitchens for copper pots, pans and kettles and beer-making equipment. It was this scrounging which had offended the abbot, and the reason for his diary entries was because he thought that they not only left with too large a party, but had also overpacked or at least that they were well supplied at Engelberg's great expense (143).

By November 17, 1882 the Gervais parish was well organized and the parish house had been converted into a priory. The monks took up their parish duties immediately along with going about the business of establishing their monastery. It was not until March 1883 that Adelhelm finally gave to the abbot some accounting of their spiritual work: "With all this temporal business, I almost forgot the principle thing," he wrote, and then enumerated that since

January 1, 1876 the Benedictines in Oregon had performed 247 baptisms, officiated at 34 weddings and 38 confirmations (the latter since 1880), and had three conversions in 1882 and another two during the first three months of that year (144). It was the "temporal business," however, which occupied most of the prior's time and his letters to Engelberg. Fr. Barnabas, the procurator, occupied a farmhouse at Fillmore on property purchased for the eventual site of the priory, and Fr. Mark began work at Sublimity in the foothills. Meanwhile Abbot Anselm, through Adelhelm, finalized an accord with Abp. Seghers on December 15, 1883 to insure the permanent retention of the three parishes assigned to the Benedictines, since these were to be the mainstay of the community's initial support. Deeds to parish property were transferred to the monks, who in turn promised to abide by the diocesan statutes and observe their Order's regulations for maintaining parishes. Pastoral assignments were the right of the prior, subject to approval by the diocesan ordinary. Furthermore, all of the rights and traditions of Engelberg were guaranteed for Mount Angel, and these privileges were to be extended to the sisters as well. The latter, who were able to build a convent by 1888, were to run the parish school at Fillmore (145). By 1883 the total Benedictine community in Oregon, monks and nuns, numbered twenty-eight; by November 13 one year later, augmented by American recruits and reinforcements from Engelberg, there were 27 members in the monastery alone: six priests, five candidates, and sixteen lay brothers (146). Among them were two shoemakers, a weaver, two cooks, two tailors, a gardener, a mason, a blacksmith, a painter, a baker, farmers and teamsters, and several who considered themselves to be musicians (147).

After the immediate task of assuming responsibility for the forementioned parishes, the second order of business was to put the foundation on a more permanent financial basis by building a nuclear estate for minimally subsistence farming but hopefully for more, to be able to generate surplus revenues to support a building program and expanded mission work. Fr. Adelhelm concentrated his attention on the Fillmore site where previously he had received assurances that land could be had through solicitation and purchase. The "Yankee" landowners of the hill and adjacent land had in 1881 responded favorably to Adelhelm's approaches, but now was the time to turn promises into reality (148). One landowner promised a donation of ten acres, and three others five acres each: "that would be 25 acres on the top for nothing but a building site". The area's Catholic families pledged $1,200 for additional land acquisitions, and they had promised to raise a total of $3,000 if Fillmore were selected as the site for the new monastery. Adelhelm reported that even before his return to Engelberg, the collection had obtained another $2,000 in pledges plus the promise of two cows to begin a dairy herd (149). Consequently, within the week after their arrival at Gervais, the small corporation plunged itself into debt with complete optimism about local support. On November 16, 1882 Adelhelm agreed to purchase from Josephine Schwab 215 acres at $28/acre ($6,020), and another contract was drawn up with Wilhelm Glover for a $5,000 purchase of 140 acres (ca. $35/acre). This meant that the community almost immediately assumed debts for considerably more than the total of the pledges. That was only the beginning of its indebtedness.

When Adelhelm on December 4 reported back to the abbot, with a separate letter enclosed for the community, he again apologized for the "turbulence" he created before turning to the business at hand, namely securing the hillsite and its surrounding land (150). Engelberg was apparently financing the initial purchases by loaning the necessary money to the priory, and the pledges were to be used to repay these loans. These were perhaps perceived as short-term rather than long-term credit, and negotiations between the prior and abbot appear open-ended; there does not seem to have been any agreement regarding the amount of backing the motherhouse could or would extend to the new foundation. The Swiss francs were converted to American dollars by financial brokers, the firm of Lussy and Falk in Lucerne, which continued to act as a middle-manager for the next decade and longer. The initial purchases of the Schwab and Glover land allowed Adelhelm to secure the butte itself and the wooded southern slope. He next moved to acquire the homestead of Benjamin Cleaver, and then worked on an adjacent property owned by the Gibson family which remained illusive. The father and son resolutely refused to consider selling, much less bargain with Adelhelm. Thus the prior asked the Engelberg community to intercede and pray for some superior persuasion: "Do pray, all of you, that the Lord may soften their hearts and make them favorable to us". Whatever the tactic, the homestead was later acquired. However, these purchases created a mini-speculation of its own, with the Benedictine prior in its midst. One landowner held out for dearer prices; John H. Palmer finally made an offer to sell 475 acres at $60/acre or $28,500—an unheard of price until then! Moreover, when his neighbor who owned land near the hill offered to sell it to the monks for $35/acre, Palmer went after it, apparently in an attempt to hold it for resale at the higher price to the Benedictines. Adelhelm, adroit as he was in such bargaining, moved quickly to secure the latter deal so that land on the east of the butte extending toward Abiqua creek (with water rights going with these land purchases) was assured. There remained, however, the Palmer property which blocked consolidation of the monastery's land to the southwest. Adelhelm described his dealings with Palmer in detail, taking some pride in his ability as a shrewd businessman (151):

> Afterwards [securing the neighboring acreage at $35/acre] I went to Palmer, and he was furious because I put one over on him; but I said that naturally I first bought what was cheaper so I would not have to pay $60 for that property too. He had already said that if I did not take his land today at $60 [per acre], it would be more tommorrow, nearly $80-100 [per acre]. I asked him how long he would wait for the money. 'Until April' [he replied].

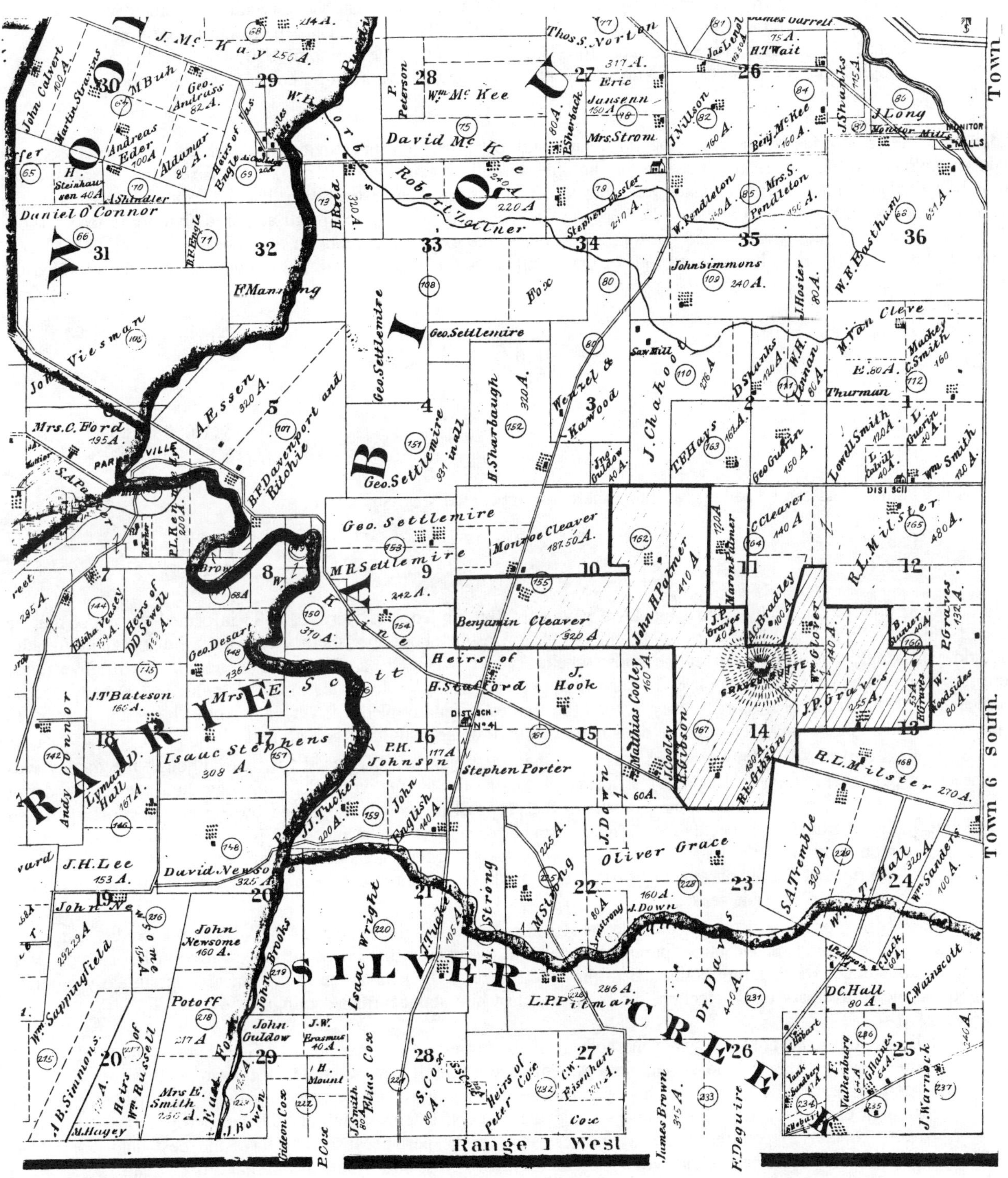

Fig. 5. Homesteads around Grave's Butte, 1870s. Land ownership survey of Oregon, 1870. Courtesy of Library of Congress Geography & Map Div.

> I took the farm because for us it is best and most necessary. He [Palmer] almost wept and wished that I would take back the money which I thereupon paid. I did not do it, so that he would be bound [by the transaction to sell at $60/acre]. Immediately afterwards he wanted to buy Cleaver's [farm] from me. I said: '$60 an acre' (although I had just paid $35 a few hours earlier). He offered me $47 an acre for Cleaver's, which comes to some $10,000. I acted as though I did not hear it. He had set the price for land in the neighborhood. Now he should pay it too.

Adelhelm's letter is in fact vague about the exact sum paid to Palmer, and presumably the exchange just described was a down-payment to bind the deal. It seems that he did pay $60 an acre, but it is not known for sure how many acres were bought; later small parcels of land were shaved off the original homesteads, so that the exact boundaries of the original estate seem unclear. In any case he kept the Cleaver farm as well, and in all acquired five homesteads, those of Glover, Davis, Palmer, Graves, and Gibson, according to the extant title deeds in the abbey's archives (152). In a letter of November 16, 1882 he itemized four of these purchases for the abbot, giving the acreage and the rounded-off price:

Homestead:	Acreage:	Purchase price:
Davis	140	$4,000
Schwab	215	$6,000
Glover	140	$5,000
Cleaver	320	$11,000
Subtotal:	815	$26,000

To this the Palmer deal can be added, assuming the entire farmstead was purchased:

Palmer	475	$28,500
Total:	1290	$54,500

It is not clear how much Adelhelm had for down payments, but his letter of April 1, 1883 informed the abbot that he needed 209,500 francs or $41,900 as soon as possible. Unsure about the abbot's response, he hastened to add: "Would you kindly and very soon let me know whether and how much can be raised at home. I will investigate here... and report what can be obtained...". If the above accounting is accurate, then Adelhelm had already bet on more than $12,000 from local sources, way beyond the figures originally pledged; yet, if need be, he would attempt to raise more funds. Interestingly enough, he does not indicate how; he may have had no real idea.

The financial outlay Adelhelm negotiated was more than the abbot had bargained for, and although the money was forwarded, it put severe strain on Engelberg's finances. Among the alternatives Adelhelm suggested later to the abbot as a means of alleviating this burden was to resurrect the proposal previously suggested by Baron von Stotzingen and to join into the local timberland speculation, "There is timber on almost all the pieces of property; millions of trees too many. In the mountains (perhaps 15-30 miles distant) thousands and thousands of acres are for sale at $2.40 per acre" (153). It is doubtful that the abbot wanted to hear about further expenditures as a means of getting out of debt, even though in hindsight the plan made sense.

The extant correspondence does not indicate what limit Abbot Anselm set on Prior Adelhelm's credit, but since Engelberg supplied capital for the initial purchase, Adelhelm discovered that he could tap local sources of credit with the land as collateral. He therefore continued to play the market. On January 25, 1882, in a congratulatory letter to the abbot on the anniversary of his election, the prior informed him about further dealings (154):

> Dear God could not have given me and all of us greater joy... than to send Saul Gibson here [to Gervais] from Fillmore—and indeed, converted! So it was possible to reason with him because death is staring out of his eyes and the Lord himself has softened him up! A terrific amount of money, true! Father and son together have 451 acres which at $60 [per acre] comes to $27,600. ...I consider these two homesteads the cheapest because they have the best land and the best buildings... and without them, the rest of the hill would never have been really satisfactory.

The prior had paid for the deeds to five farmsteads and was then caring for insurance and arranging local loans. Perhaps he resold some of the acreage, since an additional 451 acres added to the accounting of November 16, 1882 would have made 1741 acres for a total purchase price of $82,100. However, in February 22, 1883 Abbot Anselm noted in his diary that the prior's efforts had resulted in a consolidated block of 1,250 acres, and the priory's indebtedness was estimated at 370,000 francs or $74,000. Engelberg drew tremendously on its own reserves, putting off its own building program for another twenty years; it also borrowed for Mt. Angel from its Lucerne bankers and from neighboring monasteries. Because of the communication time lag and gaps in the communication itself, it is obvious that the prior and abbot had to act first and often second guess the other's intention. The abbot was frustrated with the whole affair, as his diary attests, but his letters and official actions were supportive and always encouraging. If anything, Anselm Villiger's diary tells of a man who assumed tremendous responsibility by himself, without being able to share the burden with his confreres. With that burden came worry and sleepless nights, as he admitted more than once. Because Adelhelm was doing business with California investors through a Portland bank as well as working through Engelberg, the total financial picture of the priory was not made clear until an accounting of 1892. Meanwhile, the abbot simply noted: "I am surprised that our Fathers have so much credit at the banks in America. But perhaps they do not have it [the necessary money] and then these purchases are void". He was mistaken: Adelhelm covered all of his commitments one way or the other even though in 1883 the priory faced bankruptcy, thus making future financial independence possible by encumbering the community's meager earnings for the next generation and more.

Adelhelm's initial purchases which plunged the priory so deeply in debt were seen as necessary by the prior, but not by everyone else; there was criticism that he went beyond the community's needs. His argument was that one had to invest substantially in the future; his investment in land was partially to avoid the escalating prices resulting from speculation, and as part of the speculation itself. One of his most controversial moves was to risk further debts by investing in the nearby timberlands of the western Cascade range. As already indicated, he was captivated by the long-range potential of such investing as a means to liquidating the debts incurred for the home base, and during 1883 his interest became even more keen as the monks sought out highland pasture areas. Because of their limited manpower, they could not produce enough hay and fodder to support a large herd, and it was thought that if natural grazing land could be found their meager animal husbandry enterprise could be developed more rapidly without simultaneously developing all of their farmland. In one report to Engelberg, Adelhelm revealed that fifteen miles from Fillmore "we found pasture land where the cattle are round as a ball, yet throughout the year they get no hay nor anything else other than what they themselves hunt and find in rich abundance in the brush and on the mountain, along with the best spring water. We found a level area, a meter long, with abundant grass along with magnificent, endless forests—partly government, partly railroad land and forest" (155).

This scouting for grazing land led to the further acquisition of land along the Cascades subsequently known as the "milk ranch" because it ostensibly was to aid the monastery's dairy industry, but in reality brought the monks into the lumber business as well. In June 1883 the prior informed the abbot about a fascinating American scheme called homesteading. He explained that for a $34 title fee one could get 160 acres if it were thereafter occupied and developed. His intention was to homestead the milk ranch. He learned then that the railroad was divesting some of its land, selling whole sections (640 acres) at $2.50/acre payable at one-tenth of the principal at 7% interest. Adelhelm conjectured: "If we could get some brothers or candidates who could live on it [the homestead]...we could soon take up a fine piece of mountain land and beautiful forests at a ridiculous price". Within a month, in a letter of July 11, the prior stated his "urgent" need for $3,000, not for land purchases, but for a steam-engine and power-driven saw as well as a threshing machine. As an after-thought was an added need for some more land "with some cows" referring to the milk ranch he had already gone after. The Benedictines were by then homesteaders! The saw had dual purposes, no doubt, to help with the construction of a permanent priory at Fillmore, and subsequently to be used in a mill should the monks engage lumbering for profit beyond their immediate building needs.

The community thereafter acquired over 2,000 acres of timberland on the west slopes of the Cascades, one section by establishing four homesteads, and another 1360 acres by purchase from the Oregon and California Railroad Company and three individuals. The accounts are somewhat contradictory, because Adelhelm in one instance cites 2,000 acres in total. Abbot Anselm on September 30, 1883 commented on two land deals, each amounting to 2,000 acres (which cannot be confused with the farmstead in the valley, which was finally calculated at 1250 acres. Later, on February 13, 1886, Adelhelm would estimate the monastery's timber acreage at 3,400, and then stated that the farmstead amounted to 1,400 acres. Apparently the figures fluctuate in the records from year to year, reflecting not so much inaccuracy but instability as parcels were added and substracted in continued trading.

While acquisition of the milk ranch was a sound investment for highland pasturage, there were doubts about its potential lumber value and reasons for caution. Then as now the Oregon highlands turn quite dry during summer and are plagued by forest fires. While still at Gervais on July 11 and contemplating the purchases from the railroad, Adelhelm wrote (156):

> Right now the whole valley is full of smoke (like fog in the fall at home) from forest fires in the hills around us. In the mornings and evenings, one can look at the face of the sun (which is blood-red), for hours through the smoke.

The milk ranch, then, was a high-risk venture. The monks were teachers, pastors, farmers, homesteaders, ranchers, and now lumbermen as well; above all, they were debtors.

As though this gloom during the forest fires in 1883 were not enough, a genuine crisis developed. Adelhelm borrowed most of the $3,400 needed to buy the railroad land without waiting for Abbot Anselm's advice or assurance of backing. Some of the money from American creditors carried an inflationary 9% interest, so less expensive sources than the local banks were sought. Abp. Seghers, according to Adelhelm's report of February 18, 1883, had recommended a California investment firm which was then operating in Portland, since it was lending at 7.5%. After contracting a loan, a novelty of the state tax laws which Adelhelm had thought to be a break, turned into sudden misfortune. He commented once: "There is one consolation we have in our debts, that because of them, we do not have to pay taxes. According to state law, the money lenders to whom the land still belongs are taxed". This was a modification of Oregon tax law of which the California investors were unaware when they took title to the lands as security for their loans. When the Portland firm reported that their profits would be diminished by the property tax, the investors demanded that their funds be transferred from Oregon to a state where their investments were not liable to such a tax penalty. As a result two banks recalled short-term notes totalling $56,000 or 280,000 francs payable by New Year's Eve, 1884. Otherwise, as Abbot Anselm understood in his diary writing, the farms at Fillmore could be sold at public auction.

This bleak picture was painted brighter by Adelhelm in his attempt to secure help from Engelberg: in reaction to the grim situation, he promised "Things will get better once we have survived the first, hardest few years. But as yet there can be no rosy prospect this year or the next. Why? Because we, as far as I can see now, still will not even make the American interest". The abbot was distraught upon hearing the news and demand for more money. He recorded in his diary on September 30, 1883 (157):

> The worst has now happened for our foundation at Fillmore. With the encouragement, especially of the Abp. of Oregon City and some American banks, our Fathers bought about 2000 acres of grazing and pasture land, for which the banks gave them the money. In addition, they bought a big amount comprising 2000 acres!

In a continuing dialogue with himself, the abbot wrestled with the dilemma placed before him by the prior's most recent correspondence. It was then, during the summer and fall of 1883, that Adelhelm rode from door to door with Mr. Butsch and other influential laymen, begging for additional help from the area's Catholics. At the same time he asked for laborers in an effort to harvest some profit from the farms, and he contemplated a trip back to Switzerland in an all-out effort to recruit the twenty-five lay brethren he thought were needed to operate the farms at peak capacity in order to allay the impending financial crisis (158).

The monks could not be assured of any substantial income beyond their own subsistence and what was committed for developing their Fillmore site. The parishes produced some revenues, but hardly any significant amount to help them out of this crisis. The pew and stall rents from Gervais totalled $1200, Fillmore provided another $500 and Sublimity $300, or $1700 a year which barely covered the expenses of the pastors and maintenance of the parish-house/priory at Gervais. Other than extra donations, the only real potential source of income were the farms. Fr. Fintan Packer has arrived on December 23, 1882 from Conception Abbey with his wagon, three horses, and 150 sheep (159). These had grown into a sizeable flock which could be thinned for some profit, but the dairy herd and beef cattle were still too few to do any good other than support the community. The key, thought the prior and his confreres, was to cultivate as much land as possible and pray for a good harvest. This was not entirely realistic, however, because the added indebtedness and loan cancellations came after spring planting and little could be done to increase productivity. The monastery did not have the manpower to cultivate all the cleared land, say nothing of putting more into production. If the land were leased out, or laymen were hired, profits would dwindle. Adelhelm realized that the labor shortage would be crippling even before the bank crisis occurred. Fr. Barnabas reported that the prior by February 19, 1883 was trying to recruit lay brothers and volunteers to help with planting, and once the crisis hit, he had to beg again for help in harvesting. Although no more farmland could be put into production, if the labor problem were even temporarily solved, Adelhelm hoped to add to the community's income by fully harvesting for the first time all of the nut and fruit orchards which had been planted by the original homesteaders. Despite seemingly overwhelming odds, the prior seemed undaunted because of his belief that the land was indeed a worthwhile and necessary investment. He optimistically described the farm's potential to Abbot Anselm (160):

> Everyone says we are in possession of the best grain, meadow, and pasture land far and wide, and also that the hill is suitable for raising grapes.... A part of the hill is excellent pasture land for our cattle. We likewise have several very productive orchards with enough apples and pears, very lucious for desert.

But large tracts had to be leased out because of the labor problem, so that in addition to money, the prior appealed for more recruits from the motherhouse. "Anyone can easily see that the whole complex of property will really pay off, if only a group of brothers is available so we can farm it ourselves." He thus prayed for vocations to the lay-brotherhood both in Switzerland and in Oregon, and speculated about the possibility of recruitment in Europe. Fr. Barnabas estimated that their immediate need was for sixteen horses for eight good work teams and at least fourteen hired hands. The animal husbandry enterprise was less labor intensive than farming, so this may have also played a part in the prior's purchase of the milk ranch. He envisioned the day when the community could expand both kinds of pastoral work it had undertaken; he wanted to raise more sheep, pigs, cows, and horses, so "that eventually the livestock will repay our expenditures". For now, however, he had to rely on a rather modest projected harvest. The wheat and oats were estimated to bring in only $4000 to $5000; this is why he thought of relying on a bumper fruit crop. One plan was to dry and pack whatever apple crop could be picked, and to market this outside the region. Howevee, a letter in June 1883 revealed that a late frost hit the valley after most of the trees had blossomed, killing most of the germinating fruit. Then afterwards it was unusually dry, thus putting the wheat harvest in peril. Adelhelm was resigned: "We must hope for the best; otherwise, we shall suffer heavy loss" (161).

The situation was past the point of embarrassment by fall 1883 when the prior took to itinerant mendicancy. Adelhelm had to ask Anselm for any immediate help that was possible, in addition to a long-range solution to their larger problem. A case in point was the general store in Gervais (162):

> As far as I can judge offhand, we owe $300-400 to the store for current bills, and when these bills are repeatedly sent, we are greatly embarrassed and hardly dare show ourselves anymore without money [in hand]; and this is especially hard on us, because we are considered rich and we must keep secret that we are so [deeply] in debt. Dear Pappa [Abbot Anselm], for your sake, and for the weal and honor of the motherhouse, we had to risk so much, to plunge so far into debt. Help us as much as you can, something extra too, from time to time, to give renewed courage to us. For that is indispensable with all the unspeakable difficulties [we face].

Although one can sympathize with Adelhelm's critics who blamed him for the crisis because he had over-expanded too quickly, even recklessly some thought; one can also empathize with the prior who sought to be opportunistic, making the very modest resources of the monks go as far as possible. Nobody could have foreseen the coincidental hardships visited upon the community that memorable summer: killing frosts, extra dry spells, manpower shortages, forest fires, loan recalls and threatened foreclosure. It must have seemed that God had put their faith to the test. Certainly Abp. Seghers was behind the scene working for the cause of the struggling priory, but there is no evidence that he came to rescue the Benedictines. It is doubtful if he had the means to do so. Instead, the burden again fell on Abbot Anselm Villiger at Engelberg.

Abbot Anselm's diary reveals that he and Prior Adelhelm had in the meantime decided to seek help from the southern German landed gentry which had been interested earlier in investments in Oregon. The abbot approached Baron von Stotzingen to float an emergency loan to Engelberg, using as collateral the Oregon farmstead. He in turn was to approach the same nobles and landowners he had contacted previously. Later entries for October 15-21, 1883 recount the abbot's visit to Wonnenstien and Leiden Christi, and thereafter to Steisslingen, to meet with the prospective investors who were then the baron's guests (163). They were tentatively agreeable to a loan, but would not be satisfied with a mere contract of obligation. They wanted a full mortgage agreement. This, of course, was unacceptable because the farmsteads were already partially mortgaged, and Engelberg did not want to mortgage its property. Apparently thereafter the abbot was excluded from their deliberations, and he returned to Engelberg from where he pursued other possibilities. One avenue was through the abbey's broker, Falk and associates, to solicit loans from the company's investors. By November 1 Falk reported that indeed some money could be raised this way, but not everything Mount Angel needed. The abbot also wrote Nicholas Benziger in Einsiedeln for help, and tapped other personal friendships in the search for the needed finances.

Then, as Anselm's diary puts it, "a star of hope suddenly arose". On November 5, 1883 the Baron von Stotzingen wrote that the nobles he had contacted had come to an agreement and presented the abbot with the following package of five pledges (164):

Investor:	Investment in marks:	Conversion in dollars:
Count Gundt	30,000 RM	$7,500
Count von Gallen	15,000 RM	$3,750
Baron von Bodmann	25,000 RM	$6,250
Baron von Hornstein	10,000 RM	$2,500
Baron von Stotzingen	20,000 RM	$2,000
Total:	100,000 RM	$22,000

The terms were 5.5% interest, and the whole arrangement was to be finalized in Contance at a later date. The abbot found this unacceptable, but his reasoning is not articulated. He perhaps reacted to the interest as too high, although it certainly compared well with that paid by the American priory. Later, beside this entry in his diary, the abbot scribbled "The nobles failed to do anything at all!" Indeed, the accounting of 1892 showed no indebtedness to the nobles mentioned in the baron's proposal.

On November 14, the abbot expressed his increasing anxiety about not being able to raise the money: "The fall of 1883, so replete with worry, will be unforgettable for me". Yet, he indicated that Falk was proceeding with his efforts to rush some money to Prior Adelhelm. The firm sent some promisory notes to the latter, but upon receiving them they had to be returned again because they had been signed incorrectly. Or perhaps Adelhelm's signature required subscriptions or witnessing. In any case, the abbot now worried that the pending deadline could not be met, or if the Oregon banks would accept Falk's banknotes. "Thus I shall remain," complained the abbot, "on the rack until the end of January when news may arrive". Three days later Falk sent his banknotes to the prior so that they would arrive before Christmas. They were received with joy in Oregon on December 20, 1883 and were cashed immediately. The foundation was saved!

Abbot Anselm's diary does not detail the exact amount of Falk's credit or the terms, but the 1892 accounting nearly a decade later listed Mt. Angel's indebtedness to the firm at $20,000. In fact, the entire loan was supposed to be repaid by Engelberg directly, and indirectly by Mt. Angel through the motherhouse, within five years (i.e., 1888) in five equal payments. The priory defaulted, and Engelberg carried this debt beyond the due date. Not knowing this in 1883, Abbot Anselm closed his diary on December 20 in relief: "Praise and thanks to God! Thus liquidation has been happily averted. I end this year with most heartfelt thanks to God for helping in the American crisis and directing everything so well. This fall this business almost crushed me". Later, on February 11, 1884, on his sixtieth birthday, while meditating upon his own death, he wrote a confession and admitted (165):

> I really would like to die, if only I were better prepared. But so many, many cares still bind me to this life. Especially the foundation in the state of Oregon lies heavily on my heart, and if I wish to live a few years yet, I wish it for the sake of the Oregon foundation. Once this business has been completed, I shall gladly say my *Dimittis*.

He thereafter tried to speed the process by taking from Engelberg's revenues to send a check for $40,037 which arrived at Gervais on February 26, 1884 to help build a priory at Fillmore.

A little while later, perhaps as a conspicuous sign of faith that the crisis has really passed, Adelhelm and his 27 confreres on May 11, 1884 laid the cornerstone of their new monastery's basement at the Fillmore site (166). The problems of the year before and the lingering financial constraints, forced the monks to reconsider building on the hilltop. There the edifice would have been more impressive, but also more expensive to build and maintain. Instead, the cornerstone was laid at the foot of the mount, simply, as Adelhelm explained to Anselm, because "our means did not permit it". The wooden structure designed by Otto Kleeman, a Portland architect, was, however, envisioned already as a temporary structure one day to be replaced by stone, "If only we once get together under one roof, the entire family, we shall be satisfied and can take our sweet time slowly but surely getting stone ready for a building of stone on the right spot. Time will tell!" (167).

Adelhelm described the dedication ceremony as a simple affair, without fanfare, but one of inspiration to the community. He then reassured Abbot Anselm of local support, convivial and financial, by remembering that the few faithful in attendance left a collection donation of $44 or about 200 francs for the building fund. The sum seems to pale in light of the four-digit figures dominating the previous year's correspondence, but it is significant, and was felt to be so then, because it attested local good will. Moreover, these petty donations tended to add into larger sums, and one can trace throughout the correspondence to Engelberg numerous references to contributions showing a widespread base of support. Indeed, Adelhelm noted that Fr. Barnabas as business manager had just reported receiving $600 (3000 francs) from the archbishop of Minnesota in whose jurisdiction St. John's Abbey was located. Some of the letters, very conversational, reveal interesting circumstances for the help received. He told about Aaron Grunbauer, a German Jew from Geisa, Saxony, who converted to Catholicism and made a contribution: "It was a hard job to drive the Jew and Methodist out of his Nathaniel-soul. But the Holy Spirit—by whom he claimed to be guided—triumphed and gave him light...". Grunbauer, a tailor and basketweaver, donated first $150 to the building fund, and promised another $100 more when it was repaid by by a third-party debtor. Other contributions, one time referred to as a "patch" (or "band-aid" as the translator, Fr. Luke Eberle, OSB, suggests) or "drops into the vast ocean of unavoidable expenditures," were always appreciated.

In one passage Adelhelm wished that monies could be sent to Engelberg to send candidates from Switzerland to Oregon since he still felt that they lacked sufficient numbers to meet their tasks. In another, he recounts how charity could be combined with fundraising for the mutual advantage of the community and the donor, in an arrangement reminiscent of medieval confraternalism (168):

> So too, dear God, sent an old man here, Jakob Ringel from Baden Aargau; he had $480 in gold sewn into his vest pocket. You will all believe me whan I say that I was happy to play the tailor and my scissors quickly liberated the wad of gold. The venerable old man (75 years old) still works diligently in the garden and knows alot about raising grapes. We are taking him in for the rest of his life, and he is bequeathing his money to us in writing. *Deo gratias*!

The prior, in humor which should not be mistaken for avarice, was genuinely fond of the old-timer, but taking on the responsibility of caring for the aged and homeless was beyond the monks ordinary capability. The nuns at Queen of the Angels went into such charity work, and continue to do so presently. A confraternity as such, therefore, was never founded at Mt. Angel; this was simply an instance of mutual convenience and opportunity. The monks, with no real home of their own, could hardly promise shelter for others. They preferred to bring laymen into the lay brotherhood, as in the case of another "old-time citizen," Marcus Richards, who professed in 1888 and took the name of Conrad after Engelberg's lay patron and founder.

During these two formative years, the monks tried to live a resemblance of cloistered life as they remembered it at Engelberg. Fr. Barnabas, in a nonextant letter of December 11, 1882 to Abbot Anselm was abstracted into the latter's diary; he described Fillmore so that, according to the abbot, "it makes one's mouth water" (169). He also described community life at Gervais as "very congenial" with adequate facilities and liturgical culture exemplified by Sunday Mass "in chant and four-voice harmony". Adelhelm once complained of his quarters as "the attic," but in other correspondence the housing and church were described as "tasteful," "clean," "neat," and "acoustically sound". The temporary 'priory' had been described by Adelhelm before moving into their quarters as an "annex to the church for a sacristy and rectory 50 feet long and 30 feet wide, consisting of seven rooms on the first floor: [the] sacristy, parish room, three small bedrooms, a big dining room, and [the] kitchen. The second floor, not yet finished inside, could be arranged for large and small rooms to make the whole clumsy American structure usable and habitable". Presumably it was indeed made comfortable. Consequently, life for the monks seems to have been no harder than it was for the other settlers in the valley.

There are occasional glimpses in the surviving records of daily life in this new monastery, such as Fr. Barnabas' remark that as he was writing to the abbot, his confreres "are at present chopping wood and are fetching whole wagonloads of apples from orchards abounding in fruit". An anonymous article by one of the monks for the *Catholic Sentinel* in 1884 commented further that "very often, especially during harvest, Fathers and Fraters have to act the part of farmers and cowboys" (170). Adelhelm went into some detail about the monk's day (171):

> We have the same order of seniority as at home, together with all the customs. However, we all have breakfast in common with the exception of the weekly server; moreover, during it silence is observed in an exemplary manner, perhaps better than ever before at any time.

In contrast to such an idyllic picture of gathering plentiful fruit and sharing communal meals, Fr. Maurus later recalled his being a novice under the prior's tutelage. He remembered that Br. Theodul, who was "cook," had never before made bread. "The bread he made was as hard as brick. There was not much to eat but bread, and water to drink, at meals. I felt hunger very much, suffering as I did from growing pains then being 17 years old" (172).

The priests among the community took charge of the candidates' training and the continuing education of the brothers. Adelhelm explained (173):

> Besides the other Fathers who help with the teaching, I give the Frater Novices one hour on the Holy Rule and one hour of exegesis of the Psalms every day, the Brothers one extra hour on the holy Rule, hence three hours of instruction on top of everything else. If the Fraters do as I teach them daily, they will have enough work for the novitiate, besides English and Latin.

On July 11, 1883 four candidates received their habits; one was a hand-me-down from Adelhelm who was surprised that one candidate had "grown so much that he is wearing my habit without alteration!"

The *Catholic Sentinel* on July 9, 1885 described a typical day, beginning with the morning bells at 3:30 AM for offices, followed by meditation, morning chores, and Mass at 7:30 AM; then a day filled by the canonical hours interspersed with assigned manual labor, classes, study, and meditation. The schedule on July 14, 1884 was typical: 4:45 AM, Matins; 6:30 meditations; 7:00 breakfast; 7:15 Prime; 7:30 conventual High Mass (the brothers heard Mass at 5:45 and had breakfast at 5:45 in order to do necessary farm chores, especially to tend the dairy cows); then work and assorted duties until noon offices and dinner; then afternoon work before 4:00 PM Vespers; 6:00 supper; 7:15 Compline; and spiritual reading before retiring by 8:00 PM. The schedules were published with a description of the workday at the priory to counter anti-Catholic propaganda circulating in the valley and rumors about "lazy monks". The *Sentinel* provided the means for one of the monks to practice modern apologetics, but not to engage in a real polemic (174):

> Often have the monks been accused by ignorant or malicious people, of being lazy. Let those, if any in this country think that the monks are good for nothing, go to our monastery at Mt. Angel and see what change has been brought there in less than two years in that heretofore deserted country. You find there under the shade of the monastery the beginning of a little village, settled by people who know how to appreciate the beneficial influence of that great civilizing order of the Catholic Church—the Benedictines, of which the great Protestant historian [Maitland] is not afraid to say that the world owes to it [the Order] a great debt of gratitude because of its many services rendered to religion, civilization, and literature. We hope that also the young monastery of Mt. Angel, following the path of older institutions, may be to Oregon a real God-send.

Such an admission of local antimonasticism balances other accounts which refer only to the Catholic immigrant population and suggest that everyone welcomed the Benedictines to Oregon. The monks had found a land "of milk and honey" but like any paradise on earth, it had its blemishes and required work to come to fruition.

The psychological stress in resettlement, a necessary defensive guard because of their foreign and monkish ways, financial stress and continued economic uncertainty, and the lack of a genuine monastery, all took their toll on the monastic life at Mt. Angel priory. It was ideally the "New Engelberg" as Abbot Anselm called it, but could hardly come up to standards of the motherhouse. Some of the descriptions of life at Mt. Angel are written to assure the abbot that despite hardships, everything is basically all right at the priory and that the foundation is not only Catholic and Benedictine, it is Swiss-Benedictine. Some of the passages hide underlying fears, and hint at problems which lay just under the surface of some correspondence. In other cases, troubles are in the open.

There were major dissensions between Fr. Adelhelm and Fr. Nicholas, his cohort and travel companion through the 1870s, which were brought into the open in the 1880s when Fr. Barnabas, soon after his arrival from Engelberg, was made procurator. Apparently Nicholas had initially served in that capacity, perhaps unofficially as a carry-over from his previous work with Adelhelm. At one point Nicholas threatened "to resign from the monastery". Adelhelm reported that supposedly Nicholas told Fr. Barnabas that he "was not going to write to you [Abbot Anselm] anymore,...". The trouble involved Fr. Beda as well: "Both think Fr. Beda has been frightfully unjust to them, whereas Fr. Beda says his whole crime lies in his being loyal to me...". The reasons for or resolution of this feuding are not revealed, but it does illustrate the tensions underlying what externally looked like a peaceful if difficult monastic life. Fr. Maurus recalled later that Nicholas left in the summer of 1883 to escape Fr. Beda, and thereafter he left the community to work for Bp. Jungers in the diocese of Nesqually around Vancouver. He eventually became pastor at Uniontown in 1885 and later at the old mission site of Cowlitz. In 1902 he decided to return to Engelberg via the Pacific and Indian Ocean routes. He died and was buried in Calcutta. Others were caught in this bickering and left the priory as well, such as Paul Fundman who in September 1883 left the novitiate to become a teacher at an Indian mission school at Grand Ronde. But few losses created such sadness as Fr. Nicholas' disaffection.

Prior Adelhelm attributed these problems to the insecurity of the foundation in a foreign land, and was sensitive to word back at Engelberg about internal dissension. He hoped that the abbot would not react by non-support, since that would surely exacerbate Mt. Angel's problems. Adelhelm explained that when he appointed Fr. Barnabas procurator, the latter resisted and wanted "two weeks to think it over". Adelhelm thought (175):

> He is afraid that we may be left in the lurch by everyone, even by home, which I denied and said that if we Religious do our duty and all stick together and work fraternally, you [addressing Abbot Anselm] and our motherhouse will not abandon us in our need.

Not only does this correspondence tell something about the emotions and tensions underlying the foundation of this new monastery, thereby adding to institutional history a rare human element not ordinarily seen in monastic portraits, it is equally illustrative of the prior's adroit diplomacy in being able to suggest, however discreetly and indirectly, that it was the abbot's duty and that of Engelberg to assist this struggling community in Oregon to the fullest extent possible. The abbot was all too aware of Adelhelm's tactics and as abbot was no idealist about the problems of community governance. Still, such news about internal problems on top of the external and financial issues surrounding this foundation, was cause for additional worry. Moreover, his diary entries suggest that such internal problems described by Adelhelm for 1883 continued after the move from Gervais into 1886 and still later. Anselm's diary entry for January 3, 1886 reads (176):

> The course of the past year brought me many a secret concern about Mt. Angel which still weighs heavily upon my mind. They are young people, inexperienced and unhardened, who

> must be entrusted with all too important matters there. If there were people available, the worry could be cut in half. But bitter things come also from within the cloister....

Indeed, the abbot continued to hear about such problems from the prior, and complaints about the prior, for the next eight years. Yet, Abbot Anselm remained resolute in his support of Prior Adelhelm.

The problems in organizing the original community, internal dissension, and the manpower shortage which the Benedictines faced in view of a dire need for priests in the valley's churches, prompted ambivalent feelings about the monks' parish work. The new archbishop of Oregon City, William Gross C.SS.R. (1885-98), was then busy reorganizing the diocese and moving the archiepiscopal residence downstream to Portland itself. After this relocation in 1885, the archbishop, even though he needed all the men he could get, felt that the monks could be of better service as a centralized community aiding him in Catholic education. Prior Adelhelm, judging from his experience in Engelberg and at Conception Abbeys as a parish pastor, thought of pastoral work as natural for the Benedictines. Moreover, parish work provided initial revenues as a means of support for the nascent community (177). The prelate, however, began to think differently, especially as some of the clerical shortage began to ease with recruits from the East Coast and seminarians trained in Baltimore. There was no institution for educating clergy in the Pacific Northwest, so that Abp. Gross urged the Benedictines to phase out their parish work and concentrate their efforts in education by establishing a combined seminary and college. That, the prelate speculated, would enable seminarians to study locally at decreased expense to the dioceses, and perhaps also would encourage more vocations and speedier preparation. A local seminary, then, would be a long-term solution to the shortage of clergy in Oregon. Ostensively he sought to protect the monastic community from further splintering, a natural phenomenon when monks begin to live and work away from their monastery and any resemblance of cloistered life. Sometimes monks who have served as parish priests, and therefore have lived a secular life under the guise of the regular, have problems in the transition back into monastic routine and community living. Moreover, in the early history of Mt. Angel, its monks were at times spread out as far as Spokane, Washington, to Cowlitz north of Vancouver, in Portland, and later along the coast beyond Grand Ronde at Tillamook as well as in the original territory from Gervais to the piedmont country around Sublimity. Such extensive parish work, unlike the local pastoral obligations undertaken at Fillmore for the Mt. Angel parish church, could create a classic dilemma for the individual monk and the community as a whole in compromising the focus on communal life and service of the individual through that common bond. This is why some Orders in their reforms, such as the Cistercians of the Strict Observance or Trappists, shunned parish work altogether.

Consequently, after 1885 and his first visit to Mt. Angel on August 1, Abp. Gross attempted to curtail the monk's parish work. His position was clear (178):

> I consider it to be a very great mistake to allow the Fathers to look after parishes. Each Fr. who has such a parish is left to himself. He is not able to keep the rule and is not under the supervision of a superior. Whether he makes a meditation or does his spiritual reading, or whether he does not, no one can say. Naturally he is always among the people of the world, and what this leads to, God alone knows. The great inclination toward freedom and independence in America is enough alone to penetrate a man's thinking, even though he is not in the midst of it, but when he is, he will lose without noticing it, all love for religious life and all interest in the choir and in the school. He does not even wish to think about returning to monastic life with its choir obligation and other usages, and step by step he loses all the spirit of a Religious. Everything that I mention has already long since come to the attention of many bishops in America. For that reason too, no religious order that has a good spirit will allow such a thing any longer. All of the orders have come to know the bitter results through sad experience. For this reason I advise you, Fr. Abbot, in all politeness to send a command to Fr. Prior Adelhelm that he is call all of the Fathers who are entrusted with parishes back to the monastery and not allow the same in the future.

First in 1887 Abp. Gross returned Gervais to the administration of a secular priest, directly under diocesan control; then in 1888 he moved against Benedictine control of the adjacent parishes as well. It is unclear whether the monks willingly acquiesced in the changes he enforced, but at least there was no argument over the matter in general. Differences between the monks and archbishop seem to have been particular; Adelhelm in a letter of March 4, 1888 revealed that the prelate was especially "angry" at Fr. Wehrner who may have been assigned temporarily to duty at Oregon City, but "behind my (the prior's) back and against my command" came back to Sublimity "where he did all sorts of pastoral imprudences until it aggravated the bishop to the extent that he has taken away all our parishes and will have nothing more to do with Fr. Wehrner. Here he [an ambivalent reference, possibly to the prelate, but more likely to the monk] has harmed us greatly" (179). Fr. Wehrner was an Engelbergian, not really under Prior Adelhelm's direct authority because his oath of stability was never transferred to Mt. Angel. Whatever the prior thought then, his worst fears were subsequently quieted by the archbishop who explained his motives and rationale in limiting the monks' parish work. In a letter of February 24, 1888, he assured Prior Adelhelm and indirectly therefore, Abbot Anselm, that the Benedictines in Oregon had "an outstanding spirit and all the Fathers with one exception [alluding to Fr. Wehrner] are excellent". The archbishop elaborated that "Upon my suggestion Father Prior has opened a college" (180).

The correspondence never specifies what Fr. Wehrner did to alienate the archbishop, and Fr. Maurus later contradicted the notion that any of the community did anything wrong. He maintained that the prior had asked to have the parishes returned because of the monastery's manpower shortage (181). This is unlikely in view of the documentation just cited; moreover, parish work was Adelhelm's great love, the parishes produced revenues, however modest, which the monks greatly needed to build their monastery. In any case, relations between the monks and archiepiscopal administration remained cordial without lasting damage by Fr. Wehrner's behavior. It seems instead that the latter's imprudence simply provided the occasion for the archbishop's action. In fact, in contrast to the condition of the parishes as they found them under itinerant missioners, the monks left these parishes well-organized and stable. Their pastoral work was so credible that when the local ordinary again had a shortage of diocesan priests with which to contend, he would again seek temporary assistance from the monks to either take over parishes or lend themselves for weekend duty at a church in need. The monks retained the Fillmore or Mt. Angel parish, and in 1894 Adelhelm would himself take over Sacred Heart parish in southeast Portland.

After the settlement at Fillmore was ready by July 14, 1884 for the community's move from Gervais, a vigorous building program was undertaken in part to enhance the monastery itself but also to accomodate the college. On February 13, 1886 the Abbot Anselm quoted a non-extant letter of the prior which provides a summary of the monastery's economic accomplishments and future hopes despite enormous debts (182):

> In order to reassure us regarding the burden of debt, Prior Adelhelm writes: '1,400 acres near the monastery will be worth $100 an acre, hence $140,000. Building[s], livestock, and inventory, $30,000. The land in the hills (3,400 acres), only after 25-50 years to be sure, will be worth $72,000. Hence around 1,200,000 francs in all.' If only this statement were correct. Father Prior shows himself ready to go collecting throughout America.

The statement may not have been accurate, the acreage for both the farmstead and timberland differ from the survey data in previous correspondence and the acreage of the homesteads bought as recorded in the 1878 land survey in Oregon. It may have been slightly exaggerated, or else the prior had indeed acquired some more land which was later sold.

Apart from the land itself, an earlier accounting of March 27, 1884 provides some idea of the development of the monastery (183):

> Mt. Angel lies at the foot of the hill. All around it are grouped the drier, cheese plant, carpenter shop, cider press, flour mill, machine shop, fruit house, sheep barns, several cow and horse barns, pig pens, hay and straw barns, living quarters for hired hands, [a] large lumber shed, two smokehouses, a bakery, kiln, smithy, bee house, [and] chicken coop. The land complex, consisting of seven farms lies all around the hill.

Thus one has a remarkable account of tremendous accomplishment in just a few years. Granted that many of the buildings enumerated were built by the original owners of the land and were rather modest structures, but their existence attests the readiness of the monastic estate to produce and turn a profit which could in time allay the large debt which encumbered it. One must be impressed with this daring venture amidst financial adversity; it was a corporate endeavor, more than could be accomplished individually, which took hard work, skill, and luck—or as the monks assumed, spiritual intervention.

The Benedictine community was indeed incorporated under Oregon state law and was recognized as an educational institution. Abbot Anselm was informed by the prior on December 13, 1886 that Abp. Gross expected a Latin school to open with a year as the nucleus for the subsequent development of a combination college and seminary. Adelhelm had agreed to hurry the school along because, as the archbishop reminded him using the same tactics as had Archbshop Seghers before, the next prelate could be an Irishman, not nearly so favorable to the Swiss-Benedictines or to the German communities. The prior's immediate plans were less grand than the archbishop's, perhaps because it is not clear if the prelate contributed any funding for the school. Adelhelm envisioned a preparatory school with two secondary curricula beyond that, one in business or "Commercial arts," and the other in liberal arts following the classical model. It was also decided to let boys work with the brethren on the monastery's farm in order to study agriculture and to learn farming, thus constituting an "agricultural school".

The *Prospectus* stated the institution's objective "is to impart to young men a thorough moral and mental training so as to fit them for any position in life" (184). It described a six-year course of study for each program, classics and

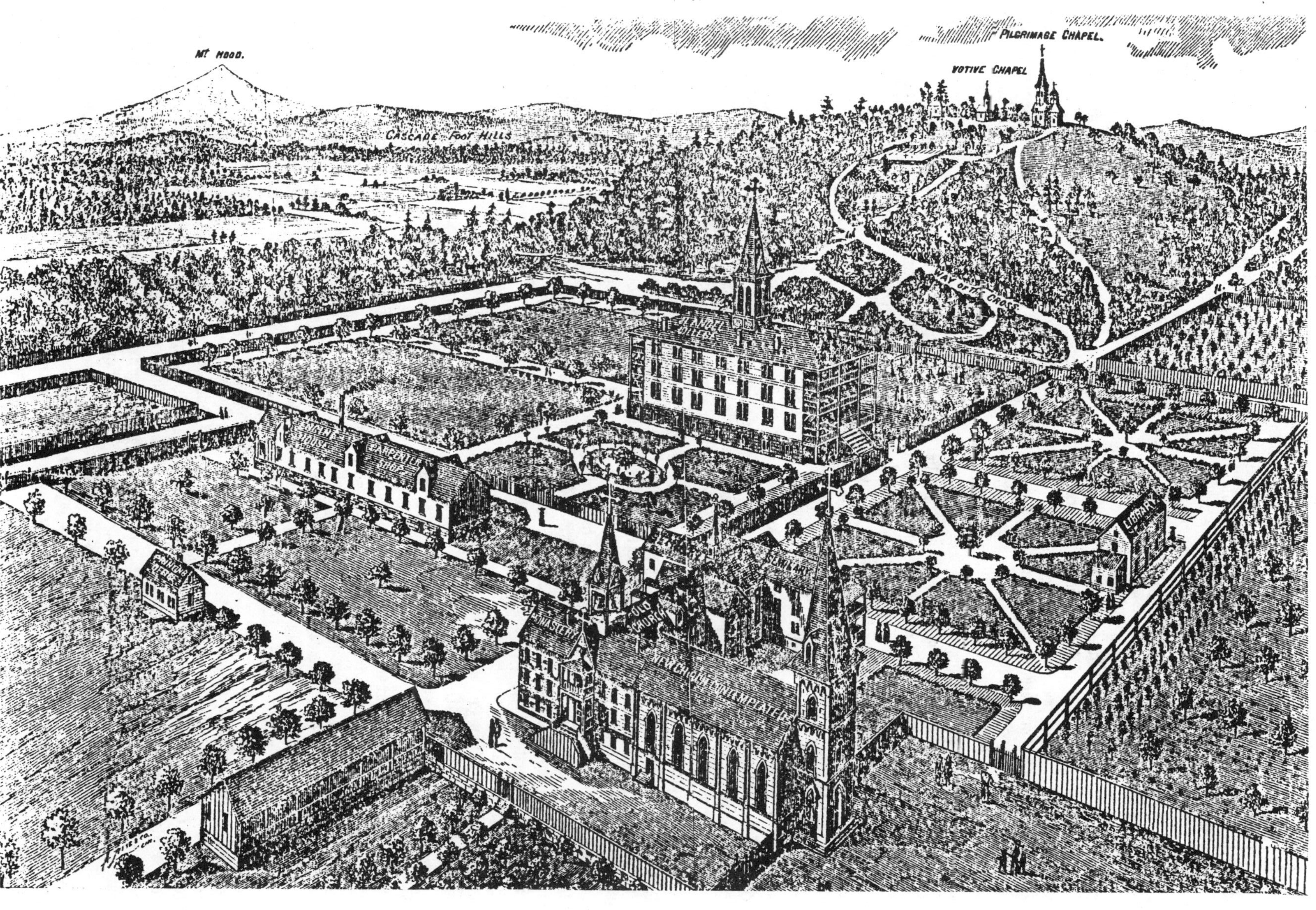

Fig. 6. Mt. Angel Priory, Seminary, and College, ca. 1890. Engraving by A. Rize & Co., MAA, s.n., looking towards the butte.

commercial arts. The school year consisted of two five-month semesters running from September to February, and from February to June, with examinations formally scheduled at the end of each. Reports on academic progress and behavior were promised to all parents and guardians. "Certificates and academic degrees are conferred on those that have merited them, according to the customs of the country [USA]". Admission standards were not immediately clarified, except that placement into an appropriate class was by examination. Non-Catholics could enroll "provided they be willing, for the sake of order and uniformity, to be present with propriety, at the ordinary religious exercise". Twenty-three special regulations were stipulated, including silence during study hours; inspection of students' mail; prohibition of tobacco, profanity, etc.; and any expression of "contempt or ridicule of religion" was grounds for dismissal as were possession of "immoral publications or pictures," intoxication, and the procuring of "ardent spirits" (which omitted beer, of course), "habitual idleness," and "absence without leave". The preference was for boarders to study in residence, but local "day students" were tolerated. The costs were negligible by modern standards: tuition was a seemingly mere $30.00 per session, but this was substantial enough considering time and place. Room and board was $90.00 per session, with a $5.00 entrance fee, and there were $5-15.00 surcharges for special courses requiring individual tutoring such as music and laboratory support for courses like chemistry. Still, the average student could attend this young men's preparatory school and college for less than $300 a year, all expenses included.

This school, a simple frame building 35 x 50 feet, opened on October 22, 1887, with Fr. Barnabas as its rector. By 1890 the curriculum had expanded into the advanced studies level, and it enrolled over one hundred students. It was the first of its kind in the Pacific Northwest, being modeled largely after the German-Swiss gymnasium tradition. The main exception was the inclusion of agriculture as a trade-school component and a remedial course of study for those not ready to embark immediately into the two major curricula. On February 24, 1888 the archbishop was able to praise the "college" as filling a critical need in Oregon, and he again voiced his preference for the monks to concentrate on this educational effort. He still wanted to develop the college into one of "grand style" with a reputable seminary in order for the Northwest to gain self-sufficiency in the training of its own clergy (185).

Although the college could serve the entire Oregon population, that was never the real intention; Abp. Gross, in any case, envisioned it primarily as a clerical training center. The enrollment of young men who never entered the clergy was inherent in the college's auxiliary purpose of letting young people explore the possibility of a priestly vocation. A better educated Catholic lay populace was an incidental benefit of the school.

A grounding in philosophy lay at the core of the college's liberal arts curriculum, constituting a general studies program; thereafter students could specialize somewhat by electives in religion, education, science, and art. The teachers-training program was approved by the state in 1889 at the onset of the college (186). The college had twelve faculty members, some of whom achieved notariety as they expanded their teaching and their own educations into areas far afield from their training, in contrast to the modern tendency toward specialization. A report in the *Catholic Sentinel* for October 8, 1888, described one unnamed faculty member as fluent in fifteen languages, who in addition to these taught "typewriting, his own system; drawing, and fancy penmanship" as well! In addition to his musical talents, Fr. Placidus Fuerst was depicted as "the author of several useful inventions" who "hopes to surprise the world shortly with a kind of flying machine which works first rate" (187). Later, other monks would be moved throughout the curricula to such an extent that after a lifetime of teaching they indeed seemed to be "walking encyclopedias," but no heralding invention or scientific breakthrough came from their efforts. Instead, their main contribution was in the everyday business of teaching Westerners who until the school opened had little opportunity, unless their families were wealthy enough to send them East, to gain any comparable education.

The college gained a widespread reputation, partially because there was little competition; the state was just beginning to establish its system and other private, and denominational schools were in the area were yet to develop any advanced curricula. The college also publicized itself, if not through its students, certainly by a sense of publication relations and periodic fanfare whenever there was proper excuse. At the commencement exercises of the academy, seminary, and college on July 4, 1889, for example, there was a special excursion train routed from Portland, hauling three hundred passengers to Mt. Angel. They were greeted at the train depot by the newly uniformed college band under the direction of Fr. Barnabas Held, escorted in parade to the monastery, and were treated to a full afternoon of festivities and a taste of Benedictine Old-World hospitality. The day included not only the graduation exercises themselves, but the play *Thomas Moore*; addresses by the state superintendent of schools, E.B. McElroy, Governor Pennoyer, and a visiting professor; lunch prepared by the Benedictine sisters; and an enthusiastic send-off back at the station. It was by all accounts a grand occasion! And subsequent programs were even more daring, bringing high culture to the valley in ways not previously common. In the 1890 exercises, Shakespeare's *Julius Caesar* was performed before a "spell-bound" audience, partially to demonstrate the students' work (and the monks' abilities to coach them) in English (188). Likewise, the music program became more elaborate with the development of an orchestra. And the college boasted of a new theater which opened in 1888, complete with a fully equipped stage, backdrops, and acoustical design, as "one of the finest theaters in the state, Portland excepted" (189). By 1889 the college had grown to 115 students "with almost daily additions," and had several organizations developing: the Young Men's Institute which resembled a Catholic YMCA, a militia, and a drill team (190).

The envisioned archdiocesan seminary opened two years after the college, on March 21, 1889; it was the first west of the Rocky Mountains to serve exclusively the new dioceses being organized above California (191). Fr. Dominic Waedenschwyler (d. 1932), who had just arrived from Engelberg in fall, 1887, when the seminary was opening, became its rector. The seminary was a wood frame building adjacent to the priory itself. The two schools were run separately. The seminary, following the model set by the Sulpician seminary of St. Charles in Baltimore, was further divided into the major and minor seminary. A separate building for the latter, often called the "little" seminary, had its cornerstone laid in 1899. The prior then assumed the post of rector himself, and Fr. Dominic became the director of the new college. The seminary began with only five students in its program, but expanded to nineteen seminarians during the second year; it continued throughout the decade with modest enrollments never exceeding thirty students at one time. It was served by a faculty of nine. Dedicated to St. Anselm as its patron, it continued to receive the benefaction of Abp. Gross who not only visited the priory after 1889 to conduct retreats, but to preside personally over some of the examinations being given to his future clergy (192). The earliest catalogue in 1889 describes an intense curriculum of six years in classical studies, along with such extras as basic bookkeeping, liturgy, and music. After this preparation, seminarians for two years more engaged formal courses in mental, moral, and natural philosophy; chemistry, astronomy, geology, and natural history; mathematics; and Hebrew, Greek, and more Latin. Then only did the seminarian enter his advanced studies: liturgy, canon law, and also medicine. Thus the usual course of studies lasted nearly a full decade.

Certainly the continued financial strain on the community while it developed its college and seminary was bad enough, but just when the foundation was achieving a momentum of its own and the critical years from 1883-85 seemed to be behind them, the monks of Mt. Angel faced continued challenges during the 1890s. Their lands were on high ground, so the monks escaped the ravaging flood of the Willamette River in February 1890; yet the damage was so extensive that the entire valley was affected economically thereafter. River commerce, the milling industry, and lowland farms were especially hard hit, and the damage to Oregon City and Portland at the mouth of the river was calamitous. Relief efforts, rebuilding, and loss of incomes resulted in an inability of the secular church to help defray much of the costs for the Mt. Angel schools. Later in June, 1890, the monks narrowly escaped being burned out when a fire was discovered in the college waiter's hall, apparently caused by a half-burnt cigar carelessly thrown into a spitoon filled with dry sawdust. The damage, estimated at $500, was covered by insurance (193). They were not so fortunate on May 3, 1892, a memorable day when fire broke out in the kitchen chimney and swept through the wooden frame buildings, destroying almost everything—the church, priory, seminary, mill, and carpentry shop, leaving only the college and the farm's outbuildings intact (194).

Abbot Anselm received the bad news by cablegram on May 5, but the full report was not available to him for another two weeks. "So our priory in Oregon burned down! At first the news hit me," he wrote, "like a bolt of lightning". While anxiously waiting to ascertain the extent of the damage and disbelieving that it was total ruin, he again turned to his diary to work out his thoughts (195):

> I am tormented by the true homesickness for the place [with] the fire at Mt. Angel, or much rather for my confreres, whom I see in my mind as despondent, forsaken, and in complete bewilderment.. Oh, if I could only help them! But it is not possible. I have already dared too much. There God must help.

He recorded on May 20 the worst news, that by 4:00 PM on the day of the fire, the main buildings had been reduced to their foundations. Insurance covered the school for only $100; the priory was insured to only $7000 (35,000 francs) more. The latter was applied by the prior to the community's California debt rather than to begin a rebuilding fund; perhaps he thought that would at least earn more credit (196).

One eye-witness described the Mt. Angel fire in his diary (197):

> ... at 2 PM, just as the classes had taken up, the terrible cry of 'Fire' was heard in the monastery and seminary. The smoke coming out through the roof told us that the cry was only too true. We all rushed for our clothes and books, as the brothers and students were active in combating the flames that made rapid progress on the monastery roof.... In two hours the monastery and our beloved seminary were reduced to a heap of smoking ruins. Sad is the site of our happy home....

There were no fire engines, only whatever volunteers which could be mustered. The college roof also caught on fire, but it was saved by a student firefighting brigade and by, as one anonymous monk wrote, "help from above. No doubt the pious Sisters helped a great deal by their prayers, for they were praying earnestly during the whole conflagration". Adelhelm later praised the students: "During the fire the students from the biggest to the smallest helped along like family members and worked until they collapsed.... Fortunately there was no death or injury of any consequence".

The monks took refuge with their parishoners and were not to be reassembled as a cloistered community for another decade when in 1903 a new monastery would be completed. However, the community proved very resilient. As attested by both the Mt. Angel *Banner*,the college's newspaper, and the *St. Joseph's Blatt*, the community's German newspaper, as well as Adelhelm's communication of May 5 to the abbot, the school and college continued on schedule, first in Mr. Oswald's village hotel while the faculty lodged in the nearby home of Mr. Butala. Local residents invited everyone into their homes for supper, but on the next day the Sisters of Queen of the Angel's Convent set up food services in the college. Adelhelm made arrangements for the twenty-four seminarians to move into the college with the hundred or more students. Its recreation rooms were converted into two refectories or dining halls, a kitchen was established on the main floor, and some of the fathers doubled up in spare rooms made available by a wholescale cleaning and economization of all available space. Some of the brothers made housing arrangements on the farmsteads.

Although local benefactors came to the community's immediate aid, the magnitude of the loss threatened the monastery's survival. The seminary catalogue of 1889-90 had already admitted that "The archdiocese is still too sparsly populated to come to our relief and the institution [the seminary] itself is of too recent growth to have secured the practical interests of wealthy, generous Catholics". Mt. Angel's rescue would depend on the small donations of many, rather than the largess of a worldly benefactor. Immediate responses were encouraging; Adelhelm recalled that one neighbor "came to me right after the fire and pressed $100 into my hand". The mayors of both Portland and Salem made appeals on behalf of the monks, and of course, Abp. Gross, who inspected the smoldering site the very next day, rushed to the monastery's support. His pastoral letter to the province's clergy announced: "The Benedictine Fathers of Mt. Angel are now homeless.... The Seminary of the archdiocese was under the same roof as the monastery..., at four [o'clock], only the stone foundations remained" (198). Adelhelm, in keeping with his amazing optimism, was confident about the help the monks would receive, as if the disaster could be turned into a proverbial blessing in disguise (199).

Sister M. Agnes Butsch, OSB, in 1935 recalled Adelhelm accompanied by her father, Mathias Butsch, and Robert Zollver "going from farm house to farm house on horseback, soliciting subscriptions (i.e., pledges) of help for the Benedictine Fathers" (200).

> The loss is great but God knows how to make the best of it all. Everyone sympathizes with us, our neighbors are helping as much as they can.... He [Abp. Gross], Portland, and all of Oregon will not leave us in the lurch. After this fire we can go out soliciting much more optimistically—especially in the East, where the bishops can hardly refuse us permission to collect.

In another instance, after counting the losses but assuring the abbot that the sacred vessels and Blessed Sacrament had been rescued from the sanctuary, he again rebounded to his seemingly undaunted self: "The loss is in any event very great, but God and good people, to whom we are grateful for every charitable gift, will not forsake us, just as our dear Americans will not". His unthinking admission that he never thought of himself as an American, and even distinguished between "good people" and "Americans" is interesting, but more to the point, he was correct in anticipating relief from a broad spectrum of American society, Protestant and Catholic, Oregonians and those throughout the country who responded to the call for help.

The disaster created a shakeup in the community's organization. Prior Adelhelm resigned his office and set out on the first of several fund-raising tours throughout the United States. Fr. Leo Huebscher became the acting prior during Adelhelm's absence, and also the temporary rector of the college until 1893 when Fr. Placidus Fuerst (1868-1940), a recruit in 1882 while a young novice at Engelberg, took charge. The crisis also prompted the organization of an alumnae association to help promote the college; it would have its first reunion on June 27, 1894 under President John Kavanaugh (201). Fr. William Kramer wrote to Abbot Anselm on December 17, 1892 that the new administration was working well: "He writes," wrote the abbot in his diary, "that under Fr. Leo as subprior, things are going well, that living together practically has never been more beautiful than now. The college is flourishing at least in spirit and good discipline. Debts are decreasing. Bequests and legacies contribute to the priory's income. The prior may stay away as long as there is anything to collect" (202). In the face of adversity and in the absence of Prior Adelehlm, previous internal dissensions seemed to have vanished.

Meanwhile, Adelhelm's whirlwind tour, coupled with an express trip back to Engelberg to ask the general chapter for further help, took only a year. He had always had a flair for public relations and was a gifted preacher. His aplomb was captured in one delightful instance when the railroad finally switched in 1890 from narrow to standard gauge and the first standard-gauge train arrived in Mt. Angel on November 11. This was a public occasion upon which the prior knew how to capitalize. As engine No. 10 pulled its ten cars (eight box cars, a Wells Fargo coach, and only a single passenger carrier), it was heralded by the college's band, a throng of enthusiastic townsmen, and the prior with his confreres. In a style now seemingly overdone and foreign, as it may have been then too, Adelhelm waxed eloquently in his oration, taking care to praise the innovative leadership of railroad magnate Collis P. Huntington before the local railway officials (203). The *Sentinel* preserved the text of his speech and captured something of that day's excitement; it also depicts an adriot politician at work. The prior's technique was the same as when he convinced the railroad and everyone else to rename Fillmore "Mt. Angel". Now, in his mission to save the monastery, his ability in public relations stood the test beyond the confines of rural Oregon.

In countless contacts he distributed St. Benedict medals throughout his journey as Catholics rallied to the priory's rescue; in one instance he even managed to make Cardinal Gibbons an oblate of St. Benedict. Fundraising was hardly an easy task, however. On November 11, 1894 in response to news from this wandering monk, Abbot Anselm commented: "Serious worry about Mt. Angel still weighs heavily on me. The collections in America are not doing well. The debt in California can hardly be wiped out". Adelhelm's correspondence thereafter brought news daily, good and bad. In New York city the prior received several hundred dollars from the Benziger Brothers publishing firm, and in Newark, New Jersey, the local ordinary, Bp. Wigger, allowed the prior to travel from parish to parish begging for his cause. According to Abbot Anselm, Adelhelm substituted for pastors, preached, took over confessions, and even made sick calls to earn his way and make even more contacts. Apparently on November 28 the abbot learned about the whole experience, since Adelhelm had time to write at length while recovering in a hospital from exhaustion and illness. Slowly, however, the crisis at Mt. Angel began to subside as alms trickled in and a more positive response to the archbishop's appeal took effect. Hope grew stronger as the prospect of rebuilding became more evident.

Despite reassurance from Oregon and intermittent good news from Adelhelm's campaign, Engelberg bore some of the priory's burden. On December 25, 1892 the subprior had already informed the abbot that the monastery had only enough liquid capital to pay the interest on the debts owed to Falk & Co. and to pay off its American creditors, so that Mt. Angel would default on the loans to the motherhouse. Now that disaster had struck, the abbot knew he could expect little repayment from Oregon and would have to extend the loans at least until after the prior could rebuild (204).

> That could take years. It will mean big deficits in my accounts. But in the Name of God, when I think of their situation, consider their poverty, I must, so as not to discourage them completely and force them to disband, grant their request and try to find the help for myself from another means. If the capital is made secure in this way [a loan extension], the interest can be dispensed with for the time being. But what this enterprise in America has already cost me in worry, suffering and sleepless nights! Some day there will surely be peace!

Far from reconciled to the *fait accompli* presented to him, the abbot subsequently wrote "The most recent reports from Mt. Angel have left a wound in my heart which makes itself felt over and over, fifty to a hundred times a day, especially as soon as I wake. Oh, why so many worries?" Despite the problems created for Engelberg, its loans to Mt. Angel were indeed extended and the interest was reduced to 1.5%. The priory's debts in 1892 were listed at $198,624, of which $137,957 were owed to Engelberg. Anselm's worries were to worsen because Conception Abbey was likewise in arrears; its debt of $30,000 had to be refinanced after 1884 by Einsiedeln, although at a rate reduced from 7 to 4.5%—still higher than the preferential treatment shown Mt. Angel at this time of crisis. Conception Abbey's fifteen-year repayment cycle was only half-finished when on June 21, 1893, so soon after the Mt. Angel disaster, Conception was hit by a tornado. The damage, once thought to be more, was only $10,000; but this still necessitated more loans (205). Engelberg was hard-pressed to help both houses at once.

Adelhelm had always wanted to build a monastery on top of the volcanic outcropping rather than at its base where the old priory had stood, not only for increased solace, so he said, but to create a shrine site perhaps reminiscent of Einsiedeln in Switzerland. Abp. Seghers, it was pointed out, had also wanted the monastery to be on top of the butte overlooking the valley as a visible sign of Catholic presence in the Willamette region. Certainly the intention of moving to the hilltop eventually was one reason for buying all the encircling land. It was now decided to leave the college where it stood on the farmstead below, but to rebuild on what symbolically had become "Mount" Angel. After extended debate, on October 25, 1893, construction began, this time in stone, at the northern, highest point of the butte where a small table of land of a couple of acres provided a miniature campus elevated 450 feet above sea level and about 250-300 feet above the surrounding prairie land (206). The building required every dollar the community could raise.

The recovery of the community from this disaster cannot be reconstructed in detail; the bookkeeping was less than adequate, and the account books were later lost in another tragedy. Moreover, the abbey archives *per se* are not open to research. No doubt, however, its success must be attributed largely to the indefatigable efforts of its founder and the coherence of the community itself, despite expected dissensions, through these trying times. While the archbishop, it appears, concentrated on helping the archdiocesan seminary, the Benedictines fended largely for themselves. In seven years Adelhelm raised enough money to liquidate a $30,000 mortgage and other debts to American creditors, pay interest on the European loans secured by Engelberg, and put $12,000 into the rebuilding fund. For the same decade the loans made by Engelberg herself were left largely untouched. In later correspondence of April 13, 1901, Mt. Angel's debts were calculated at $190,000, only $8000 less than in 1892. That debt reduction of $1000 was with American creditors and investment firms, while during the same time the priory's indebtedness to the abbey increased by $2000 (207). Even so, Abbot Anselm had to remark in his diary, with obvious amusement, "Prior Adelhelm is a master in contracting debts, and in collecting money at the same time". Indeed, it was later alleged that at the turn of the century Adelhelm's gift at 'development' as fundraising is called today, still produced an average of $10,000 a year in donations, and in a record year as much as $14,000.

Despite such expressions of confidence in Adelhelm, the abbot was always wary of the prior's seemingly reckless spending despite the latter's constant assurances that these debts were absolutely necessary. When the abbot was told that the community thrived in the prior's absence during 1892-93, it caused him to reflect that "The prior will probably never become abbot; he is suitable as prior, but not as abbot". His reservations were reinforced when Adelhelm returned to Mt. Angel; subprior Leo resigned almost immediately and requested permission to return to Switzerland. The abbot in late 1893 noted simply, "Fr. Leo Hübscher is coming home to stay. He was subprior at Mt. Angel, but could not control his temper and he did not get along with the Prior". Moreover, in that same annotation of December 17, 1892 in which Anselm thought poorly of Adelhelm's prospects for the abbacy, his diary reads: "Practical considerations and costs will probably dictate that the new monastery not be built on the hill, but at its foot; however, that will be put off for years yet" (209). One can imagine his surprise that despite the default on Engelberg's loans, within a year after the prior's return the Mt. Angel chapter agreed to start building and to do so at the summit. The abbot subsequently recorded that "Most of the Fathers seem, in opposition to the Prior, to want to build on the lower level. In general, the attitude of the fathers toward the prior does not seem to be friendly, whereas the big majority of the brothers are loyal to him". It is not known how accurately the abbot assessed the situation so far away, but Adelhelm, for all his charm and zeal, could be difficult. In at least one instance, the prior was reprimanded by Abp. Gross for meddling into the affairs of the convent and trying to influence the election of an abbess. Not only did this bring adverse reaction from the nuns and censure from the archbishop, but it must have influenced the abbot as well in decisions he made during 1894.

In May the abbot appointed a new prior, Fr. Benedikt Gottwald, who arrived from Engelberg that summer to govern the community until 1899 when he returned to the abbey because of poor health (210). During this time the founder spent much of his time in Portland, continuing to raise funds from his base at Sacred Heart parish (covering Milwaukee and Sandy, Oregon, suburbs southeast of the city), where he resided as pastor. In order to take charge of this parish and receive its property deeds from the archbishop, Adelhelm in 1892 had taken on another debt of $6000 which soon increased to $10-12,000. Later accounts, largely stemming from the reminiscences of Fr. Maurus, confuse this picture. It seems that the parish had an initial debt for its own building program and that another house was built in order to bring nuns there for a parish school (211). Although it was presumed that these debts would be paid by the parish, the abbot may have regarded this decision as unjustified in view of the priory's indebtedness, or that the prior had simply taken too much upon himself. A parish so in debt could hardly generate revenues which would have helped the priory. Adelhelm had appointed a surrogate, Fr. Maurus, as subprior after Fr. Leo left. In any case, most accounts suspect that the decision to replace Adelhelm with a new prior directly from Engelberg was motivated by the cautious stance of the abbot and the perceived need to impose a more conservative administration on Mt. Angel. Anselm had stood by Adelhelm for over a decade despite constant doubt about the wisdom of his financial dealings and the adverse criticism which the Engelbergians relayed to the motherhouse. Indeed, there was almost a mounting lobby effort to dislodge the prior. In 1894 during their visit to Engelberg, Fr. Beda and William personally expressed their frustration with Adelhelm, making Anselm reflect back on the problems which had surfaced before Fr. Nicholas left Gervais. The testimony of Fr. Leo must have convinced the abbot finally that a change in command was needed. Those who remembered Adelhelm recalled his warm, personal humor, and his piety, but moreso his zeal, vigor, and boundless energy. This made Fr. Ambroze Zenner, after reading in 1949 Adelhelm's extant correspondence and the abbot's diary, to characterize the founder as "that pioneer time which bulldozes ahead often to the pain of his class associates" (212). Others have contrasted the prior to the quiet, demuring Abbot Frowin of Conception Abbey, who in 1891 had conducted, and would do so again in 1901 and 1904, the visitations to Mt. Angel on behalf of the Engelberg abbots.

The new prior, Fr. Benedikt, was a sound businessman, well suited to supervise the foundation's reconstruction. The Engelberg community still regards his administration (so thought Fr. Ambrose in 1951) as crucial for Mt. Angel's survival, but such historical judgements about his effectiveness have been complicated by the paucity of documentation and the ambivalant attitudes of the monks under his guidance. His was a difficult administration, not only because of the financial worries, but because of factionalization in the community over the difficult decisions which had to be made. Fr. Maurus recalled incidents resulting from a split between those wanting to adopt Americanizations, and those holding onto European traditions, which suggest a temporary breakdown in monastic discipline and community life in the 1890s following the destruction of the monastery. There was some estrangement between the Engelberg overseer and the local recruits into the Order, and a parallel schism between the members who favored a more liberal lifestyle anb those who adhered to old ways and strict discipline. Accounts recorded much later recall some unruly pranks such as when a German flag was dipped unceremoniously into a closet pit as a protest by the new against old-world attitudes evident in the cleavage among the monks. Parties with local laymen, convivial as the monks had to be during their diaspora, were resented by others as laxity and signs of degradation of monastic life. It is not clear, however, whether some of these stories refer to students, novices, or to the monks themselves. More explicit is the condemnation of Fr. Anselm Weissenborn, who in the folkart watercolor illustrations of two calligraphed liturgical books produced at Mt. Angel in 1910-11, depicts card playing, beer drinking in the local pub, and political gossip, as the main temptations visited upon the monks during these difficult times (213). Abbot Bernard recalled: "In 1884 I think there were about five houses in Mt. Angel, in 1889 there were about a dozen.... Mt. Angel had a bad reputation for drinking in those days. It was only a small town, but there were four or five saloons" (214). He remembered some of the owners, Klinger, Fred Schwab, and Barney Oswald, as friends of the monastery. One can see here the process of Germanization, as in the town's celebrated Oktoberfest of today, when the beer, sausages, and German bakegoods are consumed in abundance by crowds from up and down the West Coast. Of course drunkenness was censured, but not beer drinking as such. German and American values sometimes clashed within the community as in its surroundings as the country headed toward prohibition. Fr. Maurus recalled his amazement that when the Engelberg party was traveling across country it was hosted in St. Louis on Sunday, October 15, 1882, by a German tavern keeper who served them beer in the privacy of his garden behind his establishment. The jovial monks began singing as they were about to enjoy their draft, but they were hushed by their host who explained that Blue Laws forbade the sale of liquor on Sunday and that he was afraid their merriment would attract the local police. The "surprised greenhorns" unaccustomed to thinking of beer as a liquor, could hardly believe their host that such a law would be thinkable, less so enforcible. It seemed blatantly anti-German, quite uncivilized (215). Yet, apparently Fr. Anselm thought that beer drinking had gotten out of hand. Indeed, there were instances which seem to support his inference, but never involving the monks themselves as depicted in his drawings. One candidate for the brotherhood, Joe O'Brien, a former sailor bent on amending his ways after surviving a shipwreck, "wasn't always prohibitionist" as one recollection puts it. "We were having a lecture in the college once by Fr. Brabant, a missionary to the Indians. Some of the older boys had gone downtown and got a bottle of whiskey, and had given Joe too much, so he got up during the meeting after one of Fr. Brabant's stories and shouted 'thats a damned lie!'" Joe never became a Benedictine, although he periodically volunteered to help in the kitchens. Nor did most of the brother-candidates who entered Mt. Angel in 1889; Abbot Bernard thought "lots of them were merely tramps" (216).

The reminiscences of the older members of the community in the late 1940s and during the 1950s provide numerous anecdotes which portray, not the spiritual life of the monks, but a pleasant social life which was neither overly ascetic and strict nor lax and debased. It was characterized by Benedictine moderation, and despite arguments, personality clashes, and factionalization as common to all communal organizations, there is ample evidence of humor, enjoyment of a reasonably comfortable life, and appreciation for the natural setting of the monastery. Abbot Bernard's recollections shed considerable light on the monastery's prospering dairy industry. He recalled that the main barn used to stand near the present hop drier site, and there was another barn 500 years to the northwest of the hill. There were winter pastures there, but in summer the cows would be driven to highland pasturage at the Milk Ranch (which he had first visited in 1889). This transmigrant ritual was repeated twice yearly, and while the herd was upland, the brothers had to bring the milk back three times each week by horsedrawn wagons. Mt. Angel's famous Swiss cheese was often made at the Milk Ranch and brought down as well for temporary storage in the cheese house before consumption. The journey back and forth took nearly a day. Abbot Bernard recalled that the caravan would stop for lunch at an old battlefield in the foothills, before the two to three-hour climb to the ranch. It was isolated there, although some people lived in an adjacent meadow, Grassy Flat, in a village called St. Bernard by everyone but Adelhelm who insisted on calling it St. Benedict. While one brother was entrusted with the milk runs, another was stationed there to tend to the herd, keep up the property, and make cheese. There was a small cabin on the ranch, the cheese or milk house, and a separate chapel built by Joseph Speldrich who was also responsible for deeloping some of the land. In summer 1900 the prior conducted a long foray up into the mountains behind the Milk Ranch to see if the water falls there could be harnessed for electricity. The proprietor, the owner of Scott's Mills, had agreed to share his water rights with the monastery, but it was decided that the whole project would be impractical because of the uneven flow of water from spring to fall and transmission lines over that distance would be too expensive. Abbot Bernard remembered, though, that about $100,000 had gone into this highland investment over the decades: "Old Father Prior wanted to have a place like the Alps" he thought (217). Yet taxes were minimal, amounting to only about $300 each year on all of the monastery's real estate.

Abbot Bernard also recalled the other parcels of land outside the main farmstead to which they used to travel. The monastery's coffers were helped in 1899 by a donation of Mrs. Chapman of a 400-acre farm located at Wrentham, eight miles southwest of the Dalles on the other side of the Cascades. The prior wanted to farm the land and sent Fr. Berchtold and two brothers there for more than nine months, but the distance and poor roads through the mountains proved prohibitive. It was sold for $6000. Another donated farm at Crates Point was also sold. The farmland was divided when the Union Pacific railway straightened out a sweeping curve in its roadbed and enforced its right-of-way to cut the farm in two. Moreover, Abbot Bernard remembered that the house was built so near the creek that when it flooded "salmon were swimming around the porch". Mt. Angel's diaries, letters, and recorded reminiscences thus provide some indication of life at Mt. Angel at the turn of the century, partially compensating for the inaccessibility and lack of official records.

As always in monastic history, a community's spiritual life is the most difficult to document and is almost impossible to assess objectively. The daily routine of prayer in Benedictine life is so well integrated that it scarcely attracts attention; it is almost too commonplace. Nor does the historian have privileged access to the dialogue between man and his Creator. In the absence of scandal, it is possible to suppose that the community's spirituality was exemplary. There are scattered references in the documents to special liturgies, celebrations for special events and major feast days, but these tell of a cultural aspect rather than spirituality as such. Mt. Angel has produced no canonized saint, no great spiritualist author, no modern Thomas Merton. Instead, the picture which emerges out of the monastery's record is a group of men, all too human, striving for salvation by engaging in communal work, prayer, and play. The nature of the records, of course, emphasize the work and economic aspects of the monastery's welfare; narrative sources often reflect personalities, particular situations sporadically recalled, unique perspectives, and often biased testimony. It is the historian's difficult task to assemble these into a holistic, balanced view; when the subject studied is an organization dedicated to spiritual values and objectives, and one cannot adequately document the latter. This task seems impossible. Moreover, modern sensibilities do not insist on the same standards or expressions of spirituality which may have characterized bygone years. Yet, a few impressions can be offered from the documents.

Certainly there is ample indication of a deep conviction about the necessity of formal learning in the age-old monk-scholar tradition as well as in the informal, personal mode of continuing education and spiritual development. Adelhelm's care for the formation of the junior members of the community is noteworthy. It is known that the monks conducted retreats, not only for others, but also for themselves. Guests preached before the community, while others lectured about a wide range of topics. Periodically the archbishops led retreats themselves. Until 1901, as Abbot Bernard later recalled, the Mt. Angel monks continued the Engelberg custom of observing the Grand Silence during their main annual retreats; then there was no preaching, lectures, or special events. Everyone followed a prescribed "order of the day, so many meditations, so much spiritual reading, etc., and all kept perfect silence" (218). The same held true for observance of Holy Week. These were times to clear one's mind, settle one's conscience, and in the Christian tradition of mysticism, let God do the talking. Rigorous asceticism was not practiced, beyond the usual fasting and abstinence common before Vatican II among all Latin-rite Catholics. There were, of course, the special penances and the rigors imposed by the hardships faced by the community in the wake of their series of disasters: floods, fires, near bankruptcy, and occasional poor harvests. There is no evidence about self-imposed penance, except that some monks may have been known to be more strict than others; there are no examples of fanaticism. Traditional Benedictine moderation seems to have prevailed.

The monastery provided solace and privacy for the monks as individuals, but the priory and community as a corporation was very public. Naturally it became a center for laymen as well as secular clergy to seek renewal, even though without proper facilities during its early existence retreat work was limited. Local parishes occasionally made pilgrimages to the hilltop where a small chapel, still standing overlooking the monks' cemetery, was the scene of an outdoors Benediction service. The south slope of the hill, forested with magnificent Douglas firs, came to be regarded as a better place for human retreat and the comfort of nature than for pasturage. The hillside was changed first by building an outdoor altar dedicated to the Blessed Virgin Mary; by 1918 this was enlarged to become an imitation Lourdes' Grotto. There were also Stations of the Cross constructed by artisans from Munich which lined the winding pathway up the hill; each station was depicted in a mural within a small wood chapel just large enough to shelter an individual from the rain or hot sun. Slowly the hillsite was transformed from its primitive naturalism to a more developed shrine site reflecting the folkloric religiosity and traditional devotionalism of Old World Catholicism as remembered from Switzerland. Such reconstruction, perhaps seen as unfortunate by today's conservation standards and modern sensibilities, was then responsive to the ethos of immigrant Catholicism in the Willamette Valley. In addition to the New Engelberg at Mt. Angel, lay settlers a little way south named their village Little Switzerland. As in other parts of the country, their parish churches rose above these settlements as miniature Gothic cathedrals, monuments to their faith and reflections of their attachment to their homeland. Mt. Angel was no different.

Life on the summit was hardly all prayer and seriousness, however, and it is the good-hearted humor and play which sometimes reveals an inner confidence and spirituality as much as the perseverance characteristic of this Benedictine community. At times events seem to contradict totally the stereotype of the solemn, strict religious community of the previous century. For example, one tradition famous for its resounding impact on the valley as much as the monastery's bell ringing, was the periodic and ceremonial firing of a five-inch Civil War cannon. It was used each feast of Corpus Christi among other occasions, during outdoor processions uphill to the chapel. One memorable occasion was this feast in 1903 (219):

> ... the cannon was placed in front of a huge fir tree. In order to insure as much noise as possible, the brothers, after charging the old cannon with a great deal of powder, rammed in a large amount of soft earth. The consequence was that when the charge was fired, the whole cannon exploded with the roar heard for miles around, hurling fragments in every direction. Altho[ugh] about 300 yards from the windows of the chapel, one large fragment weighing several pounds was hurled through the air, and striking the upright joist between the windows was deflected into the confessional door which it reduced to kindling wood. This broke the force of the missile which otherwise would have struck the celebrant as he knelt before the Blessed Sacrament. Thus ended our famous cannon of olden days!

Abbot Bernard's recollections thus provide a very human note to what otherwise is unrealistically pictured as a superhuman enterprise.

Other recorded reminiscences retell a story of a congenial life at Mt. Angel which put into proper balance the previously examined financial problems of the community and the dissension which periodically became so divisive. These recollections are mostly anecdotal, but deserve telling in part to illustrate the ability of these monks to appreciate situation humor and to laugh even at themselves. Abbot Bernard, good story-teller that he was, recalled the first encounter of a German nun with an American striped skunk while on a picnic in the lowland pastures during the spring when the cows had been herded off to the Milk Ranch. She spied "a beautiful black cat with six kittens [trailing] behind it. She ran to catch it, but got something else instead!" She later wrote back to her motherhouse, swearing "I'll never touch a 'cat' in America again!" There was always such humor in the early years of the community arising out of the differences between Old World behavior out of context in the Oregon frontier, communication problems, and the interesting personalities involved. Fr. Maurus recalled their train trip across country in 1882, made more miserable for the Swiss German-speaking Benedictines who did not know what Americans called a water-closet; they did not immediately asssociate a toilet with a bathroom and were somewhat embarrassed to ask. With obvious amusement Fr. Maurus told about a stopover in Council Bluffs, Iowa, where "Edmund Schnyder distinguished himself by finding out the English designation of W.C.. Triumphantly he went to his friends and told them the name was 'For Ladies,' but was met with hearty laughter from a couple of Sisters sitting nearby and overhearing the conversation" (220). They presumably set the young man straight! In another instance, a "blunder" of Prior Adelhelm and Fr. Anselm was retold when, arriving at Portland they first wanted so much to impress the archbishop and local diocesan clergy. They were visiting St. Vincent's hospital, and Fr. Anselm was asked to celebrate Benediction for those present; he did so using the familiar Engelbergian rather than Roman rite, so that only the "foreigners" knew what was happening or how to respond to his out-of-place intonation of the hymns *O Salutaris hostia* and *Tantum ergo*. This was understandable enough, but it clearly illustrated to all that these Benedictines faced a long process of acculturation.

There was also the somewhat eccentric Br. Melchior Durer who regarded manual labor as the only real "work," and "in his funny Swiss dialect" (so thought the American storyteller) one day confronted Prior Adelhelm at his desk with the charge: "Although you are prior, you are a lazy dog! You don't work at all. I work for five! Praised be Jesus Christ". He stomped out of the office to return to the barn, fortunately leaving Adelhelm in tears because of laughter rather than anger. No doubt the outspoken monk could have been more diplomatic had not language problems been in his way. In fact, even when the monks spoke in English, there were always nuances of meaning lost and more than once apologies had to be offered as the monks tried to accomodate English-speaking visitors. After a piano and vocal concert on December 8, 1901, the musicians were invited to dinner; in the conversation Fr. William was invited by the soloist, Mrs. Abrahams, to guess her weight. After trying unsuccessfully to get out of it, he finally made a guess within three pounds. She was surprised, and jokingly asked how he did that. The student waiter, "Willie" Cronin, undiplomatically blurted out: "You must remember, Fr. William is the procurator—he's used to gauging the weight of hogs!" The conversation quickly turned to another subject. Of course, such social occasions or church services often, in hindsight, make an incident more humorous. Fr. Dominic recalled Fr. Frowin one day absent-mindedly began reading from the wrong place in the *Rituale* when he was about to "church a woman kneeling at the altar rail". Not only did he plunge the aspergillum upside down into the holy water, but the text being read was no blessing but an exorcism! Fr. Dominic, notorious in the community for his sleepwalking, was certainly not immune from circulating anecdotes, such as when he prepared a homily in English for a nuns' conference. Since English was still a foreign language to him, he wrote it in German and translated it with the use of a dictionary; when trying to express that the sisters needed 'mortification' during their retreat, he opened the sermon by telling them "Now my dear Sisters, you must be very 'rotten' [but] you are not 'rotten' enough!" And so the stories proliferated, perhaps with usual embellishment; and even today the monks at Mt. Angel enjoy a chuckle over the situation humor reported in their own newsletter. Amidst adversity, a sense of humor survived; the Benedictines did not confuse sobriety with spirituality.

The Benedictines from Engelberg never made the transition totally to American customs, language, and attitudes; many retained their oaths of stability in Engelberg, regarded the motherhouse therefore as home, and after some mission duty in Oregon sought to return. Others were more accommodating, but were hardly deeply sensitive to their new American citizenship. If the process of aculturation did not obliviate nationalism, their values did. Attachment to their "roots" is reflected in the naming of Mt. Angel after Engelberg. The nomenclature is still confusing. The priory itself was called St. Benedict, and this name still remains as the local postal designation for the Benedictine settlement and the U.S. Geological Survey in the mid-twentieth century continued to refer to the monastery as St. Benedict rather than Mt. Angel at St. Benedict, Oregon. The community renamed itself after the motherhouse, allegedly because of Adelhelm's persuasion in a difficult vote when the chapter decided to move to the summit. The village of Fillmore, named after a railroad agent, had previous names after leading settlers, and at one time had the non-descript designation of "Roy's Place". The railroad and townsfolk agreed to rename Fillmore as Mt. Angel in honor of the monastery (221). Thus, one can find references to this foundation as either 'St. Benedict' at Mt. Angel, or 'Mt. Angel' at St. Benedict which is correct, or confusion between the town and monastic site. The name-change does not reflect accomodation of 'Americans' to the monks, since it was bitterly contested; it was largely the German and Swiss immigrant population which made the change. However, despite such signs of attachment to the Old World, distance, language, and natural cementing of ties with the locale, prompted the priory to grow more and more independent of Engelberg. Had the priory been able to achieve financial independence, it would have received *de jure* independence long before it did. The reconstruction of Mt. Angel monastery on the hilltop, therefore, may be seen as deference to Engelberg, but at the same time it marked a maturity and a local *de facto* independence not apparent in the first decade of the priory's existence.

Prior Benedikt tried to regularize the financial relations of Mt. Angel with Engelberg; what initially was treated like a family matter, increasingly was a matter of business and contract. In 1895, after conferring with Pope Leo XIII, all interest on the Mt. Angel debts owed to the motherhouse was cancelled. On November 16, 1900 Abbot Anselm as one of his final acts, formally requested: "For our loans of $140,000 to Mt. Angel, I ask them for a legally valid first mortgage on land, forest, buildings, moveable goods, and at the same time declare that we are renouncing any interest, [but] request only an annual repayment of $1000". This was agreed to by the procurator, Fr. William Kramer, the prior, and the abbot, and was confirmed by Mt. Angel's chapter in 1904. Adelhelm, who was recalled by Mt. Angel in 1899 to serve a second term as prior (1899-1901) after Benedikt retired, asked the new abbot of Engelberg, Leodegar Scherer (who succeeded Anselm after the latter's death on January 4, 1901), to make Mt. Angel an outright gift "of the few crumbs *(Paar Brosamen)*" that fell from the rich table of the mother abby (referring to the $140,000 debt)(222). The prior's boldness may have been inspired by his keen awareness of the community's continued economic difficulties and unawareness of Engelberg's tight position. His hope that the debt would be cancelled like the interest perhaps became more acute when the monks experienced another fire on September 20, 1901. This was a spontaneous combustion fire in the hay stacks next to the cattle barn; the hay and straw reserves were lost, as was the barn, but the brothers managed to free all of the livestock (223). Fire was to strike again on August 20, 1907, destroying the mill at the base of the hill, where later a granery and storehouse were built (but the place is still called "the mill"). Engelberg, however sympathetic with the priory and these calamities, never cancelled the debt; annual payments of $1000, usually in quarterly installments, continued uninterrupted until 1941 and the outbreak of World War II (224). Mt. Angel continued to earn its independence, but some of the American recruits tended to regard this debt liquidation as a kind of tribute and this partially explains some of the factionalism which occurred between the so-called Engelbergians and the rest of the brethren. The misunderstandings may have resulted from false expectations, and certainly from an over-estimation of Engelberg's ability to subsidize the priory. In fact, Engelberg let its own building program lapse until the 1920s after the long-lasting effects of the American venture were healed by a decade of financial recovery. Engelberg had ample reason for wanting its daughterhouse to become truly independent.

At the turn of the century Mt. Angel's community numbered 45: 14 fathers, a novice, and 30 lay brothers. It had grown considerably from local recruits as well as reinforcements from Engelberg, yet there was always a manpower shortage and inability therefore to do everything. There was special concern for a six-year span in which there were no professions of choir monks, although there had been the addition of four brothers. Even so, the community was hard taxed to keep up with its activities; it was barely able to maintain its farms. Abbot Bernard recalled that in summer 1900 Fr. Maurus was serving temporarily at an Indian mission on Vancouver Island, Frs. Placidus and Frowin were completing their studies at Catholic University of America, as was Jerome at the Sant Anselmo in Rome; Anselm and Berchtold had returned to Engelberg for a visit, and Fr. Barnabas, rather than returning to Mt. Angel, set out for Engelberg; Fr. Urban was conducting a retreat in California; the procurator then, Fr. Gregory, was visiting his parents in Kansas; two monk-priests were stationed at Sacred Heart parish; and Fr. Dominic, who had taken over St. Lawrence parish in Portland, had contacted typhoid there and was out of commission for several months (225). The number of choir monks at the priory was therefore cut in half.

The chapter of Mt. Angel conducted its first canonical election on July 11, 1901 of its own superior, thus ending twenty years of direct subservience to Engelberg's abbots. According to Fr. Maurus, this memorable conclave required twenty ballotings before a decision could be reached (226). The change did not bring about total *de jure* independence, only that the monks at Mt. Angel could elect their own prior instead of having one appointed by the abbot. The latter retained the right of confirmation, and therefore also veto power. This was accomplished under the watchful eye of Abbot Frowin Conrad of Conception Abbey, who served as Abbot Leodegar's delegate in this last abbatial visitation. Prior Adelhelm stepped down and the Swiss monk Thomas Meienhofer, who in 1903 would supervise the move into the new building, was elected prior. Subsequently, at Prior Thomas' urging, Abbot Leodegar and the chapter at Engelberg voted to give Mt. Angel full independence and to raise this daughterhouse to abbatial status. Subsequently, the Mt. Angel chapter on October 16, 1902 to incorporate itself into the Swiss-American Congregation of the Benedictine federation (227).

The change in administration during 1901 at Engelberg had important consequence for Mt. Angel because the new abbot had never shared his predecessor's predeliction to continue indefinitely the dependence of the American priory on the Swiss mother abbey. Moreover, Abbot Leodegar lacked Anselm's familiarity with Adelhelm, but knew and admired the newly elected prior, Thomas, who had studied at Engelberg (228). In fact, the abbot was the *Geistlicher Vater* at Fr. Thomas' ordination (229). Leodegar had requested Mt. Angel to choose as*abbas praesentandus*someone whom the Engelberg chapter could confirm, and this may explain why the founder never became abbot of Mt. Angel. All of the priors had complained about the distance between Oregon and Switzerland, the problems of communications, and how impractical it was for the now well-established community to remain under Engelberg's canonical jurisdiction, but it was Prior Thomas who was able to present this case most convincingly. Moreover, the worst fears about Engelberg's suppression had been abated during the last decades of the nineteenth century, and the motherhouse had achieved enough stability to reconsider its original motives in founding the American house.

The formal request for Mt. Angel's total independence apparently originated during Abbot Frowin's visitation, partially at the instigation of the new archbishop of Portland, Alexander Christie. It was Abbot Frowin who again presided over Mt. Angel's chapter on February 3, 1904, and he kept Abbot Leodegar informed about the deliberations. "All were unanimously in favor [of independence]," he wrote, "...on the ninth ballot the majority of votes fell to P. Thomas Meienhofer, and with that a stone fell from my heart. Although the election was a hard one, all were happy about the result and showed themselves ready without any hesitation to sign the petition which will be sent to Rome. I consider the election to have been the best that could have been under the present circumstance...". The abbot-elect or *praesentandus* in his letter to Engelberg reflected on the affair which "went smoothly" (149):

> What was held against me more than anything, is, or was, that during my administration, I took things in hand very resolutely and that in many things I acted independently, God knows, simply because it was so necessary if the great work... was not going to topple over into the river. I thank God that He gave me the courage and the grace to do what is now accomplished, and I must confess, that except for some harsh words that I uttered on occasion, I have nothing to regret and I can say with tranquil conscience and before God, that I have done everything *ut omnibus glorificetur Deus.*

Abbot Leodegar responded with relief, as his diary attests, and by presenting to Mt. Angel the abbatial pectoral cross, one in Roman style with ruby settings in silver filigree, which is still worn at Mt. Angel on special occasions.

Canonical independence came finally in 1904 with Mt. Angel's elevation from priory to abbey as approved by Engelberg's chapter on February 5, 1904. As expected, Prior Thomas was appointed by the Holy See to be Mt. Angel's first abbot. In completion of work begun in 1902, the new abbey was fully incorporated into the Swiss-American Benedictine Congregation (232). A Roman brief dated March 24 to Engelberg confirmed this, as did another confirmation sent to Abbot Frowin (although the *Ordo* at Mt. Angel recorded the date erroneously as March 23). The first abbot was blessed on June 29, 1904 by Abbot Frowin officiating for Abp. Christie who had taken ill, and acting as *praeses* for the Swiss-American Congregation (233). He was assisted by Abbots Athanasius Schmitt of St. Meinrad and Vincent Wehrle from Richardson, North Dakota. In addition to the Engelberg cross, the new abbot was presented with an abbatial crosier from the workshop of the Benziger brothers—a gift from the diocesan clergy. Thereupon a new era began in Mt. Angel's history.

Mount Angel Abbey, 1904-21

Mt. Angel Abbey has been governed by seven abbots during the twentieth century:

Thomas I Meienhofer (1904-10)
Placidus Fuerst (1910-21)
Bernard Murphy (1921-34)
Thomas II Meier (1934-50)
Damian Jentges (1950-74)
Anselm Galvin (1974-80)
Bonaventure Zerr (1980-)

It is traditional in monastic histories to divide chronology according to abbatial reigns, as if the abbots always personified their communities. This presumption is often unfounded, and such periodization more than for its intellectual merits is practical because so often specific events are not attributable to any other individual in the community. Such documentation seldom exists for any collective activity, but monastic records are especially problematic. If a monastery's history is not retold according to a succession of abbots with its implied continuity, then usualll a discontinuity or catastrophic interpretation of its history is held. In the case of Mt. Angel Abbey, there is a propensity to divide its history if not by abbots, then by major disasters, namely the fires of 1892 and again in 1926. Such periodization becomes somewhat strained, however, since no catastrophe of similar magnitude has struck the community in the past half-century. Moreover, such an emphasis is on the monastery itself, as a building or a physical entity, rather than on the monastic community—a social organism which is at worst a political and economic corporation only, and is at best a spiritual entity invested in a *corpus* of a different kind, the Mystical Body of Christ or the Church, which is beyond the competence of a mere historian to assess.

More balanced perspective on Mt. Angel's history can be attempted by focusing on the years 1904-21 as a continuation of the priory's history, with the obvious difference of *de iure* independence. Hence, likening the institution's development to an individual's life cycle, the abbacies of Thomas I and Placidus follow the community's childhood or growth and development as a priory, and mark adolesence after gaining recognized independence from its parent. The governance of Abbot Bernard Murphy, whose reminiscences of earlier years have already been cited, appears most like a transition period, reflecting development into young adulthood. Such periodization is convenient for a history which artificially stops at 1982 to celebrate a centenary, but it implies that somehow after this comes old age, deterioration, and death. Mt. Angel shows few signs of the latter tendencies, although it exhibits all of the expected problems in meeting the challenges of a monastic community in the modern age. That is inherent in the process of survival; that is life. Consequently, one must understand that any periodization is thus provisional. In the institutional histories of some communities which have survived for centuries, the first century of existence may strike the present historian as a growth and development stage. So too with the monks at Mt. Angel, who in future centuries might reflect on this brief history and its chronological divisions as encompassing only the origins of this religious house.

Although the monastery's cornerstone was laid by Abp. Christie in June 1899, the roofing on the main structure was not completed until 1902. At the chapter meeting of March 1903 it was decided to add a four-story wing onto the monastery to house the seminarians close to the monks and apart from the college students who remained at the lower level. A gymnasium was added as well. These changes delayed completion of the building despite continuous prodding by Prior Thomas. The move to the hilltop was set for Christmas Day, 1903, ending what was compared with the Old Testament diaspora of the Jews. To others, the interim had been more like the Babylonian Captivity. The move itself was likened to the Hebrews leaving Egypt (*"in exitu Israel de Aegypto"*), as furnishings and goods were gathered from the college, storage throughout the town, and from farm buildings, to be carried into the still unfinished monastery. The interior and trim work went on for another couple of years, long after the building was occupied. The monastery's water supply system was not completed until summer 1907 after a new 230-foot well was in 1905 sunk north of the old one and when a 1500-foot conduit of wooden piping was finished to pump water to the hilltop (234).

The first two abbots not only supervised the occupation of the hilltop, both the move into monastery but also continued site development and landscaping, but also fostered the development of the abbey's educational institutions which so dominate its history. It was Abbot Thomas I who while still prior had initiated the rebuilding of the college in stone, a new 204 x 40 ft. (with the center section 70 ft.) structure designed by a Portland architect, Joseph Jacobberger. Much of the stone slate-colored basalt was quarried locally, with help from Br. Magnus Plarer, a stone mason from the old country. Work was completed in one summer (May 4-October 18, 1902) by the contracting firm of James Barret, for the modest cost of $16,000. The money was raised by advertising in the *St. Joseph's Blatt* for benefactors to invest in the Mt. Angel enterprise. The short-term loans of the investors were to be repaid at 4% interest (235).

The college and seminary of Mt. Angel were both natural extensions of the missionary ideal and parish work originally undertaken by the Oregon Benedictines, and they were responses to the archbishops who patronized the Black Monks primarily to enhance Catholic education in the state. The Swiss monks had brought with them a tradition of activity in such education and parish work from both Engelberg and Conception abbeys. As already noted, expansion into parish work was curtailed by the monastery's lack of manpower and conscious policy decisions by the archbishops once parish revenues did not appear so necessary for the community's support. The move to the hilltop, at first apart from the college and separated moreso from the town, was at least symbolic of an attempt to retain a cloistered lifestyle distinct from the secular diocesan clergy. For the first time a monk moved into the rectory of St. Mary's parish in Mt. Angel; the former intimacy between the parish and monastic communities since 1892 started to dissolve. St. Mary's was still used by the monks, not for daily offices, but for special occasions when more lay seating was needed. The monks continued to work at other parishes as well, in far-away Spokane, in Portland, and on the coast at Tillamook. But these were increasingly mission activities to support the archdiocese when it lacked manpower to staff its churches, rather than means to gain economic support for the monastery. Yet, it was the diversity of the early economic basis for the monastery in farming, education and parish work, which had provided the stability needed to survive the financial crisis of the priory years. As the monastery grew more stable, the latter functions produced less revenue and in time roles were reversed, i.e. the monastery was supporting institutions which previously had helped the community get started.

The entwined destinies of the college and seminary with the abbey, brought closer together after having to share the same facilites in the 1890s, is most apparent in the grooming of abbatial candidates in the arduous administrative post of rector for the seminary. Abbot Thomas I had served as rector after 1898 before becoming prior in 1901 and then moving into the abbatial chair in 1904 (236). Only Placidus, who was elected upon the resignation of the former on May 25, 1910, escaped this administrative apprenticeship, but he had been in charge of the college for several years after 1894 (237). Both had the opportunity to expand the abbey's educational efforts. After the death of Abp. Gross, his successor, Abp. Christie, offered to help the monks take control of the floundering Methodist college of Portland as well as the Indian school in his former diocese of Victoria. Fr. Ambrose Zenner claimed that these options were seriously discussed and that Adelhelm had suggested separating the college and seminary, keeping the latter only with the monastery and transferring the former to Portland. Fr. Maurus thought that this proposal had in principle been accepted by the chapter (238). A separation already had occurred when the seminary moved to the hilltop and the college remained below. The monks regarded the seminarians as tolerable, but the students' behavior was considered too "wild and rowdy" for proximity to the monastery. Zenner mentions that "Difficulty because of Protestant opposition in Portland killed the issue" (239). This may be, but plans to establish an urban Catholic college proceeded anyway, leading to the University of Portland under the Holy Cross Fathers. Such developments never coalesced with the archdiocesan plans for development of the seminary, and they impacted Mt. Angel by diminishing the importance of its college. Cooperation was never a cardinal characteristic of Catholic educational institutions in this or any other area; secular and regular clergy have traditionally gone their own ways, often at their own and each other's expense. The abbey's college cooperated only superficially with the Sister's school because of the traditional segregation by sex in Catholic education, so that was no barrier in moving the college to Portland. More inhibitive would have been the

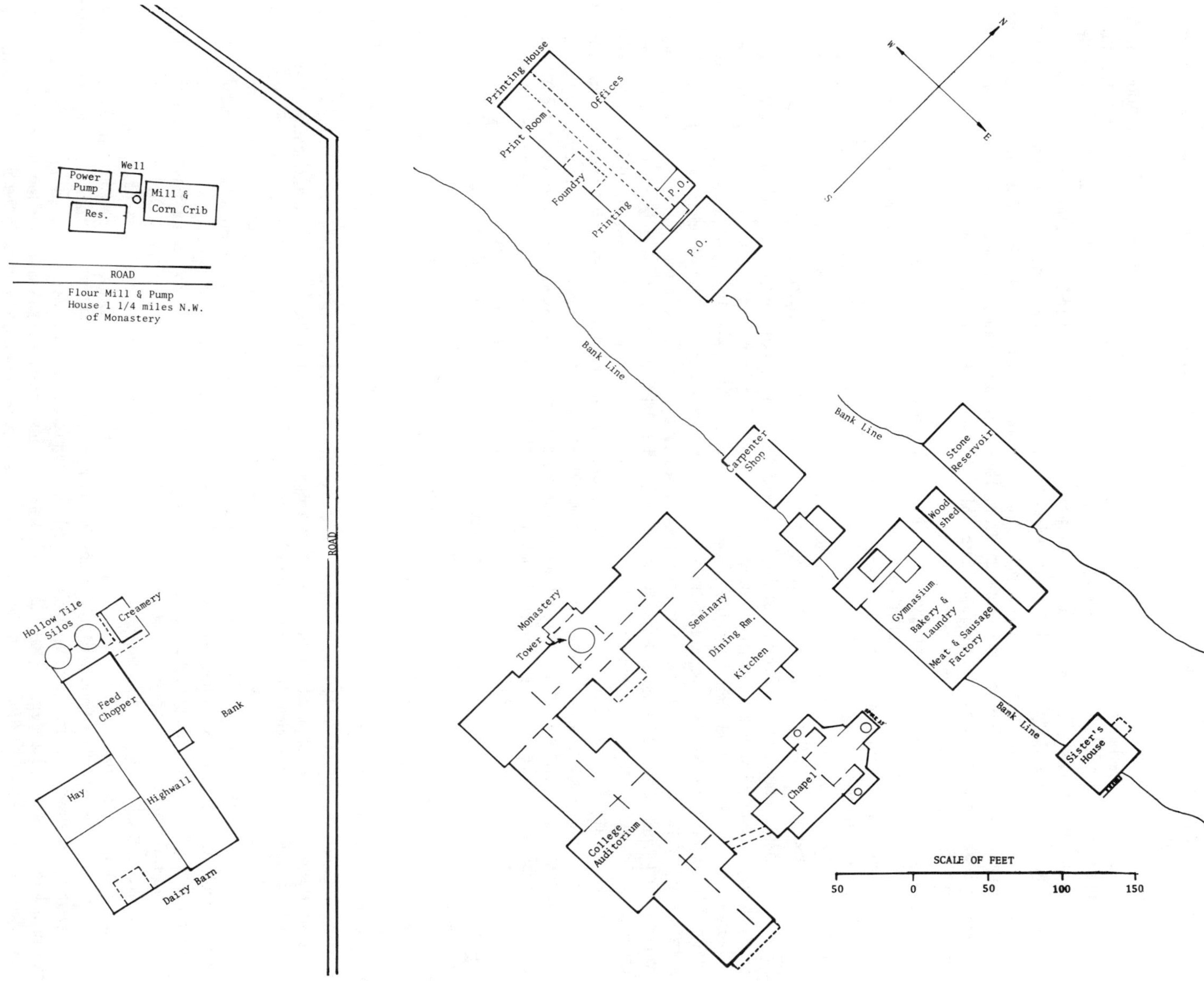

Fig. 7. Mt. Angel's monastic complex ca. 1910. Based on tracing from the Fire Insurance maps for Oregon by Sanborn Co., N.Y., 1909, in the Library of Congress Geography & Map Div.

problems already encountered by the monks in doing parish work by having their members take up residence outside the monastery or commute on weekends. The proposal held risks of creating a splinter group even if the abbey had the necessary manpower to maintain a core of faculty in two places at once. The prognostication for recruits was not encouraging, and the archbishop's motives in running a larger Catholic college so as to recruit diocesan priests would hardly support the monks' best interests in securing vocations for their own community. Finally, the timing was bad, since the community had just invested in the hilltop site and in new college facilities. The lack of common goals and coordinated effort between the archdiocese and the monastery better explain the failure of the Benedictines to take over the Portland college than any Protestant opposition. In any case, the proliferation of Catholic colleges in Oregon and the development of other seminaries by local ordinaries, had grave implications for the future of the Benedictine institutions at Mt. Angel.

The college and seminary have been combined at various times, and at others have retained an autonomy, but always the former supported the latter. A full-scale, generic undergraduate four-year college never developed, and in essence, the seminary was the graduate school. Slowly the college lost its competitive standing as other area colleges began to grow, although the quality of its education program was always considered excellent when compared with other small colleges. The monks taught in both the college and seminary, often the same monk in both depending on needs and capabilities. They often taught in several subject-areas at once, and always seem to have been overburdened. Despite financial problems, the seminary from 1889 onward produced a steady trickle of one or two graduates each year for the archdiocese. After rebuilding, Abp. Christie pressured the monks constantly to improve their seminary, and this necessitated in turn improvements in the college. Thus the community continued to select promising young men from its ranks to do graduate study in major universities here and abroad, especially in Rome at the Sant Anselmo. This established early a scholarly tradition in the community, more advanced than ever exemplified by the pioneer community. In turn, such efforts required additional expenditures for faculty development, building library collections, and attempts to improve other resources as well such as science laboratories, a museum of natural history, and eventually facilities for physical education and recreation. In short, the monastery complex took on the character of a small liberal arts college and the hilltop began to be regarded as a campus.

When rector Thomas became abbot, Gregory Roble assumed the former post until 1903 when Berarnd Murphy became the seminary's chief administrator. It was shortly thereafter that the monks moved to their new quarters on the hill and celebrated on Christmas Eve their first truly communal Mass in a decade. The new building, a massive grey stone structure (210 x 88 ft.) towering five stories high, when totally finished could accomodate both the monks and 250 seminarians and/or students. It had two communal dormitories and sixty private rooms, plus an infirmary; and as previously noted, a gymnasium (129 x 60 ft.) was added to this. The edifice certainly seemed to be a monument to self-confidence and hope for future enlargement. Yet, enrollments in the seminary remained small. In 1889 of 115 students in residence, only 12 entered the seminary. After 1906 under rector Fr. Gall Eugster, the seminary enrollment increased only to 36. The reputation of the program, however, rested partially on this small enrollment and the ration of faculty to students; this individualized learning situation was a hallmark of the Benedictine program at Mt. Angel. The curriculum steadily improved with the impact of new faculty, particularly Fathers Notker Maeder in classics and dogmatic theology after he completed his studies in Rome, and Urban Fischer in languages and sciences. Moreover, since the 1890s Abp. Gross had begun to recruit secular priests from East-coast seminaries to supplement the faculty (as in the case of Rev. Joseph O'Connor and Rev. Bernard Feeney who in 1890 had been brought from Philadelphia precisely because of their specialty in English!). Visiting faculty became a tradition at Mt. Angel from then onward. The college too remained a relatively small, select affair, increasingly catering to preseminary education. Yet by 1914 the monks had taught over 4000 students in an era when college educations were still relatively rare, especially in the Pacific Northwest.

The growing regional reputation of Mt. Angel, especially among immigrant communities which valued access to traditional, European-oriented educational opportunities at reasonable cost, was enhanced by the monastic press. Mt. Angel like most monasteries of any size, inherited a private press tradition at the time of its foundation. Yet it was not until 1889 that the Benedictine Press was active in Oregon, and then as a job press rather than a scholarly publishing house. The first press operated in a cramped 25 x 15 ft. building some 300 feet west of the old horsebarn. In the mid-1890s it moved into a remodeled granery and had its old handpress replaced by an Optimus press. Then in 1900 it moved to the second floor of the carpentry shop, to more spacious quarters required by the increase circulation of its newspapers. It was run primarily by Br. Celestine Mueller (d. 1929) who in 1909 was appointed director of the press. He had previously worked as typesetter, pressman, and foreman under former editors, Frs. Leo Huebscher and Barnabas, and eventually went deaf after a lifetime of listening to the clanging of presses. The monks were usually assisted by three sisters hired from Queen of the Angel's convent, and part-time student labor. The newspaper business did well for a time, and as circulations increased Fr. Maurus could honestly refer to the printshop as a "goldmine" in a letter to Abbot Leodegar (240). Br. Celestine was instrumental in developing the monastery's three main newspapers. The *St. Joseph's Blatt* was a local German weekly paper begun in Portland; the monks bought it in 1900 and widened its scope to embrace the whole diocese so as to appeal to the valley's immigrant population. As its choice of patron suggests, the focus was on labor, family life, and Christian welfare. In the early 1900s it had over 50,000 subscribers! This circulation increased even more when it incorporated two other German-Catholic newspapers, one from the North Dakotan Benedictines and another in Philadelphia. Its coverage became nationwide. Then came two world wars with Germany, and anti-German reaction, and a rapid decline in the U.S. of German-Americans who continued to speak German. Moreover, the *Blatt* was suppressed by the federal government during the war years because it was supposedly too pro-German; when it was restored afterwards, it could not recover its former subscriptions. By 1965 its circulation stood at only 5500 and this continued to drop radically to only 3600 in 1967. It was sold therefore in January, 1968. The *Armen Seelen Freund* suffered the same fate, but it had never developed into more than a local paper so that retained a more enduring relationship with German-Americans in western Oregon. Finally, the *St. Joseph's Magazine*, which began in October 1900 as the *Mt. Angel Magazine* changed its name in the 1930s. Like its German counterpart, it was very popular; its cirulation climbed to 40,000. Although it did not have the same problems as the monastery's German publications, its ability to cultivate a large audience was dependent in part on the regional reputation of the Mt. Angel college and seminary. As the former contracted and focused on clerical education, a wide lay readership was lost. By 1965 its circulation had dropped to 18,000 and it too was discontinued in 1968. The *Mt. Angel Letter* was begun in July 1949 to serve as an alumnae newsletter. It was issued six times a year, with each issue being about eight pages; its circulation runs about 26,000. In addition there was *The Angelus* after 1948, an organ of the seminary; and the *Pacific Star* served for a time as a local Catholic newspaper.

The press ultimately became a job press only, doing the monastery's business and supplementing its income by selling Christmas cards. The latter amounts to 140,000 boxes a year. It also does a variety of catalogues, fliers, religious vocation pamphlets, and keeps a staff of six religious and thirteen full- and seven part-time laymen employed. But it has never aspired to the same printing traditions as Einsiedeln or other monastic presses of the famous German houses. Nor did the community grow to such size that it could support the same kinds of enterprises as did the Cassinese Benedictines of St. John's Abbey, or like St. Benedict's Abbey in Atchison, Kansas, associated with the Order's publications. Mt. Angel press productions were and are eminently practical, reflecting the nature of the monks' parish work, educational endeavors, and public relations.

In contrast to this stands the remarkable achievements of Fr. Anselm Weissenborn who continued the monastic scriptorium tradition into the twentieth century. His was a one-man studio producing liturgical books commissioned by Abbot Thomas I, but which were not completed until after his administration. Four such codices are extant; all are folio size bound in gold-tooled red Morrocan leather, written in black uncials for Latin with red rubrication and incipits, and in fraktur for German and Roman for English text. They were used for nearly two decades on special liturgical occasions at Mt. Angel, especially at professions. Two of these are decorated with miniatures depicting standard iconography, but also the previously mentioned sketches of the old monastery and of the monks' temptations during their time of troubles. Equally interesting is one scene with the lone scribe seated at his writing desk, facing the window with his back toward the viewer, working on these Mt. Angel codices. They are anachronisms harkening back to when Mt. Angel was a little of the Old World set into the New, produced when the monastery was making its transition from a Swiss-German implant to an indigeneous American institution. They also provide some continuity between the manuscript arts and the monastery's publicity publications which are usually tastefully enhanced with fine calligraphy. As in several monasteries throughout the United States, and in keeping with the local Oregon revival led by Professor Reynolds at Reed College in Portland, calligraphy is still taught at Mt. Angel. It is now a studio art, however, to support graphic production, not simply "fancy penmanship" as described in the 1890s.

In addition to the local education work, farming, some lumbering, and the few parishes run by the Benedictines, Mt. Angel took on a major commitment in the early 1900s to aid missions for the Indians. Such missionary work was common to several of the American Benedictine houses, including the Swiss monks at Conception and the Cassinese of St. John's who worked among the tribes of Minnesota and North and South Dakota. As already noted, mission work played into the archbishop's thinking about bringing the Benedictines to Oregon and in trying to get them to think about a settlement at Grand Ronde in the Yamhill Valley. The Benedictine sisters were active there, and often the monks served a chaplains and helped in other ways. This effort led to their involvement at the Tillamook mission. But in 1900 such missionary efforts expanded beyond the Willamette Valley to aid in developing the nascent church along the Pacific coastline of Canada. The cause of proselytizing among the Indians and organizing the Church on Vancouver Island, in British Columbia, and in Alaska, had been hallowed in 1886 by Abp. Segher's murder (241), and since Abp. Christie had served previously as ordinary of Victoria before his elevation to the archiepiscopal see of Portland, there was continued interest in promoting this cause. The area was, however, as Abbot Bernard recalled, "a very wild, rough country that could be reached only by water" (242).

In a lengthy letter of August 14, 1902, Fr. Maurus wrote to Abbot Leodegar recalling the monastery's early history and expected participation in Indian mission work, and described in detail a two-week exploratory journey made to Victoria and to "Clayoquat" on Vancouver Island (243). Later a colony of two priests, Maurus Snyder himself and Charles Moser (whose reminiscences in 1926 recall the venture), plus two brothers, Leonard and Gabriel, and three nuns (Mary Placida, M. Frances, and M. Clotilde) from Queen of the Angel's convent, took over a poor mission school at Kakawis. Fr. Charles lived among the Indians at their village of Opitsat, "rarely seeing a white man". He fell heir to the tradition of Abp. Francis Norbert Blanchet and Fr. Modeste Demers who in their efforts to convert the Oregon and Washington Indians to Christianity, studied their customs, languages, and religion (244). Likewise, Fr. Charles took many notes, transcribed Indian prayers and songs into Roman characters, and translated into their tongue several instructional aids and catechisms. Some of these are extant today in the abbey's archives. The Benedictine's work on the island would eventually involve them on the mainland as well where they made a significant contribution to the organization of the Church in British Columbia.

The monks of Mt. Angel were stunned when on May 25, 1910 Abbot Thomas I resigned his office and thereafter left the religious life. Although there was a defensive posture for a time, partially created by the adverse publicity given by the Oregon newspapers to his departure, the community regained its spirits. By then the monastery had largely recovered from its losses in 1892, and had rebuilt a stable economic base upon which to grow. Abbot Frowin paid one last visit to Mt. Angel at the election of Placidus Fuerst (1868-1940), a musician at heart who had no predilection for the abbatial role. He too would resign the office. Despite such blows to its collective ego, the community portrait of August 30, 1910 exudes confidence and vitality. When Abbot Primate Hildebrand de Hemptinne subsequently visited the monastery, the community was still growing with new recruits despite the hiatus at the turn of the century. Men and funding from Engelberg were no longer forthcoming, and the new abbot was the last of the Engelbergians to be elected to a senior post. The gradual transition of the Swiss-Germanic character of the foundation to a mature institution of the American Church was occurring simultaneously with the passing of the predominantly immigrant culture of most of the valley's towns, a growing cosmopolitanism in Portland, and the development of large-scale fishing, lumber, and commercial industries in Oregon in addition to agriculture. The monastery was not immune to the social and economic pressures exerted by these changes or by World War I which accelerated Oregon's growth and the passing of Little Germany from the scene. The war certainly sped the de-Germanization of Mt. Angel by creating a different identity with its locale and forcing an admission that past ties to the old country were then more historical than anything (245). Even the town lost some of its rural country charm, which had to be recaptured much later for the tourists and Oktoberfest goers.

The college's enrollments dropped dramatically during the war, cycles of inflation and recession threatened even the seminary, and the noviate also dwindled. Longstanding hopes for an expanded lay brotherhood and confraternal support system among the laity were abandoned. The monks' attitude toward America's declaration of war upon Germany was ambivalent, and tensions began to mount once again as the monastery's heritage seemed somehow contaminated by the Old World culture they once clung to so proudly. Bernard Murphy recorded in his diary that during the administration of Abbot Placidus latent ill-will between the Irish-Catholic and German-Catholic elements in the community began to surface, and that the abbey's own past and flaunted, ostentacious association with German-Swiss culture was suddenly regarded with suspicion if not with contempt. Morale declined further with the onslaught in December 1918 of Spanish flu which reached epidemic proportion in the valley; one monk and three students were fatally stricken.

As with other old-world settlements in the United States, the war years brought about a psychological reconditioning, a reorientation, and a pervasive Americanization which would be finalized in the experience of World War II. In that process Mt. Angel Abbey's *de iure* independence became *de facto* as well.

Mount Angel Abbey in Transition, 1920-34

The passing of the old regime at Mt. Angel and the coming into prime of the young newlanders in the monastery's political life is evidenced by two symbolic events in 1920-21. The first was the death on November 6, 1920 of Mt. Angel's founder, Adelhelm, at age 76. The second was the election on October 21 and blessing on November 17, 1921 of Abbot Bernard Murphy, a 47-year-old Irish Catholic from Portland, Oregon (246).

Fr. Adelhelm had continued his parish work and fundraising for the monastery, but he was never elected abbot. This was perhaps because of his advanced age, but also his disposition while the community reoriented its affairs to accomodate its American setting. The records never fully explain why, after having served for two terms as prior, at the turn of the century he did not become abbot. The lingering influence of Engelberg, if not directly then indirectly through Abbot Frowin, may have been responsible. There is little doubt that everyone recognized that Adelhelm's dominating personality had shaped the early history of the monastery; while he was given due credit for the foundation and saving it from bankruptcy, he was blamed for precipitating the crisis in the first place by so over-extending the community's resources. This was perhaps an unfair assessment, since the prior had been able to argue sincerely that the risks were necessary or else the foundation would have had even a harder time getting started. Nor could he be expected to have foreseen the problems of a fluctuating economy over a twenty year period, the effects of land speculation in Washington and Oregon, and the inner motives and politics of the bishops with whom he had to contend. Opinion may have been divided, however, just enough to exclude him from serious consideration for the abbacy. Suspicions at Engelberg were obviously running against his appointment, and he was already too old by the time the Mt. Angel monks were really holding their own independent elections. Consequently, more likely than by design or any conspiracy, the circumstances of the reconstruction period after 1892 just worked against his election. As founder he was much respected, but when present he had ruled with a firm hand; and while prior, much of the time he was not in residence. His association with the monastery's indebtedness, his predeliction for pastoral work, his old-world convictions and loyalty to monastic life as he remembered it at Engelberg, and his reputation for political meddling, all must have played against him in the 1904 election. Given his age, that was really the only time he could have moved into the abbatial office and that appointment was manipulated from Engelberg. Moreover, there is little evidence that the prior actively sought the office; he was content with his pastor position in Portland. He was nevertheless obviously proud of the honor in being named titular Abbot at the fiftieth anniversary of his ordination. In keeping with his lifelong boundless energy, he made another trip to Engelberg in 1919 despite the war, and returned to celebrate a postponed Golden Jubilee on September 29, 1920. He died suddenly on November 6 after suffering a stroke. His passing seemed to demarcate the end of an era in the monastery's history.

Within a year of Adelhelm's death, on July 5, 1921 Abbot Placidus resigned. He chose instead to live out his days as pastor to the German parish of St. Joseph's in southeast Portland. On November 17, 1921, Bernard Murphy (1874-1934) was installed as abbot. He in turn appointed as prior Fr. Jerome Wespe, an able Benedictine who then had been living as a hermit on the monastery's Milk Ranch. Contrary to this seemingly inadequate preparation for administration, the prior proved to be an able manager and a meticulous record keeper. He became increasingly responsible for the abbey's governance during the last years of Bernard's abbacy when the latter went blind. Fr. Benedict Barr became rector and after 1921 began to rejuvenate the seminary. Likewise, the college was reorganized with separate divisions for a junior college which in 1922 and 1925 was accredited by the Northwest Association of Secondary and Higher Schools. It was also recognized in 1925 by the state of Oregon, and its teacher-training programs were in accord with state guidelines. The traditional course of classical studies was not diluted, but the junior college offered two-year, preprofessional training in medicine, dentistry, journalism, law, and engineering. These were augmented by the preparatory school with its special programs in liberal arts, classical studies, sciences, and commercial arts. In 1933 the combined college and seminary was accredited at the level of a four-year college by the same organization, now called the Northwest Association of Secondary and Higher Education. The pursuit by the monks of advanced studies in Europe continued, and faculty members were also recruited from other houses, as in the case of Fr. Augustine Bachofen, a well-known canonist, who transferred from Conception to Mt. Angel Abbey to teach canon law and church history.

In the evening of September 20, 1926 such progress was brought to a dramatic halt by a second disastrous fire. The blaze started in a short-circuited Model-T parked in a garage adjoining another outbuilding. It was discovered about 12:30 AM as Fr. Luke Eberle recalled some years later. The custodian raced around yelling "Fire!" and the rector aroused the sleeping seminarians (247). The fire was first confined to the car but when it caught onto the garage, the monastery was evacuated as a safety precaution. The Mt. Angel municipal fire department was summoned. The garage was in flames by the time it arrived; the brigade consisted of one Ford truck with a chemical tank and volunteer firemen. When the tank was emptied, the fire was still burning. By the time the nearby Silverton fire trucks arrived, winds had fanned the fire so that it spread to a wooden chapel, from there to the gymnasium, and then to the monastery itself. In desperation, there was an attempt to dynamite the gymnasium because it provided a bridge for the fire to travel to the monastery proper, but caps for the sticks could not be found in the confusion (248). The Woodburn fire department arrived by this time, but the water supply on the hilltop was inadequate and the pumps which supplied the reservoir from the wells below the hill were rendered inoperable by the fire. The Salem firemen arrived as well, and stretched 4000 feet of hose to the nearest pressured hydrant in the town of Mt. Angel. By the time the water reached the hill, having to travel nearly a mile and then uphill, it lacked adequate pressure to be effective. Only the press building and post office could be sprayed. The wind whipped the flames on the hilltop until the monastery itself became a gigantic holocaust, visible for miles around. By 7:00 AM the fire burned itself out as a crowd of monks, seminarians, students, townspeople, and firemen stood around in exhaustion and disbelief. Each recalled the loss of something dear, as one monk lamented seeing the church organ "burned in a pool of blue flames" as he snatched missals and breviaries from the pews (249), or the librarian who endangered his own life by lingering in the monastery's uppermost floor hurling books out of the windows in hopes that something of the library might survive.

The monastery was totally gutted, and only two outbuildings were saved. Fr. Bachofen's diary records the memory of that awful night (250):

> It [the fire] started soon after 12:00 AM and went rapidly. At 12:30 AM I heard a noise that sounded like 'FIRE!' but was not sure until about 1:00 AM when the blaze lighted the whole building. It was a ghastly sight. Although my nerves were somewhat affected, yet I tried to help the refectory Brother as well as I could. At about 3:00 AM I left in a car with some of my belongings for the Mount Angel Hotel where I was able to stay for a few days, thanks to Mr. Berchtold (the innkeeper). On the very morning of the fire, the Fathers contrived somehow to continue the Divine Office in the parish church of Mt. Angel. Then they sought shelter in the Old St. Joseph's school and a few rented houses. For the refectory we used the dining room in the basement of the new St. Mary's school.... In the meantime, we arranged for a theological class for which a room was made ready in the old St. Joseph's school.

Other accounts labor more on the fire itself, and less on its aftermath. The canonist's calm reflection stands in contrast to the emotional description released later in the *Mt. Angel Magazine* (251):

> Alas! What a period of grief and terror followed. From all parts of the building Fathers, fraters, brothers, students, and townsfolk snatched furniture and belongings that were near at hand and tried all too late to save something from the blaze. Driven from floor to floor, from room to room, by the advancing circle of fire, they could do but little, could save but little of the valuable furnishings, personal belongings, books, and materials within.

The pastor of St. Mary's parish, Fr. Dominic Waedenschwyler of Mt. Angel, made the church readily available to the dispersed community. Most of the eighty monks had toiled through the night trying to salvage what they could from the debris, but little could be saved because of the intense heat of the blaze, crumbling walls, and then, just too late to do anything but more harm, a rain shower and continuing drizzle until the next day. The books, linens, and small furniture which had been hauled or hurled from the building landed too close to the structure to be removed. What the fire did not destroy, the heat and rain ruined. The book heap was saturated with mud and ash, and only a few metal utensils and tools could be saved.

The losses were later ennumerated, down to such details as the store of 9000 gallons of canned prunes in the cellar, and there were stories of students who had lost their entire summer savings in the fire. Ironically, registration for fall classes had just been completed, students were assigned their rooms only days before, and many had not yet gone to the bank to cash their checks or they had bills with them in their travel bags which could not be retrieved from their rooms (252). The loss was estimated at more than $1,000,000, and worst of all, the building was mortgaged still and was underinsured at only 10% of its replacement value.

The whole affair reminded everyone of the 1892 fire, as if it had been but a rehearsal for this second recovery effort. This time, however, the 200 students and seminarians at the monastery were sent home; the classes of Fr. Augustine were for the Benedictines themselves. The core of the community remained in Mt. Angel town, parcelled out as before, in 1892, among local townspeople and nearby farmers. Others with parish assignments were told to stay in their rectories. Plans began immediately to rebuild, resolute as the monks were to repeat their efforts of the previous two decades. The new archbishop of Portland, Edward D. Howard (1926-66; formerly auxilliary bishop at Davenport, Iowa), rushed to the abbey's rescue with a massive campaign coordinated by Rev. J. H. Black to raise funds in Portland and throughout the ecclesiastical province. On the next Sunday, a pastoral letter was read in every parish under the prelate's jurisdiction (253):

> A dreadful catastrophe has befallen the Benedictine Fathers at Mt. Angel. During the night of September 20, a fire destroyed their magnificent abbey, college, and seminary, thus sweeping away the results of 25 years of tireless energy. These good Fathers have labored in the interest of God and His Church in the archdiocese for 44 years. We deem it, therefore, our duty to ask your charitable aid in the disaster that has befallen them. To this end, we order that a collection be taken up in all parishes of the archdiocese, Sunday, October 3.

Help was also solicited from other religious communities, and the most immediate aid came from the Benedictine Sisters at Mt. Angel who, as before, took over food services for the monks in the local Catholic grade school. The parishioners of St. Mary's raised $5000 in a single collection. Local groups like the Knights of Columbus pledged over $1000 each. Subsequently a massive letter campaign was directed toward Catholic organizations, such as the solicitation of 1928 to all chapters of the Catholic Order of Foresters (254). Other Benedictine foundations were also quick to respond; on September 20, 1926 Abbot Athanasius Schmidt of St. Meinrad's had a $1000 bankdraft sent to Mt. Angel even before appeals were heard (255). Even so, in imitation of Prior Adelhelm before, several Mt. Angel monks traveled about the country as itinerant beggers in search of alms in order to rebuild.

The appeal was ecumenical. The Oregon *Daily Press* solicited help for the homeless community, reminding Americans that recent fund drives were successful in aiding the starving Armenians, educational institutions in the Near East, and hurricane victims in Florida, "but here are stricken people and a worthy education institution in our midst that deserves not only our sympathy but our cash" (256). The *Oregon Daily Journal* on September 23 broadened the appeal: "There is no room for sectarian differences in the regret that must be felt for a loss so great" (257). The *Capital Journal* of Salem reminded its predominantly Protestant citizenry how they rallied to help Willamette University recover from a fire that destroyed Waller Hall; it suggested that the Chamber of Commerce organize a relief effort throughout Marion County: "Here is a chance for Salem to show toleration as well as benificence" (258). Finally, the Portland *Oregonian* reported how one philanthropist, Tom Turner, owner of the Portland Beavers, began a surge of local giving with a public $100 pledge; the ball club's secretary-treasurer pledged another $50 more, but after a 4-2 win, he "raised the ante!" (259). Consequently, recovery began immediately and by January 1927 pledges were sufficient to plan a new monastery.

Meanwhile, the seminary resumed classes in rented quarters downtown. Mt. Angel itself became a temporary monastery complex with monks living in laymen homes but assembling for Offices in the parish church, meeting in the schools for communal meals, and carrying on as if the monastery were still intact. It demonstrated to everyone that a monastery is more than a mere building, but a fraternity which could preserve its sense of community even under these adverse circumstances. Classes for the students also reconvened, scattered wherever space could be reserved. This interface between the town and community of Mt. Angel's monks cemented relations between the religious and the local lay citizenry which survive to this day.

On May 10, 1927 the hilltop began to be cleared of debris and made ready for reconstruction. This time the summit was landscaped for a modular campus rather than a centralized complex. The emphasis was, of course, on the monastery itself in order to reassemble the community. Originally a four-story structure was envisioned, but funding prevented this, so that the building was reduced to three stories. On July 17, 2500 people gathered on the lawn to witness the laying of the cornerstone. By March 1928 the monks were able to dedicate their new church, or at least its sanctuary and a choir section with a small temporary nave, and to move into the north wing of the monastery which

Fig. 8. Mt. Angel Abbey restored, after the 1926 fire. Architect's plans for a hilltop campus. MAA, s.n.

spread out behind the church. Much of the finish work in the church itself, such as the mosaic floor, was done by the monks themselves. Br. Gabriel Loerch died in 1932 while still working on the choirstalls. A second wing of the monastery was added later to house seminarians and secondary day students; this was occupied in October 1930.

On October 22, 1932 the monastery celebrated its Golden Jubilee: fifty years had passed since the Benedictines had come to Oregon. The community was still struggling against great adversities hardly to be expected after a half-century of labor. The austerity of the Great Depression was certainly not conducive for reconstruction and total recovery, not to mention expansion. What might have become a major college and university now seemed doomed to remain a small college devoted largely to clerical education. Whatever ambition there may have been to develop more than this was now tempered by the reality of manpower shortages, continued financial hardship, and a loss of a competitve stance with other institutions. Even so, the college had no difficulty gaining reaccreditation in 1933 and approval of the expansion of its four-year curriculum for a basic bachelor of arts degree. Its teacher's education program was designed to help its seminary program as well as continue the support of Catholic education in the area's secondary schools. In 1936 a gymnasium was built opposite the monastery, providing definition for the hilltop campus.

The Benedictine schools enjoyed modest enrollment increases, and by 1934 there were 164 resident students, of whom 78 were seminarians. Not all diocesan priests studied at Mt. Angel. It was still customary for many to complete their theologate at St. Edward's Seminary in Kenmore, near Seattle, Washington. But as the Mt. Angel curriculum developed, seminarians were attracted from over a greater radius even though the other bishops began their own local seminaries. The concentration of graduate studies in theology made Mt. Angel competitive, but it also meant that the college was permanently subservient to seminary education and that the abbey's history was hitherto entwined ever more tightly with the archdiocesan administration which had a vested interest in this seminary even though it was owned by the monastery. During the decade of the 1930s, 138 seminarians were to graduate from Mt. Angel. This greatly helped the secular church which in turn began to lend more and more support to the seminary's maintenance.

The community itself continued to grow, and given the relatively sparse population in the Western states and that Catholicism was a minority religious preference, vocations were fairly plentiful. Moreover, the presence of other Benedictine foundations in Washington and California by this time meant that Mt. Angel drew its recruits primarily from a contracting area. A registry in the abbey archives records correspondence from 1900 to 1945, largely applications of interest in joining the Order (260). Applications came from Oregon and Washington predominantly, but also from the midwestern United States, New England, and even from German-speaking countries abroad. Most came from a mid-section of America in which nineteenth-century Catholic immigration settled, namely from Massachusetts to New Jersey, cutting westward to include Pennsylvania and Ohio, then to the upper Midwest: upper

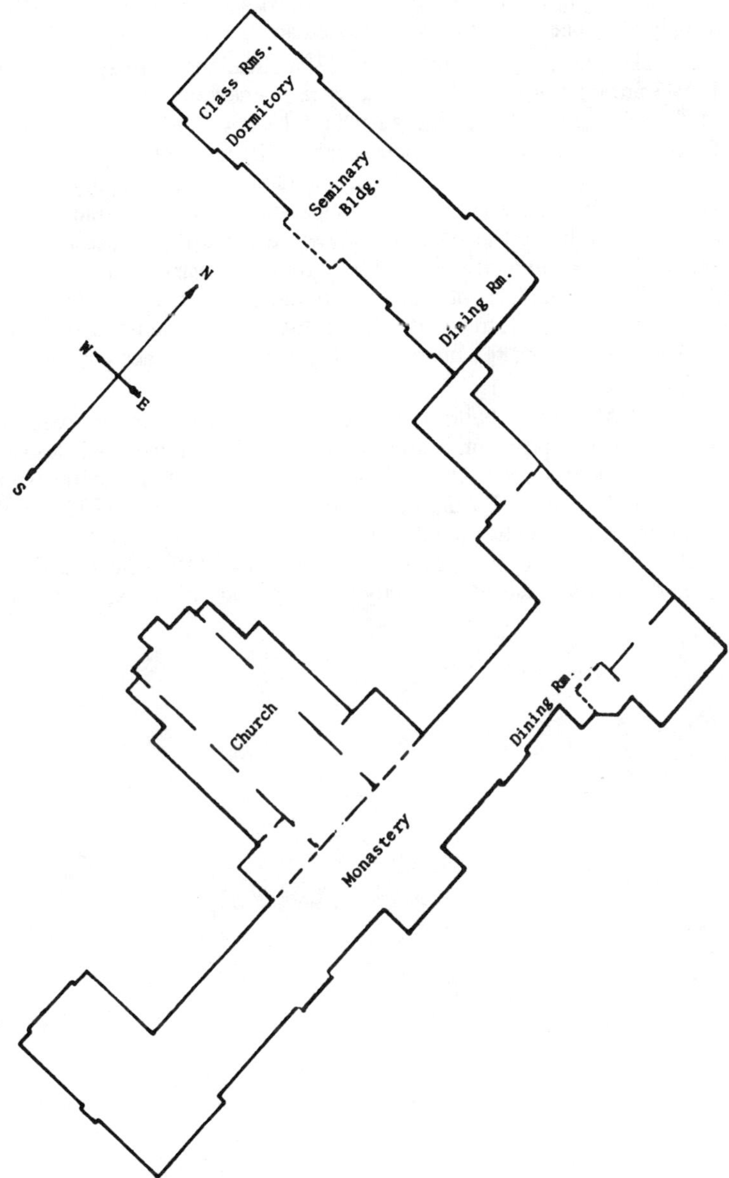

Fig. 9. Layout for the new monastery according the Fire Insurance maps of Sanborn Co., updated in 1949: Library of Congress Geography & Map Div.

Indiana and lower Michigan, Illinois, Wisconsin and Minnesota. There were also petitions, usually not approved, for transfers from other houses, and a few applications from Canada. The sample, however, can be misleading and is incomplete. The letters of those who eventually joined the community would have withdrawn into their personal, private files. Nonetheless, the register provides a sample to indicate something of the nature of a monastery's recruitment activities. The normal process was for an interested party to approach the community by letter, express his desire to either get better acquainted or to join the Order, and to provide biographical information about himself. In some cases inquirers were advised to apply formally, others were dissuaded. One could always learn more about the monks simply by asking for their hospitality for a few days. Such preliminary inquiries were handled by the guestmaster, not the novice master, and this correspondence was in a different record group. Those who applied formally and were accepted could decline, or enter as a beginning postulant before making a commitment as a novice when one's formation and training began. Even after the novitiate, the profession was for temporary vows only; final vows were professed only after one's vocation was assured and a lifelong commitment could be made.

The correspondence and registry reveals that over 127 applications were reviewed before 1945 (the years 1902-07, 1909, 1911-20, and 1943 are missing). 34% of these were rejected outright or were "disadvised". Of the 83 tentative acceptances, 34 or 41% never came, and of the 42 who did show, all but seven left within a year's time. This does not provide any information about those who entered the novitiate; over fifty did make their professions in that time span. Only 1 in 5 applicants could be expected to become monks, and generally after a trial period most of the young men could be expected to leave. There are natural fluctuations during this time showing periodic peaks of interest in the monastic life, and declining interest at others: there was a decided increase in inquiries at the advent of the Great Depression (1932-33), and an equally marked decline during the wars with Germany. Given the uneven nature of recruitment, a novitiate of 5-8 candidates at one time would be normal, but there were droughts of up to six years when no professions were made. At all times, it was felt that the community's size was an inhibiting factor on what it could accomplish. The larger it grew, the more work it set its mind to accomplishing. God's work on earth seemed to know no bounds.

The ability of Mt. Angel Abbey to rebuild, continue its educational program even in diminished fashion, and more, to attempt some expansion of this program, within a half-decade after the total destruction of the monastery, is truly indicative of the monks' resilient spirit. Abbot Bernard directed most of the recovery operation, but long hours of work and failing health took their toll. By the deepest of the Depression in 1933 the abbot, now nearly blind, needed more assistance than Prior Jerome could provide. Consequently, on August 1, 1934, a coadjutor, Abbot Thomas II Meier, was elected (261). He guided the community through the difficult depression and World War II period until 1950. During that time the abbey regained a stability and a molding of character which persists to the present.

The Modern Community, 1934-82

In 1938 Mt. Angel hosted an Apostolic Visitation by the papal delegate, Bp. Aloisius Münch (later cardinal) of Fargo, North Dakota; and one year later, in 1939, the seminary celebrated its Jubilee. Damian Jentges became its rector, and James Koessler as the new college director began to refine the latter's curriculum. Together these two administrators dissolved many of the distinctions separating the two programs. This meant increased attention to the theologate, concentration on seminary training, and less attention to lay education except at the secondary level.

This specialization in seminary education was reinforced by the takeover of the struggling seminary at Ladner, thirty miles from Vancouver city in British Columbia, largely because the Benedictine nuns were now managing the Indian schools and the province's population was growing so rapidly that there was a chronic shortage of clergy. Moreover, already ordained priests could not be spared to travel south to Washington and Oregon for residency in one of the American seminaries. Establishment of a West coast Canadian seminary was also in accord with the realignment of ecclesiastical boundaries which conformed with the border between the United States and Canada. Abp. William Mark Duke (1931-) of Vancouver when he was still coadjutor had encouraged the Mt. Angel monks since 1932 to focus their efforts on seminary training and to leave the mission schools to the sisters. Since 1938 Mt. Angel monks, such as Fr. Leo Walsh (1884-1967), had begun working with the Oregon seminary's alumnae to alleviate the shortage of clergy along the upper West coast. Msgr. Edgar Gallant worked as far north as Pius X mission at Skagway, Alaska (262). When Mt. Angel officially assumed responsibility for the school at Ladner, it was renamed "Christ the King" seminary and was relocated to Deer Lake, eight miles south of Vancouver. Fr. Eugene was appointed its first rector. A colony of monk-scholars left Mt. Angel on September 14, 1939 under Fr. Cyril Lebold as prior to found a priory which would sustain the seminary. The latter opened its doors in 1940 to begin training clergy for Western Canada, and the proto-community became the nucleus for the future Westminster Priory, Mt. Angel's first daughterhouse. It became independent in 1948, was elevated to abbatial status on February 12, 1953, and today in 1980 it had 29 members. At the same time Mt. Angel became a parent, it transferred its missions along the West coast of Vancouver Island to the Oblates of the Immaculate Conception, a Canadian missionary congregation specializing in such work.

Although Old vs. New World tensions had been resolved, World War II had a dramatic impact on the community not unlike the polarization which had developed during World War I. The most visible external effects were the deterioration of the monastery's flourishing German newspaper industry and still another blow to the abbey's educational efforts. In one monk's words, "By 1944 the Selective Service Act had begun the final decimation of the college at Mt. Angel". As the college's enrollment declined, the seminary's increased. Young men got deferments to study for the priesthood, but they had to attend school year around. Consequently the monks shifted teaching loads to the seminary and began offering summer programs for full year study. The college was never to recover from the war years because World War II also adversely affected the growth of the community. Since the Benedictines were by 1945 operating two seminaries, there was little manpower to devote to an expanded college curriculum as America's young men came home. Moreover, the college could no longer compete with the state system of higher education without a massive infusion of funds and a major decision to expand the college. That would have been unwise even if possible, since in Washington there were now two Jesuit schools, Gonzaga University in Spokane and the University of Seattle; and there was a third Catholic liberal arts college, St. Martin's at Olympia, run by the Cassinese

Benedictines. In Oregon itself the University of Portland, run by the Holy Cross Fathers, was responding to the needs of the urban area by expanding its curricula and attracting greater numbers. Moreover, laymen now preferred coeducational programs and monastic schools continued to exclude women. The Holy Name Sisters had begun a four-year liberal arts college at Marylhurst in southwest Portland, and the Benedictine nuns at Mt. Angel had developed their academy into a college as well. Finally, the Jesuits maintained their own house of study at Sheridan, Oregon (263). The state system grew tremendously after the war with the influx of federal funds for which the Catholic schools were ineligible. Because of old state politics, the state needlessly duplicated its institutions with schools in Portland, Monmouth, Corvallis, and Eugene, i.e., every thirty miles up and down the valley, and another in Ashland. Lewis and Clark College in Portland and Willamette University, although sectarian, provided nearby alternatives. None of these schools commanded the resources necessary to develop into first-rate institutions of higher learning, and their numbers were far beyond the real needs of the population. Moreover, Mt. Angel's rural setting could be expected to work against development of a college, although then the population shift toward American cities could not be foreseen. The subsequent history of the women's college in Mt. Angel suggests that the monks were wise in consolidating their programs rather than trying to expand them to become competitive with other institutions for general enrollments. The Benedictine sisters had been more successful than the monks in maintaining their college from 1882 onward, partially because they suffered no serious setbacks such as the fires which plagued the abbey, and also because without a seminary they developed a full liberal arts program without divided interests. It was perceived as a full-service women's college, not as a preseminary program; and a rural setting with proper moral upbringing of young women was traditionally considered very desirable. Even so, in the 1950s the sisters' college suffered declining enrollments, and to counteract this it went co-educational in the late 1950s thereby entering into competition with the monks' programs. The college's enrollments continued to decline in the 1960s to only 299 full-time students and a faculty of 37 in 1964, and this tendency was not arrested by improvements of its physical plant. The new buildings apart from the the convent were sold to become the Collegio Cesar Chevaz, which had no affiliation whatsoever with the Church or the Mt. Angel Benedictines. Most likely an expanded men's college could not have lasted as long, except by the infusion of tremendous funds. The subsequent concentration of the monks on seminary training was more compatible with the pastoral commitments of the community than any attempt to go into general higher education. Consequently, as Conception Abbey's college was after 1940, by 1947 Mt. Angel College was seen exclusively as a preparatory school for the seminary.

The curtailment of the college's expansion and continued concentration on the seminary allowed the community to shift some increased resources in 1945-46 to its secondary school. This preparatory school had been housed in space formerly devoted to the college, but after the athletic field was cleared along the eastern base of the hill, the school was related there in temporary quarters. Four military-surplus frame buildings were purchased to house 110 students and another temporary building was added for a gymnasium. In 1960 these were replaced with a new school. The move of the school meant that the hill was now the reserve of the monks and the seminarians. The latter numbered 50 in 1944-45, but by 1946 that increased to 81. The California Dominicans began sending some of their seminarians to Mt. Angel, and the improved theologate continued to attract students from outside the archdiocese. Enrollments built slowly from 87 in 1947 to 105 seminarians in 1950, 157 in 1951, 172 by 1952, then a decline to 153 in 1953 and a temporary leveling off, but up again to 229 by 1955-56. This meant that the seminary outgrew the capacity of St. Thomas Hall and required the construction of another building, St. Anselm Hall, and that the seminary was becoming one of the largest in the U.S..

The monks also revived their pre-1897 efforts in continuing education by hosting annual retreats for the diocesan clergy. Such activities, ultimately provided for the laity as well, led by 1960 to the construction at the cost of $494,000 of still another building, St. Benet's Hall, as a retreat center and guest house. It offered overnight accomodations for forty people plus conference and seminar rooms. By 1968 nearly 750 guests used this facility annually for their retreats. This is why the Trappists of Our Lady of Guadalupe Abbey near Lafayette, Oregon, jokingly refer to Mt. Angel as the "Benedictine Hilton!" This surge in construction also included finishing the still incomplete center nave of the abbey church. Plans had been approved in 1949 and in spring 1950 the old temporary nave was demolished; a central nave was designed to seat a congregation of more than 200, but this was extended even further. The new church was dedicated on March 21, the feast of St. Benedict, 1952, by Abp. Howard. It would be remodeled again in 1981-82, when the high altar against the rear wall would be removed and replaced with a simple table-altar in the center of the sanctuary, in keeping with post-Vatican II changes in the liturgy.

Thus the hill-top campus had grown considerably, embracing of the following additions (264):

1908	Benedictine Press and office building
1918	Post Office and editorial office building
1928	Monastery
1928	Abbey church sanctuary
1931	St. Thomas Hall (School of Theology)

1937	Gymnasium and auditorium
1938	Sister's house
1946	4-acre athletic field and tennis courts
1947	High school
1951	St. Joseph's Hall (brother's housing)
1952	Abbey church central nave and crypt
1954	St. Anselm Hall (Liberal Arts College)
1960	St. Benet Hall (retreat house)
1968	Swimming pool

The upper two floors of the monastery itself were the cloisters or monks' personal quarters, and the refectory and administrative offices were on the first level, while the basement housed the science laboratories (biology and chemistry) for the college, the natural history museum, two library rooms and the bindery, a nascent archives then storing mostly blueprints, and some equipment and maintenance areas. The back of the monastery was a private garden for the monks and a forested area before a steep drop in elevation to the farm below. The farmland amounted to 1,250 acres, with 840 acres immediately adjacent to the hill. The hilltop and slope was a 43-acre preserve for the monastery complex.

The completion of many of these projects was left to Damian Jentges who on August 16, 1950 was elected coadjutor for Abbot Thomas, who was suffering from glaucoma and high blood pressure. Abbot Damian, a theologian trained at the University of Salzburg, had been a professor at Mt. Angel since 1931, and thereafter (1939-45) he served as rector. He was blessed on October 1 (265). It was under his leadership that the community, which grew to over a hundred monks as one of the largest Benedictine monasteries in North America, achieved its dream of a fully developed campus. July 4, 1954 marked the ground-breaking ceremony for a new seminary building to go with the older one; it had a sizeable capacity for 200 students. St. Anselm and St. Thomas halls framed in the north side of the hill; they were situated with their fronts facing south and this south side of the hill was left undeveloped except for the athletic fields below, so that there was a magnificent view of the Cascades rising in the distance. It was at the time of this new building that there was a constitutional restructuring of the school; it was divided in two, a major seminary in St. Anselm's Hall and the minor seminary combined with the theology school moved into St. Thomas Hall. Half of the cost ($300,000) for the latter construction was born by the cooperating dioceses. At the same time, the crypt of the abbey church in 1951-52 was remodeled for the seminarians, and the central mall was beautifully landscaped with rose gardens and a reflection pool in front of the church. Finally the sisters' house near the monastery itself was remodeled, becoming instead an onion-domed chapel, Our Lady of Tikhvin center, for a special ministry under Br. Ambrose to serve the area's Old Orthodox Russian community which today numbers about 4000 members. This essentially completed the campus, except for the retreat and guest facilities which came at the end of the decade. Still lacking was a long-desired but financially elusive central library and cultural center.

Under Abbot Damian the governance of Mt. Angel was articulated in a revised charter of incorporation. Its articles specified that the abbey had complete charge of the seminary, the college, and the school. These enterprises were governed by four corporate officers: the president or the abbot himself elected for a life-long term; and the vice-president, secretary, and treasurer, who were elected for three-year terms. The accreditation visits of 1956-58 resulted in ranking Mt. Angel college and seminary among the best of their kind (266). Although the two were then combined, in 1962-63 they were again divided administratively. Since then the secular clergy has played a more active role in the governance of and instruction in the seminary, often by having a diocesan priest serve as rector. The faculty, however, had its strength in the monk-scholar tradition of Mt. Angel Abbey. The Benedictines continue to send their members to major graduate schools for advanced degrees: among them are still the Anselmianum in Rome and Catholic University of America, but also Harvard, UCLA, Notre Dame, University of Southern California, the universities of Oregon and Washington, Oregon State University, Stanford, Fordham, Toronto, Munich, Louvain, Edinburg and Oxford. A fifth-year program in theology, called a "pastoral year" was added to the curriculum with offerings focusing on pastoral medicine, psychology, lay apostulates, publishing, Catholic action, and other innovative subjects. While most of the seminarians returned to dioceses in the Pacific Northwest and Alaska, others were being sent to Mt. Angel for subsequent service in the American Southwest, in Mexico and Peru, and Vietnam. In keeping with changes made in the continuing education programs for the clergy, the basic curriculum was also modified. Structurally it changed from a "6 + 6" program (six years consisting of four years of high school and two or the equivalent of junior college in the Minor Seminary; then another six, i.e., two more of college to complete the bachelor degree level plus another four of graduate study in theology) to one described as "4 + 4 + 4" (that is, four years each of high school, college and graduate studies). In the later 1960s about 75-90 students enrolled in the preparatory school, and only slightly fewer (60-75) matriculated into the college, while the theologate averaged about 45 seminarians each year. In 1968, for example, over 197 students enrolled in the seminaries programs altogether, down slightly from the 1950s. Enrollment figures continued to decline as the Church came into another cycle of chronic shortage of clergy.

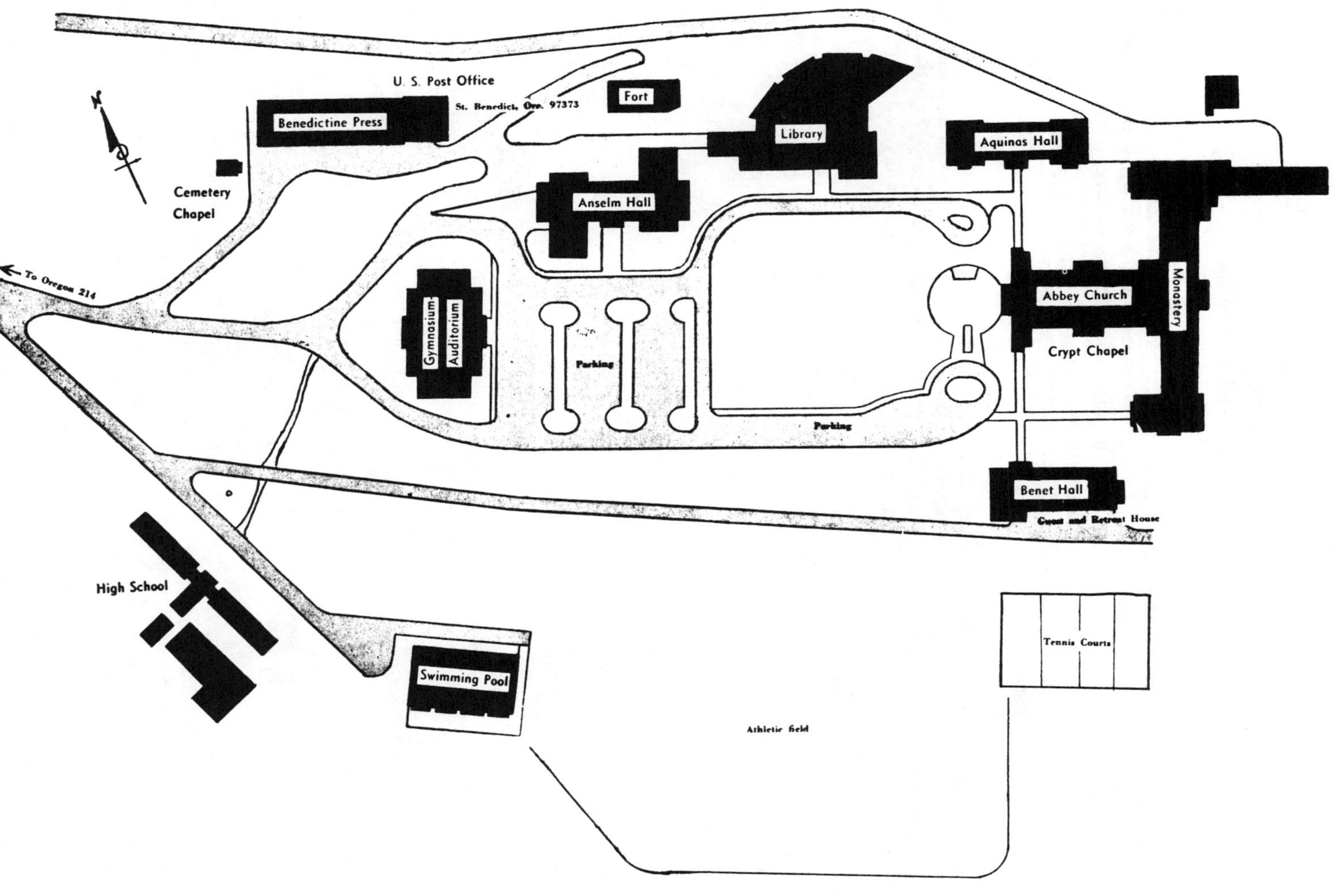

Fig. 10. Plan of the Mt. Angel hilltop campus, 1934-74. MAA, s.n.

The development of the advanced studies programs necessarily entailed the contraction of other programs, mainly in secondary education. Since 1959 the monks had run the lay-oriented Mt. Angel High School in town, but in 1964 this was made co-educational by merging it with Mt. Angel Academy. Later this school was closed in accord with the archbishop's wishes and a general shift in Catholic education throughout the United States to a focus on either elementary education or college, graduate, and continuing education. Instead of operating secondary schools, which had become a tremendous drain on diocesan revenues with no tax relief or federal support, many secondary schools were being closed and their workloads were shifted to the public systems which Catholics had to support through property taxes. Religious instruction at this intermediate level was supposed to be supplied by new programs, such as those associated with the Confraternity of Christian Doctrine. However, the preparatory school remained in operation for several more years under the direction of a single president-rector who worked through a layer of appointed deans, each in turn responsible for various subject-areas in the curricula. Thus the school's programs were streamlined into those of the college and seminary. The reorganization of 1967-68 separated the liberal arts college from the secondary preparatory program to conform more closely to the state and other private systems of education. Consequently, it was no longer so necessary for young men considering the priesthood as a vocation to make decisions at such an early age to leave home and attend the abbey's school. This meant decreased enrollments and less importance of the secondary program for the college and seminary, so that the school was finally discontinued in 1979. It was, in effect, replaced by the "Pre-theology" program.

Another major change was introduced in 1969-70 when the college began to offer an M.A. program in theology apart from the theologate leading to ordination. This was to accomodate laymen, and now women too, who sought advanced studies in religion, as the Church moved toward greater use of the lay ministry to supplement the shortage of priests. The first women admitted were religious, especially because the Benedictine sisters closed their college, but subsequently lay women enrolled as well. In fall 1981 the seminary enrolled 108 students from nineteen dioceses and two religious communities besides Mt. Angel Abbey. With its 44 faculty members, it could boast of a 1:3 faculty/student ratio (267).

The annual budget for the seminary now crests over $1,040,000 with 48% of this devoted to direct costs of the academic programs. The combined contributed services of the monks and the community's direct monetary subsidy of $133,000 accounts for 44% of the seminary's income; the rest comes from tuition (23%) born by the seminarians themselves with help from sponsoring dioceses, "auxiliary enterprises" (room and board operations, for 12%), for about 35% from student-derived sources; and 21% comes from gifts and grants (268). In the past two years the abbey has contained the impact of inflation by dipping deeper into its own reserves, since the burden on students and sponsoring dioceses is becoming prohibitive. At current costs and rate increases, each seminarian requires an outlay of $17,000 in order to reach graduation and ordination. Like most private education institutions, the seminary has therefore turned to development programs of planned giving as a means of gaining immediate aid and for building an endowment to cope with long-range development. The current recession and decreased vocations represent a modern threat to this enterprise.

Such limitations on the seminary itself have been counterbalanced by a much greater outreach effort since the reforms of Vatican II. In 1973 there began special summer programs for both the lay and ordained ministries, with specially tailored offerings in theology within or independent of the Master of Divinity program; philosophy, and other related subjects. In 1977 this broad focus was augmented further by the scheduling of evening classes in various ministries, education, and theology, thus providing an accessible set of programs both in advanced studies for the Masters degree and in continuing education. The Ministries Education program has been very innovative, attempting as it does to utilize not only the hill's theological resources but the whole area's Catholic community—the parishes, schools, hospitals, retirement homes, orphanages, and aid programs for the urban poor, the migrant workers, and the imprisoned. Finally, the seminary has developed a special Hispanic ministries program, with its first full-time administrator in 1981.

Today the college or the undergraduate curriculum is still closely related to the seminary's offerings in theology and ministry-related programs. The college's stated objective is to provide "an academic formation optimal for the development of Christian men" (269). Its curricula are divided into the divisions of: Behavioral Science, mainly Sociology (12 courses) and Psychology (9 courses); Communications, mainly Speech and English (7 courses); Fine Arts, subdivided into music, art, and drama (26 courses, with tutorials and workshops in orchestra, choir, piano, theater, and calligraphy); and History (16 courses). One can do graduate work by extending these fields in four areas: Canon Law and Communications, History and Pastoral Psychology, Sacred Scripture, and Theology (doctrinal, moral, and liturgy). In addition to the use of internships through the Ministeries Program, these curricula are enhanced by visiting faculty (22 professors since 1973) and association with the school's 22 emeritus faculty. Usually special offerings are built around four to five visitors every year, each staying in residence for varied periods up to full-year appointments. Often the secular clergy invited to teach in the seminary are rotated, so that these methods counter the natural tendency toward inbreeding in faculty development around the monastic community alone.

The abbot as corporate president is both the chancellor and chairman of the board of trustees; he and the administrative officers are assisted by a governing board of ten members, all Benedictines. There is a separate board of regents chaired by the archbishop of Oregon, now Cornelius M. Power, composed of the archbishops of Vancouver, Seattle, Anchorage, Santa Fe, and the cardinal-bishop of Samoa, plus the eighteen diocesan ordinaries within their provinces. The prelates are joined by twenty-four priests associated with the diocesan ministerial and educational programs, and by an additional advisory board of prominent Catholic laity, often civic leaders in Oregon. This seemingly unwieldy, over-grown administrative structure, especially in view of the comparatively modest size of the operation, reflects the problems of making the seminary with the supporting college programs responsive to the secular church while preserving the autonomy and proprietary rights of Mt. Angel Abbey.

Another thrust of Mt. Angel's efforts has been outreach to the lay communities, Catholic and non-Catholic, in keeping with the 1977 expansion of the formal education programs to include evening coursework and to admit laity of both sexes into its theology programs. Much of this falls under the rubric "continuing education," for credit, but there are also non-credit workshops and educational programs tied into the community's retreats. To accomodate more non-resident students and retreatants for short-period board during these programs, both St. Benet and St. Anselm Halls were recently remodeled (1980-81) in a $325,000 capital improvement project (270). St. Benet Hall gained a roof-top chapel and a conference level. Increasingly these facilities have been used by non-Catholic groups as well as the more traditional clientele served by the Benedictines. Guest-master Bernard Sander, OSB, after years of experience with the seminary and college programs, has developed a rewarding series of retreats. Perhaps no new program reflecting the community's outreach efforts has greater appeal that the abbey's annual summer Bach Festival. This concert series owes its creation to the vision of Abbot Damian Jentges who wanted the abbey to be a cultural center providing something special each year to the people of the valley. With the help of a lay board of trustees and especially the efforts of a local patron, Mrs. Alastair MacKay, as executive director, since 1972 a three-day series of concerts on the hill has earned widespread acclaim. Leading artists from the entire country, as well as those on tour from abroad, are invited. In addition to the musical delights, in an informal summer atmosphere concert goers enjoy picnic baskets filled with wine and whatever the changing menu bring, on the mall in the company of the monks and in view of the Cascade range. It is a festive 5ocasion which more than any other event, allows laymen to acquaint themselves with this interesting community (271).

In addition to these educational and outreach activities, the monks continue to do some parish work despite repeated attempts to curb any tendency to splinter the community. Periodic shortages of clergy have created situations which demand at least temporary parish duties as one means of the diocesan church to staff its churches. The recent rejuvenation of the lay deaconate is another, and this in itself provides motivation for some of the changes in the seminary and theology programs of the abbey. The monks had administered the Tillamook parish for years, but it returned to the bishop's direction in 1979; the nearby mission at Rockaway has continued under the monastery's care, but this will most likely cease when the last monk-pastor retires. Sacred Heart and Mt. Angel parishes are the only two which have developed a long, continuous history of having Benedictine pastors. St. Agatha's is also served by the monks with Sacred Heart, but both of these may return to the secular clergy. Now seven monks reside at parish rectories, but in the near future it is expected that only Mt. Angel will be served by the monks. Additionally, three monks are loaned to the archdiocesan chancery, the Hispanic apostolate, and a mental hospital chaplaincy. Periodically another serves as a military chaplain; four monks (Frs. Ildephons Calmus, Lawrence Eskay, Bertrand McLoughlin, and Leo Rimmele) have done so. Br. Ambrose Moorman continues the abbey's service to Oregon's Russian Old Believers. Consequently in the past decade ten to twelve monks may be assigned to offsite duties at any one time, but the trend is definitely away from such outreach by individual monks and more toward a wider range of services by the community as a whole.

The community in the last decade has been expending considerable resources on the above services; this requires that the monks generate enough income to support themselves and still have time left over to devote themselves as they do to education, parish, and outreach work, and more, to produce surplus revenues which provide financial backing for these activities. Their services are not compensated in full, and each activity costs more than any income thereby derived. Consequently, the monastery's health as an economic corporation is extremely important for the continuence of this work.

The farm has always been the mainstay of the monks' income (272). It consisted in the late 1960s of a dwelling, a dairy barn, a shed, three hops storage bins and a dryer, two hog barns, two barns for beef cattle, a poultry house, a feedmill, a silo, and a maintenance and equipment garage. Of the 1250-acre central tract, 850 are cultivated by eight employees, a lay brother, and a farm supervisor who is a member of the community. The tendency has been for the monks, because of their commitments and the decline of the lay brotherhood, to do less of the farmwork themselves and to rely on hired hands. This cuts into cash revenues, but the farm supplies the monastery and its schools with most of their food and since the mid-century began to produce increasing surpluses. In 1968 the farmland was divided into 350 acres of grain (wheat, barley, and oats), 140 for hops which became an important cash crop, 120 of hay, and 230 of corn. The latter two crops were for silage and fodder to sustain the dairy farm and the beef herds. The herd, which until the 1950s numbered about 150 head, in 1968 consisted on 264 head (102 Holstein milking cows of which

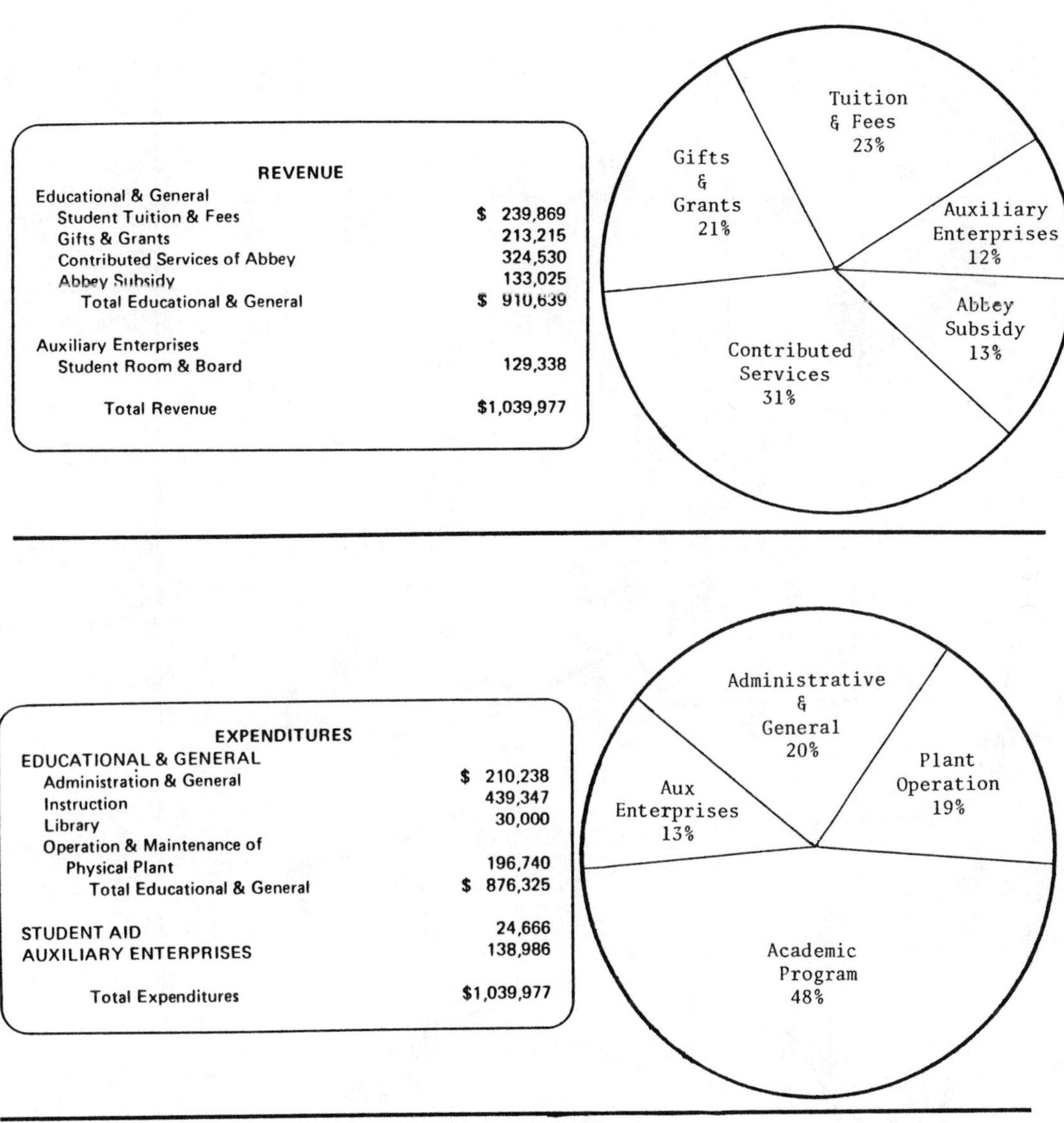

REVENUE	
Educational & General	
Student Tuition & Fees	$ 239,869
Gifts & Grants	213,215
Contributed Services of Abbey	324,530
Abbey Subsidy	133,025
Total Educational & General	$ 910,639
Auxiliary Enterprises	
Student Room & Board	129,338
Total Revenue	$1,039,977

EXPENDITURES	
EDUCATIONAL & GENERAL	
Administration & General	$ 210,238
Instruction	439,347
Library	30,000
Operation & Maintenance of Physical Plant	196,740
Total Educational & General	$ 876,325
STUDENT AID	24,666
AUXILIARY ENTERPRISES	138,986
Total Expenditures	$1,039,977

What Does It Cost To Educate A Seminarian?

Fig. 11. Mt. Angel Seminary financial report summarized, 1980-81 from the *MA Newsletter* 1980.

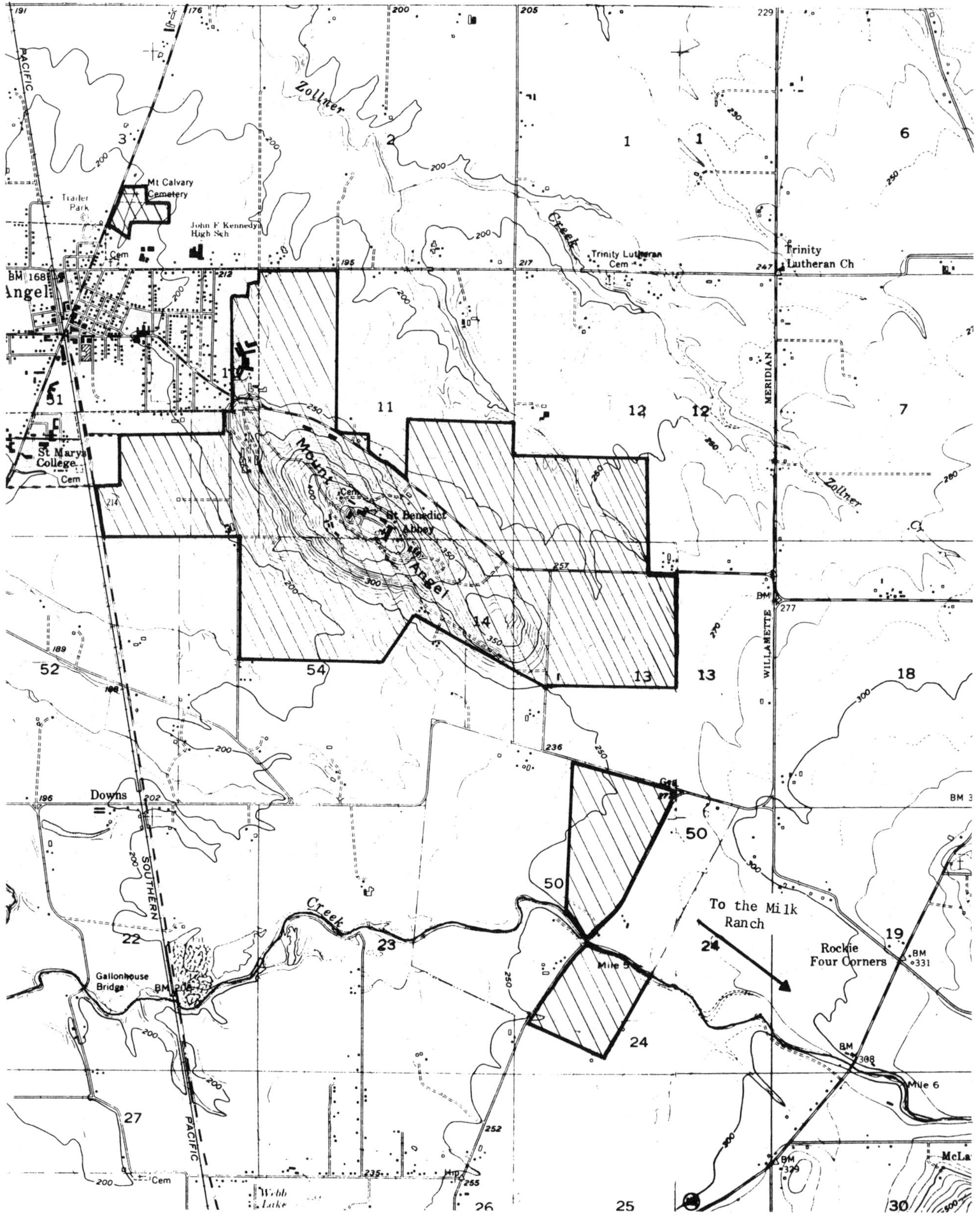

Fig. 12. Mt. Angel's farm, founded on the original homestead purchases of 1882-3. Based on current land ownership maps for Oregon by Metsker's Map Co., 1981, traced onto the U.S. Geological Survey map of the area.

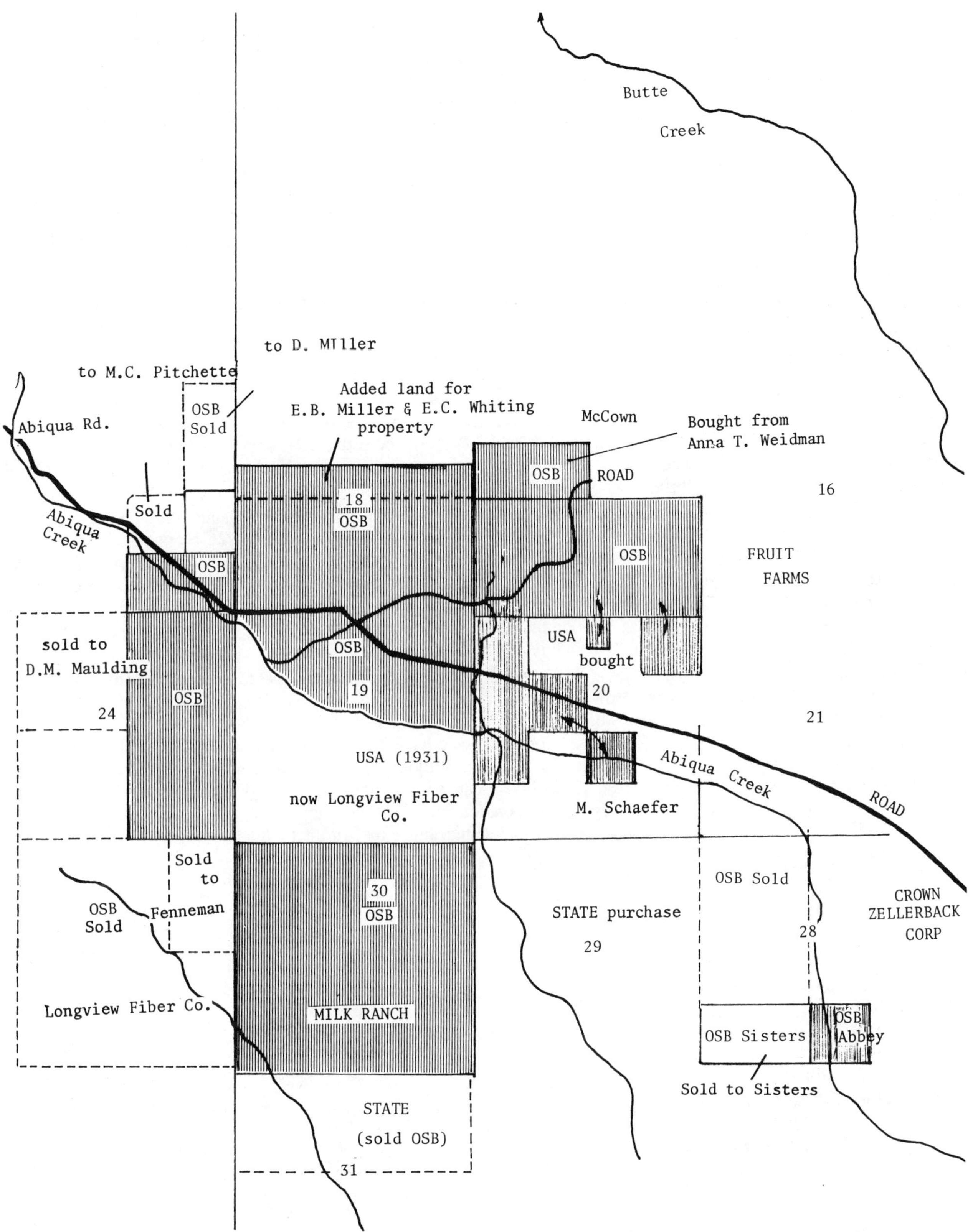

Fig. 13. The Milk Ranch up Priest's Creek into Section 30, and appendages. Based on the current land ownership maps for Oregon, Metsker's Map Co., 1981, for Marion Co. OR.

3/4 were usually producing at any one time; 7 breeding bulls, 85 steers, and 70 heifers). Ordinarily about 3000 pounds of milk were produced per day, of which ca. 240 were consumed by the community. However, when the seminarians and students were in residence, consumption jumped up to 640. Otherwise, this class "A" milk was sold to the Mt. Angel Creamery, generating a major source of income for the monastery. From 1965-67, the 525 tons of grain raised on the farm was consumed entirely by the corporation, without surplus for sale, so that the hops (168,431 lbs./year) were the only cash crop *per se*. The livestock operation likewise consumed as feed most of the 2,360 tons of corn and 600-700 tons of hay grown annually, but this in turn supplied the hilltop with about 100 beef each year. The monastery's hog farms, however, did produce surplus pork in the three years just cited; consumption averaged 252 annually, leaving about 532 hogs for the area market. Thus the monastery was almost self-sufficient and produced enough income to free the monks from farm labor and to provide some liquid capital as well. This operation continued to grow until recent years when labor prices and changes in the tax laws and Internal Revenue Service regulations made it more advantageous to reduce direct farming to the level needed for yearly consumption and to lease the rest of the land and rely on the rents as income. This reflects another adjustment to a manpower shortage and changing internal make-up of the community. Unfortunately, the leases were made too long and at fixed rents, without proper precaution against current spiraling inflation, so that the farmland does not generate the income it might have for current operations.

In addition to the farm, the abbey owns 2,598 acres of timberland along the base of the Cascade range fifteen miles east of the abbey. Some of this had been acquired by homesteading in the early years, other acreage was bought piecemeal over the years, but the core tract is the old Milk Ranch. The monastery generates a modest supplementary income from cutting selectively the Douglas fir on this land. Parts of the estate are in reforestation for future income, and other tracts are periodically leased as job lots to commercial loggers. The monks themselves maintain only a D-4 caterpillar, a jeep, and chain saws for their limited timber operation.

Finally, the monastery owns some scattered tracts, and small parcels within the main landholding, were intensive truckfarming primarily for local consumption and markets is practiced. There are a total of 26 acres of orchards which in the late 1960s produced 140 gallons of black cherries, 900 pounds of pie cherries, 700 bushels of apples, 300 gallons of peaches, and 200 gallons of pears (amount canned). Four acres of berry bushes annually produce 140 gallons of boysenberries and 140 of raspberries; blackberries grow in wild bogs and add to this variety, but not in such a way that they are included in any accounting. Finally, the estate's nut trees produce 35 bushels of walnuts annually, and there is a 2.5 acre vegetable garden which is cultivated at the foot of the hill for fresh produce.

Other than aggregate figures released in annual reports, the abbey's financial records are closed to research to protect the community's right to privacy. However, detailed accountings in 1966-68, when the abbey embarked on an ambitious ten-year development campaign, were made available after a thorough audit of this multi-faceted monastic corporation. Then, as more recently in 1980, the monastery was judged by the auditors to be financially sound. At the end of the 1960s the monastery was generating just over a million dollars annually, mostly from the labor of the monks themselves. Only 10% or between $80-120,000/year came from such sources as donations, interest, dividends, and annuities. The intricacies of the abbey's financial operations need not be described to gain a general picture of the whole enterprise; the following table simply rounds off income and expenditure to the nearest $1000 to provide a summary of the main accounts (273):

Accounts:	Income:	Expenses:	Balance:
Monastery general	27	36	−09
Kitchen	78	122	−44
Masses	43		+43
Missions	26	4	+22
OSB Scholastic	9	13	−04
Parish	23		+23
Post Office	11		+11
Medical/Hospital		22	−22
Alms & Charity		2	−02
Vehicle maintenance		8	−08
Travel		5	−05
Maintenance		6	−06
Sacristy		8	−08
Utilities		13	−13
Library		14	−14
St. Benet Hall	15	11	+04

Accounts:	Income:	Expenses:	Balance:
Seminary	210	183	+27
Farm	193	165	+34
Press	270	273	−03
Miscellaneous	26	21	+05
Donations	9		+09
Notes & dividends	35		+35
Annuities	19	13	+06
Securities	18		+18
Life insurance	7	4	+03
Capital expenses		35	−35
Totals:	1015	958	+57

In general net income in the late 1960s was declining, especially the margin generated from the seminary, because costs were rising, certain traditional revenues such as parish support and Mass stipends were falling, and as part of deliberate policy there was a major shift in all ecclesiastical finance during those years. As expenses cut deeper and deeper into the margin between gross and net income, there were fewer funds for capital improvements. Moreover, although the abbey itself and its educational programs were tax exempt as charitable, non-profit institutions, the farm, timber operation, and improvements in the latter, were taxed by the state. In the 1970s tax regulations became more stringent, cutting further into the community's net income. Afterward, the abbey's farm and timber lands were leased rather than worked directly by the community as had been done until now. This necessitated the great financial campaign of the 1970s, and partially explains in general the efforts toward consolidation of the education programs in order to maximize the resources and talents of the abbey. As adjustments were made in programs, of course, budgets shifted as well. The parish accounts became smaller, the press was made cost-effective by selling and eliminating the abbey's newspaper business, the seminary became a debit, and the expenses for the library increased considerably.

As part of this financial inspection of 1968-69, the property of the community was surveyed and appraised at its replacement cost, and the content of the monastery's buildings was appraised for insurance coverage by the Insurance Company of North America (274). Thirty-two buildings were included, mostly those on the hilltop and the farm, but also two offsite properties—a residence in Mt. Angel town, and a beach house in Lincoln City . The total capital worth of the corporation was considered then to be (rounded to the nearest $1000):

Land (without improvements)	$1820
Buildings (1967 replacement cost)	$6731
Contents	$968
Equipment	$130
Livestock	$127
Total:	$9776 = $9,776,000

At that time the community had 123 members and there were 285 students on the hill. Since then, in 1974, the monastery reorganized its fiscal administration with Fr. Andrew Baumgartner in charge of the business and procurator's offices. Investments were turned over to an outside firm, and the accounting system was revamped to protect the community from future employee embezzlement and to maximize corporate income. Finally, a development office was established under John Degnin, father of Br. Benjamin, to enlarge Mt. Angel's endowments for both the seminary and the community itself. In addition to alumnae, there are several special groups acting as "friends" of Mt. Angel, such as the parents of those entering the community. All of these measures are attempts to confront continued financial constraints on what could be done with ideal funding, and to struggle with the new problems of spiraling inflation and recurrent recession.

It was not, therefore, until the 1950s after World War II that this monastery was economically stable. Once this was finally achieved, two foundations in addition to Westminster Abbey were undertaken. On August 3, 1965 the Mt. Angel Benedictines established Ascension Priory under Fr. Patrick Meagher, first in Twin Falls, Idaho, from where it moved to a farmstead at Jerome, Idaho. Its first permanent building was completed in 1979, and the priory was blessed on August 3, 1980. The monks there under Prior Simeon Van de Voord have enjoyed the continued patronage of Bp. John Walsh of Boise. It is now planning to build a retreat center. One year later, on August 15, 1966, the monks founded a third house under Fr. Ambrose Zenner—Our Lady of the Angels Priory in Cuernavaca, Mexico. This priory is prospering despite difficult economic conditions and relatively low education levels of its entering postulants. In 1980 Fr. Louis Charvet succeeded Br. Boniface Arechederra as prior. Both of these latter foundations remain dependent on the mother abbey and constitute a drain on its economic resources and manpower, just as in any family (275). Now Mt. Angel is playing its role in the propagation of the Benedictine Order, just as Engelberg did a generation ago. The demands of these foundations, coupled with a general decline in vocations during the late 1960s and thereafter, have prohibited Mt. Angel from responding positively to invitations to undertake other foundations in Alberta, Canada, and in Samoa. During the 1970s the slow but constant growth of the community leveled off; its membership consisted of 124 monks (including 67 priests), of whom 30 resided at the two dependent priories. About 70 monks would be in residence at any one time, busy with the farm, college, seminary, and, as always, the *Opus Dei*.

The Community Today, 1982

Much of the change in Mt. Angel's educational programs and economic base came about under the abbacy of Anselm Gavin who succeeded Abbot Damian Jentges in 1974 (276). The latter died of spinal cancer while still in office, having governed the community for 24 years. It was Abbot Damian who had envisioned Mt. Angel becoming a seat of advanced learning and study, a regional cultural center, and a focal point of international Benedictinism. He certainly was responsible for the abbey's major growth, expansion of its programs, and the completion of the hilltop campus. He governed the community during an era of relative economic prosperity and lived to witness the revival of Catholicism through the reforms of Vatican II. It was Abbot Anselm, however, who after years of teaching and pastoral work, had to lead the community's response to a new era of economic entrenchment and recession, a decline of vocations, and the needs of a revitalized church which was rapidly accomodating itself to the modern world. He governed ably for six years, but resigned in 1980 because of failing health. The new abbot, Fr. Bonaventure Zerr, was blessed by Abp. Cornelius M. Power of Portland, on August 28, 1980 (277). The new abbot is a robust man, congenial and well educated. He grew up in Sacred Heart parish in Portland where the Benedictines had done much of their parish ministry. Abbot Bonaventure made his profession in 1957, and afterwards spent six years studying theology and Scripture at St. Boniface in Munich. He has subsequently studied at Berkeley. He is known throughout the province because of his previous work as novice master, teacher-scholar, librarian, and subprior. He is at once a linguist who could converse with the Soviet dissident author Aleksandr Solshenitsyn when he visted Mt. Angel as a possible residence in exile; a bibliographer who is largely responsible for building up the library colletions in theology and philosophy over the past decade; a Civil War buff and avid Western fan; and a theologian and Scripture scholar trained in Munich and known for his work on the Psalms. He now guides, as of the beginning of 1983, 118 monks: 67 priests, one deacon, and 20 brothers in final vows; 17 monks in temporary vows; plus one oblate, three novices, and nine postulants. As in most religious orders, vocations have waned. Although here has been a continual flow of candidates, so few have entered the Order that there are stretches of drought, such as from 1961 to 1972, in which no permanent members were added to the community. This diminished rate of recruitment and replenishment of the community's ranks has serious implications for the future; it will have fewer men to spare for outside work, diocesan clergy or lay faculty will play a greater role in the seminary and college, and the current work will not necessarily become less but will be redistributed over fewer laborers. A call to religious life, therefore, can be extremely demanding but also rewarding. Mt. Angel's monks are hoteliers, administrators, librarians, archivists, farmers, scholars, teachers, counselors, printers and publishers, editors, designers, applied artists, etc.. Their roles are multifaceted, and often their careers include several roles at once or at least a change in succession as the needs of the community are assessed and the talents of the individual monks are developed to accomodate those needs. Still, the primary job of Abbot Bonaventure and his monks is the *opus Dei* as expressed in the motto *ora et labora*.

This Benedictine community has played an integral role in the development of the Pacific Northwest over the past century. Its educational programs alone at the college level and above have enrolled nearly 6000 students and 600 priests; of its own graduates, 425 seminarians have been ordained. Its alumnae organization keeps in touch with over 3000 members. There is no way to estimate the extent of the monks' impact through their parish work, missionary efforts among the Indians, and outreach to educate a new kind of Catholic laity. Its major activities have been: 1) educational, focusing increasingly on seminary training and a variety of ministries, and now adult education as well; 2) pastoral, in serving local parishes first for its own support, and more so to supplement the diocese's lack of secular clergy; 3) evangelical, first in working with the valley's immigrant settlers, then the Indian missions, and now with the disadvantaged such as the Hispanic-American population, as well as with the modern non-Churched believers and those who through retreats and counseling need their faith renewed; and 4) cultural, by fostering the arts in primitive frontier conditions, then in embedding the arts and humanities into a liberal arts educational program, and finally in promoting studio arts and music such as the study of calligraphy, Gregorian chant, and liturgical arts—and now sharing this traditional Benedictine love of the arts with the entire region by attracting internationally acclaimed artists to the hilltop for the annual Bach festival (278). Mt. Angel thus exemplifies several Benedictine traditions, and its history attests vital contributions to Christian life and culture in America.

Why this historical overview of such a small, relatively minor organization in our modern times when big is considered better, the temporary to be relevant, and the material ethic the only obvious value? Above all else, the history of Mt. Angel Abbey portrays a struggle to realize the ideal against grave adversity. There is here no stereotyped myth of a monastery hoarding the wealth of ages, of a way of life which was possible only in the past, or of super-human religiosity, mysticism, and asceticism. Instead, the records portray an all too human institution suffering the problems common to all humanity, with occasional glimpses of individual personalities and conflicts coming to the surface of the protective cloak of common identity. In retrospect, one must respect this Benedictine community for its perseverance and conviction in the monastic way and for keeping the faith. Given the obstacles confronting this foundation, Mt. Angel strikes one as remarkably resilient and robust, especially considering its context. Note, for example, that Oregon was never a fortress of Roman Catholicism. Catholics in Oregon have always been a minority. In 1926 the state's Catholics numbered 61,036 or about 15% of the total population of only 900,000. Catholics became even a smaller minority as European immigration was replaced by immigration to Oregon from other, predominantly Protestant, states. In 1952 only 28.4% of the state's people were members of any church, whatever the denomination, and only a quarter of these (25.8%) was Catholic. Consequently, the percentage of Catholics in the state's total population was only 7.3%. Today, most Oregonians are still unafilliated with official religion, perhaps in keeping with the state's reputation for independence and non-alignment in politics, and the use of the state as a testing ground for new products and advertising campaigns. Indeed, not only is Oregon no stronghold of Catholicism, organized religion as such has little hold there. It is, from the viewpoint of a missioner, still an open mission field. At the opening of the 1980s the Catholic church has made a comeback; Catholics now constitute about 13% of the population, but Catholics have never had the proportional representation as they had in the late nineteenth century after the influx of the German and Irish Catholics. It is, therefore, somewhat remarkable to find in the midst of this rather areligious populace, a flourishing Benedictine monastery. If one were to prefer a theological interpretation of history, Mt. Angel's very survival and existence is providential.

1.1 Mt. Angel before the 1892 fire: the college, seminary, priory, and church

1.4 Abt. Anselm Villiger of Engelberg Abbey, patron and protector of Mt. Angel

1.2 Mt. Angel in 1908: the monastery rebuilt on the hilltop

1.3 Mt. Angel Abbey in ruins after the 1926 fire

1.5 Prior Adelhelm Odermatt, titular abbot and founder of Mt. Angel Abbey

2.1 Abt. Thomas I Meienhofer, 1904–1910

2.2 Abt. Placidus Fuerst, 1910–1921

2.3 Abt. Bernard Murphy, 1921–1934

2.4 Abt. Thomas II Meier, 1934–1950

2.5 Abt. Damian Jentges, 1950–1974

2.6 Abt. Anselm Galvin, 1974–1980

2.7 Abp. Francis Norbert Blanchet, Oregon's first prelate

2.8 Abp. William H. Gross, patron of Mt. Angel's seminary

2.9 Community of Mt. Angel Abbey in 1910

3.1 Abt. Bonaventure Zerr, 1980–, the ruling abbot

3.2 Mt. Angel's Abbey Church

3.3 Community of Mt. Angel Abbey in 1977

4.1 Mt. Angel College library before the 1926 fire

4.2 College library, rebuilt, in 1933

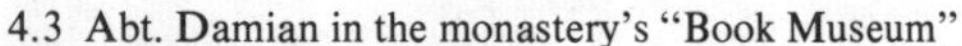

4.3 Abt. Damian in the monastery's "Book Museum"

4.4 Prior Jerome Wespe, archivist and librarian, in 1954

4.5 Library stacks in the monastery's attic, early home of the Aachen Collection

5.1 Fr. Mark Schmid, professor, librarian, and "conservator"

5.3 Mt. Angel Abbey's new library by Alvar Aalto, in 1970

5.2 Fr. Luke Eberle in 1975

5.4 Fr. Martin Pollard, rare book librarian, in the library's vault, 1981

6.1 Fr. Barnabas Reasoner, Mt. Angel's first professional librarian

6.3 Library's interior: the reference and circulation desk on the "deck"

6.2 Alvar Aalto, noted architect of Mt. Angel's library

6.4 Fr. Anselm Weissenborn, scribe and calligrapher of the Mt. Angel codices

6.5 Aerial view of the Mt. Angel complex, 1970

7.1 Richard Fall Rare Book Room of the Abbey Library, 1980

7.3 Abp. Dwyer of Portland blessing the abbey library, 1970

7.2 Library lecture and public programs' hall, 1970

7.4 Library interior in 1970: levels 1 & 2 plus the mezzanine

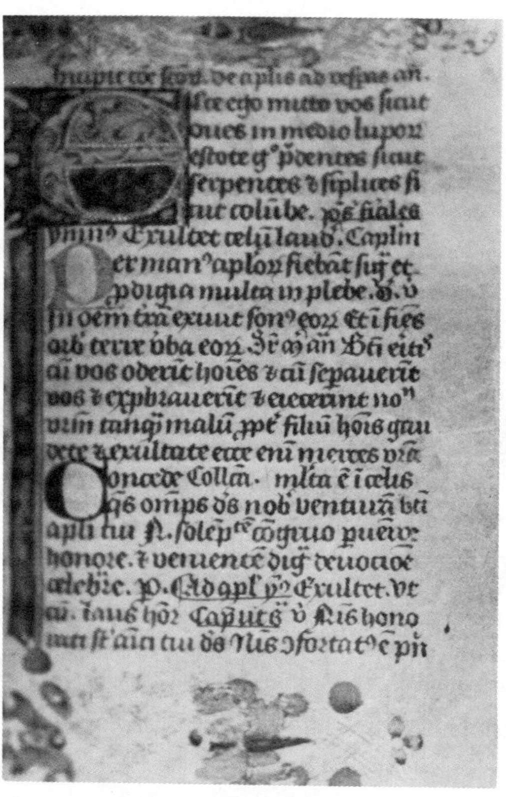

8.1 Manuscript illumination enlarged from the 15th-cent. Cologne *Breviary*

8.2 Illuminated initial in the printed Sensenschmitt *Bible* of 1476

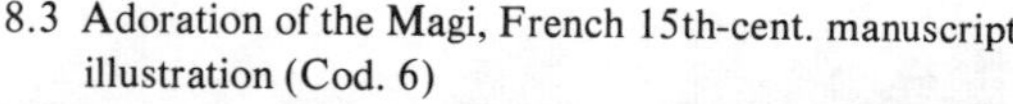

8.3 Adoration of the Magi, French 15th-cent. manuscript illustration (Cod. 6)

8.4 Monks celebrating the Mass of the Dead in 15th-cent. France (Cod. 5)

II.
THE MOUNT ANGEL ABBEY LIBRARY, 1882–1982

The Monastic Library Tradition

The monastic library tradition predates St. Benedict of Nursia and the foundation of the Benedictines, but the Order has had a particular devotion to libraries and book-oriented culture. St. Benedict's Rule placed emphasis on spiritual reading, private and collective, and offered ample justification for devoting a monastery's resources to library development. However, monastic libraries are not peculiar to the Benedictines, nor were or are they always Catholic; they may not be Christian. However, the scope of this essay is limited to the Latin Christian tradition in tracing in brief outline the origins of the monastic library and its continuing role in Western Civilization. The find of the Dead Sea Scrolls of the Qumran community uncovered a non-Christian but nonetheless monastic library and archives which attests the roots of later Western developments in ancient civilization. The idea of a monastic library not only helped to transport the Judeo-Christian heritage across cultural borders and through time, but it became part of that heritage in the process of cultural transmission and dissemination.

The early Christians who fled to the desert to find their salvation and solace individually, in imitation of Christ and the Baptist before him, had no Biblical model for taking books with them and establishing libraries for their comfort and spiritual aid. The formal schooling of Jesus is not well known, although there is ample speculation about his family's connection with the scribal schools of his time. The training might have been oral in keeping with the times; certainly his disputation of Scripture was memonic and oral. Library historiography, especially recently with studies about the oral antecedents of Greek librarianship and increased awareness of the multimedia and multipurpose character of ancient institutions of learning, and perhaps also because of several contributions to science fiction literature along similar lines, is less confined than it once was to investigating conventional libraries which like archives and less like information centers, were repositories of books in scroll or codex form. People themselves are information resources and disseminators, and certainly the early proclamation of the Gospel was oral and visual. The early Christians turned toward books and formal documentation largely upon contact with classical cultures and to use the communication systems devised by the Roman empire. There is especially noticeable throughout history the tendency to document in book form whatever information is needed when the original source of that information is no longer accessible. The book is more than a container for information transferred from place to place, it is a storage medium designed to transport messages through time. Scripture was very early converted to some book form, most likely scrolls in imitation of prevalent Jewish technology, but later into codices to adopt a form better engineered for easy transportation and storage. It is understandable how almost naturally custodians of the books or Bible became *bibliothecarii*, or librarians from the alternative term derived from the Roman term *liber* for book; and that simultaneously the place where books were kept came to be known as *bibliotheca(-ques)* in Romance language or later, libraries—a generic term for anyplace books could be gotten, often referring to commercial vendors of books and book supplies. The Christians, with their strength in the curial and scribal classes rather than the peasantry or aristocracy, almost naturally adopted Greco-Roman media and institutions for their purposes in spreading Christianity and safekeeping its written records.

Early monks were not isolated from such developments, but rather contributed substantially to the evolution of the codex as a particularly Christian format of communication, and after the state's recognition of Christianity in 312 as an official religion and not just another fad or temporary cult, they were involved in developing archives and libraries.

Even the desert father tradition had its bookish aspects, not so much in the mythography of the earliest monks, but certainly in the iconography surrounding St. Jerome's translation work. Cenobites were of course more capable of library development than anchorites and hermits, simply because of the aggregation of individual resources in communal living needed to support and maintain a library with its attendant scriptorium or publishing house. Most libraries, except those assembled by the few wealthy bibliophiles throughout history, have been corporate endeavors. Monastic communes were ideal social, economic, and political organizations to promote library development. Conversely, in the same way single books served as spiritual aids for individual monks, libraries became the mainstay of a monastery's cultural life. Just as the church was the focal point of spiritual attention and entrance into the next world, the library was a means of existing intellectually in this world despite cloistered life and the attempt by monks to insulate themselves from the secular through the order of their codes of communal conduct. Monastic libraries, then as now, provided alternatives to experiencing all of human life and conditions first hand, just as books were mechanisms of accumulating human experience and thought without the restrictions of time and place. Books and libraries were, therefore, natural allies of the contemplative life.

The association of books and libraries with the most fundamental notions of culture in Western Civilization is one of the unique characteristics of the West and this is largely a Christianized Roman response to ordering human affairs. Without libraries and books, things would return quickly to their parochial contexts now as when before there was massive destruction of these learning centers. Just as within libraries, the collections change as the old books are replaced with new; or within monastic communities the monastery and monasticism survives the passing of individual monks; so too, libraries have come and gone but the library tradition lives on. A sense of overall continuity of this tradition in general, and specifically that of monastic libraries, is often lost when focusing in institutional history on specific books, libraries, and communities. Moreover, there is a tendency in all historiography to write about the unique, exemplary, and heroic, at the expense of the commonplace, the pervasive, and the persistent aspects of life. Libraries and archives, which are dedicated to the recording of history, so often leave such few traces in history of their own record, that we know little about them. In some of the most famous cases, historians cannot even discover where the library stood since they have disappeared without physical trace. Their contributions are remembered, but they pass into a continuum of tradition as do all things human and material. They live on intellectually, spiritually, and effectively, only so long as that tradition is maintained.

Little, if anything, is so pervasive in early Christian iconography and mythography, apart from things relating to Scripture's content, than attention to the means by which Scripture and all recorded knowledge is disseminated. There are countless examples attesting the importance of scribal technology and institutions to Christianity; more than pictures of men reading, there are numerous illustrations of Christians proclaiming the Gospel orally from a Bible or clutching at a book as the authority for their words, and of those in authority as *authors* writing and copying books. As an alternative to direct intelligence and experience, the Christians relied on oral teaching based on a written, verifiable record of the Truth they proclaimed and its means of transmission. Just as scroll forms were associated with classical learning, the codex was identified increasingly as a Christian form. In its early development, it was little more than the Roman diptych modified to serve as a protective covering for a set of collated parchment folios, often with an outer leather mail pouch complete with flap for transportation. It was fundamental. The very term 'revelation' has an inner meaning reflecting on how Truth is learned by taking it out again from the calfhide or *vellum* on which it is preserved. From St. Jerome on, saints and especially doctors of the Church who taught officially, were pictured holding codices; indeed, the most common representations of St. Benedict of Nursia shows him holding his Rule in codex form. Indeed, the Rule like law, was preserved in a codex—it was codified.

It is not surprising therefore, to find throughout the manuscripts of the Middle Ages scenes of monastic scribes seated at their writing desks in supposed imitation of the Gospel writers themselves, with their *armaria* or book cupboards in the background, playing their role in the transmission of the Christian heritage. Nor is it strange to see in library and archival architecture until today the resemblance of a temple, often the basilica or forum model; or to discern in library plans the characteristics of layouts for early monasteries. Preserved and reconstructed floorplans of many monasteries indicate that the scriptorium and the main book cabinets were usually placed in a central location in the monastery complex. In Benedictine monasteries and priories it was customary to have stone benches aligning the northern arm of the cloister against the church for open-air reading. Likewise, the architecture historian Braunfels calls attention to the characteristic high windows in the dormitories of medieval monasteries, which served as skylights if not for individual cells then at least for individually defined living areas in a communal dormitory, where monks could read at small desks or lying down could read during their rest periods as St. Benedict advised (Chap. 48).

Few early monasteries had the resources for very many books, so that reading aloud for the community as a whole became a standard monastic custom. A few scholarly communities, like that gathered at Vivarium by the statesman-turned-monk, Cassiodorus, supposedly had very fine collections large enough to warrant organization into subject collections. Not only did Cassiodorus teach young scribe-scholars at the monastery to read and how to analyze a text, but in his *Institutes* or basic methods textbook, he laid down the principles of broad subject classification based on the classical division of the liberal arts. Indeed, much of the intellectual effort of the medieval scholar was in the

Fig. 14. Scribe-scholar teaching canon law in his medieval library. From Mt. Angel's *Decretales*, frontispiece.

organization of knowledge and the assimilation of non-Christian culture into Christianity. There was a great part of the classical inheritance lost, not so much from intentional destruction, but by more widespread neglect as the Christian scriptoria and libraries spent their limited resources on their main priorities, namely the Christian corpus. Thus the Bible survived in plentitude, as did the commentaries of the Fathers, and even the texts of Christianity's greatest foes, while the Roman histories of Livy survive only in part, or those of Tacitus by chance. The pagan authors which were transmitted by systematic copying were those, to paraphrase St. Augustine, which were the unjust possessors of Truth who had not realized their salvation through Christ. Some of the Stoics and ethical philosophers, Cicero himself and certainly Seneca, "should" have known Christ; the fact that they did not never stopped their works from being transmitted, even if sometimes in apocryphal form.

Most medieval libraries were small by today's standards; a collection of 300 volumes was considered a large library, 150 was substantial, and most collections were under 100 volumes. Book production was too costly to produce libraries of greater size and the times were too chaotic to insure the continuous growth of any one library. Most books were stored flat on cubboard shelves or were lined up in rows if their weight and size allowed upright storage. In either case, cataloguing involved little more than inventory control or basic shelf-listing in the flyleaves of the first books acquired for whatever class was stored on a particular shelf. The entries consisted of no more than short-title entries, and only later, authors' names. There was no standardization of imprint data—the very term suggests such innovations after the invention of printing. Catalogue terms or "catch words" were assigned by the bibliothecarius whose main task was to make sure the community had access to an official Biblical text, a selection of commentary materials, and only incidentally peripheral reading. Often the main set of Scripture like all official documents, were not kept in the reading room which one now associates with a library, but in a treasury more nearly resembling an archives. Likewise, liturgical volumes in use were in the custody of the sacristan, not the librarian. Consequently, books could be located in several places in a monastic or cathedral complex; the medieval library was not so much a place as a function. Moreover, bookstocks were not static. Books circulated from house to house just like bishop's letters or encyclicals were circulatory; most likely they followed similar circuits, just as all interlibrary lending uses well-established mail routes. Often the scribes built encyclopedia by abstracting these traveling books in order to build a non-circulating reference collection immediately at hand. They also collected cuttings from sources, developing anthologies then called *compendia*, primarily devoted to commentaries and criticism. Compendia were often simply accumulated signatures of folios like fascicles pressed together from first copied to the last; as these expanded or were bound, they required internal access and hence were indexed. Only authors like St. Augustine could be copied *en toto*, and it took a considerable reputation to warrant the costs in the editing and reediting of the *opera omnia* sets. Some of the books still extant would have cost enormous amounts when one considers labor of several scribes, specialists like illuminators and rubricators, and a binder, plus the investment in skins and hides, their processing, and the loss of subsequent residual produce such as wool as a flock was thinned for parchment procurement. When one understands the limitations of scribal technology, the economic support of medieval publishing ventures, and the kinds of financial outlays necessary for library development, it is not surprising to have so few remnants of bygone libraries. Nor is it surprising that these libraries were so small, but instead, it is remarkable that they existed at all and it is astounding that they flourished under such hostile conditions in such numbers.

The many contributions of monastic scriptoria and libraries to the preservation of the classical inheritance and elaboration of the Christian literary corpus are well known, but monastic archives are less well studied. Yet the basic elements of record keeping, formating of legal instruments and evolution of diplomatics, and systems of governmental accountability, were all developed by the high Middle Ages. Monastic archives number as many as libraries, and sometimes their systematic records series are truly impressive. Sometimes the records exist in loose parchments, while at others the records were copied into formal legal codices called cartularies, or literally charter books. When this happened, the appraisal mechanism took its toll, and only the more valuable documents were preserved. In other cases, both formal cartularies and the original series survive; the Cistercian abbey of Poblet saved a remarkable series of *pergaminos* from the tenth to eighteenth centuries numbering more than 60,000 documents. Like libraries, however, archives are vulnerable if the parent institution failed. Some famous houses left no documentary heritage to posterity, while the records of others were scattered and scholars have had to recollect them into artificial research collections lacking the cardinal virtues of original order and a chain of custody or provenance.

The previous dominance of literary and cultural scholarship over documentary historical research has resulted in a traditional imbalance between what is known about archives and libraries. The latter are better known, although they were less numerous than archives and perhaps less used. The tendency to focus on the few exemplary art production of medieval scriptoria and fine calligraphy as much as on the narrative text, has resulted in a history of libraries which is like a great books survey at the expense of archives, educational libraries, communication systems, etc., and the daily operational aspects of information exchange. Thus the abbeys of Lindisfarne, Jarrow, Sankt Gallen, Bobbio, Luxieul, Corbie, etc., and the whole circle of foundations made or inspired by the so-called 'wandering saints' are famous, made so by the few rarities which survive from their scriptoria. The greater mass of medieval documentation has been left until this century for scholars to explore. It is now better recognized how archives and libraries had interchangeable roles, and that the distinction was one often of function rather than place or different personnel. Books and official records traveled widely, not only as part of normal communications and trade, but as integral instruments of diplomacy, and often as spoils of war. The most celebrated cases are, however, the exception rather than the norm, as in the transportation of whole libraries from Rome to northern England by Benedict Biscop, or in the case of Visigothic productions arriving in Italy and southern France with monks and churchmen who fled the onslaught of Islam in Spain. The process of regularized exchange or interlibrary loan is less well known; it was not so spectacular and is more difficult to study. Yet the monastic congregations like the episcopal organizational structure of dioceses being governed as aggregates or provinces, provided communication links which guaranteed some regular exchange in normal times. Moreover, these links were often extended in the very process of colonization, and it was customary then as still today for a motherhouse to endow a daughterhouse with a small nuclear library and to document its foundation with formal charters. The spread of medieval monasticism guaranteed the spread of libraries. Slowly scholars are coming to understand that more important than the few presentation copies of great books is the underlying system of book exchange which was made possible by the organization of monasteries into families, congregations, and orders.

Although the meager survivals from monastic libraries through the rough transition from ancient to medieval worlds heralded greater accomplishments in the rebuilding of learning institutions during the so-called Carolingian Renaissance, and monastic scriptoria, archives, and libraries played a significant role in this as recognized by all modern scholarship, it is also axiomatic in most accounts that afterwards, certainly by the twelfth century, monastic centers of learning were in decline. They ceased to be the primary centers of medieval scholarship. This alleged decline is not because they ceased to function, but that their earlier accomplishments bred other institutions which began to compete with monasticism for different specialization in their activities. The urban focal points of commerce, industry, and public administration spawned cathedral schools and thence medieval universities. Historians have tended to focus attention on these academic institutions and hence on research libraries. Monastic libraries were communal, sometimes serving very large communities of several hundred members but their total integration into monastic life makes them difficult to study. Daily readings were often communal, and the number of books held in a depository or recorded on an inventory is no measure of use, the oral repetition of the text, or to what audience beyond the monks themselves the text was made known. The very finest books known for their artwork, may have been the least used and actually of less importance than the tattered remnants of a heavily used commentary. Heavy use perhaps destroyed books, so that over generalization from the extant exemplars in our rare book repositories provides no little distortion when trying to reconstruct the development of medieval learning, the spread of literacy, and the indirect influence of libraries through oral communication based on their contents. Much of what has been written on such subjects echo the pioneer studies from the 1880s onward based on fragments of medieval book catalogues and can be dismissed for the improper use of such evidence. In any case, the monastic libraries of the Middle Ages do not fit modern paradigms where size and quantified measurements of use are considered more important than quality and intensive use of texts; nor do they fit the modern distinctions between public and private, popular and academic, children's and adult libraries. It is more understandable that monasteries, reliant as they were mostly on an agrarian economic foundation, were largely rural institutions, catering to specific clientele, with parochial vision, and were generalized collections multi-functional in purpose. They stand in contrast to today's emphasis on specialization, higher learning, urbane and cosmopolitan institutions. Consequently, there is a tendency to see monastic libraries as displaced in importance then, when the displacement may really be in modern historiography rather than historical reality.

The urban university libraries may have been then, as today, important for their support of advanced studies and higher learning, but they are elitist and exclusive when one considered the mass of population. Monastic libraries because of the rural, parish mission of so many monasteries, may have been equally important but simply for different reasons and for service to different clientele. Monastic schools retained a local focus on basic education, and their libraries, if one thinks of more than the reference and central repository, may not be well documented because the thrust of the activity was so commonplace and the low key production of inexpensive and hence non-preservable textbooks never accounted to anything deserving of documentation in inventories, catalogues, and the like. Moreover, several monastic libraries did play an extensive part in the rise of university libraries. In some cases, especially where the monk-bishop office remained (i.e., Canterbury) traditional as in England or at such famous scriptoria as Tours, the distinction between cathedral and monastic libraries is not possible. Where monastic centers of learning are identified with the rise of universities, their houses often evolved as separate colleges and houses of studies within the university system. The modern distinction between secular university libraries and private religious libraries does not hold. Thus monastic libraries are too often dismissed as though they were supplanted by newer centers and organizations, when more realistically they may have been integrated into larger systems. Rather than a process of replacement, the phenomenon may have been one of library proliferation and specialization with the expansion of European education and learning. To therefore suggest that monastic libraries were everywhere in decline is indeed misleading.

It is well established, however, that certain orders, houses, and communities at different times and in different places went into periods of decline characterized by a lack of discipline, a breakdown of order, abandonment of older ideals, uneven flow of vocations, and blatant moral corruption. It is equally well known that Christian monasticism, like the Church of which monastic communities were a part, is a process of continuing reform, so that the cycle of decline and reform is ever present. When one area or order was in decline, another was in revival; the monastic tradition is full of inner-dynamics which defy over-generalization. It is to be understood, therefore, that monastic libraries would follow similar patterns of growth, intensive use, vitality, and perhaps even notoriety, followed by reduction in collection size, decreased use, cold storage, and perhaps abandonment and decay if the parent organization disbanded or was destroyed. Libraries are highly artificial creations, depending on their livelihood and continuous sustenance from their creators which are also their chief users. In any case, the static images of medieval libraries formed by James W. Thompson's *The Medieval Library* should be discarded at long last, with realization that his pioneer scholarship after the turn of the century was a prematurely attempted synthesis permeated with Victorian notions of libraries and librarianship, based on initial data gathering from the 1880s. One might think of monastic libraries as well studied; in fact, we know so very little about these important institutions and their role in communications and information dissemination. Our best insights are just that, glimpses through peekholes, provided by such provocative essays (not documentary histories) as those by the humanist-philosopher Dom Jean Leclercq, OSB, who entitled one of his many books *The Love of Learning and the Desire for God* to underscore the traditional nexus between monasticism and the learning process based on books and in libraries.

Late medieval monasticism still suffers from its own form of the Black Legend in Anglo-American thought, despite the efforts of late nineteenth-century romanticists to rehabilitate the Middle Ages. This association in Protestant thought of monasticism with Catholicism, despite the persistence albeit in diminished number of Protestant monasticism, has contributed to the mythology of monastic decadence which somehow justified the politically motivated suppression of so many monasteries in the course of the Reformation. Of course from the Catholic viewpoint, one must reflect on what instead appeared as massive theft and a breakdown of law and order based on legal custom and tradition operating through time. Or, one must consider that suppression, dissolution, and extinction, are odd methods of reform. Rather, reform by its nature requires continuity and mandates revival, not death and discontinuity. This was essentially the case argued by a series of Catholic historians in reaction to the historical classification of what they saw as a protest and rebellion (only partially successful enough to be a revolution) as a genuine 'Reformation'. They disliked more the term Counter-Reformation for the Roman Church's reaction to Protestantism, and would have preferred such nomenclature as the Protestant Revolt and the Reformation. Moreover, from the vantage point of continuist historiography, this like "the" Renaissance was one of many revivals and reformations. One's persuasion along these divided Protestant and Catholic lines of interpretation influences one's understanding of monastic history through the turbulence of the period from the plagues of the mid-fourteenth century through the final peace at Westphalia in 1648 ending the Wars of Religion. Regardless of one's persuasion, it is undeniable that the course of Western Civilization's history was dramatically altered, that the ideal of Christian unity was permanently fractured, that the regular church was permanently reduced to secondary importance to the secular church, and that the Church itself was toppled from its once paramount position by the rise of the modern nation-state.

The prevailing Renaissance-Reformation historiography has indeed affected library historiography. As expected, over-generalization has resulted in a widespread belief that monasteries everywhere were in such decline that they could not support centers of learning, their libraries were being neglected, and that suppression and dissolution was little more than a final act to the incipient abandonment of monastic ideals and lifestyles which characterized most houses in the fourteenth-fifteenth centuries. Indeed, this does seem to have been the case in several of the most celebrated monastic libraries in history; everyone can empathize with Petrarch's lament as he explored the neglected library of Monte Cassino itself. The loss was tragic for modern scholarship in its attempt to reconstruct pre-modern history and culture. It was then, and is now, blatantly assumed that somehow these monasteries had the overwhelming responsibility to preserve classical learning for all time simply because they had once provided this valuable historic preservation service through the ninth century. The failure of these monasteries to do so might be explained better by the general failure of society as a whole to support historic preservation of such magnitude, and if one is to succumb to such presentism in historical thought, then one might at least balance the viewpoint by looking at modern society to ascertain if current secular institutions are doing much better in such preservation efforts. In the U.S. national archives system it is estimated that only 3-5% of all official records are to be permanently preserved. In libraries which systematically weed on the basis of use statistics, 80% of the collection can be destroyed after five years of immediate, intensive use. Thereafter space and personnel costs per volume become very expensive, without measurable cost-benefit ratios, for each use. One's attitude about monastic libraries performing supra-institutional service to mankind in general soon changes when such modern comparisons are made.

One is also prone to change traditional stereotyped thinking when considering the results of modern historic preservation surveys of manuscript holdings even after the massive destruction of World Wars I and II. In England where most of the great abbeys were suppressed, monastic bookstock supplied the antiquarian trade for nearly a century and helped to form the nuclear private collections which ultimately formed the core of the British Museum or British Library's research collections. Other libraries were formed anew from the collections of old, in a seemingly never ending cycle of death and rebirth with the continuing library tradition. Such libraries perhaps should not have been saved at all, if in fact the parent organizations were as corrupt and unstable as they have been depicted. Professor Paul O. Kristeller's *Iter Italicum*, a modern humanist's Petrachian journey, is remarkable for the wealth of manuscript material still preserved, even if unused, from monastic centers which collapsed under the impact of plagues, wars, famines, economic fluctuations of rampant inflation and depression, and growing secularization. Where

Catholicism retained its ground and monastic institutions remained operational, there is little to suggest the decline of monastic libraries. The Hill Monastic Microfilm Library surveys of monastic and monastic-related libraries in Austria and Catalonia in that case could not have found the extraordinary bookcount, over 60,000 extant medieval codices which have come to light in this modern historic preservation and micofilming effort. Its findings reinforce the surmise that monastic libraries although never large, were numerous. Such a focus on manuscript codices, of course, does not discern the shift from manuscript to printed book production and collection development; neglect of the great humanistic manucript holdings in monastic libraries may have been partially the result of changing priorities, when limited funds were spent instead on currect print materials. What is described as a decline and neglect may be none other than the change created by changing technology, just as in modern libraries when book budgets provide far more funding for modern acquisitions than preservation of already acquired materials and are now under pressure to buy as well several kinds of multi-media products. Print collections in current libraries may survive the current technological revolution to electronic communications no better than medieval manuscript collections fared in the transition to print during the Renaissance and Reformation. Will the indictment of future humanists of modern libraries be similar to the disparagement of late medieval and early modern monastic libraries for their neglect of their retrospective collections?

It does seem clear that as secular institutions grew in size and number, monastic libraries by comparison suffered; they had not the size, means, or inclination to compete with the new mega-universities and libraries of Gargantuan size. The Reformation left whole parts of the monastic networks devastated, and monastic libraries did recede in general importance. It was the proverbial case of the big fish in a relatively small pond being less important when placed in a lake or sea with many schools of much larger fish. That is different, however, from assuming that because of the new environment and perspective, they ceased to have any importance whatsoever.

In the post-Reformation era monasticism itself went into a series of reforms. Not all of the various reforms supported library development on the same grand scale as pre-Reformation houses or the Benedictines. Some of the more severe strains, the Trappists for example, would not foster large-scale libraries. Even the Benedictine congregations of the early-modern period with continued emphasis on parish duties and secondary education which required some library activity, did not necessarily promote the growth of universal libraries or the continuous building of research collections. They tended to keep what they had, convert these in time to little-used but much valued rare book repositories, and to rely on the current acquisitions for most of their work. The contemplative tradition, the rekindled focus on manual labor, and the diminished size of the communities with the decline of the lay brotherhoods (which never provided library users, but certainly contributed to the means by which libraries were maintained), did not require major research libraries but instead smaller, practical, reading libraries with perhaps some minimal reference capability in religion and philosophy. Individual scholars have risen from the ranks of modern monasticism, even from the non-library oriented Cistercians and Trappists, but not on the same scale as the production of scholars by such new non-monastic orders as the Jesuits. In any case, monastic libraries continued but their most famous cases are hardly representative of the trends in modern monasticism; they are instead like book museums or monuments to past learning and intellectual activities, of interest primarily to the historian, not the contemplative monk. Consequently, little attention has been paid to the modern monastic library tradition in historical literature. The standard surveys of library history by E. Johnson, even as revised by M. Harris, or that of Sydney Jackson, for example, fail to mention the monastic library tradition, monastic libraries by typology, or famous monastic libraries by name (that is, which are accessible via the index). A search of the current secondary literature indicates that there is little research on small religious or theological libraries at all, so that one cannot expect to find much information about monastic libraries in particular. Ecclesiastical archives, if one were to jump to conclusions based on the absence of anything in the literature, would seem nonextant; monastic archives and scriptoria appear to be phenomena of the past, except for the commercial reminders from Xerox Corporation about the miracles of modern reprography!

The libraries of the Benedictine houses connected with the reforms of the 1700s were the most important. Most of the Benedictine congregations like that formed around Beuron Abbey, retained a deep sense of continuity in the tradition of monastic libraries. These Benedictines continued parish work, ran schools, and came to dominate the elementary and secondary education systems of some areas until the rise of public state-supported and controlled systems in the 1800s. Many of the larger houses developed small liberal arts colleges and seminaries out of their original academies, designed primarily for teacher education and to train diocesan clergy as well as their own recruits. Some of these Benedictine academies, such as at Salzburg, developed into well-known theological and canon law graduate schools. These were often incorporated as colleges with other such institutions into city universities. Their libraries then served as academic research facilities, often as branches of a larger university-wide network, with a special focus on the particular teaching and research strength of its resident faculty. Perhaps the most famous of these "think tank" operations rooted in a monastic library was the central house of studies maintained by the Benedictine Congregation of St. Maur in France, at the abbey of St. Germain-des-Prés. This center was exceptional in its collecting of manuscripts to support what Dom David Knowles has described as one the world's great historical enterprises. Another example would be the Sant' Anselmo College of Rome which was primarily an international graduate school for Benedictines, but it relied primarily on the Vatican library rather than on its own monastic library for support of its programs. Other centers such as at Solesmes, unattached to a university, became known in its own right for other specialties, in this case music, which was reflected in the monastery's development of its library.

For the most part, however, these libraries like other larger research libraries, were divided into two sections; the older, pre-1500 Latin and Greek manuscript and incunabular collections became rare book libraries within the framework of the whole library. The generic collections were printed works, and serials were often treated like newspapers with general and immediate reference. Abbot Johann Tritheim's famous appeal to monks everywhere in his *In Praise of Scribes* to continue the scriptoria of the past was not heeded specifically; many houses followed his dictates generally by continuing publishing activities, often out of their libraries. But the scriptoria gradually gave way to noisier presses which had to be separated from the libraries. Spiritual reading in unison while copying instead gave way to the hustle and turbulence of printing shops and a greater specialization separating as well authors from editors and publishers. Archives likewise tended to become more distinct from libraries, both in treatment of materials and methods of access, but also in location. The archives, that is official records, were part of the administrative machinery of the monastery so that it was often controlled by the secretary or treasurer in one of the offices related to the treasury and sacristy. Manuscripts in the library were for inspection if not actual use, accessible rather than secret as were the records of most archives. Thus the manuscripts were treated more like personal papers today in a research library, more akin to rare books and special collections than archives were. This meant that the library itself, without the former functions of archives and book production, specialized in the reading and research functions common today.

Much of this publishing and collecting activity of the Benectines relied on the old patronage system of the *ancien regime*. It was severely challenged by the French Revolution, and monastic libraries therefore often asociated with the old aristocracy and antiquarian interests, and an elitism which brought widespread condemnation. Some of the Baroque libraries built by such patronage systems were indeed ostentatious, and their holdings consequently were seen as forms of wealth rather than learning resources. Like most artworks, manuscripts and books kept for posterity, cannot be converted readily to liquid capital without the destruction of the library itself; a library without its collection is a mere framework, a hollow structure capable of sustaining little intellectual activity. Consequently, these libraries if they were to be maintained, were not sources of wealth, but rather were drains on the liquid assets of the communities. When the patronage system decayed, it became more and more difficult to maintain these libraries and many indeed were hollowed out, abandoned, or became book museums once again.

The post-Revolution cross currents of radical liberalism and equally reactionary conservatism wrought almost as much destruction to monastic libraries and intellectual institutions as did the Reformation. There was again widespread expropriation of lands and revenues which added to the crisis created by the loss of aristocratic patronage, and conditions were hardly conducive to cultivating new patrons among the rising middle class. There was also the removal of so many schools from church governance in widespread secularization even in countries traditionally Catholic; more accurately, the liberal political reforms encompassed nationalization of hitherto private resources. Not only did this cut into the financial basis of many monastic libraries, but it undermined the very rational for their existence. Coupled with decline in vocations, and the outright suppression of many houses especially in Catholic Germany, Austria, Italy and Switzerland, there was a general inability of the monasteries to protect their own cultural resources amidst an era of continued social unrest. The wave of anticlericalism which hit Europe was more antichurch than antireligion, but the largest of the monasteries with their formal libraries, were conspicuous targets for mob riots. This was especially so when the monasteries retained their land holdings for economic support, and consequently were seen as more than grand ecclesiastical institutions, but landlords as well. More than one monastic library suffered the fate of that of the Cistercian Sta. Maria de Poblet in Catalonia which was abandoned and sacked after seven centuries of existence. Its library and archives, built over these centuries, was destroyed. The parchments were saved because the peasants could see no value in them, but the royal tombs were desecrated, the corpses were stripped of their jewels, and the library was treated similarly. Its black ebony shelving was destroyed, and the books of former nobles associated with the extensive patronage system of Poblet, reportedly all bound in red gold-tooled Morrocan leather, were hauled off to be sold for whatever could be gotten on the streets of Barcelona. Story after story repeat such grim spectacles. After two centuries of rebuilding, many monastic libraries were again despoiled.

When monks of threatened communities sought refuge in sister monasteries, in exile abroad, or in relocation to the New World, seldom could their monastic libraries be saved or transported to new locations. The uprisings were too sudden, too violent for that, and unrest was too widespread. Moreover, the economic means to accomplish such relocation of the monastery *per se*, more than the monks themselves, were not available. Rather than the libraries themselves, the most important thing carried across the Atlantic was the monastic library tradition, an intellectual commitment to library development as a necessary component of monastic spirituality. Initial efforts in the foundation of daughterhouses in America were directed toward economic stability, understandably so; library development in these new foundations would come only in the twentieth century after decades of struggle in rather desperate pioneer conditions. Many of the American Benedictine communities founded small colleges in imitation of activities in their fatherlands, and these in turn fostered the growth of monastic libraries. But their collections were small, contemporary, and hardly comparable to the libraries these monks left behind in the Old World.

The pattern of development of the American houses is essentially similar to that of the post-Reformation era, except that on American soil few have been able within one century's time to achieve the size, corporate structure, or patronage system to expand their schools much beyond the four-year liberal arts college. The largest schools, associated with the larger communities such as St. John's Abbey in Collegeville (Minnesota), St. Meinrad's in Indiana and St. Vincent's in Latrobe Pennsylvania, or St. Benedict's in Kansas, have graduate programs mostly in education and theology. They have not developed comprehensive higher education programs comparable to secular universities or those associated with the more famous universities founded as Protestant colleges. Despite the relatively large number of Catholic colleges and universities in the U.S., only sixteen have developed nationally recognized graduate programs and, therefore, major research libraries. Catholic education in the U.S. has remained largely parochial, aimed modestly at post-secondary college education extending from earlier programs in secondary and two-year college teaching. None of the larger institutions developed from monastic centers as in Europe. Consequently, although several monastic libraries in the U.S. grew into academic and research libraries, they resemble small college libraries rather than the large multi-library systems of modern universities. Their uniqueness lies in the presence of core libraries, special collections, catering to their special interests in religion, church history, canon law, theology, and philosophy.

As in ages past, therefore, one can easily overlook the importance of monastic libraries in America if the main focus is on size and outstanding accomplishment. Such institutions, of all types and in all ages, are always the exception to the norm. Yet they dominate our cultural history in general, and library history in particular. The present study of Mt. Angel abbey and its library is in part an effort to provide some balance to this common distortion resulting from restricted emphasis on the great. Instead, attention here is deliberately focused on an institution noteworthy in its own right, which is more representative of the small Catholic, monastic library in the U.S. which supports parish and educational endeavors in a quiet, persistent manner, with a regional rather than national impact. Most importantly, this library's history is placed in the context of the community's history, and then into the larger field of library and cultural history. It explains what happened in the spread of monasticism to America, provides an example of what happened to make American development somewhat less grandiose than in Europe but nevertheless significant, and gives some insight to a relatively hidden but pervasive and continuing tradition transmitted to the New World in the process of its incorporation into Western Civilization—that of the monastic library. The continuation of this tradition is, I suspect, more important than any single library.

Early Developments: 1882-1926

Little is known about books and libraries in the Pacific Northwest until the mid-nineteenth century. Just as printing came late to Oregon, so did the development of libraries as institutions instead of private, small collections. The latter, of course, provided the basis for subsequent library development in the territory. The earliest libraries were family collections brought from the East by the wealthier of Oregon's settlers; most 'libraries' were merely small collections of practical books carried over the trails to provide enroute education for pioneer children. They often consisted of a family Bible, some handicraft or do-it-yourself books, cookbooks, basic grammars, perhaps a history book, and more rarely some classics. Most of the fiction was adult literature, and even the children attacked classical tomes as the only available formal literature. Conversely the grammars were often used by the adults for whom English was a second language. Otherwise reading was limited to newspapers and journals, or the numerous magazines which were just beginning circulation during the period of Reconstruction. Such literature was consumable and expendable, and seldom contributed to the development of libraries. Professional people, of course, had small working libraries related to medicine, law, or religion, which were more important for institutional collection development. The earliest institutional libraries therefore seem to have been ministerial and legal collections, and the earliest public libraries were mercantile collections. In general library development followed patterns already well established on the East coast, but the lag time was nearly a century.

There was a traceable booktrade between Seattle, Portland, and San Francisco in addition to the overland transport of household libraries to the West. However, there are few collections deserving the designation "library" until the last quarter of the nineteenth century. Indeed, the personal library of Abp. Francis Norbert Blanchet served as the institutional library of the archdiocese for more than two decades, but it was a small collection of fewer than a hundred volumes, mostly pocketbooks for easy transportation. Consequently, one cannot find in Oregon's history much evidence of library development until the growth of the public education system, secondary and higher, after the turn of the century. Although few collections constituted formal libraries, the omnipresence of books is documented. They did serve to inculcate functional literacy and keep the idea of book-related culture alive. The ideal of cultural preservation in libraries and their essentiality to education was reinforced by the northern European immigrants to Oregon, but most of Oregon's settlers were traders and farmers without immediate needs to build libraries. Even when they did so, their collections were emminently practical; likewise, until the twentieth-century private press movement, the history of books and printing in Oregon is largely that of a job press, not large-scale publishing. Just as the best families educated their children back East, so too did the West rely on Eastern production for its books. Hence, books remained expensive, libraries were small, and collections were mainly didactic, practical, and popular. So too, the Catholic Church in Oregon educated its clergy in Eastern seminaries or tried to import already educated priests and religious as in the case of the Benedictines. It could be expected, however, that the Swiss Benedictines would bring with them a tradition of library development such as they had known in the Old World.

The model of Engelberg suggested the building of a Benedictine library in Oregon, one along classical lines which would therefore stand in contrast to the territory's other libraries. Moreover, the Benedictine's support of a college meant development of a teaching and research library beyond more common grammar school collections or personal devotional books. Abbot Frowin certainly respected Engelberg's library tradition, and in one letter lamented the thought that if the motherhouse were ever suppressed that its library would fall into the hands of secular authorities who could or would not use it to good advantage. Books were sent from Engelberg to Conception, as attested in Abbot Anselm's infamous letter threatening in 1876 to depose Frowin as prior. However, the development of a monastic library was not dictated by such action, and indeed, the emphasis in the pioneer settlement was on the very practical. When Frowin advised the sisters of Maria Rickenbach about what to bring to the New World, he told the mother superior "most of European school books should be left behind" (1). His diary and correspondence contains little about how a library developed at Conception Abbey, but one did—presumably in conjunction with the diocesan seminary. However, that came after the Mt. Angel founders had left Missouri. Conception Abbey, therefore, provided no concrete model for library development in the founding of a new house. The founders themselves, Frs. Nicholas and Adelhelm, were not bibliophiles or scholars, but were eminently practical men, activists and innovators, and later administrators. The monastic library was not an artificial implant at the very beginning of the priory, but was developed as part of the overall institutional growth of the monastery. Adelhelm had a classical education and advanced seminary training, and he demonstrated docility in languages, but his correspondence reveals no scholar here. Adelhelm had taught at Engelberg, but at Conception Abbey his main involvement was parish work rather than the establishment of New Engelberg College. His letters seldom mention reading anything but his Offices and what little news of Europe he could glean from the American newspapers. Yet he no doubt appreciated book learning and libraries. There is, for example, the incident he recalled while visiting California; he remembered having seen the remnants of an early Franciscan mission library among the ruins of the church's outbuildings at Sta. Ynéz. When his Christian Brother guide allowed him to inspect the site, he was sufficiently impressed to remark later in his letter of August 15, 1881 to Abt. Anselm. "In one of the still intact rooms of the ruins, I found to no little surprise, a little library containing books and papers, fortunately not badly gnawed by mice. I hope someone will save the books that are worth saving." (2).

Apart from this passing observation, there is little hint of intellectual curiosity, even in the history of this valley in which he was contemplating making his home. His own reading needs were slight in those days, perhaps only his Breviary, some devotional literature, and something for sermon preparations. Yet there is no reason to assume that his homilies were researched beforehand, or even carefully prepared. He was a gifted extemporaneous speaker, an inspirational man with an outgoing personality and an infectious laugh, whose preaching was built around his recall of training at Engelberg, his own religiosity, and an appreciation of the limited theological needs of his listeners. Although no theologian or contemplative mystic, he was by nature at home in the Oregon frontier without the trappings of serious scholarship. Libraries may have been implicit in Benedictine communal life, but the need is never made explicit in Adelhelm's writings.

It is therefore significant that the great impetus for a college along classical lines, something more than the kind of secondary education first envisioned by Adelhelm at Sta. Inéz or Jacksonville, came from Abp. Charles Seghers. This was reinforced by Abp. William Gross, and the Benedictines seem to have responded to archiepiscopal pressure rather than to initiate the college on their own. Financial limitations partially explain this, but also, the first prospective educational effort was with the Indian mission schools, not a grand college. Abp. Seghers was well aware, however, of the reputation of the Black Monks for fostering higher learning in the Old World. His letter to Adelhelm on February 1, 1881, after having visited Monte Cassino, displayed indignation that "the very library, which is an admirable monument to their [the Benedictines'] intelligence and patient research, is supposed to be the property of the Italian government" (3). His assumption was that the prior shared his appreciation for the Benedictine library tradition. The stereotype of the monastic scribe and scholar was widespread and enduring.

When the colony left Engelberg for the New World, as Abbot Anselm's diary attests in contrast to the "limited supplies" sent initially to Conception Abbey, a great many books were included in the thirty crates which were shipped with the monks (4). Books continued to come from Engelberg from then until the present, in keeping with the traditional spread of libraries with each monastic foundation. A few trickled into Mt. Angel from Conception Abbey, but there was no bountiful warehouse there. Its library was a twentieth-century development. The ideal, however, survived even if the reality of a monastic library could not be supported in the American West until this century. The idea was reinforced by the motherhouse. In retrospect, it was this tradition which was celebrated when Engelberg's abbot presented Abbot Anselm Galvin on his blessing with the Missal from the motherhouse's library which the founder had used at his first Mass. This modern presentation volume reminds the American community today of the core library sent from Engelberg a hundred years ago. There is no record about the contents or even the exact count of books in this initial library, but presumably many were liturgical and prayer books, some music, and the rest were textbooks considered useful in the monks' own training of their novices and in their secondary school endeavors. Rather than Adelhelm himself, Frs. Anselm Wachter and others, who would have been more prone to pack more scholarly materials. Sister Agnes Butsch recalled her early years when her father was helping the community build its monastery. She remembered that the Gervais parish house, the temporary priory, included a 10 x 12 ft. room on the first floor which was "the library" (5). Prior Jerome later recalled also that the so-called library also served as a tailor and shoemaker's shop during daytime working hours (6). The nuns too, had brought with them books from their motherhouses, and altogether a small collection was maintained for both teachers and preachers. The buildup of a nuclear research collection, however, came only after the college was underway and when the community was in its new facilities. Whatever this library contained, much of it was lost in the 1892 fire. Abbot Anselm noted then in his diary that "they saved a lot of books and household utensils, but a lot more were burned" (7).

No doubt the dominant influence in the monastery's library development was Fr. Benedikt Gottwald after 1894 when he became prior. Before coming to America, Fr. Benedikt had been the librarian at Engelberg abbey, and in that capacity had studied the history of Engelberg's medieval scriptoria and produced a reputable book-catalogue of the abbey's manuscript codices—a work of recognized scholarship still used to this day (8). Apart from periodic raiding of Engelberg's library, as evidenced in the provenance marks in some of Mt. Angel's extant collection, acquisitions came from the following main sources.

First there were local patrons who began donating their few volumes to the monks. One of the earliest such donations recorded came from Fr. Francis X. Blanchet, then pastor at St. Paul, who on July 25, 1889 gave some books for use in the Minor or Little Seminary (9). Secondly, as had been customary among Benedictine houses since their very beginnings, there was an interlibrary network within the Benedictine congregations and loans across organizational lines as well. The largest single donation to Mt. Angel came from St. Benedict's abbey in Atchison, Kansas, which had enjoyed the patronage of the mad castle builder, Ludwig I of Bavaria. St. Benedict's Abbey began building its library in 1875, not from collections at its motherhouse, St. Vincent, but from St. Boniface in Munich and the abbey of Raegern. The latter, for example, sent 857 volumes, including several incunabula, to Kansas. In 1907 St. Benedict's Prior Thomas presented Mt. Angel with over 300 volumes, mostly in history, literature, and biography (10). Thirdly, whenever the priory's monks went to Europe for graduate study, they acted as scouts and scroungers seeking out bargains in the local antiquarian shops and bookfairs. Since most went to the Benedictine Sant' Anselmo in Rome, classics and theological works from Italian dealors began to trickle into Oregon. One of the most active monks in this regard was Fr. Notker Maeder who in 1889 was also the procuror of the painting of St. Benedict by Velter of Sankt Gallen which adorned the high altar of the priory's original chapel (11). Other sources were developed throughout Europe in typical Benedictine mechanisms. Sometimes books came as gifts in return for Mass stipends sent abroad; at others from friends and family in the old country. The archives contain occasional letters with scattered references to shipments of books, as in the case of Benno Lindenbauer of Metten, Bavaria, who on September 3, 1922 corresponded with the librarian at Mt. Angel and subsequently on February 27, 1923 mailed a parcel of wanted titles to the Oregon Benedictines (12). The trade went both ways. When Fr. Nicholas left in 1902 for Engelberg, he carried with him books being returned to the motherhouse. When he died in India, the abbot had considerable difficulty retrieving them (13). These scattered references do not depict a coherent, systematic acquisition policy or even continuous collection development, but they do provide indications of how a monastic library would be built naturally by exchange within a larger system.

It is doubtful that the early students had access to the priory's small library. They would have instead relied on books purchased especially for them. Since students, according to the *Prospectus* of 1887, were not allowed to keep money on their persons, parents and guardians deposited at the beginning of each term enough funds to cover anticipated personal expenses, desk supplies, and textbooks. The books used were those ordered by the faculty ahead of time, and the students themselves were prohibited from buying, selling, or trading any "personal effects" (14). Of course the college's code of behavior censored immodest pictures along with the use of tobacco or intoxicating drink, but the rules went further to control reading habits and the choice of books. Rule 12 stated: "Books, papers, periodicals, etc., may be read only with the approval of the Prefect, and only at such times as he shall specify" (15). The college favored boarders but accepted non-resident students from the local area. To enforce the same discipline, a special prefect was appointed to visit homes unannounced to make sure they, like the boarders, spent the required time at their studies and consumed the appropriate literature. It was a liberal arts education, but hardly liberal by today's standards. Nor was the curriculum structured around library usage.

As in the case of St. Benedict's and other abbey libraries, most of the books acquired were not really useful for such an educational endeavor. They were in Latin focusing on moral and dogmatic theology, canon law, and Greek and Latin patristics. Most of the church histories were in French, as was the bulk of pastoral theology perhaps because so many of these general titles came as donations from local clergy on the French Prairie. Finally, the general collections, largely devotional, were in German, often in Fraktur type. There were also miscellaneous volumes of hagiography, collected sermons, and homilectic illustrations. There was very little in English, except perhaps grammars which were in constant need to help the monks master English. For most of the community before the 1920s, English remained a foreign language. Consequently, the monks' library itself was not suitable for the American students. As in most monastic libraries, devotional literature, prayerbooks, and breviaries were kept in individual cells and in the choir stalls; they were not considered part of the library proper. Likewise, liturgical books were often housed in the sacristy. All books were scarce and valuable. When Br. Stanislaus' pet crow in 1894 flew inside the chapel, the nusance was all the more irritating because the bird tore a page from one of the breviaries (16). Even common breviaries were difficult to replace.

Until 1892 there were no official archives kept, but thereafter some of the early materials were stored in the library and correspondence, especially that from back home addressed to the whole community, was preserved in letter books (17). Important official papers and documents such as property deeds, as well as most of the accounting records, had been kept in Prior Adelhelm's desk and after the fire in a safe in his room. From 1892 until 1928 this safe served as the main archival depository, the so-called Secret archives as distinct from the Public archival material kept with the library. This basic dychotomy between closed and open-access archives was typical of most ecclesiastical institutions, including the Vatican, and remains the practice today. The prior took some personal interest in preserving some records; it is his copy in his own handwriting of Leo XIII's bull of July 16, 1882 which survives today in the abbey's archives (18). But Adelhelm by nature was hardly an orderly nor organized man. Abbot Bernard recalled later the frustration of young Jerome Wespe whose first exposure to administration was basic record keeping for the founder, "He [Adelhelm] had no sense of order. Once the present prior [Jerome] went in and picked all the letters up and filed them alphabetically, but it was no more than three days after Fr. Adelhelm's return home, than they were just as bad as ever." (19). The safekeeping of Mt. Angel's early records and many of the library acquisitions resulted from the industry of Prior Jerome who in 1902 became the community's secretary and treasurer, offices which he held for more than a decade. He later served Abbot Bernard faithfully as prior when the latter went blind, so that this monk was a dominant influence on the development of Mt. Angel Abbey. Jerome's character was described in a 1901 memoir as, "...a man of exemplary exactitude in every sense of the word, and his [account] books were a model of neatness. This was of prime importance during the time of the erection of the buildings, as a very close watch had to be kept on the finances, [so] not to overstep the bounds of discretion." (20). Subsequently, when Jerome was consumed increasingly with the overall administration of the monastery, Fr. Urban Fischer served as secretary and thereby as archivist. Fr. Maurus, after having searched the chapter's records to argue some contention or another, and missing them, later reflected that in contrast to Prior Jerome "Fr. Urban in my observation was not at all scrupulous to keep the chapter's meetings and decisions duly recorded. He took minutes in shorthand (incidently, a shorthand method of his own device) and read them in the next meeting from shorthand. When nothing came of a decision, he simply left the entry out...". (21). Such record keeping remained dependent on the personality of the secretaries from then until 1928 when, while reorganizing the abbey's administration during its move to new quarters, an *archivarius* was appointed separately from the secretarial-treasurer office, and thereafter the archives became more official and professional.

Of all the remnants of the original library at Mt. Angel, perhaps the most treasured volumes are four folio-sized liturgical manuscript codices calligraphed by Fr. Anselm Weissenborn from 1908 to 1921 at the request of Abbot Thomas (22). Mt. Angel never had a scriptorium as such, although until the last decade its press played a significant role in the monastery's history. However, calligraphy and design were taught then as now for improved penmanship and to improve a student's writing, but also as part of studio arts to support graphics. While calligraphy remains a distinctive feature of Mt. Angel's arts program, as it does in several religious houses, and the monastery's brochures display infinite variety in admirable design work, the Mt. Angel codices were a special effort, a unique commission, reflecting Old World tastes somewhat out of context in the Oregon abbey. They were executed in a formal Gothic bookhand (*littera gothica textualis*) for Latin text, a Gothic bastard for English, and a tasteful Germanic fraktur lacking the overly ornate capitals of contemporary typefaces for the German. The tri-lingual rendition of the professional vows is symptomatic of Mt. Angel's transition in accomodating its American environs. The books are written in black ink with red rubrication, within borders copied from the latest imported printed Missals. The folios are decorated with black initia, music notation, scattered emblemata, and several half- and full-page illustrations featuring life at Mt. Angel during the community's difficult years after the 1892 fire. Some of these are commentaries, if not indictments, as stated before, of the laxity of monastic discipline fostered by this declaustration. While the monks fervently pray and recite their offices, under the care of guardian angels, demons and devils of all sorts tempt the Benedictines with card playing, gambling, tobacco, condemned books, and other distractions. Even the organist must fight the temptation to lapse periodically into popular secular music! As a final commentary, one illustration features a lone monk, seated at his writing desk with his back to the viewer, laboring away on the Mt. Angel liturgical codices. The manuscripts were carefully done, with occasional emendation, and were bound in red Morrocan leather, decorated with gold-filled borders, satin ribbon markers, and gold fore-edges. They were used by the Mt. Angel abbots from then until the 1940s, especially for the induction of novices into the community, but were finally retired to the library's rare book collection. They are now showpieces, hardly representative of the main library collection assembled after the 1894, but they provide evidence of the survival of the book arts tradition at Mt. Angel as an ideal if not constant practice. As such they provide unique testimony to the cultural aspirations of this community.

The library's growth reflected the monastery's expansion of its educational curricula in the college and seminary. In the 1897-98 catalogue the facilities were described as "in every respect all that can be desired" including two libraries. One was next to the study hall, "with works covering every department of science and literature". Especially mentioned were the expensive encyclopedia sets recently acquired: the *Brittanica, Americana,* and *Chamber's Encyclopedia* (23). The other, called the Teacher's Library, as distinct from the former student collection, housed 6000 volumes and was described as a support resource for mental training. By 1909-10, the latter had doubled in size to more than 12,000 books, which had to be housed in a separate wing of the monastery. In keeping with the split of

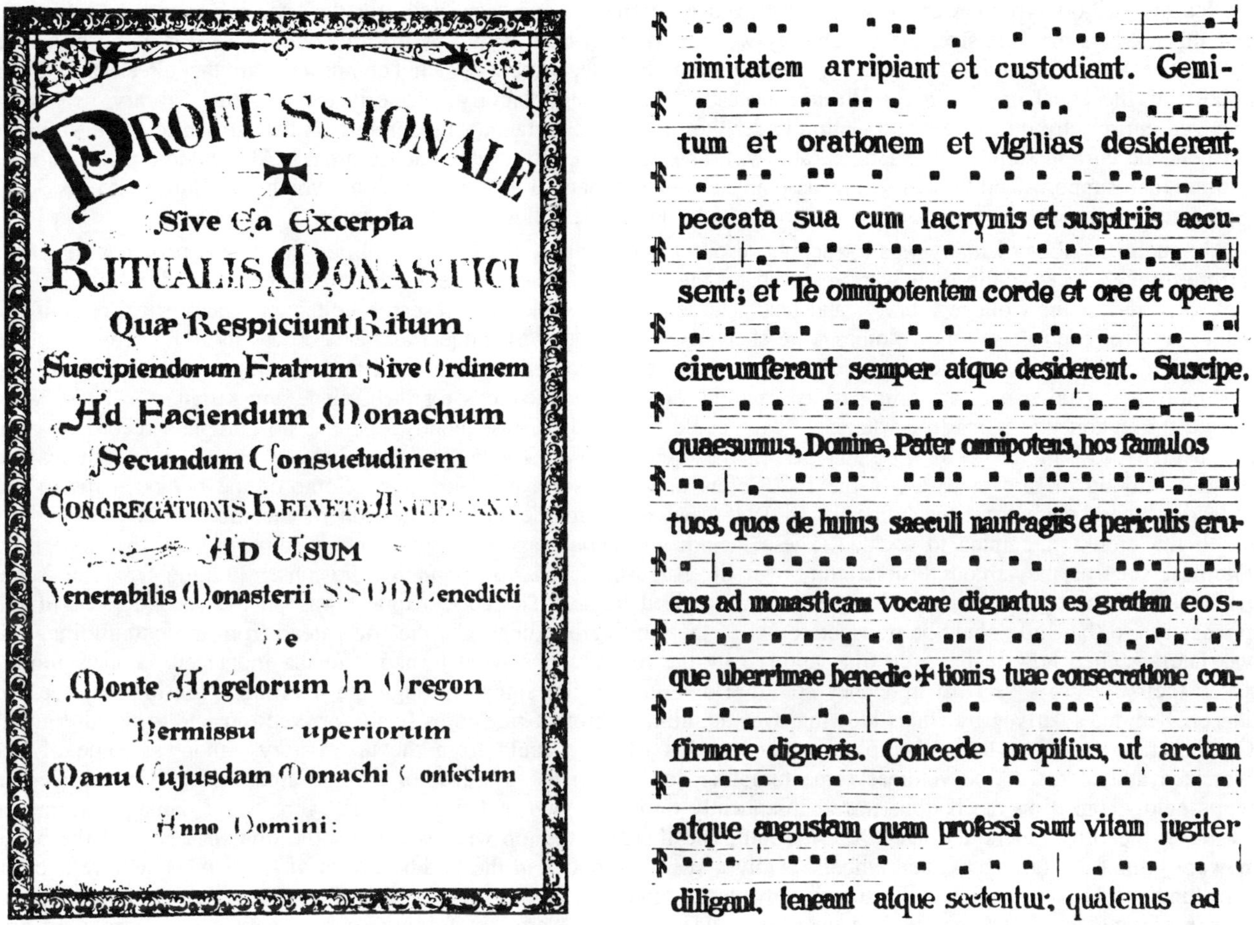
Professionale
Sive Ea Excerpta
Ritualis Monastici
Quae Respiciunt Ritum
Suscipiendorum Fratrum Sive Ordinem
Ad Faciendum Monachum
Secundum Consuetudinem
Congregationis Helveto-Americanae
Ad Usum
Venerabilis Monasterii SS. P. N. Benedicti
De
Monte Angelorum In Oregon
Permissu Superiorum
Manu Cujusdam Monachi Confectum
Anno Domini:

nimitatem arripiant et custodiant. Gemi-
tum et orationem et vigilias desiderent,
peccata sua cum lacrymis et suspiriis accu-
sent; et Te omnipotentem corde et ore et opere
circumferant semper atque desiderent. Suscipe,
quaesumus, Domine, Pater omnipotens, hos famulos
tuos, quos de huius saeculi naufragiis et periculis eru-
ens ad monasticam vocare dignatus es gratiam eos-
que uberrimae benedic ✠ tionis tuae consecratione con-
firmare digneris. Concede propitius, ut arctam
atque angustam quam professi sunt vitam jugiter
diligant, teneant atque sectentur, qualenus ad

Fig. 15. Folios from Anselm Weissenborn's Mt. Angel manuscript codices, 1905-1911.

its archives into those public and private, this library constituted a research collection reserved for the senior seminarians and the community itself. The separate library for student use, largely a reserve collection selected specifically for class purposes, marked a major change in the college's earlier approach to instruction predominantly through assigned textbooks and a carefully monitored reading program. The student's library was indeed a controlled collection, and book selection was still monitored, but now students were expected to carry out their own reading programs and significantly to contribute to their own educations by independent use of the library. By 1910 the students had formed both a Literary Society and a Reading Club. Again, developments at Mt. Angel paralleled those at St. Benedict's where much of the library was augmented by a similar student Reading and Literature association founded in 1881 (which by 1884 was known as the St. Thomas Library Association). At Mt. Angel the members of these organizations played an increasingly important role in running the college library and they took almost complete charge of their own reading lounge which had "the best daily papers, a large number of Catholic papers, magazines, college journals, and such literature on various subjects as may prove interesting and instructive"(24).

The publicity for the college and seminary boasted in 1917-18 and throughout the early 1920s of two libraries "of which Mt. Angel College may be justly proud" (25). The Teacher's Library, now called the Abbey Library, now totalled over 20,000 volumes and was still restricted to the monks and "especially for the lay professors, and advanced students". More than the size, the community was proud of its careful title-by-title selection, "a great many of which are of rare value," and in particular promoted its classical department which "comprising all the Greek and Latin authors, is the equal of any in the Western states". The College Library, formerly the Students Library, was now managed entirely by the student association under the direction of a faculty moderator. It had grown to 8000 volumes and held the current serials subscriptions, and was developing rapidly in the science areas. At the same time, another instructional support facility was being assembled, a large natural history museum which in addition to its local geological specimen, array of mounted mammals, fish, and fowl, included a herbarium of 1,500 plants.

Although the Abbey Library was a teaching resource, increasingly the College Library collected curricular materials and the limited-access collections were reserved for the few and for serious research. All reference and public services were centered in the College Library, and technical services as well. The research collection was not under uniform bibliographical control, and the volumes were shelved approximately by subject and access was more by browsing than anything else. Because this research collection was largely unstaffed, several special collections were kept apart and were not always described in the monastery's public relations' publications for the college and seminary. These were housed throughout the monastery wherever space could be found. Consequently, there is no complete record of what was actually lost in the 1926 fire, and personal estimates vary. The acquisitions lists of Prior Jerome indicate a sizeable buildup of rare materials in the 1920s, few of which survive to this day. Some of the books in the extant collections bear scars from the holocaust in 1926, and they provide some indication of the more prized collections which the monks attempted to rescue. These include incunabula and sixteenth-century imprints, mostly large folio volumes, such as the famous Froben edition of St. Augustine's *Opera omnia* by Erasmus. Judging from the scant evidence and these chance survivals, the loss was indeed tragic. The abbey library was on the second floor of the monastery, so that little could be transported out of the burning building once the fire spread from the outbuildings. It was later recalled how in the little time allowed by the fire after the wind turned it to the monastery proper, monks risked their lives to save what little they could. However, the fire spread through the main complex in what seemed like only minutes, driven by winds blowing over the hilltop before a rainstorm finally arrived too late to do any good. The librarrin rushed to the main collection and hurled what he could from the upper-story windows; some of the oversized and oldest of the volumes came tumbling down from the fourth-floor storage areas (26). They landed in heaps below; those on the bottom were subsequently buried in mud and debris, most were water damaged from the efforts of the fire fighters and later from the rain, and those on the top were seared by the immense heat of the blaze or were burned by falling ash and embers. Only a very few books in the middle layers of these piles survived, often with bindings broken in their fall. It was only in the aftermath of the fire that this library was fully appreciated; its treasures, incunabula and medieval manuscript codices as well, were lost forever. None were ever recorded in any census or even briefly described bibliographically in any catalogue. Their destruction was total.

The descriptions of the Mt. Angel fire and the destruction of the library remind one of the great fire in 1887 at St. Meinrad when 10,000 volumes were lost. There was a similar scene of panic and hurling rare books frantically from upper-floor windows to cement patios below where the piles of broken books were damaged further by falling firebrands (27). The archabbey saved only a tenth of its bookstock. Although all accounts agree that Mt. Angel's loss was tragic, there is disagreement about the exact status of the library collections at the time of their destruction. The Oregon *Daily Journal* of September 23, 1926 reported "the priceless medieval manuscripts gathered from the Old World and the wonderful library can never be replaced...". Fr. Luke Eberle repeated the claim: "The loss was extreme. From the library a priceless collection, some 15,000 volumes along with priceless medieval manuscripts, had been consumed. Nearly the entire museum collection, which rivaled any in the Northwest at that time, was destroyed" (28). These and most other accounts were capitulated in an emotional article, "St. Benedict's Abbey is a Mass of Ruins!" in the *Mt. Angel Magazine* on September 30, 1926, which estimated the library loss at 16,000 books plus "several thousand" unbound volumes (29):

> ...today but a few hundred old books remain out of a collection that would have graced any institution in either the Old World or the New. Handwritten manuscripts, treasures of ancient and modern times, magnificent sets, rare editions, and files of inestimable value—all are part of the smoking ashes.

Prior Jerome later, when beginning a new library appropriately enough with a copy of Boethius' *Consolation of Philosophy* (1771), noted therein as "Bibliothecarius": "Dono dedit Bibliothecae S. Benedicti post incendium quo tota antiqua biblioteca descructa est. Die 21 Sept. 1926".

Ironically, given the lost treasures alluded to in these tales of woe, the one loss specifically mentioned by one report, to illustrate how valuable the collection was, was hardly valuable compared with medieval manuscript codices; it was the complete run of the *Dublin Review* back to 1848, for which the appraisal value was set at $50.00 per volume. Perhaps the most immediately felt loss was not the scattered rarities in the collections, but the destruction of the working library which would have allowed the monks to resume their college and seminary programs with proper support. It was this practical need which required the immediate restoration of a library as a collection, even before a library building could be had. The emphasis would not be on the rare and beautiful, although the abbey was to acquire a few manuscripts in time. However, the paramount goal for all was to rebuild a working, general education library.

Restoration of the Library, 1926-53

A 16,000 volume library built slowly over nearly a half-century but wiped out in one night, was hardly easy to restore when so little means were at hand. The economic structure supporting the library was so hard pressed afterwards, that conditions seemed like those experienced in the 1890s. Then, with the onslaught of the Great Depression immediately thereafter, recovery was slow and painful. The students in both the seminary and college had to rely mostly on their own textbooks again, and small subject-area collections were assembled by their professors. A general reference and reading library was the first priory, but there was no main repository, technical facilities, or means of good bibliographical control. Nor was there any capability for research except by reliance on nearby facilities, such as the growing state library in Salem. Understandably, when new facilities were planned for the hilltop, the main concern was for the teaching collection. It would take much longer to recover any of the library's former capacity to support advanced studies and research, and from this time on the monks attributed the inability of the college to compete with area institutions of higher learning to the 1926 fire.

Prior Jerome was responsible for rebuilding the monastery library. Soon after the community was resettled and the college had returned to near normal, at least in schedule, the prior began seeking help in obtaining needed books. Because the major development campaign was for the building fund, solicitation for the library ranked a poor second priority. His effort was therefore not to seek monetary donations, but gifts of books themselves from whatever source possible. He turned immediately to "gift and exchange" librarians in the state and asked for duplicates from their collections. Locally many of the diocesan clergy responded generously, giving what books they had on subjects relevant to the teaching interests of the community. Few, however, had the kind of older, research material which really replaced the lost library. One significant donor was Fr. John Waters, who after studying at Mt. Angel continued a lifelong correspondence with Abbot Bernard and Prior Jerome from 1928 to 1943. When he became pastor at Albany, Oregon, after 1933, he began donating several pre-1800 imprints to the abbey's collections (30). Other alumnae were equally responsive, but few were bookmen as such or had the means to possess large personal libraries. The archbishops likewise tried to help, especially the seminary; among the collections received to sustain research were those of both Francis X. Blanchet and Abp. Francis Norbert Blanchet. Duplicate materials were sent from the archdiocesan archives, and the cathedral's small library was likewise given to Mt. Angel. There were also the almost spontaneous gifts of single books left by visitors and parents of students, often old Bibles belonging to Oregon's early families but which were no longer used except as heirlooms. Occassionally, as in the case of the parents of Donald Toepfer, a Mt. Angel alumnus who died still a young man, coherent collections (in this case, the Latin classics) were donated to the abbey in memory of the deceased.

Not content with passive acquisitions, the prior worked for a decade in rebuilding the library. Among the vast correspondence file left by Prior Jerome to the abbey archives are several letters such as those dated October 12 and December 8, 1926 to and from Athanasius Dengler of Conception Abbey arranging for book shipments. There are also letters of December 5, 1926 and January 18, 1927 to the abbot and prior of Assumption Abbey in far-away Schyern, Bavaria, asking for any of their duplicate books (31). Fr. Maurus Snyder helped Jerome by contacting his associates in Europe, especially in Rome, and the other monks were pressed into similar service. Fr. Maurus wrote to Prior Jerome on December 5, 1928, notifying him of books being mailed to Mt. Angel from Beuron Abbey, and on

September 3, 1929 P. Lambert Krahme of Maria Laach contacted Fr. Maurus about duplicates in its monastic library (32). Before then, since October 18, 1928, Fr. Bonaventure Dressback of Maria Laach had been selling duplicate books from its collections to the Mt. Angel library. Indeed, the Prior Jerome recorded that by 1929 he had already sorted out 948 pre-1800 imprints for a rare book collection (50 from the 1500s, 202 from the 1600s, and 796 from the 1700s)—not all of which survive today in Mt. Angel's collections. Another letter dated February 23, 1932, from P. Romanus Rios notified Fr. Maurus of books by Bp. Salvado being sent from Barbastro, Spain (33). These two Mt. Angel monks continued to search for interesting and relevant titles through the Benedictine network which existed in the congregations and the informal international contacts developed by the monks' associations in various university's and abbey schools. Another link was to follow leads provided by the abbey's charitable connections to Europe. As economic conditions grew worse, numerous communities solicited funds from their better off American sisterhouses. The Redemptorists, who had just received Mass stipends that year from Mt. Angel and would through 1937, on October 5, 1926 reciprocated with a shipment of books from their libraries (34). Despite Mt. Angel's own plight, this monastery also received requests for alms and the monks responded as best they could, often by forwarding Mass stipends to their European confreres. In return, they asked for whatever books could be spared.

One such contact was made at St. Matthias abbey near Trier on the Mosel River. Its abbot and Fr. Johann P. Hau (d. 1951), its librarian, had been fellow students of Abbot Bernard and Prior Jerome in Rome. This German community was struggling to restore its ancient monastery which had been abandoned after the French Revolution. Its lands had been expropriated and redistributed under the Napoleonic regime, leaving only the monastery precinct itself for the new Benedictine colony. During the 1930s with the onset of the Great Depression, there was some chance of buying back some of the original monastic estate, if only the monks themselves could find surplus funds. The abbot appealed to the American communities, and calls for help were exchanged across the Atlantic at about the same time. Mt. Angel began to send some of its Mass stipends to St. Matthias, but the latter had no library to share with the former. The favor was later returned. Fr. Hau contacted Prior Jerome about a "Catholic collection" which might be available cheaply in nearby Aachen (35). The acquisition of this collection is an interesting episode in the restoration of Mt. Angel's library; accounts are preserved in the journal of Fr. Luke Eberle and the reminiscences of Fr. Martin Pollard, the two young monks responsible for the transaction at the orders of Prior Jerome (36).

Johann Hau's overture to Mt. Angel was not entirely altruistic, since he hoped to keep much of the collection for St. Matthias abbey. The community could not afford the asking price, 4000 RM. He therefore offered to secure the collection for Mt. Angel Abbey, if the duplicates and local history materials in the Aachen collection could be kept by St. Matthias in repayment for its services as agent. Upon Prior Jerome's confirmation of interest, since Hau described the collection as especially germane for a Benedictine monastery, the librarian agreed to act as the intermediary. It was Fr. Luke's impression later that the initial contact came while Dr. Hau was searching for a "flush" abbey to buy the collection (37). The librarian of St. John's abbey at Collegeville, Fr. Oliver Kapsner, had been contacted as well and urged his superiors to buy the collection, but it was assumed that there would be too many duplicates between the Aachen collection and titles already acquired by the Minnesotan Benedictines. Fr. Kapsner was ordered to rescind his earlier statement of interest. Actually, Hau never provided a detailed description to make such a determination, and financial difficulties everywhere were more likely the reason for St. John's caution. The depression was now tightening its grip on the United States as much as on Europe, and none of the American foundations were "flush" enough to act without reservation, including Mt. Angel. The Oregon Benedictines were more desperate than most, however, in their search for library acquisitions.

It is not understood how Prior Jerome thought that Mt. Angel could buy the collection without dipping into its precious building fund. Nevertheless, the prior contacted Martin Pollard who was completing his studies in Rome before his ordination on July 10, 1932, to negotiate on behalf of the community to acquire the collection. Meanwhile, the prior himself began his own library development campaign, one of extreme "bibliophile mendicancy" as Lawrence Thompson called it, to raise the necessary money. He collected nickel and dime donations in coffee cans, and obtained the largest donation from the meager savings account of his own family. Fortunately negotiations in Europe took time, and this provided some opportunity to scrounge for funds.

After his ordination, Fr. Martin traveled to Maria Laach on a tour of Europe's famous monasteries, but on order of the prior, proceeded to Aachen. He was joined by his confrere, Fr. Luke, who was to help him in case the collection were actually purchased. The prior already sent word to Fr. Hau, and the latter had whittled the price down by 300 RM. The pressure was on, however, since now the owner said that a third party had expressed interest in the collection. Fr. Martin was charged with the responsibility of appraising the collection, since the descriptions of Fr. Hau were too general to determine whether this was a good buy. The Mt. Angel monks arranged to meet Fr. Hau at Anernack, there to settle on a strategy before going to Aachen. Unfortunately Fr. Hau's schedule changed at the last minute, and they did not meet as planned until all arrived at Aachen.

The provenance of the so-called Aachen collection cannot be reconstructed in full, yet more is known now than did the three Benedictines in 1932. Most of the extant books seem to have been the remnants of the suppressed Jesuit college in Cologne, and of other suppressed religious houses in the Rhine and Mosel valleys which had lost their libraries in the chaos of the Napoleonic Wars. There were collections from the Discalced Carmelites of Trebizond, choir books from Rolandswerth, and devotional literature from countless ministerial libraries. After the political settlement of 1815, many of these libraries were literally homeless. They were either in storage with no clear ownership evident, or were in abandoned religious houses where they were rescued (or stolen, depending on one's viewpoint) by opportunistic antiquarian dealers in the area. One of these was Anton Creutzer (sometimes spelled Kreutzer), who in 1898, according to one Aachen register, owned an antiquarian shop, the forerunner of the modern bookstore—the Creutzer's Sortiments-Buchhandlung G. m.b.H. at Elisabethstrasse 4 in Aachen. The only surviving sister of the three who owned this store in 1975, Fraulein Hanny Cloth, supplied information about their family business (38). Anton Creutzer had been a collector for some time, having both his personal library and his bookstock. He had assembled after the 1850s a large collection of 16-18th century imprints as well as some incunabula, manuscripts, and exempla of decorative arts, before going into the trade wholeheartedly. Most of Mt. Angel's Aachen collection can be traced to his collections by his hand-inserted five to seven-digit inventory numbers on the front flyleaves. His business was passed to his son, Hans Creutzer, who was subsequently in a partnership with another antique and art dealer, M. Lempertz. Together they ran the Antiquariat Lempertz on Theaterstrasse and another shop on Kapuzienergraben in the historic old section of this medieval city, in addition to an old bookstore at Hindenburgstrasse 49. The partnership failed; Lempertz moved to Bonn where his business continued until 1954, but Hans Creutzer was forced into bankruptcy. One of his chief creditors was Herr Alvin Neuber, an Aachen businessman who owned among other properties an auto garage and a 'Fleischkonservenfabrik' or sausage factory at Peterstrasse 44/46. The second story of these buildings had been leased to the Creutzer firm over the years for overflow storage of its bookstock, but Hans Creutzer owed rent in arrears for five years. In the backruptcy settlement, Herr Neuber was left with the upstairs bookstock in compensation for his loss. The Protestant sausage dealer was left with over 25,000 books, mostly remnants of Catholic Counter-Reformation libraries. It was, in Fr. Luke's use of the American colloquialism, a "white elephant".

Neuber sought to unload the collection as quickly as possible and was not interested in the booktrade or in what happened to other parts of Creutzer's collections stored elsewhere. As Fr. Martin learned from Fr. Hau, Neuber approached St. Matthias of Trier and offered to sell the entire bookstock very reasonably just to recover some of his lost rent. He had already let some English dealers into the warehouse to scrounge for individual bargains, and had sold most of the incunabula to them at prices supposedly totally unrelated to their actual value. He could not get good prices at that time, even if he had known their normal market value. He realized, however, that it would take forever to recover his money by selling a book at a time and that in the meantime he could not use his own warehouse space for his own business. Money was increasingly dear, buyers were becoming scarce, and he shared the widespread but seldom founded conviction that all monasteries had wealth hoarded from ages past. When he learned that St. Matthias could not afford to buy the collection *en toto,* he came down in price by 300 RM if Fr. Hau worked out the deal with Mt. Angel Abbey. Fr. Hau, of course, was eager to secure a buyer in America which would consent to let St. Matthias keep some of the unwanted books, duplicates, and the local *Trevirensia*—which Fr. Martin agreed to do.

The American Benedictines arrived in Aachen in the early afternoon and rendevouzed with 'Fr. John' at the local Redemptorist house. The Redemptorists had no room for them, nor did the Franciscan nuns or Alexian Brothers, so on Fr. Johann's insistence they checked into the Hotel König von Spaniens, which even with a discount was, according to Fr. Luke's diary, "Catholic true, but pretty high class, ...prices were steep...". They were able, however, to refresh themselves for the next day of business. Neuber, whom Fr. Luke described as "a small trim business man, very polite and friendly," had agreed to hold the unidentified third party off since Fr. Martin had first indicated in writing his intent to buy, but the asking price now went back up 300 RM. Fr. Luke recalled (39):

> ...we inspected the books after the introduction and before closing the deal. First, we were led into a room where several thousand books were stacked about, on architecture, medicine, general science, and French and English books. These were the less valuable assortment. Then we went upstairs and almost fell back in amazement at the shelves and shelves containing thousands upon thousands of books, about 700 'Folianten,' [or] grand folios, predominantly from [the] 16-18th centuries...; several were handwritten books; thousands upon thousands of books on theology, philosophy, history, ecclesiastical and profane art; sermons and ascetical works; the Fathers [of the Church] works and history; juridical works, liturgy and ritual; scientific books in every branch; Bibles in every tongue; dictionaries and lexicons, publications bound and unbound in complete series; pictures and views; in fact, work representing almost every possible branch of knowledge—predominantly in Latin and German, with a good deal in French. The first general 'Ueberblick' aroused our enthusiasm to a high pitch and completely justified our eager anticipation. After a couple of hours of examination, we returned to Herr Neuber's office and then the deal was closed.

Neuber took them at their word, refusing to draw up a contract, and in true German fashion, the deal was really finalized at Aachen's famous 'Altes Kurhaus' over several drafts of dark beer.

Herr Neuber's son-in-law was a partner with his father in the export business with the Netherlands, so it was agreed after supper to have this *spediteur* firm handle the packing and shipping around the Panama Canal to Portland, and by train to Mt. Angel. During the week thereafter, Fr. Luke and Fr. Martin helped with the sorting and packing, did some sightseeing on Herr Neuber's insistence as host, and made a side-trip to the Beuronese abbey of St. Benediktsberg and five other monasteries. When the sorting was completed by the evening of August 17, the agents estimated the bulk at 35 cubic meters and charged Mt. Angel 2800 RM (12.25/cu. meter) for crating and shipping. Fr. Luke estimates that 15,000 volumes had been set aside for shipment; depending on actual weight, the total cost would be between $1500-1700, which he guessed would be about ten cents a book! He was only slightly inaccurate: the purchase price of 3300 RM converted to $785, packing cost $7.40, and the freight bill came to 3368 RM or $802, for a total of $1594.90. The inventory completed by Prior Jerome indicates that about 13,000 titles arrived, so the cost was slightly more than a dime a book!

Fr. Luke described the sorting process in which the monks "minus scapular and collar" pitched into the labor (40):

> Fr. Martin, on the ladder, takes up every book or set, peers at it, decides to take or leave it, and hands it to Fr. John for his corroboration. Usually his decision is OK. Sometimes Fr. John says it has no practical value for our library, and with Fr. Martin's consent puts it on his pile. He takes all duplicates, when it has no practical value for us to ship more than one or two of a kind. The work is interesting and the air is punctured by cries of triumph as Fr. Martin discovers [a] volume or set that pleases him.

This scene, of course, still arouses an instinctive exceleration in any bibliophile, providing adrenalin for added energy as it did for these young monks. In retrospect, it is sad that they were not more experienced bookmen who realized the harm done in splitting collections which until then may have had their provenance in tact. In the process much of the information value potentially derived from maintaining a *respect du fonds* which could add to our knowledge about library history in the Rhineland, was irrevocably destroyed. The books were not treated as rare books *per se*, but were selected simply by first impression of potential use. Little was it realized that technically there is little chance of a true duplicate in hand-press book production. Sorting was done so hurriedly that imprint data were not considered as selection criteria; there was no concern for editions, states, or issues in any bibliographical sense, but only the rough estimate of relevance by subject to the practical teaching activities of the monastery. This overriding practicality of the selection process may be seen now to have been impractical, since the monks failed to capitalize fully on the investment potential of their find. Books then costing ten cents for purchase and shipment now have market values one to five thousand-fold and more, so that if the entire bookstock had been shipped to Oregon and weeded there in time, after proper research and with the benefit of hindsight, resale of selected portions of the collection would have more than paid for the whole transaction. The worry then, as expressed by Fr. Luke, was to eliminate "unnecessary duplicates and excessive weight". Given Prior Jerome's difficulty in raising even $1500 during the depression, such a concern is more understandable.

The Aachen collection had indeed been combed before the monks got to it, and no incunabula were to be found. The oldest book left was Justinian's *Decretals* of 1505. Of the 700 oversized-folio volumes, mostly sixteenth-century imprints, between 100-200 were left for St. Matthias Abbey in addition to all imprints from the province of Trier and books about the region, plus the so-called duplicates. Judging from the estimates of the bookstock's total volume, about 5000 books were left behind. How many of these were in fact transported to St. Matthias is unknown, since Fr. Luke returned to his studies at Maria Laach and Fr. Martin to Rome before the Aachen collection was fully crated. Abbot Athanasius Polag of St. Matthias on December 29, 1975 reported that there is no record for the abbey's library acquisitions in 1932. Fr. Hau died suddenly on December 6, 1951 without the opportunity to leave any written recollections, and the abbey archives contain no bills or other records attesting the acquisitions. Abbot Polag explained (41): "...at the beginning of World War II the community was suppressed and the library and a lot of other things confiscated. Part of the material was destroyed during the war". The present librarian at St. Matthias found only two testaments to the transactions described by Fr. Luke, namely two manuscript codices from the seventeenth century (before 1647) attributed to the Benneictine convent of Rolandswerth, which are like three such codices currently in the Mt. Angel collection. One is a hagiographic compendium in German, in which the *Translatio* of the Three Magi suggests origins in the diocese of Cologne; the other is a later antiphonal which Dr. Hau ascribed to Rolandswerth, but the contents of which suggest the provenance of the Cologne Brigittines. In the front flyleaves in addition to Anton Creutzer's inventory numbers, are the notations in Fr. Johann's handwriting reading "Geschenk der Abtei Mount Angel" (i.e., "Gift of Mt. Angel"), and this makes it even more sad that the entire bookstock was not brought to the U.S.. So little remains of the Aachen collection which was given to St. Matthias abbey. Yet, there is consolation in that as much of the remnants of these early modern religious libraries was preserved by the bargain struck in 1932. Had the collection not been moved, the total collection might have been lost. During World War II the allies bombed the industrial district of Aachen; the building complex, including the book warehouses, of Herr Alvin Neuber were totally leveled.

Fr. Hau returned to St. Matthias on August 20 after having stayed a while to check on the packing and to pose for pictures at Herr Neuber's invitation, standing in front of the loading dock and before wagons full of boxed books. Fr. Luke recalled how happy the laborers were to find work, "even tho' Aachen looks very prosperous. They are a jolly crowd and get a big kick out of the thousands of books over which we made such a fuss and which mean only paper to them" (42). This passing comment must make one wonder about the care in the collection's handling. Seven men had worked for six days, four packing and two loading, and one did all of the marking, weighing, and billing. They earned altogether 30 marks (then $7.40) for their toil!

Fr. Martin and Luke lingered in Aachen to supervise the packing and shipping arrangements, but also because they were waiting for funds to arrive from Prior Jerome. When not working with the books, they saw some of the locale's historical sights, visited surrounding monasteries, and tried to lead a religious life in their non-monastic abode. In contrast to Luke's comments about attending Fr. Martin's Masses and recollections about their walking tours, one unsavory incident recorded in his diary humorously reveals unusual perils in bookcollecting (43):

> ...after this [Benediction at the Redemptorist house], we decided to take a walk—almost an eventful one. We start[ed] for the park, go[ing] along a lovely street under huge trees, and in the park itself ascend[ed] a hill from which we [could] get a fair view of the city. Going down, we reenter[ed] the city. Fr. Martin decide[d] to take a short cut... [through] an obscure alley. From the first I felt misgivings, especially when I saw a bold female straddling the steps, smoking a cigarette—something I had not seen in Aachen. (yet among the many, very many modern American-type girls, we had seen). We passed her and struck others just as bad. It wasn't the smoking that bothered [me], but the general attitude of corruption. A couple [of them] barked "guten Tag" at our Roman collars. We hurried thru, passing a big brazen thing hanging on the neck of a man—most probably the dives of Aachen. I shuddered at the experience and felt as if I had passed right through hell!

Once getting out of the Aachen red-light district, they found their way back to the hotel. After supper Luke retired, wrote about this experience in his diary, then read in bed until after midnight. He had regained his composure and simply closed his entry for the day with "First use of the new Mt. Angel library".

The monks had to wait longer than expected because the money from America did not arrive. Communications back to Oregon were slow, and for whatever reason, when the prior responded to Martin's telegram and approved the purchase, he omitted the essential element in the transaction—the cash. Fr. Martin thought that the prior misunderstood the criptic message, but it could also have been that the money was not yet collected. However, the monks needed to make at least a deposit to the shipping company, but they had only their travel monies. Luke wrote: "Fr. Martin is all up in the air about the failure of [the] money to arrive; it should be here according to telegrams from Father Prior. Patience is the only ticket—and it is not [the] lack of that from which Fr. Martin is suffering; [it is] simply the nervous suspense of waiting". It was Fr. Martin who had to assure Herr Neuber that the money was on its way. After another day of sightseeing, he wrote again: "...as I am writing this, Martin is rattling off calculations for shipping [by] the Spediteur. Must be an end to it sometime! Hang around until quitting time; the packers announce they are finishing tonite...". On August 24, Luke left Aachen for a visit to Beuron Abbey via Luxembourg and Strassbourg, and he ultimately returned to Andernach. Fr. Martin was there when he arrived, since the money for the Aachen collection never arrived. Finally, a bank draft came to the Sant' Anselmo and Fr. Martin rushed it to the procurator to get it exchanged so it could be sent to Aachen. Then, as Fr. Martin recalled: "we found to my dismay that he could not get another draft to send to Germany. Italy had impounded all funds due to the depression" (44). The procurator was finally able to cash the draft into American bills, which were then carried personally (smuggled?) by Luke "across the border (probably illegally)...". to Aachen where Neuber (who because of his trade with Holland was sympathetic with the problems of currency exchange, but was nevertheless anxious) was finally paid. The "new Mt. Angel library" then left Aachen on October 1 for its new home.

So newsworthy was the arrival of the Aachen collection that the *Pacific Star* later ran a feature article describing the work (45). On November 17, 1932 some 143 crates were unloaded from the steamer *Schwaben* in Portland, greeted with the herald "Valuable Shipment of Books from Europe Arrive at Abbey". When on November 28 the books arrived at Mt. Angel, the news was that "the monastery's library almost tripled its previous content". The Southern Pacific Railway Company delivered the crates by truck to the monastery's very doors, and for the next week the monks hand-carried the volumes to the monastery's basement where wood shelving had been erected in anticipation (46):

> Since that time an interesting scene has been that of Father Prior [Jerome] wrestling with one or

> the other of these boxes, eagerly delving into them, always anticipating the find of another treasure. The zest of the old Spanish gold diggers is more than equalled by the zeal of our Very Rev. Librarian as he explores the contents of this new acquisition.

By January 15, 1933 the prior had unpacked and brief-listed 1700 volumes in his ledgers and prepared by hand index cards for a catalogue. The reporters mistakenly claimed that there were incunabula among them, but at that time the earliest yet found was the 1519 commentaries of Franciscus Longus de Coriolano on Clement VIII's canon law casebooks. They were amused to see the variety of books, from 550 large folio volumes (about 15 inches high) to miniature pocket dictionaries measuring 1 3/4 x 2 inches. Included in the shipment were paintings "of the Rhineland in bright color" which were also erroneously described as "frescoes". When the prior completed his inventory on May 2, 1936, the Mt. Angel library held 19,826 titles.

More important than the inaccuracy of such student reporting was the explicit joy of the monks in replacing the library lost in 1926. Yet, from the students' perspective (47):

> ...the deficiency in the College library is still very great. Indeed, rather than alleviate the present poor condition of our college library, the very thought of those 15,000 volumes in the monastery seems only to aggravate the situation and to make the deficiency felt the more keenly. It is confidently hoped, however, that sometime, somehow, (preferably soon) this deficiency, especially in recent but necessary English, History, and Science books will be supplied.

The students recognized that the Aachen collection constituted a research library, and even though it would be accessible for special projects, the college library was their mainstay: "...the books wanted should be recent editions dealing with problems of our contemporary world". The prior's decision to purchase the Aachen books was not, therefore, without detractors. Then as always in times of limited resources for acquisitions, the allocation of funds was controversial; it is always a political process. At least Prior Jerome, because of his personal fund-raising efforts, could not be accused of using college funds to build the abbey's research collection. In fact, this budgetary distinction was as important as the nature of the two libraries in keeping them apart.

The 1195-36 Mt. Angel College and Seminary catalogue maintained, " ...the libraries of the institutions before the fires [1892 and 1926] were a credit to Mt. Angel College and Seminary. More than 30,000 volumes, including precious manuscripts and first editions, occupied an honored place accessible to faculty and students" (48).

As time went on, it should be observed, the accounts of the old library continued to inflate its size and significance, when no records survived to contradict the exaggerations. This was a natural reaction to a catastrophic loss and the subsequent hardships in carrying on without adequate support resources. Likewise, the Aachen collection in 1935 was touted as 18,000 volumes "selected by competent scholars in Europe" to ¢eable the library to surpass previous standards. The count then put the abbey library at 22,000 volumes in all, and the college library at 6000. This description remained in the catalogues until after 1939, partly hiding the real deficiencies in the ability of this collection to support fully the curricula of the college and seminary. A great bulk of the collection that was thought usable for teaching was in German, and increasingly not only did the students not read German, but nor did the new members of the monastic community. As time went on, it became more apparent to everyone that the Aachen collection did not adequately serve the immediate needs of Mt. Angel's educational programs. The book count helped to provide the illusion of a viable resource and substantial research potential, but in reality the books were little used in contrast to the smaller public collection.

The tedious work of bringing some resemblance of bibliographic control over the Aachen collection fell on the prior-librarian who worked on this project until 1936. The Aachen books were simply inventoried as they were unpacked, being assigned an acquisition number and its corresponding inventory number from the Antiquariat Creutzer. Although Fr. Martin had tried to keep sets together at Aachen, in the process of packing and unpacking, sets were broken and titles in series were often treated as separates. Moreover, the Aachen books were interspersed with the 4000 volumes of the abbey library, without regard to provenance. The 1932 resorting, the integration of collections in 1935-36, and a subsequent rearrangement of the books, all destroyed the last remnants of any original order or *fonds* which might have survived in Anton Creutzer's collection management of the previous century. There was a general appreciation for the older imprints, and for those volumes notable for physical size, binding, or engravings and mapwork; but for the time being, all were treated equally as part of a general research library.

Prior Jerome continued to scrounge for more books whenever he made another contact, and he was a prolific correspondent. In a note to Dunstan Juneman of Aberdeen, Washington, for example, on May 30, 1936, as an afterthought the monk urged him "look for old books and libraries which have them" (49). However, on August 14, 1936, Fr. Mark J. Schmid succeeded the aging prior as librarian. In contrast to Jerome Wespe, the new librarian was a dilettante. He was a character long remembered on the hill. His training at the Sant' Anselmo was in philosophy, but he taught introductory science as well. He publicized the new library and worked with its physical rearrangement over the next decade. In an address on April 3, 1939 at the state library in Salem before an assemblage of librarians from throughout Oregon, Fr. Mark described how the pre-1700 imprints had been separated from the main research collection of the abbey library, forming what he called interchangeably the "old book collection" or "old library" and the "book museum". He maintained that a few of the "twenty-pound" books extant were survivors from the 1892 fire and before "when the pioneer founder of Mt. Angel College came to America... [they] brought with their ,mager luggage heavy cradle books and manuscripts" as "a heritage" from Engelberg (50). The old book collection, according to Fr. Mark, numbered 4000 volumes, of which 1500 were "on display for visitors, whilst the rest are in storage and accessible only to special scholars". He claimed that 60% of the books were in Latin, but that 26 languages were represented in the collection, covering "every major heading in the library classification chart" (51). Included in this count were some manuscript codices, or "calligraphs" as he called them, as well as palimpsests, but he did not enumerate them. That is unfortunate, because this same number is no longer extant and there is no record what could have happened to them.

Fr. Mark fancied himself to be a scholar and an original, scientific researcher, and was interested in early book conservation even though he had no expertise here whatsoever. Undaunted, he nevertheless experimented with several of the rare books in an attempt to read the underlayer of script in the palimpsests and to arrest the acid deterioration and embrittlement of some papers by resorting to home remedies and "kitchen conservation". When discussing some of the specimen, he misinformed students that "the palimpsest was the creation of poorer scribes who could not buy the expensive new sheets [of vellum], so they just 'washed' the ink off cheaper manuscripts and used them over. Usually the acids of the first ink etched themselves into the fabric, and one can make entire lines reappear by careful restoratives" (52). These palimpsests are no longer extant, so one must wonder what "resoratives" he tried on them. A few volumes in the present collection bear the scars of his crude experiments, including a 1504 canon law text which has two folios varnished; another sixteenth-century imprint was treated with shellac; and a sixteenth-century alum-tawed pigskin stamped binding is now pure white and totally brittle as a result of being cleaned with bleach and scouring brushes. Perhaps most sad of all, several folios of the Mt. Angel liturgical codices by Fr. Anselm Weissenborn (who had just died two years before, in 1937), were treated with thinned varnish in a foolish attempt to counter the acidity of the modern wood pulp paper. These folios became so stiff and brittle that they broke along the tension line in the gutter margins, and were reattached with white medical tape. They constitute a conservator's most severe test and attest how a bibliophile, when uninitiated, can be a very poor lover. Other volumes were lost as well, either as a result of such experimentation, or weeding of the worst kind.

The collection today includes numerous sixteenth and seventeenth-century tracts, pamphlets, and treaties documenting the aftermath of the Wars of Religion and the 1648 Peace of Westphalia. Curiously, the surviving miscellany are by Catholic authors with only a few extant Protestant authors, mainly medical writings, but not theological. The collection, as Fr. Martin recalled, had been far more extensive, but presumably Fr. Mark got rid of anything that smacked of a Protestant attack upon Catholicism. Thus, although this is still a valuable research collection of Reformation and Counter-Reformation apologetics, it is not as rich an historical resource as it once was before Fr. Mark's librarianship. Moreover, the numbers given for the rare book collection size, 4000 in 1939 and 5000 in 1941, are not only contradictory for then, but are inconsistent with both Prior Jerome's inventory and the current count, which is little more than half that number. Indeed, the collection was never brought under bibliographic control, nor do the extant records explain such discrepancies. One cannot help wonder what happened to hundreds of volumes during his tenure in office.

In 1939 the Portland *Journal* carried two stories disseminating from Mt. Angel, with the caption-headings reading "Ancient Manuscripts Discovered in Museum" and "Prized Writings Found in Library" (53). As "announced... by Rev. Dr. Mark Schmid, OSB, librarian," parchment manuscripts were indeed used as stiffeners in the bindings of oversized, early-printed books. Although this is commonly known today and some fragments, such as those from Krakow analysed after World War II by Prof. Karl Weimer which attested the work of a third printer in Mainz contemporary with Gutenberg and the team of Fust and Schöffer, have been important, Fr. Mark thought that his "discovery" was more unique that it proved to be. The newspaper reported:

> More than 40 manuscript fragments, ranging in size from 35 to 50 square inches, and 20 smaller fragments from 6 to 20 square inches, have been laboriously recovered from the backs of books which date from the 15th century.... Especially designed tools were in use in carefully peeling off the inside of the books' backs to remove only a few inches. Certain of the manuscripts have been left adhering to the backs of the books because, Dr. Schmid states, 'some of the medieval glues even resist solvents'.

That, of course, explains something of the nature of Fr. Mark's experiments.

When in 1974 these manuscript fragments were examined encased in a crudely fashioned display box made from an old basement window casing, with the window serving as the cover, not all of the parchments were found. Most had been reglued to a pasteboard bottom sheet; under the latter was found a kitchen fork with its prongs bent apart and back, with one of them sharpened. This, plus a scapel from the biology laboratory, seems to have been Fr. Mark's "specially designed tools". The article closed: "He is now seeking a restorative which will allow translation of some too faded to be read". That perhaps explains why today there are not 60 manuscript fragments in the rare book collection of Mt. Angel Abbey. The incunabula from which these were removed are likewise no longer extant, but the fragments left attached to their open spines seem to refer to the *Opera omnia* of St. Augustine edited by Erasmus and printed at Basel by Frobin, which narrowly escaped the 1926 fire. Fr. Mark was correct when assuming that these less valuable manuscripts were used as book stiffeners. They are mostly from liturgical texts of the fourteenth and fifteenth centuries: i.e., a Sacramentary and a Pontifical; one is Biblical; another is an unidentified philosophical treatise, and the others appear to be largely canon law texts. They are, as he stated, interesting specimen of medieval book arts with their examples of various Gothic scripts, methods of rubrication, and marginalia. Yet they hardly deserved the attention drawn to them by the monk-librarian's news release; the Catholic *Register* circulated the story again, "Manuscripts, 800 years old, Found!" and the United Press wire service picked it up from Portland so that Toronto and Boston papers announced "Prized Writings Found in College Library—Manuscripts Used to Bind Old Books Found in College Library". The *New York Times* reported (53): "Old Writings Found in West—Manuscripts Being Read in Oregon Library Are of Great Antiquity".

Such notariety had immediate results, both good and bad. It initiated some attention of one forensic document examiner and criminologist from San Francisco, Edward Oscar Heinrich, who on September 29, 1937 took Fr. Mark more seriously than he should have, by informing the latter about new microscopic examination techniques for paintings which had been developed in Berlin (54). He had learned about Mt. Angel's library from the head of the Oakland Public Library, and they were both interested in the results of Fr. Mark's scientific research in book preservation. The latter never answered this correspondence. Other miscellaneous postcards left by Fr. Mark among the library records indicate that he received several donations to the collection because of his publicity; but others wrote from throughout Oregon, and as far away as Michigan and Indiana, hoping that the abbey would buy or recommend a buyer for their treasures—the London *Times* of June 22, 1815 announcing Napoleon's defeat at Waterloo; a 1547 edition of Horace's poetry; John Hersey's *Importance of Small Things*; the St. Louis *Gazette* of 1808; an Armenian magazine; "an old book printed in 1786"; and the London *Original Treatise on Universal Redemption*. More than once, there were pitiful letters from those hoping to sell their 'rarities' "to raise money to pay my debts" in this post-depression era. More rewarding were responses from religious houses. St. Joseph's abbey in Louisiana in 1938 and St. Meinrad in 1941, sent Mt. Angel numerous liturgical texts (55).

In February 1940 the student's library of over 6000 volumes was moved to the seminary, and the main library was then estimated to have grown to over 30,000 volumes. A small library was sent in 1939 to Westminster priory to aid its beginning seminary, just as duplicates and useable textbooks weeded from Mt. Angel's collection had been sent to the Indian schools at Grand Ronde in the Yamhill Valley of Oregon and to those on Vancouver Island, British Columbia. Unfortunately, no record survives to indicate the extent of such bookstock transfers, and the librarian at Westminster in 1976 reported that only a few of the original volumes survive interspersed with its general collection. One can assume that these were not rare books, but the gesture is indicative of a longstanding Benedictine tradition of library dissemination.

By spring 1941 the central library was rearranged because it had outgrown its old quarters. Nearly 15,000 books, and untold numbers of unbound periodicals, were moved to the fourth floor of the monastery to be rehoused in 2400 feet of newly built shelving. That was the first time that space allowed for some kind of classification; "Prior to this time the volumes which will make up the stack room library content have lain in huge stacks without definite classification" (56). A *Pacific Star* article on February 7 explained that "the librarian" then sorted the books by subject: Canon and civil law, theology, Scripture, homiletics, apologetics, Church history, general history, and literature. It was explained: "Since there is yet no general library building on the hilltop, the library is split into ten various sections of the abbey and college buildings. These function as a unit". The total bookcount was then estimated "conservatively" at 35,000.

Two thousand of these remained in the basement next to the bindery, forming the "ancient book library," of manuscript codices and pre-1800 imprints. They were rearranged over the summer so that press releases in October 1941 announced in the *Oregonian*: "Library of Old Books Opened by College... [to] librarians, educators, and book friends". The Salem *Capital Journal* raised the count to 5000 volumes in the "ancient book museum" arranged "to meet the needs of practical use and public curiosity" (57). More accurately than in Fr. Mark's publicity, it was now reported that only four incunabula were still in the collection; there were 151 volumes from the 1500s, 717 from the 1600s, and 3202 from the 1700s. From then on, there was a fascination with trying to collect one book from each year, to have a continuous run regardless of content or other valid selection criteria; collection development 'theory' was hardly very sophisticated. The canon law section was the largest, followed by Scripture which then included a collection of Bibles in 25 languages. A few facsimile editions, such as the Gutenberg Bible, were included since this was above all a museum; hence a display was set up along one wall, and visitors were regularly led to the basement for a capsulized 'show-and-tell' lecture on historical bibliography. It is remarkable that throughout the 1930s and 1940s faculty instructed students about the history of the book and communication technology, when even today in most undergraduate education students know nothing about the books they take so much for granted. More notable than the lack of professional library standards or bibliographical expertise in the handling of this collection, or its relatively small scale, is the general appreciation of the book arts and the library tradition which was inculcated in the students, clergy, and laymen who visited Mt. Angel. Visitors were proudly told: "Many of the volumes... were once the property of European abbeys which were suppressed during the French Revolution. This fact is evident from the names of various monks that still appear written in the books" (58).

Little is known about the library during World War II. The college catalogue descriptions simply repeat the 1941/42 blurb through 1947/48. These were austere times during which acquisitions were minimal, space constrained any major expansion, and enrollment declines forced a rethinking of the direction in which the curricula were to develop. The research collection remained fairly stable at about 27,000 volumes, while the college library grew to only 8000 volumes. It was sorely evident that the library was no longer competitive among those being developed by state funding 9i the Pacific Northwest, and was being surpassed rapidly by those of the larger private colleges and universities as well. The teaching programs at Mt. Angel contracted and as the monastery concentrated attention on clerical education only, any pretense of being able to offer a broad, general but higher education curriculum was abandoned. With that capitulation, there was little immediate incentive or capability radically to improve the library. With the postwar reorientation of the college to pre-seminary education and the build-up of the latter's curriculum, came some pressure to revamp the library but not to enhance its general collections so much as to develop a specialized research capacity and to support religious studies about the modern church. Those pressures became stronger, however, as the Church moved toward the renewal exemplified by the Vatican Council II, requiring a conversion of the research library from a relatively passive component in the monastery's programs to an active, central role. Slowly plans were made for a new invigorated library, and a transformation of the old museum and warehouse syndrome of the earlier period into a dynamic learning and research center.

Toward a New Library, 1953-70

The move toward a new library at Mt. Angel was inspired mainly by the vision of Abbot Damian Jentges who wanted to make the hilltop a regional cultural center for more than the clergy and to recapture for the monastery some of its older aspirations. It was made into a reality by the diligent efforts of Fr. Barnabas Reasoner (b. 1923-), the monastery's first professional librarian. Moreover, the monks of Mt. Angel were impressed by the reforms taking place in other religious houses, such as at St. Meinrad's under Abbot Ignatius, where the library was placed at the core of the seminary's activities—actually in advance of the movement in public schools during the late 1960s to place their library media centers in the center of their facilities and activities. The reorganization of seminary curricula and new focus on libraries as active learning centers, just as the church was an abbey's spiritual center, was part of a general reform in the post-war years as the entire Church adjusted to new ministerial needs and to societies now tired and disbelieving in the wake of the war's death, destruction, and shattering impact on family ties.

The Swiss Benedictines were behind the Cassinese Congregation in library development, just as they were ahead in liturgical music. St. Vincent, St. John, and St. Benedict all had good teaching collections with core research strengths and were training their men in librarianship or they were hiring professional librarians. The first Benedictine to obtain the new professional degree in library science (the MLS or MA in LS) was Fr. Colman Farrel of St. Benedict's abbey. After coming under the influence of Fr. Paul Foik, CSC, who was reorganizing the Holy Cross Fathers' library at Notre Dame, Fr. Colman enrolled at the University of Michigan. The prior of St. Meinrad's, Fr. Placidus, held a library degree also from the University of Michigan (which incidentally had an earlier influence through James Bp. on the reclassification of the Vatican library and the evolution of the Vatican *Cataloging Rules*). The abbot there released the prior from his administrative duties to devote full-time attention to the rebuilding of its monastic library which, like Mt. Angel's, had been neglected during the previous two decades. The librarian embarked on a five-year development plan in 1945 which not only called for an improved physical plant and a massive infusion of funds, but the reorganization of the 40,000 volume library itself and for the first time, cataloguing according to the Vatican rules (59). For this latter task a professional cataloguer, with experience at Yale and Brown Universities, was hired.

In this process the librarians began to struggle with the problems of compatibility in cataloguing religious materials for Catholic theological libraries and the practices commonly followed in the U.S. which soon crystalized into the *Anglo-American Cataloging Rules* endorsed by the American Library Association (60). Both the Dewey decimal classification system and the accompanying subject headings developed by M. Sears had inadequate capacity to provide intellectual access to religious material, their access points and control vocabulary were overwhelmingly Protestant in nature, and there were no uniform titles for Latin and liturgical books. The Protestant church libraries had started to follow the system devised by Julia Pettie for the Union Theological Seminary library in New York after 1905, and many academic libraries were just beginning to think about the Library of Congress system of classification and descriptive cataloguing which was almost as Protestant in its orientation (61). A system for handling Catholic titles was already devised at Catholic University of America based largely on Vatican practices, and it was at this time that Fr. Oliver Kapsner, OSB, of St. John's Abbey, went to Washington D.C. as a visiting professor at Catholic's library school to develop further standardized approaches to the handling of particularly Catholic materials. He gained a worldwide reputation not only for his *Benedictine Bibliography* but also his manual for the cataloguing of Catholic titles. Particular attention was paid to entries for the papal documents, popular devotional literature, liturgy and ritual (especially uniform entry for specific rites and liturgical books), and special genre of religious literatures and documentation (62). His tools were put into widespread use after their endorsement by the Catholic Library Association, which unfortunately did not collaborate as yet with the Protestant-oriented American Theological Library Association. Kapsner's subsequent design of a uniform thesaurus for the description of Catholic books in subject tracings, *Catholic Subject-headings*, was also widely influencial (63). Simultaneously the Catholic Library Association was beginning to create a climate for interlibrary cooperation, a forum to exchange views, and later those technical services associated with the all-comprehensive term networking (64). The American Benedictine Academy was formed to promote monastic scholarship and joined this movement to improve Catholic libraries by sponsoring bibliographical projects such as those pioneered by Fr. Kapsner. The problem of compatibility between this developing system for the bibliographic control of Catholic materials and the larger systems designed by Dewey or the Library of Congress under Herbert Putnam's administration was not resolved fully until later, with the design of the Lynn-Peterson "alternative classification" schedules for the arrangement and description of specifically Catholic materials (65). The Benedictines were encouraged to participate in this general movement to improve library and information services within the Church, although Mt. Angel neglected to contribute to early calls for cooperation. But St. Meinrad Abbey like St. John's was more responsive, and Mt. Angel was slowly coaxed into participation. Both St. Meinrad's and St. John's abbeys began to send some of their members to the new library schools; Fr. Simeon Daly of the former went to CUA and four monks from the latter began working on their Master of Library Science degrees to continue the work of Fr. Kapsner.

Br. Barnabas Reasoner and Fr. Ambrose Zenner of Mt. Angel Abbey visited St. Meinrad's in the summers of 1947 during its five-year effort to rejuvenate its library and at the very beginning of this Catholic library movement. They were impressed with this reform which refocused so much attention on the monastic library tradition of the Benedictines, and their subsequent reports to the community were so favorably received by Abbot Thomas that he sent Fr. Barnabas after his ordination in 1949 to Rosary College where the latter in 1951 earned his M.L.S. degree (and subsequently did graduate work at the University of Chicago). Fr. Barnabas recalled that in 1949 Fr. Clement had already urged the abbot to get a trained librarian for Mt. Angel, and how, remembering the enthusiasm of Barnabas in his reports, the abbot approached the monk and "told me I would like library work—wouldn't I" (66). Barnabas was off to Chicago soon thereafter.

On December 12, 1952 Fr. Barnabas sought to bring the reformation of Catholic libraries to Mt. Angel; he began his campaign by presenting a seminar paper to the community on "The Library" (67). He reported on his visit to St. Meinrad's and its library efforts, the library science training undertaken by St. John's monks, and his own experience; then he attempted to place Mt. Angel in a larger context by noting "the American Cassinese Congregation is about 25 years ahead of our own in their library programs". He prodded his confreres to action by referring to Kapsner's Benedictine *UnionCatalogue* project in which Mt. Angel was unrepresented: "I don't know of any other abbey which had not cooperated in this important work for Benedictine studies". Apparently the abbey was criticized for such inactivity at the recent meeting of the Catholic Library Association and Fr. Barnabas, sensitive to the attack, now used it to shame his confreres to do something about such inactivity. When, as he explained, his defense was the community's lack of manpower, it was pointed out that other abbey's shared this perennial problem but responded nonetheless. Moreover, the desire and need for more devoted manpower was a constant in Benedictine existence as in all Christian endeavors where the ultimate goal is conversion of the human race. Mt. Angel's excuse was inexcusable. The second line of defense was to take shelter behind the calamity of 1926, but the fire was now part of history and the community would be hard pressed to explain its current lack of fortitude and perseverance in library development. Fr. Barnabas made a convincing case and had strong supporters, including the abbot, who sought to overcome the natural inclination to regard any major attempt to improve the library as unaffordable. It was a question of priorities. Barnabas noted that St. Vincent's abbey under Fr. Shoniker was developing an excellent library; St. Benedict's at Atchison, Kansas, had three professional librarians; St. Procopius now had two and had had full-time librarians since 1923, and its Fr. Adolph Ardlicks had taken charge of the Benedictine Academy's union list of serials; and Conception Abbey had just put up $300,000 to erect a library with a capacity for 100,000 volumes. In contrast, it was reported, Mt. Angel's library acquisition expenditures were less than modest: $643 in 1948/49, $856 in 1950/51, $927 in 1951/52, and was increasing, but not nearly enough, to $1296 in 1952/53 (68). Fr. Barnabas had done his homework and laid a masterful case before the community that now was the time to eliminate the lethargy which had overtaken the Mt. Angel library and to reverse the years of contraction. Rather than to retreat further in face of the problems of the modern church, the argument was to confront these agressively and that a fully active library was one means to do so.

Apart from the ever present shortage of men to do everything the community might ideally accomplish, as well as the equally persistent lack of infinite funding, a library development program faced four major problems as Fr. Barnabas explained. The first was space, namely for a new reading room capable of seating between 28 to 70 students based on ratios of 10-25% of projected enrollments, with another faculty research room to accomodate 45 clerics and monks associated with the seminary. Until then serials were part of readers' services, so periodicals including bound back issues, had been shelved around the reading room; the journals were now occupying all available space. He recommended a separate periodical stackroom for service directly into the reading room. He also advocated establishing an audiovisual center which would combine equipment storage with collections of slides, maps, prints, etc., plus a display area for the rare books. The latter, it was thought, could be adjacent to an area doubling as a seminar or lecture hall which the abbot had always wanted for public programs. Based on the current bookstock of nearly 50,000 volumes, the new librarian wanted a stack capacity to be expanded to accomodate twice that number. Finally, he made a case for a librarian's office to be adjacent to the reading room, big enough for a work room and to have a security or restricted access, not so much for rare books, but so that "Forbidden books could be kept here...". He went further to advocate "some provision for visiting scholars, men or women," and special lavatories therefore. Fr. Mark added to this want-list the needs of the bindery of which he was still in charge.

Fr. Barnabas was likewise critical of the lack of a systematic acquisition program which had left certain areas of the curriculum without proper support. This problem, like that of cataloguing, was tied to that of the libraries' poverty in current reference tools, especially bibliographies. "Our library will have to be completely recatalogued and reclassified," he informed the community after carefully avoiding any criticism of Fr. Mark's tenure in office. The previous practice was described (69):

> Because of the pressure of work, he [Fr. Mark] adopted the expedient of listing a skeleton of information on library cards. His classification was by broad areas. The cards were typed by anyone who happened to be assigned to help him. There was no chance or thought of training. He was fortunate if he had assistance. As a result, the cards are frequently inaccurately filed, contain sketchy and inaccurate information, and are limited to an author and title entry. Subject and analytics have been ignored completely.

In the remarks of Fr. Barnabas lie some indication of the neglect the library suffered during an era of continued austerity when the Aachen purchase was the only real positive step taken to remedy the long-lived harm of the 1926 fire.

Fr. Barnabas coaxed his confreres by mustering every possible argument: Benedictine tradition expects a monastery to be a cultural center; the Catholic Education Association and many of the bishops were calling for more scholarly clergy and for American scholarship to fill the gaps in the Church's theological tradition left by World War II's destruction of so many Catholic libraries and institutions of higher learning in Europe; the Catholic population in Oregon was increasing and Mt. Angel was the only Catholic resource of any potential other than the developing library at the University of Portland, but that was not predominantly a theological library; Catholic organizations like the Benedictine Academy were interested in Mt. Angel's collections; and, there was the threat of nonaccreditation of the college if the library were judged incapable of adequate support for the monastery's teaching programs. He emphasized how nearby Willamette University had expanded its library staff; Albany College upon moving to Portland as Lewis and Clark College improved its library; and the University of Portland was planning a new libary building. In another meeting he provided statistics about library expenditures at other nearby institutions, "not to ask for more money for the library... [but] to give everyone a general idea of the cost of a good library. We have lost our library tradition in the fire. We need some orientation. We have fourteen centuries of tradition of good libraries" (70). His urging had the desired effect. The idea of a new library, now firmly implanted, was gaining increased support. Still, Fr. Barnabas realized the difficulties in bringing such plans to fruition, when he paraphrased the prophecy of Joel (2:28): "...your old men shall dream dreams, and your young men [shall] see visions". He joked that the procurator and those responsible for funding "might think that these dreams are more like nightmares!"

Indeed, when upgrading the library was discussed, there was apprehension about the huge financial outlay required. In another, later report (1956?) Fr. Barnabas recalled that when the faculty realized that $20,565 was spent in three years to improve the library, "there was an awed silence that spoke very loudly about our awareness of the cost of modern education—and of books.... Libraries are expensive" (71). At that time he was justifying a budget which had declined in 1952/53 from 1951/52, although acquisition funds actually increased. The modest budget was for the direct operating costs only, that is acquisitions, subscriptions, and hired labor; it never counted indirect costs or non-salaried staff such as the librarian himself or those assigned, perhaps as their penances, to work with the collections. Consequently, the figures seemed high. He reminded his colleagues that neighboring institutions were spending 5-6.5% of their total budgets on their libraries, and that St. John's Abbey spent $33,103 or 6.02% of its total expenditures on its library. In contrast, the Mt. Angel library budget for 1957/58 did not reach $6000.

The 1956 Library Committee self-evaluation report counted the number of books then accessible as 23,063 (11,811 catalogued fully in the conversion project, 8385 partially under control, plus 1951 bound periodicals)—only half of the monastery's holdings. Accessions into the usable collection from the backlog and from acquisitions jumped from 284 in 1954/55 to 1295 in 1955/56. The largest subject-area collections were Religion (6936), History (4304), Classical and Christian Literature (2803), Sociology (2492), and English literature (2552), Philosophy (1003); followed by areas under 1000 volumes, namely Science, Applied Science, Fiction, General works, Fine Arts, Education, and Music. The median age of the religion collection, twice the size of any other, was three years in contrast to twenty-two years for History and Philosophy, or forty-five years for secular English literature. This reveals the big drive to build up the seminary-related collection, although in 1956 more books were being added in History and Sociology than in Religion. At the same time, the collection was being weeded for "obsolete volumes" at an increasing rate: 700 volumes in 1954/55, to 1314 volumes in 1955/56, with most discards in History, Literature, and Pure Science (only 35 books in Religion were removed). Among the discards were a great many of the books brought from Aachen in 1932. They were unfortunately not added back into 'Special Collections' but were recycled into the book market; the thinking at this time was still only for the old and rare as being special, along traditional antiquarian lines. At the same time, the library subscribed to 15 journals and received another 21 as gifts, but got only four newspapers. The budgets for 1956-58 were not only small, but they were sporadic; the outlay in 1956/57 was less than half that for 1955/56, and although it doubled again the 1957/58 figure still fell below the 1955 $7895 high. Acquisitions continued to account for nearly half of each budget; salaries and supplies (including binding costs) constituted the remainder. The unpaid librarian worked a 48-hour work-week, supported by a half-time salaried but under-paid lay cataloguer, a trained professional, and a full-time circulation desk attendant, plus an assortment of clerical assistance of about 15 hours weekly, and a half-time typist. A library orientation program was introduced in 1955/56, and the library's circulation statistics doubled from 1953/54 to 1954/55, leveling off thereafter at about 3300/year. Use by classification fluctuated, but the highest circulations were in History, Religion, Sociology and Literature respectively. Interlibrary loan requests rose to more than a hundred each year. Meanwhile, new card catalogue units, cases, cabinets, and additional shelving put increased pressure on the limited space. Slowly the library was enlivened, and more use gave Fr. Barnabas increased ammunition in his lobby for a new library on the hill.

In 1956 a questionnaire was used to poll the opinions of the community regarding the future acquisition policy and planning for a better library. Given the choice of increasing the book budget to $5000/year in order to stay abreast with new publications and to plug up holes in the collection, keeping the budget to a $3000 level with nothing extra to remedy past lacunae, or cutting back to $1500, the decision was the middle ground. A consensus was still not enough to shift resources from other areas of expenditure into library development. Likewise, for future planning most preferred to have a library incorporated into another structure, either a classroom building or in combinations with another facility, i.e., a retreat center, a gallery, or the seminary. A few favored excavation of a new building opposite the major seminary. There was, however, no strong mandate arising from the community.

Despite this lack of support for the wholescale improvement of the library, slowly converts were made and Fr. Barnabas enjoyed the support of Abbot Damian within the latter's financial limits. By 1960 the collections were improved substantially by improved budgets between $7000-8000/year (of which $6000 went for acquisitions), and the librarian was able to purchase several major research sets such as the Library of Congress catalogues, Giovanni Mansi's editions of the church councils, the Loeb classical library, and the microfilm edition of the famous *Monumenta Germania Historica*. In addition to regular purchases of the recommended titles from the American Library Association's annual *Notable Books*, and ALA's *Booklist*,the *Catholic Library World*'s "Best Reading" lists, and from the faculty itself, to maintain current acquisitions, the research collections benefited from continual donations.

Retrospective collecting was largely through donation, and the rare book collection depended on outside patronage entirely. In 1957 the Portland Cathedral collection was transferred to Mt. Angel, some 2000 volumes. Half were weeded, but half of the collection was integrated into the monastic library. The personal library of Abp. Francis N. Blanchet was collected by Fr. Sullivan and pulled into the rare book room, but it was not maintained as a separate collection. Records of its transfer from the cathedral to the abbey's research collection, and then into rare books, were so inadequate that it is impossible to tell today how complete this extant historical collection is. At least one book owned by Abp. Gross, the Chommiski *Bible* of 1826, was added as well. Bp. Francis Leipzig of Baker, the future archdiocesan archivist, donated over 500 volumes, mostly usable back issues of periodicals. Three diocesan clergy, Msgr. Bonora, and Frs. Boesch and Ildefonse Calmus, gave personal collections of 500 books each to the monastery, and a Portland architect, Ernst Kroner, added 300 volumes on art and architecture. Thereafter Fr. Derewin and Br. Michael Mau added more than 1000 literary items, and Erwin Schultz provided a collection of Protestant theology which was now welcome. Thus more than 5000 volumes came to Mt. Angel within just a few years, and within a short time the library's gift and exchange operation became an important part of its total acquisition program. The collection continued to be refined by weeding and careful selection of purchased titles, with the heaviest collecting in History, Literature, Religion, and Sociology. The weeding operation also produced two core libraries carved out of the general collection which in 1965-66 were transferred to the new priories in Idaho and Mexico, just as had been done in 1939 for Westminster—or as had been done initially at Engelberg for Mt. Angel. The tradition of library proliferation is to this day embedded in the notion of monastic colonization, and as always, monastic libraries thrive through the patronage of lay and clerical support.

Despite these acquisitions from local donors, the bookcount in the accessible collection did not swell significantly (from 23,000 to 24,624 by late 1958), but they made for a much better collection by filling gaps, replacing older materials, moving the collection toward some modern coverage, and by adding to the specialty research focus of the library. The circulation statistics began to skyrocket, up to 9345 in 1958/59. The preparatory students checked out about 20 books each, the college students 59, graduate students 29, and the faculty averaged 41. There are no comparable records for in-house use. Nevertheless, slowly the librarian was able to demonstrate need from increased use, and therefore to argue ever more effectively for still further improvement. Of all the converts to this library advocacy, the most important was Abbot Damian. He used to enjoy personally leading visitors into the old book museum and to tell them about the Benedictine library heritage, Mt. Angel's once proud library tradition until the disastrous fire, and of the community's dream someday to have a library worthy of these past accomplishments. He longed for proper facilities and a continuation of the kind of program presented in September-October 1952 when the monastery mounted an exhibition from its rare books entitled "The Bible Through Centuries," accompanied by a series of well-received lectures which drew attendance from throughout the valley. He still envisioned the library as the core of a future regional cultural center.

Progress in further development of the library was slow, resulting in a collection better tailored for the college and seminary's teaching needs, but not necessarily a larger collection. Inaccessible collections (i.e., overflow in storage, the backlog of uncatalogued books headed for the general library, the gift and exchange stock, and the rare book collection) constituted a bookstock as large as the number of books under bibliographical control. The 1958 self-evaluation study of the seminary had concluded that the library had to improve steadily, not sporadically, and this set the tone for the 1960s. In the planning for the new retreat and guest house to be opened in 1959, there was considerable thought given to adding a $300,000 wing onto St. Benet Hall while it was still in construction, in order to relocate the library along the north slope of the butte.

Within the decade of the 1960s the catalogued collection grew from 24,624 to 44,756, averaging more than a thousand additions each year beyond the weeding of obsolete volumes. Serials increased from 207 to 410, a phenomenal improvement from decades past. The average total budget rose to $43,610 in 1969, including $14,837 for book and periodical acquisitions and extra money for additional processing staff (an increase over the average $8,309). By 1968/69 the book expenditures alone equalled past combined expenditures for books, periodicals, basic supplies, and processing time ($8,879 of a total $20,069) (72). Personnel had likewise increased; in addition to the librarian, there was usually a second professional on the staff. A part-time lay professional was moved to reference. Later Fr. Augustin de Noble, who had worked in the library as a paraprofessional, in 1963 completed his M.L.S. at the University of Washington and then worked in technical services, and when the budget increased in 1968/69 to hire a technical services librarian fulltime, he moved to reference. There were also two lay-women who worked as clerk typists, Mrs. Joseph Grant who moved to the administrative secretary post when its incumbent of many years, Mrs. Mary Jarvie, retired in 1981. Mr. Richard Portal, a librarian with experience in the state library, worked through the 1970s in collection development and in organizing the public archives in the library. There was also a revolving cadre of student assistants common to all academic libraries, and the occasional assignment of a novice for internships in the library or bindery. The exact components of the staff changed, but in general at least four people worked in the library all the time, and they were supplemented by up to eleven part-time people (excluding the bindery). This enlargement of personnel resources under the supervision of a professional library administrator, explains much of the rapid improvement of the library during the late 1960s and early 1970s.

This more rapid expansion of the library's collections and the capability of the increased staff, forced the problem of space limitations into the critical stage. Throughout the 1960s the library continued to function out of cramped quarters in St. Thomas Hall. It occupied two large rooms on the main floor for open stacks with a central circulation desk, and the other was for reference and a general reading room. The reference books were shelved around the perimeter of the room. The librarian's office was adjacent to these, and while attempting to wrestle with the daily flow of administrative problems, he was called into reference service whenever the need arose. Fr. Barnabas in 1968 recalled (73): "I have probably 15,000 items stacked right outside my door that I'm afraid to touch because I can't put them anywhere". The technical service operation was in the basement of the monastery itself near the bindery, and another room there held rare books. There was overflow storage in the attic, and two rooms on the abbey's main floor served as a faculty study. The space problem became acute after 1968, as Fr. Barnabas lamented: "In the past ten years we received 30,000 uncontrolled items," that is, as he explained, items which "for lack of facilities could not be catalogued and [be] made available". By 1969 it was estimated that 50,000 catalogued volumes were split between St. Thomas Hall and the monastery, and that excluding books not intended for the permanent collections, there were another 30,000 uncatalogued items. That backlog is increasingly normal for large academic libraries today, but it was unthinkable in library science of the 1960s and unheard of for special libraries such as that of Mt. Angel seminary and college.

The self-evaluation study of 1968/69 was undertaken mainly as part of the major "10-year, 10-point" capital development campaign, initiated in 1963. Among others, the firm Development Directors, Inc. of New York, was hired to help since the total plans for the hilltop campus required an estimated $7,158,000 over the next decade.

Abbot Damian in 1968 set a new goal of $3,840,000 beyond the net income from present operations in order to finalize these plans. The library became a key issue in this expansion of facilities on the hilltop, especially so if it were to become the capstone for the seminary's programs and the envisioned efforts in Catholic continuing and adult education. The bishops were trying to raise the level of their funding for the library since it was seen as fundamental for the seminary, and not just a resource which the monks let seminarians use. Such support, while adding to the collection's growth, actually put increased pressure on the abbey to resolve the space problems. Therefore, in conjunction with reorganizing the seminary, the monastery began solicitation for monies to help build a new library. The abbot's prayers for a successful campaign were answered, mainly by the generosity of two benefactors, Howard and Jean Vollum of Beaverton, Oregon, headquarters of Tectronics Inc.; on July 4, 1967 they promised more than a million dollars to build a new facility. This donation was kept quiet for some years, and the donors anonymous, but the assurance that the abbey could proceed inspired other donations, much smaller but which by their number were nevertheless substantial (74).

Negotiations had been going on since 1962 with various firms about plans for a library, since then the abbot had in principle given permission to build a library once funds were forthcoming. The retreat house drained the development campaign, but when it was finished the monastery's officers felt that $500,000 could be devoted to one other building program. But in addition to a library, another class building was needed and there was some speculation about converting the gymnasium into a fine arts center. The monastery could not afford everything envisioned, and certainly had it not been for outside patronage the result would have been some sort of compromise instead of building an ideal library. Once the abbey's benefactors pledged their support, and with the revamping of the seminary's programs, there was all of a sudden, after decades of edging forwards, intense pressure to proceed as soon as possible. As Fr. Barnabas stated in his correspondence of 1965, "ordinarily one moves rather slowly here in matters of great importance. However, a number of things are working together to catapult us into action" (75).

While searching for a suitable architect, a friend at the University of Oregon, whether seriously or not, recommended Alvar Aalto (1898-1976), a Finnish architect of international fame who was then one of the most sought after in his field. Fr. Barnabas may have known little about Aalto at first, perhaps luckily so, since otherwise Aalto would have seemed beyond approach. Enough research was done to persuade Abbot Damian that Aalto should at least be contacted. Aalto had earned worldwide recognition already in 1928 for his Sanatorium in Paimio, Finland. Most of his early works were industrial sites, large plants with employee housing projects, model communities built between the Wars. His designs for the Finnish pavilion at the 1937 Paris International Exhibition and the 1939 New York World's Fair gave him international exposure, and subsequently for six years from 1940 onward he taught as a visiting professor of architecture at the Massachusetts Institute of Technology while also practicing in his native Finland. His first major building in the U.S. was MIT's Baker House dormitory. His achievements were recognized by Princeton University in 1947 with an honorary doctorate, and thereafter he received numerous awards and accolades, including the Gold Medal of the Royal Institute of British Architects (1957), the Gold Medal of the American Institute of Architects (1963), the Jefferson Medal from the University of Virginia, and when considering the Mt. Angel proposal, he took honorary doctorates from Columbia University and the University of California. One may have suspected therefore, that his fees would have been too high, or that a mere special library in remote Oregon hardly deserved his attention compared with his art centers at Copenhagen, Berlin, Wolfsburg, Paris, Aalberg, or Bagdad, or his grand project of urban renewal, the civic center of a revitalized Helsinki (76). Yet, undaunted and perhaps blessed with naîvité, and without the security of the Vollum donation, on March 22, 1963 Fr. Barnabas had contacted Aalto to solicit his interest in a library for Mt. Angel. The envisioned facility was projected to hold 200,000 volumes and accomodate a total user population of 550 (150 monks, 300 collegians, and 100 theologians). His approach was described later by one reporter as "disarmingly simple". He recognized then that even a million-dollar building for Aalto might be "pretty small potatoes," but writing on behalf of the community, he was direct (77): "...we need you. We have this magnificent monastic site and we don't want to spoil it. We want you to improve our site and give us a building that will fill our needs in a beautiful and intelligent way". The monk's letter went unanswered until May when the Aalto firm notified Fr. Barnabas that his letter had been held up in a postal strike and that in the meantime Aalto was back in the U.S. working on his United Nation's project, the conference center of the Institute of International Education. Then, on May 28, 1963 Aalto himself responded from Helsinki, "I have been thinking over your offer about projecting [i.e., the project of] a new library and, although my time is very limited because of all the official buildings I have under contruction, I am very interested in your suggestion as libraries are my favorite subjects" (78).

With that reply commenced nearly a decade of collaboration and friendship, and Oregon was going to get "an original Aalto". Indeed, he had designed only three libraries, one a technical library at Viipuri, Finland, and another at Rovaniemi in the Arctic, but he had designed several churches, art museums, and country houses. The Mt. Angel natural setting gave him the perfect opportunity to blend his experience and to apply his ideas on a project which became very dear to him in his later years—almost a source of personal pleasure to which he turned during a period of failing health and tremendous pressure from his monumental urban projects. Later Fr. Barnabas was told by Aalto's associates "libraries are his pets," and the librarian was to recall in March 1966 a conversation with Aalto, "he mentioned that libraries and the place of libraries in our civilization, remain constant. Other activities and buildings planned for activities have a changing role, [while] the function and place of a library remains the same" (79).

Mt. Angel's needs had been studied thoroughly by Fr. Barnabas; he had already spoken with the area's librarians and secured the consulting service of Carl Hintz, director of libraries at the University of Oregon. The proposal to Aalto was purposely vague, even as to the library's location, since one reason for approaching this famous architect was his reputation or, as Fr. Barnabas put it, "recognized competence with a landscape". By October 10, 1963 Aalto had reviewed the program and was preparing an "ideological" sketch which he intended to present to the chapter when he planned a return trip to America in April 1964. Meanwhile, communications were improved by securing the services of a Portland woman capable of translating Finnish; fortunately Aalto spoke colloquial English from his war days in the U.S., and he had an English-literate secretary. Moreover, upon taking on the Oregon project, he relied increasingly on a young Finnish-born American architect, Erik F. Vartiainen (b. 1936) who had been an intern in the Aalto firm and who had been a supervisor at its United Nations' project. He became the "on-site architect" at the Mt. Angel project after 1968, serving "as Aalto's sensitive antennae in preserving the obvious beauty and inherent humanism that typify Aalto architecture" (80).

Aalto did not make his projected April trip because of his European commitments and poor health in 1964, but a plan and layout were submitted for a library of about 44,100 square feet with forty study carrels, a stack capacity for 200,000 volumes, and a design for 550 users as specified. The plans were received by the librarians of the University of Oregon, Oregon State University, and the University of Portland, as well as the chapter. Some modifications were suggested. Vartiainen represented Aalto at the University of California and thereafter inspected the Mt. Angel site for his boss. Fr. Barnabas, reacting to pressure from the abbot and the community, was uneasy about Aalto's impersonal involvement and the delays required in getting him to take on the project. On July 18, 1965 the monk explained his position (81):

> There is a feeling of doubt and uncertainty among the monks here about effective action on the library building.... The delay... has now forced the community to begin intensive planning of the building program for the next seven to ten years without a definite picture of the library and classroom building in their relation to our finances and building dates....

After informing him that the monastery was able to proceed at once with the plans approved by the chapter (on May 29, 1964), Barnabas urged immediate action (82):

> ...we proceed as a family here in the monastery. We don't have hard and fast target dates with penalties, etc.. We have a preference for deliberate and thoughtful acting taking the time we need. [But] We are now in a rather painful need for solving our problems. The shortage of library facilities is seriously affecting our effectiveness... the uncertainty of effective action and an action date is causing the most unrest.... I cannot expect the monks seriously to depend on a few weeks really to be indeed a few weeks.... We need Mr. Aalto's help [Barnabas explained to Vartiainen]. Our site must have an architect worthy of its magnificance. We are desperately in need of a building designed with imagination and appreciation for the landscape. It would be a lasting shame to ruin one of nature's most beautiful monastic sites for want of a great architect.

With such diplomatic skill, Fr. Barnabas nudged the architect into action. In turn he minimized the Aalto firm's involvement in local squabbling about details, finances, and problems not absolutely necessary for the architect to resolve; in retrospect, Fr. Barnabas acted in anticipation of the architect's later remark, "I build, I do not talk. My building is my talking" (83) in reference to his dislike for local indecision and quarrels. When the library came into being, it was Fr. Barnabas who was described as the "midwife" officiating at its birth.

In 1965 development began to accelerate, largely because Aalto enlisted the aid of a colleague from MIT, Vernon De Mars, now a partner in a Berkeley, California, firm which agreed to act as onsite engineers and technical architects. On De Mars' advice when Fr. Barnabas visited the firm in early 1965, the monk set out for Europe to expedite matters: "the squeaky wheel gets the grease with Aalto... [who] reacts to people and personal contact. He is a warm personality with concern for persons rather than things" (84). He left on March 8 for a prearranged meeting in Zurich where Aalto was resting at his doctor's orders, and for a visit to the firm in Helsinki where Erik Vartiainen was in charge of executing Aalto's plans for Mt. Angel. There he inspected the model of the library placed on the hill's north side between the college and seminary. "They all agree in principle that the 'academic' side of the North (where the monastery is) should be a quiet side" (85). The library, far from a quiet retiring place, was thought of as a center for campus activity on the hill. At the same time, every precaution was being taken to take advantage of the site, both for the visiting motorist who wanted a "crow's nest type of vantage point" and for the contemplative scholar. Fr. Barnabas explained (86):

> ...this is how Aalto approaches the problem, and [this is] his thinking about the space in the building. A person entering the library will (on a clear day) see the most majestic element of overview, framed in the picture window of the browsing room. This will include the valley below and the Cascade Range crowned with Mt. Hood. Proceeding from this point, a person will enter a pleasant, controlled space with an emphasis on quiet and disengagement.

Fr. Barnabas personally liked that Aalto kept his buildings "light and cheerful," a feature well suited for Oregon's overcast rainy season. Aalto's own attitude toward nature is illustrated by his discovery that the planned location for the library would have required uprooting a small stand of Douglas fir on the hillside; the library was moved ten feet off-site to save the trees, especially one giant evergreen which Aalto wanted to frame his architectual creation (87).

By July 1966 all was ready to begin; the plans were finalized with Fr. Barnabas' continual prodding. The De Mars and Wells firm completed its surveying, and now with the assurance of the Vollum donation, bids were let. May 25, 1968 was set for beginning excavation and construction. The construction contract was awarded to F. H. Reimers and C. A. Jolivette, a Portland firm founded in a 1922 partnership which among other buildings had been responsible for three churchs and a convent in Portland, designed by the well-known architect, Pietro Belluschi. Contracts were let to San Francisco structural, mechanical, and electrical engineers, and 26 area businesses were used as sub-contracters and suppliers. The anticipated completion date was August 31, 1969 in time for use that fall term. Mr. and Mrs. Aalto, after he accepted the Jefferson Medal at the University of Virginia, flew to San Francisco in April 1967 to consult with De Mars, and then they arrived in Oregon on April 22. Their two-day visit was a media event which included meetings with many of the region's architects, planners, and art buffs. After unveiling his plans, Aalto discussed his architectural "humanities," explaining his often pronounced dictum: "True architecture is only to be found when man stands at the center" (88). He never fully comprehended how such an idea might clash with Christian humanism and the God-centered mileu of Benedictine monasticism, but nevertheless, his model and lecture made a lasting impression. Dr. Hintz, in anticipation of the building, remarked that "the library will quite possibly exert national influence in design of small college libraries" (89).

The plans had been detailed for the Mt. Angel community beforehand, on April 9, 1967 (90). The site would be on the north side of the hill overlooking the valley and area where the sisters' house had stood before the 1926 fire. The building was projected to encompass 33,000 square feet, at an estimated cost of $1,240,000 or about $28-30/sq. ft., some $4.00/sq. ft. more than a common building of similar space without the library's unique design and special features. It would seat 88, perhaps slightly more, at any one time: 25 at open desks, 30 in private research carrels, and 8 conference carrels. From May 9, 1964 to December 10, 1966 the master plan had been revised five times; the final plan of April 11th was executed. What was expected? Fr. Barnabas in his April library report to the community cited the text of Vatican Council II's decree, or the *Pastoral Constitution on the Church in the Modern World* (91), "...for those who question the community's selection of an externally famous architect in our cloistered corner of the world, and question it on spiritual grounds":

> Literature and the arts are also in their own way of great importance to the life of the Church.... Efforts must therefore be made so that those who practice these arts can feel that the Church gives recognition to them in their activities, and so that, enjoying an orderly freedom, they can establish smoother relations with the Christian community. Let the Church also acknowledge new forms of art which are adapted to our age and are in keeping with the characteristics of various nations and regions. May the faithful, therefore, live in very close union with the men of their time. Let them strive to understand perfectly their way of thinking and feeling, as expressed in their culture.

Fr. Barnabas, in addition to using Vatican II as a defense against his critics, adroitly cited another portion of the same constitution:

> Through a sharing of resources and points of view, let those who teach in seminaries, colleges, and universities, try to collaborate with men well versed in the other sciences [than religion]. Theological inquiry should seek a profound understanding of revealed truth without neglecting close contact with its own times. As a result, it will be able to help those men skilled in various fields of knowledge to gain a better understanding of the faith.

The librarian came back to this same theme in a subsequent interview in 1968 for the *Catholic Sentinel* (92): "All you have to do is look at the document of Vatican II... and see what it has to say about the proper development of culture...". He then explained:

> To a Benedictine monastery, and particularly one that incorporates a seminary, an adequate library is as indispensable as, say, a kitchen. Even more so, maybe. ...those things that are appreciated by the cultivated man are also appreciated by the Catholic Church and by those people who are involved with the training of priests for the modern world. We appreciate the beauty of architecture and design in principle; it is involved with our Catholicity, with our concept of man and our concept in the dignity of man.

This, in this monk-librarian's mind was justification for the library as more than a collection of books; he, and the whole Mt. Angel community, after Aalto's visit expected a genuine "work of art". It was to be a means to fulfill their monastic objectives (93): "We want very much to enter more fully into the intellectual and cultural life of the world around us".

The monastery paid the Aalto firm $18,000: $10,000 down and $8,000 upon completion. Judging from all subsequent reviews, it was money well spent. The library was completed one year behind schedule, but the wait was worthwhile. So was the increased cost, $1,272,000, or some $32,000 more than the originally projected figures. The three-level structure finally contained 44,000 square feet, with a book capacity of 75,000 in open stacks, and other stack areas for another 225,000 volumes or a 300,000 volume total. Counters were expanded likewise to seat sixty readers, and the main level contains forty study carrels. The main public area is broken by a suspended messanine level for reference and reserve books. The lower level is for book stacks, with a microform room in one wing, and an archives in the other. The entry level has a foyer with lavatories, and to the right a combination auditorium/exhibit hall used for lectures, recitals, and special events for which seating of 100 people is adequate. In Aalto's plans, this was the "Rare Book Room": so that in addition to a hidden audiovisual technician's booth there is also a storage vault for the library's treasures. To the left is an administrative wing consisting of the librarian's office with an adjacent secretarial office, a staff lounge, and a cataloguing room with easy access to the outside for delivery and to the interior bibliographic alcove and card catalogues. The inside main space is laminated by a pear-shaped combination reference and circulation desk under a unique skylight, from which a single librarian can view the entire main floor, the messanine, and can even peer down into the lower stack level. The position has been likened to that of a captain on the bridge of a ship. A periodical and current awareness or browsing room is to the right, and to the left past the bibliographic alcove was the original microfilm room which was subsequently converted to the Richard Fall's Rare Book Room. The basement level, still open and naturally lighted because of the library being built into the hillside, contains closed stacks for overstock and exchange operations, plus an insulated wing for the bindery.

The whole library is brightened by diffused, indirect light from the central round skylight and the larger half-circle skylight over the mezzanine which lets natural light drift downward to the second level, and by the band of windows which lets light radiate inward above the free-standing bookshelves. The walls are non-gloss white smooth plaster; the carpets are an earthtone grey; counters and furnishings (desks, chairs, and stools) are black leather or formica insets in natural birch, which match the birch-slat facade frontispieces on the shelving sections that radiate into their fan-shaped layout. Individual desk lamps are spaced along the counters, ceiling lights are recessed, and the carrels are all along the outer walls where light is plentiful. The natural wood motif is carried through the building and the use of strips breaking up the wave-formed wall in the auditorium and a strikingly simple oak backdrop which forms a discreet, canopied stage suitable for a lecture, a concert, or a Mass. All furnishings and decorative pieces, even details like the door knobs, were designed by Aalto and made by his firm, Artec Ltd., founded by the architect in 1935 to support his interior design work. The result is an utterly simply design, deceptive for the space provided with a feeling of comfortable enclosure befitting this monastic library. Its aesthetic appearance is almost more Cistercian than traditionally Benedictine, because of the overriding simplicity and natural forms. The library interior is almost bland, were it not for the color provided by the subtle use of wood and reliance on the bookbindings for accent.

The exterior is likewise natural sand-colored brick with dark brown trim, which allows the building despite its modern lines, to blend into the hillside with its dark green fir trees and in the summer, dry grassy slopes. The library is, as all critics have agreed, a remarkable facility. The Belgian critic for *Art d'Eglise*, Dom Frederic Debuyst, in an article carrying the opener, "The Benedictines are Not Dead," was capitivated by Mt. Angel: "...a setting with which only three or four monasteries in the Benedictine world could compare". In speaking about the "humanist organicism" of Aalto, he too remarked that the librarian's desk was stationed where "one could have the impression of being on the upper deck of a ship. For Aalto had fully exploited the levels of the ground". He continued:

> The library proper thus became a world of exploration and almost of adventure, where we rediscover the image of a ship, or rather of the voyage which carries us to the most distant regions of the world of knowledge. We are thus invited to enter into an immense spiritual abode, daringly offered for our research, where the soul can expand and deploy itself without

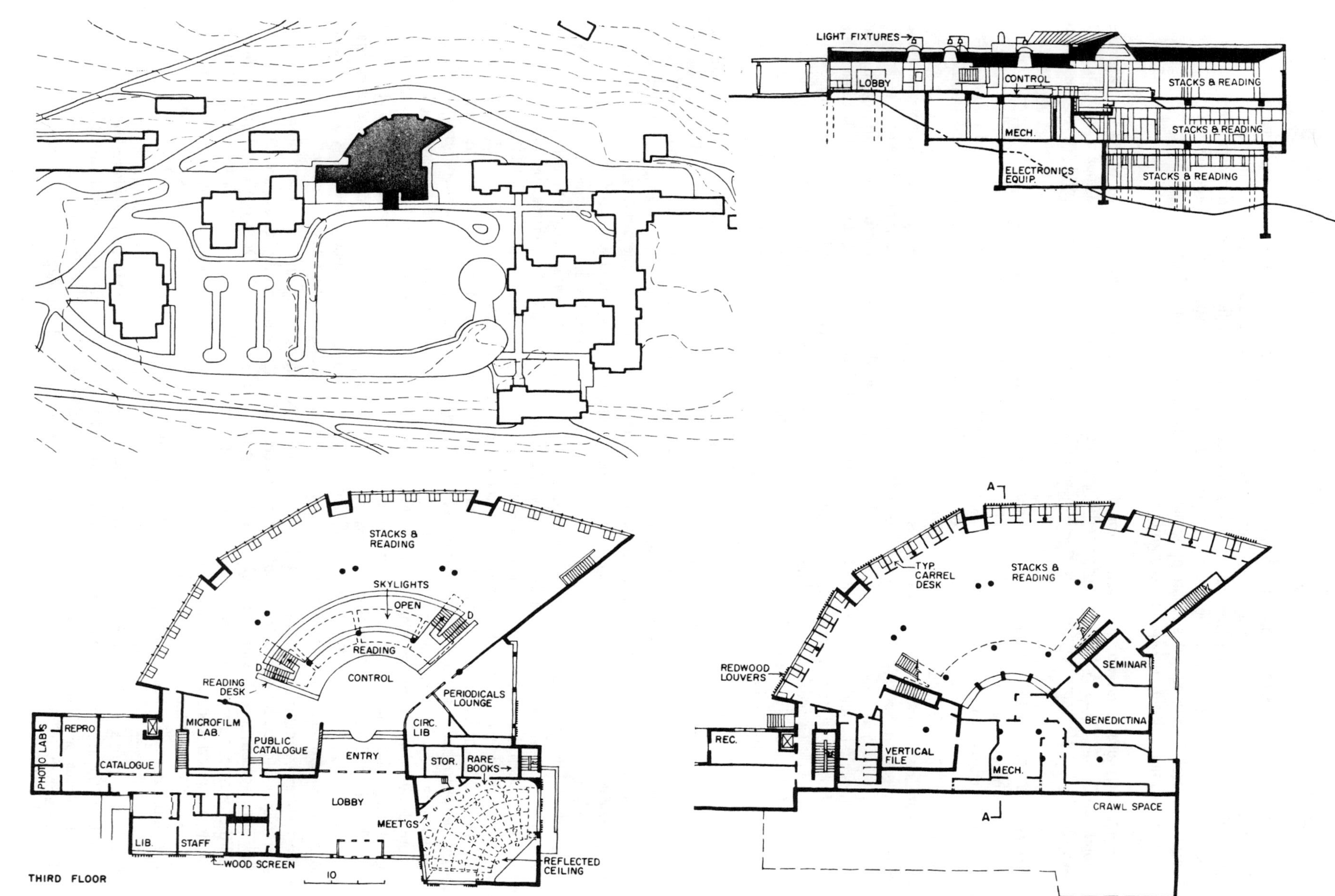

Fig. 16. Mt. Angel Abbey Library floorplans and horizontal perspective, and its location on the hilltop campus. Designed by Alvar Aalto (MAA, s.n.).

> fear of the depths above which it advances.
>
> But one must not push their symbolism too far. The essential is that we are here at the antipodes of the images to which our Western libraries have accustomed us: the neo-Greek monument in which enormous rows of shelves are crowded together without any organic link with the space that shelters them. Here the place and function are completely unified. It is the whole ensemble and detail which *is* the library, that is to say, a place for *people*, where a man for his greater job, can explore the world of books, live there, and derive from it the spiritual vigour he needs.
>
> ...the library of Mt. Angel is the culmination of a concentrated effort,... It is, above all, an absolute radical refusal of all mediocrity (94).

What praise! And in what sharp contrast this library stands to either the sterile warehouse environs of some libraries, the monumentary design of others, or the action-oriented but often thoughtless malaise of the modern information center.

Like so many others, Dom Debuyst thanked the monks of Mt. Angel for going "well beyond the sphere of their immediate needs. They have offered to the state of Oregon, and also to the Pacific coast of the United States, a unified and complete source of life, a dynamic [attraction], brimming with humanity and culture". The Pulitzer-prizc winning architectural critic for the *New York Times*, Ada Hustable, remarked (95): "Important architecture, unlike some important wines, can travel well. The new library of Mount Angel Abbey... brings a small and perfect work of the 73-year-old master of the modern movement, Alvar Aalto, to the United States".

The Mt. Angel community planned a lavish dedication celebration for the opening of the library, in contrast to the quiet ground-breaking ceremony which initiated construction. After all, this was the answer to a communal prayer for over four decades. Aalto was invited as the guest of honor, but he had to decline because of his constantly filled schedule and his failing health. Born on February 3, 1898, the architect was already 65 when he undertook the project, and meanwhile from age 67 on his health began to deteriorate. He would never see his Oregon library: Hugo Alvar Henrik Aalto died in his native Finland on May 11, 1976. There are as many posthumus tributes to him as there were awards during his lifetime. His architectural achievements were celebrated in April 16-17, 1971 at a conference hosted by Mt. Angel Abbey and again in 1979 by a traveling exhibit at the library sponsored by the Finnish government (96). A public program on June 28-29 brought architects together from throughout the West for a series of papers, discussions, the exhibit, and a tour of the library, and a chance to meet Mrs. Aalto, the guest of honor. Yet, there has been no more moving, truly Benedictine tribute to Alvar Aalto than the respect paid to his genius by Fr. Bernard Reasoner in a personal letter of encouragement dated March 16, 1965, addressed to Aalto himself after a major illness (97):

> I will ask Fr. Abbot to request the prayers of the monks that God grant you more years of creative activity. God must have a very special place in His heart for those who make it their business to understand the principles of beauty which He has laid down. Man has done so much to disfigure and squander the beauty God has brought to our lives. One who loves beauty, searches for its principles and exercises living care and reverence in those things he fashions, must find himself very close at times to the Eternal Beauty Who has placed His imprint upon all He has created.
>
> May God preserve you many years that you may design buildings which have reverence for a landscape and excite reverence in the beholder.

The Mt. Angel Abbey library was dedicated on May 29-31, 1970. It was a grand occasion! Guests were received by an impressive lineup: Abbot Damian Jentges, who was elated at the culmination of more than a decade of work, played host; Governor Thomas McCall of Oregon and his wife, with Congresswoman Edith Green; Abp. Dwyer of Portland and Abbot Primate Rembert Weakland, OSB; Mr. and Mrs. Vernon De Mars, representing the architects and builders; the artist Duke Ellington and vocalist Ann Henry who would provide the opening concert; and finally, librarian Barnabas Reasoner. The dedication opened with the Duke Ellington concert in the library itself; that, if nothing more, was symbolic of the ethos pervading this dedication and of the modern use for which this library was intended. The 71-year-old "king of jazz" featured his lead singer, Ann Henry, in another of his "musical sermons," including a premier performance of "Pockets [of Love]" composed by Ms Henry. The open house on Saturday sponsored by the American Institute of Architects was intended to give area designers a chance to meet Aalto, but they were instead provided with a detailed tour of the library by representatives of the Aalto firm, De Mars and Wells, and the contractors. After a concert by the Portland Junior Symphony under the direction of Jacob Avshalomov, there was the lecture in the abbey church by Sir Richard Southern, a noted medievalist from Oxford University, entitled "A Benedictine Library in a Disordered World" (see the following text) in which he suggested a motto for the library might be taken from the library and editorial work of the eighteenth-century Maurist Benedictines: *Ex arduis, Pax et*

Amor (Peace and Love Come from Labor). On Sunday, after a concelebrated High Mass, there was another concert of church music by the Lewis and Clark choir under L. Stanley Glarum, director and composer, and of Gregorian chant by the Mt. Angel schola under Dom David Nicholson, OSB, of Mt. Angel. One of the choir's selections was a composition of Dr. Glarum, and another combined presentation by choir and schola, Darius Milhaud's *The Three Psalms*, was dedicated to Dom David whose work in plainchant and polyphony is widely known. Following was the keynote address of the abbot primate, Rembert George Weakland, the first American to lead the 12,000 member world-wide Order of St. Benedict, and an accomplished musician and liturgist in his own right. Thereafter Abp. Robert J. Dwyer of Portland, a canonist and bibliophile who subsequently bequeathed his personal 6000-volume library to Mt. Angel's library, led a procession of diocesan clergy, the monastic community, and the several hundred visitors and dignitaries, from the church to the library where the formal dedication finalized the three-day celebration. There Rabbi Emanuel Rose of Temple Beth Israel made a presentation of books on Judaism to the library, symbolic of the library's intended eucumenism and cultural service to all faiths in the area. Finland's ambassador, Olavi Munkki, extended his country's greetings, and then the archbishop officiated at the formal blessing. His benediction for the faithful echoed the sentiment of all and brought back remembrances of the long struggle of the community to play its part in the Benedictine tradition of library development (98):

> God, Lord of all Wisdom, pour out your blessing on this library. Let it safely withstand fire and every peril, and let it increase its volumes day by day. May all who come here for work or for study grow in the knowledge of things human and divine, and grow likewise in their love of You; through Christ our Lord. Amen.

The Modern Library: A Continuing Tradition, 1970-82

Fr. Barnabas, in the tone of traditional apologetics, became unwittingly a spokesman for the Mt. Angel community, presenting a modern statement not only about monasticism in the modern world, but more especially, the place of a Benedictine library in this world. His commentaries to the press contain, if not a coherent philosophy, an articulated ideal underlying the convictions and actions of the Mt. Angel monks which makes them continuators of a great tradition.

In reflecting on how the Mt. Angel library project blossomed from a practical notion about a modest extension for increased book storage, to a vision encompassing so much more, a Benedictine library *per se,* required considerable sacrifice even with outside patronage. In a 1968 interview, Fr. Barnabas tried to explain what had happened (99):

> The Council [Vatican II] states that we are living in the twentieth century, and that we have to be involved with men of the twentieth century and with the ideas of the twentieth century.
>
> Monks in the Middle Ages had an appreciation of arts and crafts and were their greatest exponents,... they were the ones who trained our ancestors and gave them an appreciation of civilization. We [Benedictines] in the twentieth century still are working on the same basic principles of the value of the world that God has created and of man as the one who tends Creation.
>
> Man in his own way uses the talents and abilities God has given him, sees the beauty around him, and makes a statement about the world around him—in his own age, in his own way, and with his own materials.

The reporter, Fritz Meagher, rightly concluded from these remarks: "For the monks of Mt. Angel, the new library will be this statement".

Indeed, by building a library larger than the community's immediate needs, or those of the seminary, the Benedictines hoped to make a lasting, viable contribution to the cultural life of the valley and to make this monastery a center of Catholic culture.

> We have... a place in the area where people can... get information on what's happening... what's happening in the Church after the council. The expanded library facilities, with room for making available all the manuscripts, documents, and books now in the abbey's possession and providing space for adding new books as they pour off the presses, will enable not only the seminarians and monks, but all interested persons in the community to keep abreast of theological developments and to probe more meaningfully into the controversial past.

"The library, too, will be an intellectual fountainhead for Catholic students; the monks forecast" reported one newspaper, especially lay theologians, or those involved in the Confraternity of Christian Doctrine programs, revival of the deaconate and lay ministry, and the general reform. The eucumenism of the post-Vatican II era encouraged the welcomed use of this library by non-Catholics as well; indeed, since 1967 the abbey began hosting Protestant retreats and conferences of such inter-denominational groups as the Mid-Willamette Ministerial Association. In that sense, the library and the community's outreach, were intended as healing remedies for past divisions and non-cooperation among Christians.

The library was seen as a valuable resource, but not a dynamic information center in keeping with the recent movements in modern library and information science. Instead of extending itself into an area of activity and actively assuming an advocacy position more concrete than its general Catholicity, or in disseminating information alone without the other accoutrements of knowledge, this library was seen as a center attracting area patrons to it, offering and inviting, but not coercing or propagandizing. Moreover, the information sought therein was not merely data which was readily transferable as distinct units, but rather the kind of sophisticated reading and broad cultural research requiring careful thought, meditation, and the integration of knowledge from its diverse branches. This atmosphere of traditional Benedictine hospitality combined with an ambiance for reflection upon texts and penetrating thought, was in keeping with its larger monastic context. As a "center for study" rather than merely an "information center" this library would also be, as Fr. Boniface Lautz, rector of the seminary hoped in 1968, a place for "dialogue," meaning that people were to be brought together here. The communication contemplated was more than a passing of news, an assimilation of data, or even a contemporary dialogue with one's colleagues, but with one's heritage in the past and understanding of it as it is being lived at present. Fr. Boniface thought "men [will] want to come here because they have the surroundings, the atmosphere of prayer and meditation, because they want to get away from it all" (100).

How ironic, that this community in its attempt to 'go modern' established a library that was conceived as an institution first, a service second, and then an all-comprehensive domicile of the mind, but without any well-defined program for action. Even the projected clientele seemed diffuse. To the modern information scientist, the abbey library might be considered a throwback still shackled with the book-museum syndrome the monks so desperately tried to escape. The ideology underlying its purpose, expected performance, and ultimate effect, could not have been more adverse to the new librarianship of the 1970-80s which was sought reform of the library world at the same time, by thrusting libraries into the midst of action and converting them to businesses offering cost-effective information storage and retrieval for specific clientele. In this modern librarianship, about which nothing was known at Mt. Angel, there is little of the humanistic philosophy, mission complex, or cultural ethics, which the abbey library came to represent. It would be another decade before this library would enter the world of automation; it has never engaged the issues or activities of information science. Indeed, from the latter perspective, this library may well fulfill the needs of the twentieth century just as time marches into the twenty-first. So much more would need to be done. But then, perhaps the problem here is the mistaken notions in library science which confuse data for knowledge, technology for progress, and motion for productive activity. Certainly library science literature has stopped paying lipservice to the core ethic that a library is to help "in the search for truth," as Fr. Bernard Sander hoped it would do (101). Nor would information scientists readily understand what he was talking about when his students could "sense the spirit of inquiry and meditative reflection which such a facility will promote". The monks themselves in their seeking out Alvar Aalto to design a modern library demonstrated their dedication to a "modernistic approach," but their remarks reveal an all pervasive attitude that what they really sought was a timeless library. In sharp contrast to the modern secular thinking about libraries, their thinking was particularly Benedictine. To be modern, a library need not be secular.

It was Abbot Damian who tried to capture the spiritual meaning of the library, even though he talked in concrete terms with reference to the modern world and in an administrator's language which managers of all types could understand (102):

> My feeling about the library is that it is essential to the care of an educational institution. After all, we are engaged in intellectual formation, and a faculty cannot operate without a background of research information.
>
> Other disciplines are becoming more knowledgeable about their professions. Priests too, must be more knowing about the spiritual. We have to have priests who are more heaven wise.

For this purpose, a library was built: "...the creative act they [the monks] find vital to the culture of our generation...". Indeed, the monks felt it to be vital to any generation, as illustrated by the monks' allusion to the influence of the arts school at Maria Laach in Andernack, where several of the American Benedictines had studied. One could just as easily have pointed to the Sant' Anselmo, Beuron, Engelberg itself, or any of the links in a cultural chain reaching back to the origin of Western Civilization. A library, fundamental in the process of intellectual formation, was a tool for spiritualization, and hence, even of salvation.

In expectation that the library would enter the electronic and multi-media era, the new library was equipped for the use of video and television in the lecture hall, and conduits and wiring was installed so that later computers could be utilized throughout the library with only minor alterations. Untimately the library joined the Pacific Northwest Bibliographical Center, and in 1981 it also joined OCLC (Ohio College Library Consortium) to benefit from automated cataloguing and citation service from this large bibliographic utility. However, the need to rush into the electronic age has never been as acute at Mt. Angel as in larger institutions where automation is partially answer to high-volume impersonal education, to the control of increased mass in library collections, and to inflation and rising labor costs. At Mt. Angel, the most humanistic attribute of the education process is intensive human contact and personalized attention. Consequently, technical services adopted automation to economize bibliographical control operations, but online reference service, information systems for teaching support, and other novelties of the 1970s have not yet been required. The emphasis is still on a contemplative search, research, and digestion of text, and the traditional codex remains predominant there.

When the new library opened, it contained 46,770 catalogued volumes—the cumulative efforts of cataloguers since 1952 to convert to AACR standards. There were still another 30,000 volumes in backlog, and the staffing limitations remained a constraining factor on innovative service or in rapid solutions to the control problems. Classification was the expanded version of the Library of Congress system modified by the so-called Lynn-Peterson (named after the revision's chief architects) "alternative classification" for Catholic libraries. This means that most books are classified and shelved as in the L.C. system, except those falling into the religion schedules; these are modified to accomodate the "special collection" strength within the general collection. Basically, the schedules were expanded, the subject access conformed to terminology use within the Church (often Latin based, despite the Church's move away from Latin as a universal language), so that one could have even more precise intellectual control and item access than provided by the Library of Congress.

The new library remained open seven days a week except for specified holidays and Christmas vacation, until 10 P.M. and on Saturdays during daytime. Special Collections could be used only during daytime hours, when professional reference staff was available. This schedule has remained fairly unaltered to the present. Staffing remains small, but perhaps not out of proportion to its select and relatively small clientele. In addition to the librarian and his two clerical assistants, there was the reference librarian and his or her assistant, and the technical service personnel and student assistants. These three functions, reference, technical support services, and general administration, were managed directly by the librarian who in addition cared for a Friends of the Library Association. In turn, the librarian reported to the abbot who was both president of the Board of Trustees and chancellor of the seminary. Overall library policy and budget control rested in his office. In addition to the librarian, the abbot relied on a governing committee representing the interests of the community, the College, and the Graduate School of Theology. The latter committee and the library director relied on input from an advisory subcommittee for library services consisting of seven members: one faculty representative; two students, one each from the College and Graduate School; two members of the library staff appointed by the library director; and an elected member of the community. In short, the library was well integrated into the structure of the monastery itself rather than being an adjunct institution or a semi-autonomous auxiliary support service. It took its direction from the community's service roles and the schools' curricula, received broad input from all constituents, and in many ways dissolved the standard distinctions between client and patron. The Benedictines today, as during centuries past, continue to perform "penance" by library work (as distinct from doing one's own work in a library) and then change roles as users to reap the benefits of their own labors. This solid integration into the administrative structure of the abbey, close association of the library with the lifestyle of the Benedictines, and the recriprocity of the users providing service in order to be served, mark this library as peculiarly monastic.

During the decade of the 1970s Fr. Leo Rimmele, OSB, who took his MLS degree from the University of Southern California in 1974, replaced Fr. Barnabas Reasoner as librarian. The latter, after years of service, took a temporary leave from the community. Fr. Leo was also a military chaplain in demand after the Vietnam War, so he was not always in residence at Mt. Angel, nor was librarianship his major interest. Consequently the forementioned library committees played increasingly active roles in library work, more than merely advisory roles. The staff was augmented by another professional librarian, but at the end of the decade budget cuts forced a RIF (reduction-in-force), before this term was so hallowed by the Reagon administration. Sister Theresa Eberle of Queen of the Angel's Convent took charge of the circulation desk, Mrs. Mary Jarvie served as administrative secretary until her recent retirement. She was replaced by Darlene Strand, formerly technical services assistant. A professional librarian, Patricia Ann Haymaker, then took over technical services. The technical and clerical support staff is augmented annually by a half-dozen juniors who contribute many hours to library work. During this interim of committee governance, Fr. Bonaventure Zerr, then prior and now ruling abbot, became active in daily selection and acquisitions work. Collection development was boosted by a $100,000 gift to the seminary. When the rector, Rev. James Riddle announced the bequest, he specified that a high priority was "maintaining and supplementing the book collections and periodicals of the library, as well as better binding equipment" (103). Responsibility for Special Collections fell to Fr. Martin Pollard, and he was assisted for a time by an experienced archivist, Br. Michael Davis, a postulant from Boise State University, in the task of preparing finding aids for the recent acquisitions of the Vatican library microfilms, nearly 100,000 volumes, from the Knights of Columbus project at the University of St. Louis. Fr. Leo returned as acting director in the 1981-82, while Fr. Bede Partridge completed his library degree at Rosary College, presumably in preparation as the next library director. The collections themselves have continued to grow despite shifts in the abbey's income caused by changes in federal tax laws, continued financial constraints, pressing demands from other competing needs, and the toll of inflation which has more than doubled the cost of academic books over the last decade. The acquisition budget has grown annually, and in 1981 crested at the $80,000 mark. In addition, there have been several more donations, the largest being nearly 6000 volumes in the personal library of the late Abp. Dwyer who had earlier blessed the new library building. A second significant donation was made by William R. Duggan. The St. Louis microfilm collection was a gift from the bishop of Yakima, Washington. And there was a continuous trickle of smaller donations, mostly collections under 30 volumes, but which have included imprints from the sixteenth through nineteenth centuries and a papal bull for special collections. Many of the gifts are integrated into the general collection, and those not pulled into Special Collections go into overstock for exchange or sale. In 1981-82 the overstock in the basement level, perhaps 40,000 volumes, was systematically weeded by Fr. Hugh Feiss, for volumes suited for the permanent collection. The same bookstock had been weeded previously by Mr. Portal and the catalogue project director for pre-1825 imprints and remnants of the Aachen purchase. One of the largest single purchase came in 1979 when the Jesuit house of studies near Sheridan, Oregon, was closed; Fr. Hugh Feis reportedly spent over $4,000 for acquisitions from this Jesuit library (104). Consequently, through gifts and exchange, an active solicitation campaign (indeed, many volumes come to Mt. Angel voluntarily without asking), and item selection and special purchases, the collection continued to develop.

The library's budget today illustrates the impact of double-diget inflation on a small college, but also demonstrates the long-range commitment of Mt. Angel to a quality library. The 1981-82 fiscal budget was $220,684, not counting indirect costs (overhead such as utilities, building depreciation, space, etc., which in many institutions ranges from 48-95% of direct costs), or the contributed efforts of the monks themselves in time and service to the library. The Seminary's 1980-81 *Annual Report* indicated that the participating dioceses contributed $30,000 a year for library support of the seminary's programs, or 3.5% of the seminary's educational expenditures. The Seminary's subsidy accounts for only 13% of the library's direct-cost budget. The 'abbey library' is just that, largely the enterprise of the monks, operated at no small cost to the community. This is especially true when one contemplates the relatively small user population of the community and its schools. *Per capita* library expenditures run about $450/user, an extraordinarily high support level when compared to much larger academic libraries with large university user populations. The library is used intensely by some, casually by others, and continually by a steady flow of readers; but it is nevertheless underused when taking into account the library's capacity and total financial outlay. If continued services were considered in addition to direct costs plus indirect costs figured at a modest 50% (of an estimated $250,000/year direct costs), the expenditure per user would increase to $750. Much of the use is inhouse only, but the same calculation compared to circulation statistics (about 7000 volumes/year) reveals that current costs run about $55 per circulation record. Because the library has a resident clientele, such figures are somewhat misleading. However, these estimates place into perspective the great effort required to sustain such a good library by a relatively small community. This too makes the abbey library a remarkable institution.

Monastic libraries share many common characteristics with other libraries, including parallel histories. Libraries are highly artificial, sophisticated cultural endeavors requiring sustained effort and support; their welfare depends on the health of the parent organization. All have periods of growth, development, and decline, and none are immune to natural calamity as the disastrous fires suffered by Mt. Angel attest. Equally common is the sporadic documentation in library and archival history for all types of institutions; they tend to document the culture they serve and preserve, and often record inadequately their own history. It is not surprising, therefore, that only a sketch of Mt. Angel's library history could be assembled, especially in view of the library's destruction in 1892 and 1926, the unsystematic archives and records management through the years, and the understandable restrictions on access to extant documentation in the abbey's 'secret' archives. On the contrary, the very fact that this survey was possible may be special, and this history becomes even more unique when one realizes how little is known about modern monastic libraries. The greatest amount of scholarly emphasis on monastic institutions has been on libraries long gone. That is unfortunate, since writing about a library tradition and depicting a stage in its evolution is much like writing family history instead of focusing on the individual as in biography. The past obtains its relevance in the present; extinct libraries are interesting because libraries are part of our cultural life today. Yet, to the average American surely the subject of monastic libraries conjures up immediate images of medieval scribes, old books, and places resembling childhood recollections of castle keeps. Certainly monastic libraries are thought to be 'Old World' species, with little relevance to modern, technologically advanced, American life. Yet, as this study shows, the tradition of monastic libraries lives on and finds a comfortable environment within its modern context. Finally, it is doubtful that the ongoing contributions of such religious libraries to Western culture and the process of civilization itself are known, even less understood.

The history of the Mt. Angel Abbey library was presented here to counter those commonplace tendencies to ignore the history around us, and to illustrate the essential continuity in this great Benedictine tradition. It certainly depicts the immanence of the 'Old World' in the 'New' and provides a necessary prologue to the following catalogue.

Obviously this library does not rank as one of the great American shrines of the book; it does not stand out because of its great age, monumental size, lauded accomplishments, or by having great men associated with it. Rather, its history takes on significance as an extension of an age-old tradition, within the greater context of monastic history in general and in particular the corporate biography of the Mt. Angel community. This historical sketch, therefore, is offered as a modest contribution on an interesting subject, an otherwise unknown phenomenon in American cultural history.

Note how library history and monastic history are alike in that the whole must be studied as a sum of its parts. Libraries are made of library collections, which in turn are aggregates of books; yet historical bibliography is not library history. Likewise, biographies of monks cannot by themselves constitute the history of a monastic community, anymore than a portrait of abbots as prelates in long succession reveals much about the nature of a monastery or of the Church of which it is a part. The lasting impression may be the pectoral cross worn by each in succession, rather than their individuality; the office effectively cloaks the person and pictures instead the legal, official person. Similarly in monastic history, the monk individually counts so little; his *corpus* is the fabric of the corporation, and his documented personality is sublimated to that of the community as a whole. Yet, corporations, like individuals, leave traces in the course of their lives from their residual activities. These sometimes can be telling, as in the case of past libraries providing some recollection of monastic communities long since gone but which form basic components in the history of the Order. The history of the Mt. Angel Abbey library mirrors the history of the community itself, and *vice versa* the ideals of the community are reflected in its library. The library as a whole, as a century-long effort, represents a monastic ideal, a communal commitment, and a living tradition.

Perhaps less abstractly, there is throughout this story an underlying 'philosophy of librarianship' in the spirit shared by Ortega y Gasset, Archibald MacLeish, and other visionaries who could see in a library much more than a conglomerate of books, and in learning something far more subtle and pervasive than data transfer. This ideal is expressed admirably by the monks of Mt. Angel themselves in their presentation of the library to prospective students and seminarians in their recent catalogues (105):

> A library is an important extension of a monastery. It plays a special role in the Benedictine vision of education. In the Mount Angel schools the library stands at the very center of our learning task. Reading is one of the real cornerstones of learning, reading broadly and well. We think that our library is a place where a person can learn the fine art of reading.
>
> We are fortunate to be heirs of a very long and great tradition of Benedictine libraries. From this tradition we gain certain convictions about what a library ought to be. First of all, we believe that a library must be a place of peace and a place that gives certain visual delight. The physical apperarance of a libary should reflect its role as a source of liberty and refreshment. Our library, designed by the world-renowned architect Alvar Aalto, is a symbol of peace and refreshment. It houses with reverence over 100,000 volumes. It is a space which makes one want to sit and read.
>
> The collection is strong in a number of areas. In general, of course, its concentration is theological. In this field it has strengths in sacred scripture and systematic theology. But we are also convinced that a good theological library must also be strong in philosophy and the humanities. Ours is. The library also subscribes to nearly 600 different periodicals, brings students into contact with the most recent thinking in theology, scripture, philosophy, and the humanities. We believe that the first condition for a library's survival is the necessity of keeping its books in use. A collection must be used as a whole if it is to have its full effect. We want our library to be used by many people, not only by the students or only by the monks. We are gathering together many resources for a number of different kinds of work. We hope that people will come and read. We do not wish merely to be preserving books, however. We hope that research in our library can stimulate the production of books which must still be written, that gaps in thinking can be bridged, and that new combinations of thought can occur through the use of this collection. The library at Mount Angel is available to students in all of the schools' programs. Guests of the monastery are likewise free to use the library. But also, students from any place and of any age are more than welcome to use our library. We hope especially by this collection to serve the needs of continuing education among priests and other ministers in the Church. We believe that our library can be a center for learned activity, a place where systematic and well-directed work is done. Our hope for the users of this library is that with these resources and in this atmosphere they may work toward gaining a comprehensive and unbiased understanding of the Christian tradition in all its branches. This is the understanding which can lead to service and to praise.

A Benedictine Library in a Disordered World

Sir Richard Southern
President, St. John's College, Oxford

I

We have come together from all parts of the world to give what help we can to consecrate a new library. And it may well be asked whether a new library is the kind of response to the disorders of the world in which we live that we can confidently applaud. What the world needs, it may be said, is right action, and a library is an invitation to inactivity. Moreover, the things of most immediate concern to mankind at present lie in the towns, the slums, and the overcrowded countryside of many parts of the world; and a library demands seclusion, leisure, and some quite high degree of amenity, and even splendor, its purposes are to be fulfilled. Superficially it would appear that, of all the possible cures of the world's ills, a library is the least likely to provide a source of healing, and we must begin by asking in what sense and by what means the library we have come here to consecrate may hope to contribute to the healing of the world's ills.

The value of what we are doing today will only become apparent in thirty or perhaps fifty years' time; but instead of attempting to peer so far into the future, I propose to look at the past and see whether it provides any grounds for confidence in the kind of institution we are helping to bring into being, and any hints for its guidance in the future. I shall try to place our actions today, and the action of our benefactor, and of the community on which the whole success or failure of the enterprise must rest, in their historical perspective, by asking what contribution libraries, and more especially Benedictine libraries, have made in the past toward overcoming the disorders of the world.

It is an important qualification that the library we have come together to consecrate is not just another library: it is a Benedictine library. What is special about this? What difference does it make? All libraries exist for the same general purpose of the conservation of inherited spiritual resources, and for making these resources readily available to those who seek them. All libraries demand the same steady dedication of self-effacing men and women to the task of putting other people's works in the best possibly light and giving them to the world. They all require unremitting labor, humble and ill-rewarded in the scale of worldly things, yet calling for refined talents and careful training for their performance. These are virtues which are found in the world as well as in monasteries. They are rare indeed, but no great library could long continue without them. Yet the Benedictine Order may justly claim (or rather it may not claim this, but we can do so on its behalf) that humble, patient, ill-rewarded and highly skilled labor is its special contribution to the world. As an Order it seeks no esoteric virtue, but only in their highest form those virtues that are, or can be, common to all mankind. The defenders of Benedictine life in the Middle Ages used to say that the Rule of St. Benedict was not a special form of Christian life, but simply the whole Gospel distilled into a simple rule of life. Similarly as a first approximation we may say that a Benedictine library is not a special kind of library, but simply a library that concentrates in itself all the virtues that libraries should have. We shall have later to refine this definition, but first let us try to see some monastic libraries of the past in action.

In this inquiry we have a starting point which stands before us as clearly as any event in ancient history. If we take our stand in Italy at the moment of the most conspicuous collapse in ancient civilization, about the middle of the sixth century, we find a situation about as dismal for the prospects of civilization as any in recorded history. The country was torn by competing invaders—Goths, Lombards, and Byzantine armies—who differed in their claims and aims, but not at all in the destruction of social life and institutions that their military operations brought in their train. In this desolation three men stand out who took an effective stand against the decay of the world around them: St. Benedict, Boethius, and Cassiodorus. They were all men who by birth and upbringing belonged to the ancient world, but they gave different answers to the problem of the growing chaos around them. It is tempting to linger over each of them and to show how in different ways they became the founding fathers of our modern civilization, but it is only on the last and least well-known of these figures that we have time to dwell.

Cassiodorus was born a few years after the formal disappearance of the Roman Empire in the West, probably in 485. It was only after a long experience of the world that he had the idea that the foundation of a library was the best remedy for the multiple evils of his day. It was not a conclusion that he came to easily or willingly. During most of his life Cassiodorus had been one of those men who think that they can best preserve the values and institutions they revere by serving the barbarians who are destroying them. To civilize by serving is a plausible ideal, and it is one to which many men have felt called. Cassiodorus pursued it for nearly forty years: from 506 to 538 he persisted in his efforts to civilize the Goths by seeking a place at the center of their administration. He was richly rewarded. He climbed almost to the top in the Gothic administration, which still preserved a shadow of the Roman hierarchy. At his peak in 538 he was given the honorific title *Patricius* and he could look back on a long career of almost unbroken success during a time of the breaking of nations. Of course, no man can succeed in such a situation without closing his eyes to a good many things. Cassiodorus was a Catholic Christian serving an Arian ruler, and some of those in his position had been dismayed when Boethius and other Roman aristocrats in the administration had been arrested and executed in 523. Cassiodorus must have felt the shock, but these were events that he never mentioned and he was not deflected from his course; he simply rose higher in the royal service and stepped into the shoes that Boethius had forcibly vacated. Although he persisted, he was not satisfied. Despite all his attempts to teach his barbarian masters the ways of civilized Romans by writing for them model letters in correct Latin and by interlacing his correspondence and speeches with the flowers of ancient wisdom, it was clear that, intellectually as well as politically, things were getting worse from year to year. He had the idea that a university—a Christian university in Rome—might be an answer to the problem, and he tried to interest the Pope in the idea. Rome, however, was captured by the Byzantine army and the idea came to nothing.

So things might have remained till the end of his life. In 538 Cassiodorus was already quite an old man. He was loaded with honors, but he was out of office and he could scarcely hope to climb higher in his profession. He put together his official correspondence and turned his mind to the problem of the soul. The secret of an effective stand against barbarism still eluded him. Then, by a turn of events that Cassiodorus had resisted all of his life, the way to a solution was opened. The Gothic kingdom that he had served so long was destroyed by the invading army of the Emperor Justinian. As a result of this disaster, the Gothic court was transported into exile to Constantinople and Cassiodorus was among the exiles. Here he lived a life of religious retirement, and it was not until 555 that he and the other exiles were permitted to return to Italy. Cassiodorus was now seventy years old. Externally his career was at an end. To the world it must have seemed that a decayed and discredited careerist was returning to settle on his family property on the southern coast of Italy near Squillace. But it was now, at the end of his life, with his career in ruins and the whole ideal to which he had devoted his life finally exploded, that he had the idea to which he owes all his claim to our regard. He set about the task of collecting a library and gathering round it a community of monks to help in the varied tasks of building, copying, translating, arranging, and preserving. At last he had found work for which he was perfectly equipped. He was rich and learned; his years in government and exile had made him familiar with the world, and his disappointments had made him patient and indifferent to the world's rewards; he loved the cool waters of his family property, and he called his monastery *Vivarium* after the fishponds which he constructed with great elaboration in the creeks flowing to the sea—they seemed to him a symbol of the sheltered freedom of monastic life. It was in this seclusion that he set about teaching his monks, and through them the future, the elements of the Christian and pagan learning which was threatened with destruction.

The works which Cassiodorus wrote to explain to his monks the contents of the library, the principles on which it had been selected, and the purpose for which it could be used, is one of the great books of the Middle Ages. It served as a model for the makers and users of libraries until the end of the twelfth century, and it provided a guide to the fundamental studies of the early Middle Ages. It is the first library catalogue in Western history; but it is much more than this. It is the work of a man who loved books and was familiar with all the problems of finding the right books, arranging them in the right way, and making them accessible—by translation if necessary—to their potential users. His book gives us an extraordinarily vivid sense of being *there* in southern Italy with the world collapsing about our ears; it conveys a a sense of the physical presence of the books, whether they are on papyrus or parchment, whether they are large or small, how they are divided into volumes, and how they are disposed on the shelves. After a long career of sterile service, here at last Cassiodorus could employ his mind on the things that he understood.

He understood everything about books, not least the need for clarity and accuracy in their text, and the necessity for keeping the books in use, which is the first condition of a library's survival. He understood that a library exists not only to preserve the books that exist, but to stimulate the production of new books that still need to be written: his research revealed the gaps that still existed in Christian literature, and he himself set about filling some of them with works which became part of the necessary reading of succeeding centuries.

He understood too that a library must be a place of peace and of a certain visual delight, and he thought that the physical appearance of the place should reflect the role of the library as a source of refreshment and liberty within a confined space. Although his whole aim in founding the monastery and gathering together the library was to combat the growing chaos of the world, yet he forgot the strife and disorder around him when he wrote about his books. A large comprehension of Greek and Latin, an equal understanding of great questions and trivial details, pervade his latest writings. Nothing is too small for his attention when he writes about the instrument he has devised to overthrow the powers and confusions of the world. Then, having succeeded in creating the peace of a working library, he was content to let it make its way in the world without anxiety.

Perhaps, if he had known what was to be the fate of his library and monastery, he would have been more anxious; but he would have been wrong. On the face of it everything turned out as badly as could be imagined. Cassiodorus died about 582 in extreme old age, and his library did not long survive his death. Within a hundred years it had vanished from the earth, and even its site was only fairly recently discovered after a prolonged search. A few fragments of stone remain to mark the place where it stood. No single volume from his collection has survived, and few people can have read his books in a library designed to support a falling civilization. Must we then say that the whole effort was a failure? I think not. In the first place, Cassiodorus's account of his books continued to influence the world for centuries after his death. Secondly, although his library disappeared and its books have vanished, at least one of them, and possibly more, came into the hands of a man who understood what Cassiodorus had tried to do, and, consciously or unconsciously, followed his example.

II

It is to this man and his library that we must now turn our attention. He was an English nobleman from the North—a man wholly unlike Cassiodorus in background, culture, and outlook, yet like him a man who spent all his resources on founding a library and a monastic community: Benedict Biscop.

Cassiodorus had been a man of Greco-Roman origin and culture, attempting to stem a rising tide of barbarism. Benedict Biscop was one of the barbarians, born 150 years after Cassiodorus, when the barbarian grip on Europe was complete. In his youth he was a member of a Germanic war band in a part of Europe that had never been more than superficially Romanized. He was a second-generation Christian—only just, for his parents cannot have been baptized until about the year in which he was born, when the Roman missionary Paulinus baptized the royal house and a large part of the nobility of Northumbria. Biscop can have had none of the elaborate education of Cassiodorus. Until he was about twenty-five, he lived the rough life of a member of a band of military toughs. Then, when the time came for him to be rewarded with land and to settle down to found a family, he withdrew from the world and gave himself up to the study and practice of the monastic life. This was not an unusual step to take, but what marked Biscop out from all other converts to monasticism in his day was his passion for books. Among the barbarian peoples of Europe he was the first great collector of books and pictures, and he sought them where they were best to be found among the desolate remains of ancient civilization in Italy. His biographer speaks of his burning desire to visit the tombs of the Apostles in Rome, and in the thirty years after his conversion he paid no less that six visits to Rome. This was more than any other man of his age, and it shows a certain obsession with the ancient Christian past. From these visits he brought back (in the words of Bede) "an innumberable collection of books of every kind". By our standards indeed the collection was not very large—perhaps three hundred volumes or thereabouts. Still, by the standards of the early Middle Ages, it was a very large library, and it contained some wonderful books—among them a great Bible, the very volume which Cassiodorus arranged and described with special care, a fundamental volume in his organization of the library at Vivarium. More important, the books which Biscop collected contained everything that was necessary for understanding the main outlines of the Christian learning of the ancient world. He must have been an exceptionally intelligent man to have found his way to so much that the most discriminating buyer would have wished to possess. Biscop himself wrote nothing, but he understood the value of what he had collected, and on his death-bed he begged the monks to keep the collection intact, and not to allow it to decay through disuse, and on no account to break it up. Like Cassiodorus, though without any of his advantages of classical education and habitual contact with ancient civilization, he understood that books are made to be used and that they must be used as a whole if they are to have their full effect. I like to think of him as the first of the great book collectors of the type that America has so abundantly produced—practical men with an instinctive desire to appropriate or be associated with the works of the spirit, and with the resources to swoop down upon a decayed society and carry off the fruits of civilization to produce a new harvest on a distant shore.

"Our aim is both to preserve what is old and to build something new; we desire to raise things which are modern without diminishing the works of our ancestors". These are words that Cassiodorus wrote on behalf of his king when he was a young letter-writer in the royal service. It is an aim that he lived with all his life, but only finally accomplished when he built his library. So the young Biscop must have felt when he collected his books and arranged for their permanent preservation. Both he and Cassiodorus saw that it was not enough simply to collect; the collection was only a starting-point for something new. At Vivarium the community failed to produce any writers after the death of its founder. At Jarrow, Biscop was more fortunate. His monks were the true heirs of Cassiodorus. They copied, they disseminated, and at least one of them produced works of the highest scholarship which preserved the contents of the library for future generations in a usable form. The monks of Jarrow and Wearmouth seem to have been moderate in everything except in their expenditure on books. They made no less that three facsimile copies of the Bible of Cassiodorus. The one that has survived contains 2060 folio pages and weighs 75 1/2 pounds; and it has been calculated that the three of them together required the skins of 1550 calves, not to speak of the silver and precious stones for their bindings, or of the skilled labor of at least seven scribes over several years. This was only one of their many works. In the libraries of Europe there are perhaps a dozen manuscripts which found their way from Jarrow to monastic centers in France and Germany, where they became essential tools for missionaries in their work of evangelization. What remains is certainly a small fragment of what once existed, but even in their present fragmentary state, these manuscripts are, in their accuracy, clarity, and beauty of workmanship, the finest collection of books to have survived from the centuries before Charlemagne. When we consider the circumstances of the library in which these books were produced—its distance from ancient centers of civilization, the very short space of time that separated its monks from an illiterate pagan past, their complete understanding of the art of calligraphy in its finest form, and the literary culture that their efforts bear witness to, the monastery at Jarrow must appear the finest of all examples of the power of a library to bring order out of chaos. Besides, and above all, the library at Jarrow produced a scholar of the kind that Cassiodorus had dreamt of in vain: Bede.

How shall I speak adequately of Bede? All that I could say of him would fall short of his desserts. For our present purpose it must suffice to say that, writing in a monastery remote from the main centers of power, he was able to put together works of learning which show that he, alone in his day, had a thorough mastery of the learning of the Christian past. He had fewer books than Cassiodorus, he had no knowledge of Greek, and he lived in time and space far removed from the living tradition of the ancient world. Yet he wrote as one who had a full understanding of even so complex a thinker as St. Augustine; he understood the essential merits of Cassiodorus, even though he had no copy of the work in which he chiefly reveals his personality; he was at ease with the greatest pagan Latin writers; as an historian he is the equal, at least, of Livy, and he is far above the rhetorical historians of the main Roman tradition; of ancient learning, he had the justifiable ambition of filling some gaps in Christian scholarship. He is, and probably forever will be, the greatest example of Benedictine scholarship and of the use to which a Benedictine library can be put.

By the time that he was writing, the greatest crisis in European civilization, which Cassiodorus had seen growing, was over. The main lines which the recovery would follow were already laid down and could not much be altered by the work of any single man. Bede did as much as any man, however, to stabilize the tradition of Western scholarship. Quietly, without hurry and without intermission, with the clam and unclamorous insight of a scholar, he worked for forty years to draw together the threads that had been broken, and he produced books that were among the text-books of scholars and evangelists alike for four hundred years.

Benedict Biscop began to collect his library during his visit to Italy in 671; Bede died in 735; in 794 a band of Viking pirates working down the coast fo Northumbria, destroyed the buildings of Jarrow and Wearmouth and scattered the monks and their books. Biscop's enterprise had lasted scarcely longer than Cassiodorus's foundation at Vivarium. It is a salutary warning that length of survival is no index to greatness. We build libraries to last for centuries; everything about them suggests longevity—and rightly so, for if libraries cannot survive, what can? Yet the libraries that have best performed the essential service for which they were founded have often been the least long-lived. Likewise, those that have lasted longest have often done least good. This is another sign, of which we have already seen several, that there must be no delay in making libraries active centers of civilization: they must not be repositories, still less tombs, of learning, but places where systematic, well-directed work is done. Only in this way can the founder of a library be sure that he has not worked in vain.

III

Much might be said about the monastic libraries of the Middle Ages and their silent work of preserving ancient texts, and providing the necessary equipment for public worship and private devotion. I pass over them because, although they made possible a high level of literary culture in many monasteries, they do not illustrate our main theme, which is concerned with the special contribution that a library can make in repairing the disorders of the world. We must jump nearly a thousand years from the foundation of Biscop's library to get another example of what a library can do in a time of disorder and uncertain values to bring stability and order into a chaotic scene. The disorders of the world in the sixteenth and seventeenth centuries were very different from those of the sixth and seventh: there was no threat of a total breakdown of civilization, but there were widespread wars and religious dissensions, and an even more profound disorder caused by the break-up of a traditional way of thought. Briefly we may say that, whereas in the seventh century the highest function of a library was to preserve the learning of the past and make it available to a disorganized world, in the seventeenth century the highest function of a library was to expose the genuine foundation of the learning of the past and purge it from seditious accretions and confusions. As always in a struggle between old and new habits of thought, the adherents of the old often took their stands on the wrong grounds, and often relied on prejudice or force to attain their ends. They were encouraged to do this because the foundations of their thought were uncertain. The texts in which ancient and medieval learning was transmitted were often deplorably bad. Errors and misunderstandings had crept into the texts through the constant process of copying and recopying through the centuries, and the early printers had perpetuated the confusion by multiplying the texts of the nearest manuscripts that lay to hand without regard to their credentials. In addition, the histories of the Church and kingdoms, on which many controversies hinged, were choked with the misunderstandings and fabrications which had accumulated in the course of centuries.

How was this state of affairs to be remedied? Briefly, it could only be remedied by subjecting the ancient texts of Christian thought to the kind of critical investigation which was often looked on as the greatest danger to religion. Psychologically therefore the step was not an easy one. Besides, the materials and methods of examining them were uncertain. The manuscripts of ancient works were scattered in many libraries throughout Europe, they were often uncatalogued, their whereabouts were often unknown; even when manuscripts were known and accessible, there was no science to enable scholars to give a confident judgement about their date or provenance; and even when these facts were known, the art of distinguishing true readings from false, genuine texts from apocryphal, the writings of one author from those of another, was very uncertain. Above all, there was no body of men who could devote their energies to these matters. The problems of manuscripts lay outside the scope of university studies; and since they had no application in practical affairs, no professional body was concerned with them. A few individual scholars had tackled some of the problems that a lone could justify the long and severe labor necessary for satisfactory results.

To these problems, different though they were from those of the age of Cassiodorus and Bede, the solution turned out to be the same as before: the building of a library and of a monastic community to serve and make it of use. It was the vision and energy of Dom Grégoire Tarisse, president of the Benedictine Congregation of St. Maur from 1630 to 1648, which were chiefly responsible for providing the solution which Cassiodorus and Benedict Biscop had already hit upon a thousand years earlier. The life of this great man who died in 1648 after working on his great design for some twenty years, and the history of the literary labors of the community which carried on this work for 150 years, have been well described in recent years and in English especially by Dom David Knowles. I shall confine myself to a few remarks which I think are pertinent to our assembly today, about the general purpose, method and scope of the work which the Maurists set themselves to do.

Their purpose was to get back to the original words of the main Christian writers down to the thirteenth century, to construct the genuine *corpus* of their writings, and to equip them with notes and indexes necessary for helping the reader to understand a writer's thoughts as they unfolded throughout the whole body of his works. The leaders of this group of scholars were the first to give prolonged thought to the problems of making an edition of a Christian writer. It was a task that required very wide readings and a complete knowledge of the Bible, a wide familiarity with the Fathers, and a sensitive appreciations of the development of the Latin langurage. Futhermore, it required the foundation of two new sciences, paleography and diplomatic, in order to determine the dates of manuscripts and the genuiness of charters. In an important sense it required a new start in historical research. This new start was, in fact, being made all over Europe in the seventeenth century, but nowhere so fruitfully as by the Maurist monks in Paris, who gathered their materials in a library at St. Germain-des-Prés, and went out all over Europe in search of fresh materials for their work.

I may here quote a few phrases from the circular which was sent out to fellow-workers in the Congregation of St. Maur in the last year of Dom Tarisse's life (in 1649). It is a fine expression of the modesty and patience which made possible their scientific achievement:

> When you take a MS., look first for the list of contents—look inside the cover: there is often an index there—but do not give too much credence to it.... And then when you look at the beginning of a treatise (for instance, the first books of St. Augustine's *De Ordine*) you must not be satisfied, but look at the beginning and end of each section, for one often finds between two

> works of an author small pieces by someone else which are very precious.... Reject and despise nothing, even if it is only a distich or an epigram, and be careful not to fall asleep at your work, for, if you are not extremely vigilant and on your guard, you will certainly pass over many small pieces without noticing them.... And finally be on your guard against those who will have no scrupple about taking away your manuscripts, on the pretense that it is a pious theft.

It was their concentration on these small matters, which had previously been neglected, that laid the foundation of the scientific revolution in the editing of texts.

It would, of course, be absurd to say that this revolution was the single-handed effort of even so learned and industrious a congregation as that of St. Maur. Their contribution was uniquely important in bulk, range, and quality. They took in their stride every author, whether Greek or Latin, from the third to the thirteenth century. When they got to the thirteenth century, indeed their zeal flagged. As the greatest among them, Jean Mabillon, said in his *Treatise on Monastic Studies:* "After St. Thomas, scholastic theology degenerated greatly from its first state and came under the rule of vain subtlety and a low chicanery unworthy of the gravity of Christian schools".

It was left for a later century to discover, and perhaps exaggerate, the virtues of the scholastic writers. This was not part of the aim of the Maurists who sought to turn men back to the solid and well-established truths of the Christian religion, to the traditional rules of Christian life, and above all to the Bible. They saw that this aim could best be achieved, not by controversy, but by science. It was thus that they sought to raise the facts of Christian experience above the hostilities of Jansenists and anti-Jansenists, of spiritual extremists and reactionary conformists. In the controversies of their contemporaries they took, as learned men and especially learned Benedictines are apt to do, a middle way. This was not the result of cowardice or feebleness. They published Augustine when to do so exposed them to the charge of Jansenism. They were bold in the cause of moderation, because it was the cause of truth.

IV

I have now said something about three libraries and the monastic communities that were their creators and guardians. What can they teach us and how can their experience be applied to our own condition?

1. It is evident that one must not expect too much too quickly. Cassiodorus built his monastic library very quickly, but its influence on the outside world was of very slow growth, and it is perhaps only in our day that the scope and nature of his enterprise have been fully realized. Benedict Biscop's monastic community was extraordinarily precocious in producing craftsmen to make books, but it took thirty years from the time when Biscop started to collect his library for the first of Bede's works to appear, and they were not widely known for another generation. As for the Maurists, the most effective learned society in our history, their origins go back to 1611 and the scholarly design began to take shape in 1630; but it was not until 1648 that the first learned work appeared, and it was only in 1668 that the publication of the first of the really big works began. It took nearly forty years therefore, for this great organization to get into its stride. We often think that, in comparison with the past, our learned plans are very slow in bearing fruit; but we foreshorten the labors of the past in retrospect. To judge from the examples we have studied, we must plan for a harvest in thirty or fifty years time. To plant a library is like planting trees: it is an investment that only the most patient and confident institutions and families can afford. What institution has better claim to these virtues or can wait longer for results than the Order of St. Benedict?

2. When this has been said, our examples give no encouragement to lingering over our task. None of the libraries we have examined lasted very long: between their full development and their final dispersal or destruction there is a period of about 100 or 150 years,—no more. On the whole the libraries that have lasted longest have least to show for it. Yet no library is ever made in vain. The library at Verona, which has slumbered for 1500 years, has given us Catullus and Cicero's *De Republica* as a result of its rest. A vigorous librarian at any moment in its long history might have cleared out these precious relics to make way for more up-to-date volumes. So long as a library lasts, it will do something, and we can never tell when it will inspire some ardent spirit or some great discovery. Libraries have their own life and their own fruits which come by no human contrivance. But if we plan—as we must at the outset of a great library—for a definite result, we must work, without hurry or anxiety, but speedily. The history of the great libraries is the history of sudden disasters.

3. A library is nothing unless it is the center of learned activity. Libraries exist not simply to preserve the intellectual resources of the past for some indeterminate future, but also to make use of these resources in the present. Each of the libraries we have studied was formed for an immediate as well as for a distant purpose. Within a generation or so, the libraries of Vivarium, Jarrow, and St. Germain-des-Prés all inspired new works whose influences can be felt even today. Cassiodorus's little treatise on his library is still an inspiring account of what a library ought to

be; scholars still use the editions which came from St. Germain, historians still read Bede, and if nothing remained of ancient Christian literature but his commentaries, we should still have a wide knowledge of the Fathers. If a library that slleps through long generations performs a secret service to mankind by its mere existence, a library that is a center of serious scholarship can be one of the most powerful civilizing forces in the world.

4. It must be recognized that many of the tasks that a library inspires and makes possible are humble and laborious, though they require skills and talents that are more uncommon than people suppose. I mean they require orderliness, system, perseverance, and an ability to keep the end in view while dealing with a multiplicity of minute facts. In scholarly work these are not virtues that can be left to subordinates while the great men float off into an empyrean of large ideas and exciting controversies. They are needed at every level of the enterprise. Cassiodorus's last work, written in his ninety-third year, was a treatise on spelling for his monks. Bede's first work was a handbook on irregular verbs and similar pit-falls in the path of a beginner in Latin. We have already seen that nothing was too small for the attention of the Maurists. This attention to the lowliest tasks of scholarship will never have any news-value, but without this attention there can be no intellectual progress. It is to be hoped that this library will follow the example of these great and lowly men, and that (after the events of this week have been duly recorded) its name will disappear from the newspapers until—perhaps thirty years hence—the world discovers that a new force has been active in the world, growing in strength from year to year without fuss or frenzy.

5. This brings me to the last point which emerges from our examples: the special character of a Benedictineeibrary. I have already mentioned some of the virtues which make a Benedictine library different from others, but our examples encourage me to mention another. Vivarium, Jarrow, and St. German-des-Prés had one great source of strength: whatever their contribution to the world, they had the immediate and inescapable function of providing the necessary books and studies for the ordinary routine of religious life. A relatively humble function, maybe, but very necessary. All institutions need—in addition to their higher aim and hopes—a daily bread-and-butter function that keeps them ticking through good times and bad.

The existence of this kind of low-pressure incentive, operating without remission day by day, is necessary for all human activities of long endeavor. It is this gentle daily pressure that has formed the habit of patient and self-denying labor which has been one of the most conspicuous Benedictine attributes through the centuries. Without this nothing can be achieved. The healing influence of a library in a disordered world must be a matter of long and deep therapy: there can be no question of quick cures, and of all communities in the world the Benedictine Order has best discovered the secret of corporate endeavor toward a single end. The final end that the Order has set itself is peace. But peace has many aspects and modes; and it is the spiritual peace or order and comprehension that has always been the chief Benedictine gift to the world. Here, as at Jarrow and St. Germain-des-Prés, we may hope to find a comprehensive and unbiased understanding of the Christian tradition in all its main branches. It was in that spirit and toward this goal that Cassiodorus, Bede, and the monks of St. Germain-des-Prés all worked. There is no other temper of mind or goal that is more permanently necessary in the Church or in the world.

V

It may finally be asked whether there is today any area of learned endeavor that can be marked out for a Benedictine library comparable to those chartered by the great libraries of the past. This is something that has, no doubt, already been the subject of much thought and it would be impertinent to discuss any details at this moment. I shall only say that to me there appear to be a number of tasks which (though they can scarcely be called "urgent" or "exciting" in the ordinary sense of these words) will help toward a sober and realistic assessment of the fundamental documents of Christian life through the centuries, and in this way strengthen the forces of order and stability in the Church and in society at large. To specify these tasks—beyond saying that they are largely concerned with the careful analysis of texts, the compilation or word-lists and concordances, and the work of translation—would take us into discussions that must be carried on in small groups meeting and planning their work in private and with the full realization of all the difficulties that lie ahead. Let me therefore simply conclude by turning our minds back to the monks of St. Germain-des-Prés three hundred years ago.

Like all scholars of that age, they were very fond of expressing their ideas and intentions in symbolic form on the title pages of their books. These symbols give an extraordinarily vivid picture of their minds and aims. As the flow of their publications grew in volume, they used a succession of symbols; but there was one to which they were especially attached. It appears again and again on the title pages of their books from 1650 to about 1690. It consists of a crown of thorns; within it, two hands are stretched out from either side which grasp each other in friendship. Above the hands there is a burning heart pierced by an arrow; and over the whole emblem the motto:

EX ARDUIS PAX ET AMOR.

Fig. 17. Printer's device and motto used by the Benedictine Congregation of St. Maur, St. Germain-de-Prés, outside Paris, during the 1600s.

I can think of no better motto or device for a Benedictine library setting out on its career, expressing thus briefly the love and peace, the reconciling of all men through the toil and suffering that are never far below the surface in all learned endeavor.

III.
APPENDICES

Notes: Community History
Notes: Library History
Bibliography
Index

NOTES: The Community, 1882-1982

The citations below contain short-title and/or author references only. Full citations are provided in an alphabetical bibliography thereafter.

1. See *Angelmontana: Blatter aus des Geschichte von Engelberg...*, and *Engelberg: Land und Leute*, as well as the works by Frs. Gallus Heer and Albert Weiss (1946 and 1956 respectively).

2. Zenner, *Pages from Mt. Angel's Early History*, unpublished ms., Mt. Angel Archives (hereafter cited MAA), 1952. This typescript for lectures delivered in 1952 during Lent, is based on the notes compiled while Fr. Amrbose studied at Engelberg from 1948 to 1951. His notes are based on: (1) the correspondence file at Engelberg between the motherhouse and Mt. Angel (552 letters or 2,525 pages, on 96 rolls of microfilm); (2) the dairy of *Tagebuch* of Abbot Anselm Villiger, from which Zenner transcribed 94 pages relating to Mt. Angel; and (3) the memoires of Abbot Leodegar Scherrer, resulting in 21 pages of transcribed excerpts relating to Mt. Angel.

3. The following abbots have ruled Engelberg:

Anselm Villiger de Stans, 1866-1901
Leodegar II Scherer d'Inwill, 1901-14
Basilius Fellmans d'Oberkirch, 1914-29
Bonaventure Egger de Tablat, 1929-31
Leodegar III Hunkeler de Pfaffnau, 1931-56
Leonard Bösch de Ruswill, 1956-

4. I follow the account of Fr. Malone, *Conception*, closely for the materials on Mt. Angel's founder before 1880, and defer to his references to Abbot Frowin Conrad's diary in the Conception Abbey archives. I also have used his English translated excerpts of this diary, as well as his translation of Abbot Anselm's, whenever his rendering of the colloquial German and Swiss dialect parallels the text closely. When his translation is cited, no or only minor changes have been made. The German quotes are from Zenner's transcriptions. See Malone, 48-51, 61. t

5. Abp. Seghers to Adelehelm, Feb. 1, 1884 (from Rome), reprinted in *The Catholic Sentinel*, 15 no. 7 (March 13, 1884); see also Zenner's *Abstracts* for 1884, p. 12-14.

6. In addition to Malone's account of Conseption Abbey's history, see Barry's *Catholic Church and German Americans* for the best contextual background for the history of Mt. Angel Abbey. For summary statistics about German immigration, see Barry, p. 6.

7. Sister Maria Agnes Butsch fo Fr. Maurus Snyder, Feb. 13, 1935, recalling the family's move to the Fillmore area in 1878. She remembered that articles published in 1880-81 encouraged other German immigrants to follow then westward. She maintained: "Fr. Adelhelm knew about the articles written by my father in the German papers... Did that bring Fr. Adelhelm out west to look for a location for a monastery?" See MAA, Sr. Anges Butsch: memoire notes, s.n., ff. 16-17.

8. Barry, 7-8.

9. Malone, 52.

10. Malone, 61, n. 15.

11. Adelelhelm to Anselm, Aug. 15, 1881 (from Jacksonville), trans. by Fr. Maurus Snyder, MAA *Historical Notes*, s.n., p. 5.

12. See Malone, 1-46, for the early history of the Reading colony and the early Irish and German immigration to Missouri. Bp. Hogan had come to this area in 1856; his experiences were recounted in an autobiographical sketch, *On the Mission in Missouri* (1892). He was made bishop of St. Joseph's new diocese in 1868.

13. Malone, 40-41; 46, n. 55-56. He cites records from New Malleray abbey in Iowa, and Rothensteiner's *History of the Archdiocese of St. Louis*, II, 57.

14. Schmid, *Benediktiner,* 28-29. See also Frowin to Anselm, June 15, 1874, cited by Malone, 46, n. 58: Conception Abbey Archives (hereafter CAA), H-III-B-2-1873.

15. Bp. Hogan to Abbot Martin Marty, November 8, 1872, transcribed by Malone, 42 from Mt. Michael Abbey (Elkhorn, Nebraska) archives (hereafter MMAA), I-B-1872. See also Kleber, *St. Meinrad Abbey*, 340-42.

16. Frowin to Anselm, June 30, 1873, trans. by Malone, 51; CAA, H-III-B-2-1873.

17. The property had been donated by the railroad builder and banker John Corby (d. 1870). After the Holy Cross Fathers returned the land to the diocese, part went to the Alexian Brothers, and a portion was converted to a city cemetery. Frowin to Anselm, Oct. 15, 1873; CAA, H-III-B-2-1873, cited by Malone, 46 n. 66.

18. Kleber, 340-42.

19. Martin Marty to Frowin, Jan. 17, 1872, transcribed by Malone, 43; MMAA, I-B-1872.

20. Martin to Frowin, Feb. 27 and Nov. 17, 1872, cited by Malone, 43; MMAA, I-B-1872.

21. Anselm Villiger, *Tagebuch*, for Dec. 13, 1872; trans. by Malone, 47.

22. CAA, *Necrology of Conception Abbey*, cited by Malone, 61, n. 11.

23. Malone, 61, n. 16; Hess, *Engelberg*, 111, n. 7.

24. Malone, 61, n. 19 assumes that Frowin and Adelhelm were told to keep the mission quiet until they were out of the country, judging from Frowin to Anselm, May 8, 1873; CAA, H-III-2-1873.

25. Frowin to Anselm, Sept. 3, 1873; MMAA, I-B-1873, quoted by Malone, 61, n. 15.

26. Malone (61, n. 18) points out the discrepancies in the personal data in the passagenger lists and the immigration office records and corrects it; National Archives and Records Service (NARS), Mic. Pub. roll 375, May 15-31, 1873 (lists 424-509). Br. Meinrad professed at Conception Abbey on Jan. 1, 1875 and died there Oct. 20, 1901.

27. Frowin to Anselm, Oct. 15, 1873: CAA, H-III-B-2-1873, cited by Malone, 61, n. 14. Frowin later saw this property, than as now associated with the Church of St. Rock at "French Bottom" in St. Joseph, and commented that it would have been "very unsatisfactory".

28. Kleber (340-42) maintained that the bishop offered the Benedictines 300 acres, a farm house, and a church (presumably referring to the parish church, actually little more than a chapel, at Conception junction).

29. Frowin to Anselm, June 15, 1873: CAA, H-III-B-2-1873, cited by Malone, 51 & 62, n. 21-23.

30. Frowin counted 65 German and 35 Irish Catholic families in his letter to Anselm, June 15, 1873 (*supra*). It was customary to discriminate between the Irish and German Catholics, since from the 1840s onward there was considerable friction between the two in parish politics especially in Philadelphia and southern Pennsylvannia and Maryland.

31. Malone, 66-70.

32. This contract was drafted in manuscript by Frowin Conrad's brother, Fridolin (CAA, s.n.), ed. Malone, 51-52. The second documents were signed on December 31, 1873 as well, by the same candidates; additional signatures were added in 1876; Malone, 63, n. 73.

33. These instructions were given to Prior Jerome Bachmann of St. Meinrad in 1855 by Abbot Heinrich IV of Einsiedeln; Kleber, 154-58.

34. See Malone's treatment, "The Musenalp and Missouri," pp. 76-87. See also the anniversary history of Maria Rickenbach (1956).

35. Frowin to Anselm, Nov. 27, 1873: CAA, H-III-B-2-1873, quoted by Malone, 78.

36. It was when Engelberg failed to send new recruits, that Frowin turned to Einseideln for help, especially his brother. It is significant, that for his love of Beuron, there is no record of Frowin's reliance on this abbey for anything but advice.

37. Sister Beatric Rengli, *Reise*, 22, trans. by Malone, 81.

38. Adelhelm's advertisement appeared in the *Nodaway County Democrat*, Aug. 26, 1875.

39. The Benedictine Congregation of Perpetual Adoration today operates six sanctuaries in Missouri, Illinois, Arizona, and California, plus several hospitals and schools. The largest daughterhouse is Sacred Heart Convent, Yankton SD, with its 318 members (1971) and priory at Watertown SD. It alone operates 16 elementary schools, a coeducational college in Yankton, four hospitals, and furnishes teachers for four other schools.

40. Fr. Powers also arranged a 100 acre donation from the Land Assn. of Reading, and Frowin was later able to purchase 80 more acres for $400. Cf. Frowin Conrad, *Diary*, I, 31, 115; CAA, H-III-B-14-1860, -2-1873, and -13-1874; cited by Malone, 62, n. 22; 90.

41. Frowin Conrad, *Diary*, I, 24-31; Malone, 92, n. 9.

42. Note Malone's (123, n. 35) summary and estimate of Adelhelm's career; cf. Malone, 85; 87, n. 42.

43. Quoted by A. Zenner, *Pages*, f. 3

44. Anselm Villiger, *Tagebuch*, II, 180, trans. by Malone, 105. The entry refers to Frowin to Anselm, Nov. 27, 1880: CAA, H-III-B-4-1880, full-text trans. by Malone, 117-18.

45. "If Fr. Adelhelm and Fr. Ignatius (who let the cat out of the bag last summer [by writing to Abbot Anselm]) had made an honest attempt to understand my position and had reported it correctly to Engelberg, I am sure this bitterness woulld never have arisen". Frowin Conrad, *Dairy*, I, 84, trans. by Malone, 104.

46. Abbot Placidus Wolter to Frowin, Aug. 9, 1875: MMAA, III-B-3-1875; full-text trans., Malone, 100-101.

47. Frowin to Maurus Wolter, July 31, 1888: MMAA, I-C-1875, quoted by Malone, 93.

48. Frowin Conrad, *Diary*, I, 66-88, cited by Malone, 93.

49. Malone (110, n. 48) explains Adelhelm's phrase "ohne zu Schmalzen" that meat and seasoning were not added to the water to give it body and taste. He concludes that such complaints about food preparation and abstinence were "perhaps entirely justified" but tries to put the monks' living standard in perspective.

50. Malone, 112.

51. This was after Fr. Ignatius tells on his "blood-brother" who is "'hic et nunc' so obsessed with Beuron that the mere name attached to anything makes it perfect. P. Adelhelm is a man of pure gold and a man after the heat of God". Anselm Villiger, *Tagebuch*, III, 19-31, trans. by Malone, 106. Adelhelm, of course, constantly spoke as the chmapion of Engelberg's traditions. See his letter to Anselm, Aug. 1, 1876: MAA, Zenner's transcriptions, no. 6, f. 1.&

52. Anselm to Frowin, Nov. 8, 1876: CAA, H-III-B-3-1876; full-text trans., Malone, 107-08.

53. Malone, 109.

54. Frowin Conrad, *Diary*, I, 85, trans. by Malone, 108.

56. Anselm Villiger, *Tagebuch*, II, 180, quoting Adelhelm; trans. by Malone, 105.

57. Anselm Villiger, *Tagebuch*, II, 181; Malone, 112.

58. Frowin Conrad, *Diary*, I, 109; trans., Malone, 115.

59. Bp. Hogan to Pope Leo XIII, Petition of Aug. 2, 1878, copied into Frowin's *Diary*, I, 106; full-text transcription, Malone, 115.

60. Frowin to Adelhelm, Nov. 25, 1880: MAA, *Extracts & transcriptions*, s.n., ff. 1-2. Cf. Anselm Villiger, *Tagebuch*, I, 151.

61. Nicholas to Anselm, May 15, 1881, abstracted in the latter's *Tagebuch*: "Fr. Nicholas says to have an eye on the Pacific is advisable because of the favorable climate and good soil there. There is nothing attractive in Conception for him, a long severe winter, great heat in summer, poor water; he would never join Conception, as they have too many strange Beuronese customs and rules".

62. Nicholas to Anselm, April 5, 1881: MAA, Zenner's *Extracts*, s.n., f. 12.

63. Adelhelm to Anselm, Feb. 23, 1880: MAA, Zenner's *Extracts*, s.n., f. 1. "Ange es in Maryville wie es solte, wir könnten jedes Jahr wenigstens sechs bis sieben hundert Dollars von dort bezechen,... Währen in Maryville nach ähnlichen Grundsätzen von Anfäng an verfahren worden, wir könnten jetzt jährlich ganz leicht 6 bis 800 Dollars erhalten...".

64. Frowin to Anselm, Nov. 27, 1880: CAA, H-III-B-4-1880; full-text trans., Malone, 117-18.

65. Bp. Hogan to Anselm, Nov. 27, 1880: CAA, H-III-B-4-1880; full-text trans., Malone, 117.

66. Frowin to Anselm, Dec. 17, 1880: MAA, *Transcriptions*, s.n., f. 2. Malone (119; 123, n. 27) estimates that Maryville had a total debt of about $7200, calculating at 20 cents per franc. He cites Frowin's *Diary*, I, 116 for Feb. 14, 1879: "By examining his [Adelhelm's] accounts, I found that during the last year Fr. Adelhelm had paid nothing to the monastery.... With two fathers stationed there, they should have paid us at least $400". In fact, Conception Abbey had been subsidizing the whole Maryville operation, when originally the rationale in giving the parish to the

Benedictines was to help start the monastery.

67. Adelhelm to Anselm, Oct. 11, 1881, cited by Zenner, *Pages*, 2.

68. Anselm Villiger, *Tagebuch*, III, 32 (cited by Malone, 118-19) for July 23, 1881: "P. Nicolaus und P. Adelhelm sind beauftraft in Nordamerica einen Ort auszuchen, der sich durch Klima, Quellwasser, Wald, Berge, Verbindung swege, etc. für eine kloest. Niederlassung eignet. Nun schreibt P. Adelhelm darüber, wie folgt (referring to a letter of Adelhelm, June 29, 1881 from San Francisco: MAA, *Transcriptions*,, s.n.).

69. Frowin to Anselm, Dec. 17, 1880: CAA, H-III-B-4-1880; full-text trans., Malone, 118.

70. Nicholas to Anselm, April 5, 1881: MAA, Zenner's *Extracts*, s.n., f. 12. Nicholas reports that Adelhelm was raising money for the exploration of the West. The letter of Adelhelm to Anselm, May 11, 1881, indicates that the abbot had by this time approved the venture. Note Anselm's entry in his *Tagebuch* for April 26, 1881, presumably referring to the April 5th letter: "P. Nicolaus schreibt von Maryville dass sie vom Bishof von Portland, Oregon, eine Eindladung... einer Gründung erhalten haben. Pater Adelhelm und er gedenken nächstens eine Auskundschaftreise nach Oregon, Colorado, und an die Kueste des stillen Uzans zu machen".

71. Nicholas to Anselm, Aug. 15, 1881: MAA, Zenner's *Extracts*, s.n., f. 11. Nicholas refers here to the Oregon option at Jacksonville as a real opportunity not to be lost, as in the chance situation in California.

72. Data from the official census records and the state may surveys (land ownership) differ: Williams, *Oregon* (1870), 99. The total state population was 104,920 in 1870, but this figure excludes 16,000 Chinese and Indians.

73. Champoeg was an important trade factory which became a convention center for the anti-British movement in Oregon, and thereafter was important in the movement toward statehood. The exact nature and accomplishments of the Champoeg assemblies has been subjected to much debate. Although it flourished in the 1850s, it was destroyed by the floods of 1861-62 and thereafter few of the towns right on the river developed further except for those upstream which were protected from flooding. See the standard bibliographies for the early history of Oregon.

74. See Malone, "The Wild Rose and the Edelweiss," *Conception*, 182-197; and Duratschek's account (1947).

75. Malone, 119-20.

76. Frowin Conrad, *Diary*, I, 165, quoted by Malone, 119.

77. Nicholas & Adelhelm to Anselm, June 29, 1881: Engelberg archives copied by Zenner, MAA *Extracts*, s.n., f. 12. See the full-text trans. by Malone, 120-21. The letter suggests that the bishop offered him the whole of Montana! Assuredly, he meant the freedom to pick a spot in Montana.

78. Anselm to Bp. Machebeuf, Jan. 11 & Feb. 17, 1881: MAA, *Extracts*, s.n., f. 12. Note that Bp. Machebeuf is thought to have been the real-life person behind the character of Fr. Joseph Vaillant, vicar-general of Abp. Latour, in Willa Cather's novel *Death Comes to the Abp.*.

79. Nicholas & Adelhelm to Anselm, June 29, 1881 (see n. 77 *supra*).

80. Anselm Villiger, *Tagebuch*, for May 15, 1881, citing a letter from Nicholas.

81. Adelhelm to Anselm, Aug. 15, 1881 from Jacksonville: MAA, Abbot Thomas trans., *Historical Notes*, 2-3.

82. Fr. Maurus questioned that it was ever Abp. Blanchet who had contacted the Swiss Benedictines, or that Olwell had ever approached Blanchet before the latter's retirement. See MAA, Maurus Snyder, *Comments*, f. 31; Hogan (1976), 14.

83. Nicholas & Adelhelm to Anselm, June 29, 1881 (see n. 77 *supra*); cf. the version copied into Anselm Villiger's *Tagebuch*, for Sept. 22, 1881: MAA, Zenner's *Transcriptions*, s.n., ff. 2-7.

84. *Ibid.*

85. Adelhelm to Anselm, Aug. 15, 1881: MAA, Abbot Thomas, *Historical Notes*, 2-3.

86. Hogan (1976), 14. Hogan's quotations were presumably supplied by one of the Mt. Angel monks who did the translations (Fr. Luke Eberle?).

87. Nicholas & Adelhelm to Anselm, June 29, 1881 (see n. 77 & 84 *supra*).

88. Gabriel, *Christian Brothers*, 229.

89. Adelhelm to Anselm, Aug. 15, 1881 (see n. 85 *supra*), where the former expresses concern for the summer dryness: "...when [the Christian Brothers] assured us that from May to November not a drop of rain falls, we were less inclined to believe that. This may be the reason why no barns are to be seen. The cut grain is left in shocks in the field; there it is threshed and the wheat or oats put up in sacks". Still, Adelhelm's impression was not all unfavorable: "All in all, I have the very best opinion of the Sta. Inéz Valley, with one exception: the water supply is not good". He reported seeing a small creek and a good spring, but makes no mention of the Sta. Inéz river which irrigates the valley today. He was much more concerned with the lack of cold drinking water such as he was accustomed to at Engelberg.

90. Hogan (1976), 14.

91. Nicholas & Adelhelm to Anselm, June 29, 1881 (see n. 77 & 84 *supra*).

92. Adelhelm to Anselm, Aug. 15, 1881: MAA, *Historical Notes*, 5.

93. MAA, Zenner's *Pages*, f. 5

94. Nicholas to Anselm, Dec. 2, 1881; MAA, *Extracts*, s.n., ff. 10-12, esp. f. 11.

95. The land agent gave the monks $10.00 for travel money, and the railraod and steamship companies provided free passes for half-faires: MAA, *Historical Notes*, p. 4. The cost of travel, postage, etc., was recorded down to the franc by Abbot Anselm; the traveling monks seem to have been equally penurious.

96. MAA, Maurus Snyder, *Memorable Dates*, 1.

97. Adelhelm to Anselm, Jan. 6, 1881, quoted by Hogan (1976), 14.

98. *Ibid.*

99. "Da Erxbischof in Folge dessen eine grosse Anzahl Gäste zu erwarten hatte, und Jacksonville für längere Zeit ohne Priester gewesen wäre, so wurden wir ersucht, für einstweilen die stelle der hiesigen Geistlichen einsunehmen und uns gleichzeitig in der Gegend umzusehen. Die hälfte weges konnten wir der Eisenbahn zurücklegen,... Die Katholiken und selbst einige Protestanten haben nicht geringe Freude u:ber unsere Ankunft an den Tag gelegt und dringen fortwärhend in uns,...".

100. Fillmore was named after J. M. Fillmore, General Superintendent of the Oregon and California Railroad when the narrow gauge line from Woodburn went through it to Silverton. The town was originally named "Frankfurt" after Frankfurt am Main by the first settler, Settelmeier. Afterward, the Cleaver brothers called it "Roy" after someone in their family. The post office established there in February 1, 1882 used the name Roy, not Fillmore. So the name does not seem to have been well established before it was changed on September 19, 1882 to Mt. Angel. See Ochs, *Founding Mt. Angel Abbey*, 14; McArthur, *Oregon Names*, under "Fillmore".

101. The surveyors recalled in 1851 that it was a "strikingly beautiful butte some 300 feet in height and covering nearly a section of land" with a grove of fir trees at the base; it was barren at top except for a stand of twelve giant firs and a couple of wind-blown oaks. The rock formations were described as "semi-circular walls of stone, enclosing a space enough for a comfortable seat and as high as one's shoulders when in a sitting position. The seats were made of cross sticks as high as the knee [is] from the ground". The Indians traveled along the valley's Abiqua Creek rather than the Willamette which flooded, had widespread marshlands, and was where the white settlements were. The surveyors maintained that throughout the 1800s the Indians when encamped along the creek nearby would climb the butte, sit in these prayer circles, and "Commune in silence with the Great Spirit". To the west lay what they called "Chek-ta" or the "beautiful" or "enchanting land". The transliteration of the Indian name for the butte was "Tap-a-lam-a-ho," which according to the surveyors, meant "God is near the mountain top" as explained to them by an unidentified Indian from the Crooked Finger area who remembered the days of tribal migrations up and down the valley. See the land agent description of 1907, MAA, s.n.; "Tap-a-lam-a-ho," MAA typsecript, s.n., copies of 1922, 1941, and 1942. The monks were then, and were through the 1940s, taken with the idea of having built their monastery on an old, primitive place of worship.

102. Abbot Bernard recalled that the hilltop, before it was leveled for the present development, "used to be a racky ledge for what is now the campus, an there was the orifice of a volcano near where the old sisters' house was. It was like a pudding stirred up in stone". Bernard Murphy, *Reminiscences*, MAA, s.n., p. 5.

103. The Indian lore surrounding the butte was enhanced and passed on by Homer Davenport, a Silverton poet; one of his sources was a Clackamas Indian, Joe Hutchins. It was Davenport's father who had originally surveyed the land (see n. 101 *supra*); the original description of a "prayer circle" was elaborated into an "amphitheatre" in later renditions. Zenner, *Pages*, pp. 21-22. Fr. Maurus Snyder recalled also that before the hilltop was cleared, the novices would climb the butte to pick its wild strawberries, and would hold their own prayer session in the Indian semi-circles. He alludes to Homer Davenport as a cartoonist, but essentially substantiates the "oral history" project of uncovering the mystery of these rock formations. See Davenport's letter to Adelhelm, *Mt. Angel News* 10. no. 37 (Jan. 8, 1931); cf. Maurus Snyder, *Reminiscences*, MAA typscript (June 6, 1950), f. 1.

104. When the sodality of the B.V. Mary was founded and a shrine site was dedicated on the hill (May 23, 1888), the address as recorded in the *Sentinel* remarked: "What was once the hunting ground of the Indian Manito and his frantic medicine-men, where once the horrid and frenzied Wakonwas were performed among the glowing fires during moonlit nights as if shunning the light of bright day, God chose a sport for his select place, and as of old when the Pantheon opened its gates to all His saints, when Apollo's temple withits demonic oracles on Monte Cassino through the prayers and power of the blessed patriarch St. Benedict had to give way to the presanctified Baptist, St. John, now He delights in taking possession of a locality He chose in His incomprehensible wisdom, tearing it out of the claws of the insidious Prince of darkness". Such rhetoric displays continuity in a long-standing tradition of Christian conversion of pagan sanctuaries into churches and shrines.

105. Adelhelm to Anselm, Oct. 31, 1881, cited by G. Hogan, p. 14.

106. Adelhelm to Anselm, Jan. 6, 1882 (MAA, Zenner's *Extracts*, f. 11), specifies that the goal was 15,000 francs, of which 10,000 were already pledged. Once owner offered ten acres free and to sell the rest of his homestead cheaply, and thereafter provided another five acres. Adelhelm expected the price of land to rise to an unheard-of twelve francs per acre.

107. Dr. John McLaughlin in the 1830s had resettled a number of Hudson Bay Company traders along the Willamette, from Oregon City at the Willamette Falls, to a more central location at St. Paul. The latter, now known more for its annual rodeo than anything else, was then a major stopover when navigating south, upstream, to present day Eugene (i.e., Eugene City or the "Emerald City") where the MacKenzie River joined the Willamette and made the latter navigable.

108. The monks' difficulties with English continued to limit their service to non-German speaking Catholics; they were no different, however, than some of the diocesan clergy recruited from the immigrant communities. Fr. Hartlieb for example, requested transfer to Baker, in eastern Oregon, where he planned to study English at the "college" started by Fr. Peter de Roo. MAA, Maurus Snyder, "Memorable Dates," for October 2, 1881. Adelhelm in his letter of February 5, 1882 to Anselm (cited by G. Hogan, pt. 1, p. 15), somewhat maligned Fr. Nicholas: "Fr. Nicholas could hardly take care of the pastoral work in the three places [Sublimity, Gervais, and Fillmore], if only because of preaching, which he has never done and cannot, not even in German, and therefore he would be no help to the French and English and Americans". See also MAA, "Historical Notes," s.n. (1951 transcription), for 1881, p. 1.

109. The Church in the Pacific Northwest had severe shortages of clergy and had to recruit manpower even outside the U.S.. Since 1833 laymen there petitioned the dioceses in Canada and in the American midwest for missionaries. In 1879 the Catholic population was estimated at 10,000 in Washington alone, but these people were served by only nine diocesan priests and six missioners. These fifteen priests covered an amazing territory as itinerant preachers, taveling between 117 churches. By 1895 the picture had not improved; the Catholics then numbered 42,000 but had only 39 diocesan priests and 24 missioners for the province's 48 parishes and 240 "stations". See the *Catholic Sentinel* for Jan. 9 and Sept. 10, 1896 for front-page pleas for vocations.

110. Bp. Junger was under tremendous pressure from the German-speaking parishes at Tacoma and around the Puget Sound to accomodate their special needs. Parishoners independently petitioned the Abbot Bernard Lockikar of St. John's Abbey in Minnesota for missioners. Bp. Jungers did the same in 1891 and in 1894 selected a site south of Olympia, Washington, for a Benedictine College. A nuclear community was formed to run this college, and the monks received patronage from Bp. Edward J. O'Dea (1896-1932); it became St. Martin's Abbey. As a priory it became independent in 1904, and a decade later, in 1914, was made into an abbey. Its Cassinese-Benedictine monks specialized in parish work, retreats, and eventually seminary education in competition with Mt. Angel Abbey and College.

111. "...the Fathers, especially Adelhelm, had the idea of Engelberg monks duplicating in the West what Abbot Boniface Wimmer had done in the East". MAA, Zenner's *Pages*, f. 7.

112. MAA, Maurus Snyder, *Memorable Dates*, typsecript, s.n., p. 12.

113. Nicholas to Anselm, quotes by G. Hogan, pt. 1, p. 14.

114. Adelhelm to Anselm, Jan. 6, 1881; *ibid.*

115. Anselm Villiger, *Tagebuch*, trans. by Zenner, *Extracts*, ff. 7-8; quoted by Hogan, pt. 1 (1976), p. 15.

116. Baron R. F. von Stotzingen to Anselm, Sept. 25, 1881, cited by G. Hogan, pt. 1, p. 14; MAA, Zenner's transcription (1949), *Diaries*, p. 9: "In dem, was Sie mir über die Reisen Ihrer H. H. Patres mittheilen, sehe, ich einen Wink der Vorsehung, und werde nun mit aller Energie an die Werwirklichung des Planes gehen. Bis jetzt weiss ich etwa[s] 10 Familien die sich betheiligen würden, ich muss aber bemerken, dass ich erst in der allerjünsten Zeit meine Idee mit einigen Nachbaren besprochen habe. Jetzt erst, da durch ihre Mittheilung mir eine Angriffnahme des Projekts möglich scheint, werde ich die Angelegenheit bei mir befreundeten adelichen Familien in Süddesutschland, am Rhein und in Westphalen in Anregung bringen. Sobald sich wenigstens 50 Familien gefunden habe, dürste die Constitutuirung der Gesellschaft erfolgen...". 117. *Ibid.*: "Die Berichte Ihrer H. Patres haben mich sehr interessirt. Ich meine, man sollte in erster Reihe suchen Waldungen zu erwerben, da deren Administration sehr einfach und bei der sinnlosen Verwüstung der Wälder in Amerika das Holz binnen wenigen Jahren einen hohen Pries erhalten dürste; Waldherrschften wachsen ins Geld-unter den gegebenen Verhältnissen muss der Werth derselben in Amerika rasch steigen. Ich möchte mir die Bitte erlauben, dass Ihre H. H. Patres angewiessen würden auf grossere Waldkomplexe ihr Augenmerk zu richten...".

118. Zenner's translation (*Pages*, f. 7) of "Es ist nichts daraus gekommen!" Another marginal notation reads "Nolite sperare in principibus" as a motto regarding the promises of the noblemen. Only the baron's brother-in-law, Otto von Boeselager & Hessen, from Westphalia, came to invest money in Oregon real estate. Possible linkage to other investments, i.e. the Weyerhauser family, in Pacfific Northwest timberland, is unknown.

119. Baron von Boeselager built the public water works for the town. At the same time the priory got a steam engine to pressurize its water system, and the facilities were remodeled when the well was deepened to tap a "splendid

spring of cold water at a depth of 20 feet" found in the fall of 1888. See the *Catholic Sentinel* (Oct. 8, 1888), abstracted in MAA, s.n., f. 8.

120. Nicholas to Anselm, Dec. 2, 1881; this places Fr. Nicholas in San Francisco on a trip during which he acquired three paintings for Mt. Angel (St. Benedict and Romanus, St. Jerome, and the Miracle of the Loaves & Fishes, destroyed in 1892). MAA, Maurus Snyder, *Mem. Dates*, p. 3; MAA: Zenner, *Diaries*, p. 10-11.

121. MAA, Zenner, *Extracts*, f. 8.

122. Adelhelm to Anselm, March 8, 1882: MAA, Zenner, *Extracts*, f. 10.

123. Nicholas to Anselm, April 6, 1882: MAA, Zenner, *Extracts*, f. 11; cf. Zenner, *Mt. Angel's Early History*, pp. 8-9.

124. Adelhelm to Anselm, April 10, 1882: MAA, Zenner, *Extracts*, f. 11.

125. Attempts to establish Benedictine colonies at Santa Fe and in the southwest Indian mission fields likewise failed. See Beckman, *Kansas Monks*, 212-213.

126. Adelhelm to Anselm, Oct. 19, 1881, cited by G. Hogan, pt. 1, p. 15.

127. *Ibid.*; see also MAA, Zenner, *Pages*, f. 8.

128. MAA, Maurus Snyder, *Mem. Dates*, p. 3 for May 9, 1882.

129. Adelhelm to Anselm, April 10, 1882, from St. Vincent's Hospital, Portland OR. Referring to Abp. Seghers, "who was much worried that I was going to die, very willingly gave me permission today to start the trip as soon as possible. In case Fr. Nicholas would or could not come, he is prepared to steal a priest from somewhere and send him to replace me until late autum [at Fillmore]".

130. A certain P. Buchholzer from Maryville CA, for example, wrote to Abbot Anselm on Feb. 20, 1882, having heard that the Benedictines were locating in Oregon instead of California. He offered his opinion, summarizing that the land in Oregon would be "practically donated" but the climate there would be rougher than in California; whereas the Sta. Inéz lands would have to be bought, but then the climate was very mild. His observations were as facilating as the reports from Fr. Adelhelm, so that the abbot could hardly have known what to make of the situation. To add to the pressue, both reported that land prices were escalating because of the influx of settlers to Oregon and California. MAA, Zenner, *Extracts*, f. 11; Zenner, *Historical Notes*, f. 5.

131. Fr. Maurus thought that the archbishop may have offered the mission to the Benedictines, but this remains unclear. The mission in question during spring 1881 was presumably St. Helena, just north of San Francisco. Fr. Maurus inserted his own evaluation of the affair alongside his translation of Adelhelm's letter of Aug. 15, 1881 to Anselm (MAA, Maurus Snyder, *Historical Notes*, p. 4): "...Adelhelm liked the S. Ynez proposition. Why he did not act accordingly, and settled on S. Ynez, is a mystery. Could have had a donation of land at least a thousand acres; why he decided to settle in Oregon and pay from $25 to $80 [an acre]... shows that he was irresponsible". Fr. Maurus concluded that the founding fathers had made up their minds on an Oregon location before going to California, because of their "high opinion of Abp. Seghers, based on reports they read of him in papers, possibly of his trips to Alaska when Bp. of Vancouver Island". Maurus, no admirer of Adelhelm, was wrong here, since Abp. Seghers was still fairly new on the job in 1881, and was not before a widely known personality. See MAA, Maurus Snyder, *Mem. Dates*, p. 1 for May 24, 1881 in addition to his *Historical Notes*, p. 4.

132. A second brother was appointed to go, but he chose not to emmigrate. The abbot did not press the issue, nor did he select another candidate. Apparently all of the recruiting was done by Adelhelm himself, with the abbot's subsequent acquiesence.

133. Anselm Villiger, *Tagebuch*, for June 17, 1881: "Heute ist P. Adelhelm aus seiner Mission in Oregon hier eingetroffen. Er reiste 34 Tage, zürst auf dem Stillen Ozean bis Californien dann per Bahn durch das Herz von Nordamerika nach New York, & durch den Atlant. Ozean nach Cherbourg. Er schient ermattet & angegriffen, stellt sich aber in seinem schwarzen Bart gut & ist lebhaft. Seine Erzählungen sind interessant. Er bittet so sehr um P.P., F.F. & Candidaten. Wir wollen beten, denken, & Berathen, wie dem eifrigen Missionar zu helfen sei". MAA, Zenner, *Diaries*, f. 13; see also G. Hogan, pt. 1, p. 15.

133. Engelberg, although an old foundation, was not a large commmnity. In 1897 on the jubilee of Abbot Anselm I, the catalogues of it and its two American foundations listed the following memberships:

Members:	Engelberg Abbey	Conception Abbey	Mt. Angel Priory
Priests:	41(11 in USA)	24	13
Brothers:	1	7	6
Novices:	13(1 in USA)	15+1	38
Total:	55(12 in USA)	47	47

This means that the daughter houses by then had more men in residence than did Engelberg Abbey (i.e., 47 each, compared to the mother-house's 32). There were a total fo 149 monks associated in Engelberg's extended family. When Mt. Angel was getting started, Conception Abbey had no spare manpower either. According to Abbot Anselm's diary (*Tagebuch*, entry for March 7, 1884 cited by Zenner, *Pages*, p. 2), Conception had then 33 members, including the abbot, five at Mt. Angel, nine in various chaplancies, ten lay brothers, and five novices. Considering those at Mt. Angel and in Switzerland studying, there were only 13 monks and the 5 novices with Abbot Frowin. Consequently, the American settlements were a huge drain on the European community, and when this situation is understood, the effort to support two American houses at once must have been monumental. Engelberg's attitude toward the American colonization stands in mark contrast to that of Einsiedeln earlier.

134. Anselm Villiger, *Tagebuch,* quoted by G. Hogan, pt. 1, p. 15.

135. Fr. Maurus (MAA, *Comments*, s.n., ff. 25-26) maintains that everyone other than the Engelbergians paid 1000 francs apiece in advance, and that he too, although a monk of Engelberg, had paid his own faire presumably with family money.

136. Anselm Villiger, *Tagebuch*, for Sept. 8, 1882: "...in grossen Kisten verpackt, aber immer noch vollen sie mehr, immer noch sind sie nicht zufrieden. Das berührt mich ubel". under-stated in G. Hogan (pt. 2, p. 14) as "but yet they want still more and are still not satisfied. That makes a bad impression on me".

137. See the account of Fr. Maurus, *Mem. Dates*, ff. 5-7.

138. The monks' sense of distance and knowledge of American geography was still undeveloped. Abbot Anselm's diary, for example, reveals understandable ignorace about the West, except that it took Adelhelm so long to traverse it; he refers to the Pacific Ocean always as the "Quiet Ocean". Their education about America would have been the stories told by Adelhelm, which according to the Abbot were so intriging. The route across country ran toward upstate New York, then across to Rochester, Buffalo, Erie, Cleveland, and over to Toledo, Ohio. Fr. Barnabas, exited at the prospect, told everyone to listed for the thunder of Niagra Falls since he had figured out that they would pass in its neighborhood. See Maurus Snyder, *Mem. Dates*, f. 6.

139. Fr. Maurus recalled his first impression of Portland, Oregon, as they walked up the wharf to the cathedral with a welcoming party of diocesan priests, Frs. Orth, Gibony, Melayer, Glorieux, and Thibeau (in the absence of Abp. Seghers): "...we had to step into mud at every street crossing. The night was dark, and the gas lamps were few and feeble". MAA: Marus Snyder, *Mem. Dates*, f. 8. See the arrival announcement in *The Oregonian* for Oct. 27 (p. 3, col. 1) which made all the men into priests, so that later the archbishop had to explain what he was to do with so many new clergy. The *Oregonian* said simply that they "are coming to organize churches and schools," with no mention of a monastery. Its readership, overwhelmingly Protestant, perhaps would have had no more ability to distinguish between secular and regular clergy, and supposedly had suspicions of a major Catholic action front about to take over the state.

140. A copy of the bull in Adelhelm's own hand exists in the Mt. Angel archives; transcribed again by "P. J[erome] Archivist" as *Rescripta Romana* into the abbey's *Historical Notes*, s.n., pp. 9-10. Prior Jerome's notes indicate that the original petition and concession of July 2 or 3, 1882, drawn by Cardinal Simeon, were never at Mt. Angel.

141. *Monastic Life at Mt. Angel* (1936), 17-20.

142. Anselm Villiger, *Tagebuch*, quoted by G. Hogan, pt. 1, p. 15.

143. G. Hogan, pt. 2, p. 15.

144. Queen of the Angels convent was blessed on July 8, 1888. See the *Catholic Sentinel*, 24 (July 12, 1888), p. 4, cols. 5-6 for a description of the community and new foundation; cf. MAA, *Catholic Sentinel* abstracts for that date, p. 7.

145. One of the party, Mrs. Sonderegger, the mother of Sister Birgitta, was a lay woman. The original group consisted of:

6 priests	Adelhelm himself, Beda Horat, Barnabas Held, Anselm Wachter, plus Ferdinand Limberg and Fr. Nicholas who joined them at Gervais.
1 lay brother	Br. Theodul
4 choir candidates	Paul Fundman, Edmund Schnyder, John Burrs, Medard Fürst.
3 brother candidates	Joseph Eugster, John Battig, and Boniface Beurer.
3 laborers	C.T. Schetter, Mr. Kundig, & Mr. Kuhne.
7 total	
2 Maryville nuns	Mother Bernadine Wachter & Sister Benedicta.
2 Rickenbach nuns	Sisters Agatha and Birgitta.
3 Sarnen nuns	Sisters Johanna, Rosalia, and Magdalena.

4 postulants	Josi & Kathleen Battig, Clara Hess, & Marie Eugster.
1 laywoman	Mrs. Sonderegger
12 subtotal or a total party of 29.	

See the *Catholic Sentinel* for Nov. 13, 1884; cf. MAA *Abstracts*, p. 16.

147. *Catholic Sentinel*, for Nov. 20, 1884; cf. MAA *Abstracts*, p. 19.

148. The original landowners in Oregon were surveyed in 1870. The homesteaders whose land came into the monastic domain had made originally the following claims (Williams, *Oregon* (1870), 43); as entered:

John P. Graves	640 acres
Jn. W. Cleaver	280 acres
Benj. Cleaver	641 acres
Randolph G. Gibson	639 acres (claim 54)
John H. Palmer	290 acres
William Glover	600 acres

149. Adelhelm to Anselm, Jan. 6, 1882; cited by G. Hogan, pt. 1, pp. 14-15.

150. G. Hogan, pt. 2, p. 15.

151. Fr. Martin Pollard, *Mt. Angel Letter*, 30 no. 6 (Dec. 1981), 5.

152. The land ownership maps are based on tracings, with modifications, on the 1870 survey copy in the Library of Congress Map Division, which provided copies of non-copyrighted material; the coverage of Marion Co., Oregon, is based on changing land ownership recorded in the various revisions by the Metsker Map Co., Seattle & Tacoma WA (1929 and 1971 mainly), which denied the author's request of copy privileges. Consequently a tracing to scale and reconstruction are included instead of the ownership maps themselves. The land-use survey maps were by the U.S. Geological Survey.

153. G. Hogan, pt. 2, p. 15.

154. Adelhelm to Anselm, Jan. 25, 1883; quoted by Hogan, pt. 2, p. 15.

155. The "Milk Ranch refers to a square mile of land, now just called "Section 30" (see map insert). Mt. Angel's ownership of highland varies, but it has always limited its holdings to the upper Abiqua creek area where the original Milk Ranch was. Property added in the 1920s and before was sold to the Longview Fiber Company and the state.

156. Adelhelm to Anselm, July 11, 1883; quoted by Hogan, pt. 2, p. 15.

157. Anselm Villiger, *Tagebuch*, for Sept. 30, 1883. Note his accounting entries for July 23 and Nov. 1: MAA, Zenner, *Diaries*, p. 17-18.

158. G. Hogan, pt. 2, p. 15.

159. MAA, Journal of Fr. Barnabas, entry for Dec. 23, 1882, cited by Zenner, *Extracts*, f. 12. Note that Fr. Barnabas sent copies of his journal entries to Abbot Anselm on a monthly basis throughout 1883.

160. Adelhelm to Anselm, Feb. 18, 1883; quoted by G. Hogan, pt. 2, p. 15.

161. Adelhelm to Anselm, June 25, 1883; *ibid.*.

162. *Ibid.*.

163. Anselm Villiger, *Tagebuch*, entries for Oct. 15-21, 1883; transcribed by Zenner, *Diaries*, p. 18; trans. in Hogan, pt. 3, p. 8.

164. *Ibid.*.

165. Anselm Villiger, *Tagebuch*, for Feb. 11, 1884; quoted by Hogan, pt. 3, p. 8.

166. MAA, *Membership Roster*, 1884, cited by Fr. Martin Pollard, "Chonicle," *Mt. Angel Letter*, 33 no. 6 (Dec. 1981), 5: the community consisted of 27 members then (6 priests, 4 clerics or clerical novices, and 16 lay brothers).

167. Adelhelm to Anselm, May 12, 1884; Quoted by Hogan, pt. 3, p. 8.

168. *Ibid.*.

169. *Ibid.*.

170. Signed B.H., *Catholic Sentinel*, Nov. 20, 1884; cf. MAA, *Abstracts*, for 1884, p. 17.

171. Hogan, pt. 3, p. 8; MAA, doc. no. A-II-1-4.

172. MAA, Maurus Snyder, personal interview transcription, n.d., inserted into his *Chronological Notes*, for 1883-83, pp. 1-6.

173. Hogan, pt. 3, p. 8.

174. *Catholic Sentinel*, for July 9, 1885; cf. MAA, *Abstracts*, pp. 4-5.

175. Fr. Wehrner's transgressions are described simply and without detail by the prior, as "allerei Pastoral Unklugheiten". See MAA, Zenner, *Pages*, f. 17.

176. Anselm Villiger, *Tagebuch*, for Jan. 3, 1886; MAA, Zenner, *Diaries*, p. 28; quoted by Hogan, pt. 3, p. 8.

177. Abp. Seghers resigned on Jan. 1, 1884, presumably because of discussions with Pope Leo XIII beforehand at the Vatican. He was immediately appointed bishop of a newly constituted mission diocese consisting of Vancouver Island, parts of what are now British Columbia, and Alaska. He moved to his see at Victoria and there built an episcopal mansion which in 1885 gained some adverse publicity for its $17,000 cost! After setting up his administration, he set out on an inspection of the Indian missions under his jurisdiction. He was murdered on Nov. 28, 1886; the exact circumstances of his death are unknown, but Oregonian Catholics soon referred to his "martyrdom". See the reports in the *Catholic Sentinel* for July 19-20, 1887. Abp. Gross (b. 1837 of Alsacian ancentry) had done a variety of missionary work in the eastern U.S. before his appointment to the see of Savannah, Georgia, in 1873. In 1874 he was consecrated by the archbishop of Baltimore.

178. Fr. Nicholas in the late 1880s served as pastor at Colfax WA. Periodic rotation of assignments makes it unclear when the monks took over a parish for other than a short-term substitution. In the case of Sublimity, for example, Fr. Joseph Lessler, a diocesan priest, was there in 1889 so its pastor, Fr. Bolla, OSB, could intern at the cathedral and work with the archdiocesan administration. In September 1890 Frs. Kauten and Barnabas OSB were working in two distant parishes in Spokance WA, with over 5000 Catholics in dire need of clergy. There was also the Benedictine mission at Crooked Finger (named after Chief Crooked Finger of the Molalla Indians) which was settled by German immigrants after 1884 when the Niederbergers were joined by the Maloney, Paquet, and Lucus families (the latter two were descendants from St. Paul settlers). Fr. Anselm Wachter first said Mass there at the home of Anton Ettner, near Scotts Mills, and afterwards, the monks journied upland each Sunday. Fr. Frowin Epper OSB took over, and finally ac hurch was dedicated in 1898. A new church was erected in 1920, and in 1940 the parish itself was transferred to the direct administration of the abbey along with Mt. Angel parish, and the latter's assistant pastor (i.e., Fr. Hildebrand Melchior, OSB) ordinarily served this isolated community. Note that the memoires of Fr. John Plas, recorded in 1950, which recount much of the history of this parish and the settlements in the neighboring highlands, are preserved in the abbey archives (see also the two page abstract in the library archives, s.n.). Consequently, it seems that the Benedictine fathers were never permanently taken off parish duty.

179. Fr. Maurus disputed the contention that Fr. Wehrner was ever pastor at Oregon City, but that he may have helped out there. His assignments were at Sublimity, Stayton, Jordan and Aumsville OR, in German parishes, because he spoke English so poorly. He had trouble with a key parishoner at Jordan, Herr Silbernagel, but the records are just not clear about the real problems prompting the archbishop's decisions regarding the Benedictines and their parish work. See MAA, Maurus Snyder, *Comments,* f. 29.

180. Fr. Wehrner died on New Year's eve, 1888—the third of the community to be buried on the hill. Fr. Eugene Bolla, just ordained on January 11, 1889, succeeded him at Sublimity after an interim of rotated staffing from Mt. Angel. See the *Catholic Sentinel*, for May 9, 1889; *Mt. Angel College Notes*, for Jan. 13, 1889. Sublimity's new church was dedicated on Oct. 26, 1890. For the letter of Abp. Gross to Anselm, Oct. 22, 1887, see MAA, s.n.; Zenner, *Extracts*, ff. 18-19; and the transcription by Malone, Append. II [pp. 225-226].

181. MAA, Maurus Snyder, *Comments*, n.d., f. 29.

182. Anselm Villiger, *Tagebuch*, for Feb. 13, 1886.

183. Adelhelm to Anselm, Dec. 13, 1886; MAA, Zenner, *Pages*, f. 18.

184. *Prospectus of Mt. Angel College* (1887), 7 p.

185. Fr. Barnabas' *Journal* entry for July 25, 1883 in MAA; see Zenner, *Extracts*, f. 13.

186. Beck & Ass., *A Self-Evaluation Study of Mt. Angel Seminary* (1969), 4.

187. *Catholic Sentinel*, for Oct. 8, 1888; MAA, *Abstracts*, p. 8.

188. *Catholic Sentinel*, for July 4, 1889; cf. *Mt. Angel College Notes*, for 1890, p. 20.

189. *Catholic Sentinel*, for Feb. 25, 1888; cf. MAA, Zenner, *Abstracts*, for 1888, p. 2; for 1890, p. 20.

190. *Catholic Sentinel*, for Sept. 25, 1890; MAA, Zenner, *Abstracts*, p. 23.

191. Bauman, "Fr. Dominic" *Mt. Angel Letter*, 34 (1982), 3-5.

192. *Catholic Sentinel*, Aug. 13, 1885 records the archbishop's first visit. See MAA, Zenner, *Abstracts*, p. 6.

193. *Catholic Sentinel*, June 5, 1890; MAA, Zenner, *Abstracts*, p. 19.

194. *Oregonian*, May 4, 1892, p. 1; and the *Catholic Sentinel* for the same date, MA, Zenner, *Abstracts*, p. 13.

195. Anselm Villiger, *Tagebuch*, for May 20, 1892; quoted by G. Hogan, pt. 3, p. 9.

196. Anselm Villiger, *Tagebuch*, for May 20, 1892 in MAA, Zenner, *Diaries*, pp. 43-44 The abbot quotes Adelhelm, who characterized the disaster "...in kurzer Zeit ein Raub der Flammen...".

197. Adelhelm Morter, "The Fire of 1892," *Mt. Angel Letter* n.d., quoting an unidentified "eyewitness account".

198. Apb. Gross, Pastoral letter reprinted in *Mt. Angel Letter* (n.d.), p. 2.

199. See Morter's account, n. 197 *supra*.

200. MAA, Sister M. Agnes Butsch, *Reminiscences*, ff. 32-33.

201. T. J. Casey, sec., "First Alumnae meeting of June 27, 1894"; MAA, s.n., transcription by Francis P. Colets (1896), s.p..

202. William Kramer to Anselm, Dec. 17, 1892, paraphrased in Anselm Villiger, *Tagebuch*, for that date; cf. MAA, Zenner, *Diaries*, p. 46: "Prior könne so lange wegbleiben, als etwas einzusammeln sei. Prior werde wahrscheinlich nie Abt werden und tauge als Prior aber nicht als Abt".

203. *Catholic Sentinel*, Nov. 13, 1890; MAA, Zenner, *Abstracts*, pp. 24-25.

204. *Ibid.*.

205. Anselm Villger, *Tagebuch*, II, 156 translated by Malone, 129-131.

206. Fr. Maurus recalled (MAA, *Comments*, f. 28) that the decision was reached only after "much wrangling" but the Chapter book he consulted did not provided adequate detail of the discussions. At one time the vote was 6 vs. 7, the narrow majority against building on the hilltop.

207. Prior Thomas to Abbot Leodegar, April 13, 1901; MAA, Zenner's transcriptions, ff. 3-5.

208. Zenner, *Pages*, f. 20.

209. Zenner, *Pages*, f. 22. Note that Zenner in 1949 read the *Tagebuch* of Abbot Leodegar Scherer, but transcribed for the MAA only the introduction, the "Erinnerungen von Abt Leodegar" in Helft I, pp. 76-78 for 1901-04, from the Engelberg archives.

210. According to Zenner (*Pages*, f. 12), Abbot Leodegar in his memoires regarded Fr. Benedict as "one of Engelberg's most outstanding and talented men of the time".

211. MAA, Maurus Snyder, *Comments*, f . 28.

212. MAA, Zenner, *Pages*, ff. 11-12.

213. See the descriptions of the Mt. Angel manuscript codices in the following catalogue, pt. 1.

214. MAA, Bernard Murphy, *Reminiscences*, transcribed in 1951, p. 2.

215. MAA, Maurus Snyder, *Mem. Dates*, ff. 6-7: "A German student cannot enjoy drinking without singing. The young men kept on singing, therefore, *sotto voce*. But not to be allowed to get a glass of beer on Sunday in free America was beyond their comprehension! ... Fr. Adelhelm [who ordered beer for all] felt rather proud of his achievements in finding a place to get a glass of beer for the Sisters".

216. MAA, Bernard Murphy, *Reminiscences*, p. 6.

217. *Ibid.*, p. 10. Note that the priory had no electricity, but used instead coal oil lamps for light and wood for heat. Br. Philibert had been in charge of refilling the lamps and keeping oil in supply; as strict ascetic, he was affectionately known in the community as "Coal Oil Johanny" by the students. In 1900 the college and seminary switched to acetyline gas lamps.

218. MAA, Bernard Murphy, *Reminiscences*, p. 4.

219. MAA, Bernard Murphy, *Memoirs*, transcribed in 1903, f. 15; MAA typescript, p. 2.

220. MAA, Maurus Snyder, *Mem. Dates*, for Oct. 18, 1882, ff. 7-9.

221. Sister Agnes claimed in 1935 that the pioneer settler, Martin Settelmeier, "whose prejudices ran strongly in favor of German Lutheranism," disliked Adelhelm's getting the railroad to rename the Fillmore station as Mt. Angel. The latter tried to have the town incorporporated under the name Fillmore.

222. MAA, Zenner, *Pages*, f. 13.

223. MAA, Bernard Murphy, *Memoirs*, f. 11 (p. 2).

224. Adelhelm to Leodegar, Jan. 12, 1912; Placidus to Leodegar, Oct. 21, 1910 and Dec. 19, 1911; Prior Thomas to Leodegar, April 13, 1901: MAA, *Transcriptions*, f. 2. See also Leodegar Scherer, *Tagebuch*, 76-78, transcribed by Zenner, *Diaries*, 53-58.

225. MAA, Zenner, *Pages*, f. 13.

226. MAA, Maurus Snyder, *Comments*, f. 29.

227. Zenner (*Pages*, f. 13) relates that so reactionary were the early members of the Mt. Angel community against the Beuronese reform in the Swiss-Benedictine monasteries, that on May 4, 1896 the chapter voted to join the American-Cassinese Benedictine Congregation instead. Abbot Anselm's diary shows that he took this personally as a rejection of Mt. Angel's Swiss heritage, and in time, cool heads prevailed.

228. Abbot Leodegar wrote memoires rather than a true diary, as did Abbot Anselm. The former's *Tagebuch*

contains 21 pages of references to Mt. Angel. Note that this abbot had been prefect in Engelberg's college at the time of Mt. Angel's foundation, and he had then objected to a second American foundation on grounds of Engelberg's pressing manpower shortage. He had reacted particularly badly toward Adelhelm's taking to America younger men Leodegar thought were needed more in the Swiss monastery's college. Zenner (*Pages*, f. 13) refers to this as "an old prejudice against Adelhelm" and concluded "...this much is clear. Abbot Leodegar did not share Abbot Anselm's confidence in Fr. Adelhelm as being the right man to head the Mount Angel undertaking".

229. MAA, Bernard Murphy, *Reminiscences*, p. 9.

230. Frowin to Leodegar, Feb. 9, 1904; transcribed by Zenner, *Pages*, f. 14.

231. *Ibid.*, f. 15.

232. MAA, *Rescripta Romana*, no. 59931. Decretum of Pius X, dated March 24, 1904 for the enactment of the hearing before the Sacred Congregation for the Propagation of the Faith, March 23, 1904. See the transcription, MAA, *Historical Notes,* p. 12.

233. The Conception Abbey *Ordo* for 1902 notes that the priories of St. Benedict in Oregon and St. Gall in the diocese of Fargo ND (Richardson) joined the Congregation at the same time. The General Chapter continued to refer to Mt. Angel as *Prioralus qua talis* and *In abbatiam mutetur canonice* suggesting that it was still canonically under Engelberg until it was elevated to abbatial status. See Jerome Veth to Ambrose Zenner, Nov. 19, 1951, appended to Zenner's *Pages*, f. 32.

234. A stationary steam engine pumped water directly from the well to the hilltop until 1907, when the system was improved by forcing water with compressed air to a 23,000 gallon reservoir, thereby insuring a constant supply of water under pressure even during mechanical failure. The wood pipes were replaced with steel, with a capacity flow of 5000 gallons an hour. The pumping station was severely damaged by fire in 1907; thereafter an electric pump was introduced. See MAA, Bernard Murphy, *Memoirs*, p. 12.

235. MAA, Bernard Murphy, *Memoirs* for 1901, f. 11 (p. 2).

236. Thomas Aquinas Meienhofer was born in Wuppenau, Canton Thurgau, Switzerland, Sept. 18, 1865. He entered Engelberg in 1890, was ordained in 1893, and was elected conventional prior on July 11, 1901. He was appointed abbot, March 23, 1904, and was blessed on June 29. He resigned his office and left religious life on May 25, 1910.

237. Placidus Ferst was born in Bremen, in the diocese of Fulda, Germany, on June 8, 1868; professed at Engelberg on July 11, 1884; and was ordained on July 11, 1891. He was elected abbot on August 30, 1910, blessed on October 5, and was the second abbot in a row to resign (July 5, 1921). He died in Engelberg, August 16, 1940.

238. MAA, Maurus Snyder, *Comments*, f. 29.

239. MAA, Zenner, *Pages*, f. 21.

240. Maurus Snyder to Abbot Leodegar, August 14, 1902; MAA, *Transcriptions,* ff. 7-8: "Die Druckerei ist eine Goldmine".

241. Abp. Seghers had made four trips to organize the church in Alaska before his murder in the Yukon, apparently by his trapper-guide, a man named Fuller according to his two surviving Jesuit travel companions, enroute to a mission at Mulato. His last trip was allegedly to counter an anti-Catholic campaign mounted by the U.S. Government's so-called "public education" ministers. After his death and burial at Victoria, the Jesuits took over the mission work and organization of the church in Alaska, operating out of the apostolic vicariate at Juneau. The latter was raised to a bishopric in its own right only in 1951.

242. MAA, Bernard Murphy, *Reminiscences*, p. 8.

243. Maurus Snyder to Abbot Leodegar, Aug. 14, 1902; MAA, *Transcriptions,* ff. 7-9.

244. Fr. Modeste Demers, when he became the first bishop there, had only ten priests for the entire island and coastline of British Columbia. A vicariate was moved to the mainland at New Westminster (near modern Vancouver BC), where the daughterhouse of Mt. Angel would be founded. Vancouver had its first bishop in 1864, D. Herbomez (d. 1890). Much of the teaching and missionary work was coordinated by the Sisters of St. Anne, and its few clergy, 17 priests, were ll Oblate Fathers. The church was reorganized by Bp. Durieu after the great Vancouuver fire of 1899, and in 1903 it was raised to independent archiepiscopal status. Victoria, previously a suffragan of Portland, was then placed under Vancouver so that all Canadian churches were independent from American sees. By 1916 Vancouver also had suffragans in the Yukon, the see of Prince Rupert, and now has others at Kamloops, Whitehorse, and Nelson.

245. Sister Agnes to Maurus Snyder, Feb. 13, 1935, reflecting on an article by F. Lockley in the *Daily Journal* (1931): "Mt. Angel is a bit of the old world dropped down in the new. Just as in the old days, Gervais, St. Paul, St. Louis on the French Prairie, were a bit of old France in the new world, so today Mt. Angel is little Germany in the Willamette Valley".

246. Bernard Murphy was born in Portland OR, Dec. 10, 1874; he professed at Mt. Angel on Nov. 4, 1894, was ordained on June 4, 1898, and was elected abbot on Oct. 25, 1921 and was blessed on Nov. 17. He received a

coadjutor on August 1, 1934, and died on February 18, 1942.

247. Fr. Luke Eberly, quoted by S. Slemenda, "Mt. Angel Abbey a half-century ago," in the Silverton *Appeal-Tribune* (Sept. 23, 1976), 1.

248. S. Slemenda, "Holocaust engulfs Mt. Angel Abbey...". *Appeal-Tribune* (Sept. 23, 1976), 2.

249. *Ibid.*.

250. MAA, Augustine Bachofen, *Diary*, quoted in *Mt. Angel Seminary, 1889-1964*, p. 23.

251. "St. Benedict's Abbey is a Mass of Ruins!" *Mt. Angel Magazine*, s.n. (Sept. 30, 1926), 4-5.

252. *Ibid.*.

253. Abp. Edward Howard, pastoral letter of Sept. 22, 1926, reprinted in the *Mt. Angel Magazine* (Sept. 30, 1926), 4.

254. Portland *Oregonian* (Sept. 24, 1926), 1. Turner and Mack led in organizing alumnae to help in rebuilding Mt. Angel. Turnermade his appeal to sports enthusiasts saying how small-college athletic programs were scouting grounds for the large ball clubs, but hastened to add: "the high scholastic requirements [at Mt. Angel] helps to make brainier players later on when they get into bigger sports". So much for academic excellence!

255. Kleber, *St. Meinrad*, 455.

256. "St. Benedict's Abbey is a Mass of Ruins," *Mt. Angel Magazine* (Sept. 30, 1926), 5.

257. Oregon *Daily Journal* (Portland, Sept. 23, 1926), 1-2.

258. Salem's *Capital Journal* (Sept. 22, 1926), 1.

259. *Ibid.*.

260. MAA, Inventory for Drawer 6, Env. 1-5, covering 127 inqueries and applications from 1900 through 1945.

261. Thomas Aquinas Meier was born in Troy, Iowa, on Jan. 5, 1887. He professed at Mt. Angel on Nov. 1, 1906; was ordained on June 4, 1910; was blessed as abbot, Aug. 10, 1934 and received his official coadjutor on August 16, 1950. He died on Oct. 17, 1961.

262. "Fr. Leo Walsh, OSB," *Mt. Angel Letter* (1967), 2.

263. All of these institutions except the University of Portland closed during the 1970s under the impact of the recession, rising costs, decliningg5enrollments, and post-Vatican II shifts in priorities of some of the religious orders. Marylhurst has remained active as an adult and continuing education center.

264. "Facilities and Activities," in R. W. Beck & Ass., *Self-Evaluation Study of Mt. Angel Seminaay* (1969), pt. 2, pp. 1, 9-12.

265. Damian Jentges was born in Herndon KS on Nov. 25, 1902. He professed at Mt. Angel on Sept. 8, 1926, was ordained on Sept. 21, 1929, and was elected abbot Aug. 16, 1950. He was blessed on Oct. 5, 1950 and died in office, Sept. 1, 1974.

266. Mt. Angel underwent its last examination of standards and programs by the NCCB in 1981.

267. "Annual Report Edition," *Mt. Angel Seminary Newsletter* (Fall, 1980-81), 1.

268. The *Self-Evaluation Study* (1969), II, 9-10, attests that tuition was raise in 1967 from $800 to $1000 per year for the seminary, and for the college from $900 to $1200 (as also for the school of theology). Student service fees were $40 and $50 respectively, so that the total annual costs for a degree program would run $13,600 at Mt. Angel.

269. *Mt. Angel Seminary: Profiles and Catalog, 1980-83*, ed. Gregory Duerr (Mt. Angel Abbey press, 1980), 26.

270. Martin Pollard to Lawrence McCrank, March 20, 1981.

271. Abbot Damian had wanted to offer an annual program of excellent music as a cultural contribution to the people of the valley, as Abbot Anselm expalined in 1976 in the *Mt. Angel Letter*, 28 no. 3 (June 1976). Plans materialized largely through the efforts of Mrs, "Michel" Alastair MacKay, the Back festival's executive director. The series began in 1971. The fifth program, for example, featured organ, harpsichord, piano, and violin, vocal and choral conserts, as well as a presentation by the Mt. Angel monastic Scholia.

272. Beck & Ass., *Self-Evaluation Study*, I, 5; II, 16; III, 1-3. The figures here, from accounts in 1966-68, are totalled and then Saeraged, merely as a summary of the report's presentation.

273. *Ibid.*, III, 1-3.

274. *Ibid.*, II, 16.

275. The Mt. Angel community in 1980 consists of 124 members: 67 priests and 23 brothers in final vows; 26 monks in temporary vows; 1 oblate, 4 noovces, and 3 postulants. Mt. Angel is the second largest monastery of six houses in the American-Swiss federation which now has 872 members (in 1980, up from 859 in 1979).

276. Anselm Galvin was born in Saskatoon, Sask., Canada, on Nov. 8, 1916. He professed at Mt. Angel on Sept. 8, 1937 and was ordained on May 14, 1942. He was elected on Oct. 8, 1974, and resigned the abbatial office in

August 1980. He continues to be active in the community, and serves as the assistant pastor of St. Mary's church in Mt. Angel OR.

277. Bonaventure Zerr was born in Aberdeen SD on Nov. 2, 1936, and was given the name Jerome. He came with his parents to Portland in 1943 and came into contact with Mt. Angel's Benedictines through their parish work at Sacred Heart. He was educated at Mt. Angel, and in 1956 became a postulant, then a novice, and made his profession of first vows in 1957. His final vows were professed on Sept. 12, 1960, and he was ordained on May 11, 1962. Thereafter he pursued studies of Scripture and theology at Munich, both at the monastery of St. Boniface and the university of Munich under Karl Rahner. Upon his return he joined the Mt. Angel seminary faculty, served as subprior, and acquisitions librarian, before his election on Aug. 25, 1980. He is the author of *The Psalms-A New Translation* (Paulist Press), a known theologian, linguist, a Civil War history buff, and an unknown but avid philatelist. Fr. Peter Eberle was appointed prior immediately after Bonaventure's blessing by Abp. Cornelius Powers of Portland. See the biographical sketch in the *Mt. Angel Letter*, 22 no. 4 (Aug. 1980), 2-4.

NOTES: The Library, 1882-1982

1. Anselm to Frowin, Nov. 8, 1876; trans., Malone, 107. See also Frowin to Anselm, Jan. 22, 1874 (CAA, H-III-B-2-1874), cited by Malone, 78.

2. MAA, Zenner, *Historical Notes,* p. 3.

3. Abp. Seghers to Anselm, Feb. 1, 1884; *Catholic Sentinel*, 15 no. 7 (March 13, 1884); MAA, *Abstracts*, for 1883, p. 15.

4. Anselm Villiger, *Tagebuch*, for Sept. 8, 1882: "...Menge wertvoller Bücher, Devotionalten, u.s.w. in 30 grossen Kisten verpackt". See MAA, Zenner, *Pages*, f. 20.

5. MAA, Sister Agnes Butsch, *Reminiscences*, s.n., f. 19.

6. MAA, Pr. Jerome, "Prologue," *Archives Index*, XI, pt. 1, f. 2.

7. One wishes that Abbot Anselm had specified the amount and kind of books sent in 1882, other than his distinquishing between books and devotional literature; he simply abbreviated his ennumeration with the German equivalent of 'etc.'. MAA, Zenner, *Pages*, f. 20; see also note 4, *supra*.

8. MAA, Zenner, *Pages*, f. 12.

9. *Catholic Sentinel*, for July 25, 1889; MAA, "Date Sheet," *Abstracts*, 1.

10. MA College, *Mt Angel College* (St. Benedict OR, 1908) 10; Beckman, *Kansas Monks*, 108.

11. Fr. Notker Maeder continued to scrounge for books while in Rome; see the provenance index to the following catalogue.

12. Benno Linderbaurer to Mt. Angel's librarian & Abbot Bernard, Feb. 27, 1923 and Sept. 3, 1922: MAA, B-II-CC-5, env. 5.

13. MAA, Bernard Murphy, *Memoirs*, for 1902, f. 13 (p. 2).

14. MA College, *Prospectus* (St. Benedict OR, 1887), 6.

15. *Ibid.*, 1-9.

16. MAA, Bernard Murphy, *Reminiscences*, p. 6.

17. MAA, Jerome Wespe, "Prologue", *Archives Index*, XI, pt. 1, f. 1.

18. MAA, Zenner, *Pages*, ff. 10-11; Jerome Wespe, "Recollections" (1951), *Archives Index*, XI, pt. 1, f. 2.

19. MAA, Bernard Murphy, *Reminiscences*, p. 4.

20. MAA, Bernard Murphy, *Memoirs*, for 1901, f. 17 (p. 1).

21. MAA, Maurus Snyder, *Comments*, f. 29.

22. Note the request for permission to photograph the Mt. Angel manuscripts for the *Oregon Journal*, Mar. 18, 1927: MAA, B-5-2, no. 12. See the descriptions in the following catalogue, pt. 1, Manuscripts.

23. MA College, *Mount Angel College* (St. Benedict OR, 1897), 8-11. This library description remained unchanged in the college catalogues until 1909.

24. MA College, *Mount Angel College* (St. Benedict OR, 1909-10), 26.

25. *Ibid.*, 9-10, 13.

26. Fr. Luke Eberle, quoted by the *Mt. Angel Magazine* (Sept. 30, 1926), n. p..

27. Kleber, *St. Meinrad*, 376-377.

28. Fr. Luke Eberle, quoted by the Oregon *Daily Journal* (Sept. 23, 1926).

29. Note 26 *supra*.

30. See the correspondence files of Abbot Bernard (33 letters, 1928-43) and Prior Jerome Wespe (20 letters, 1928-44): MAA, B-II, EE7, env. 15; B-II-15, env. 70.

31. Athanasius Dengler to Jerome Wespe, Oct. 12 and Dec. 8, 1926: MAA, B-II-CC-2 no. 15. Pr. Jerome Wespe to Assumption Abbey (Scheyern, Bavaria), Jan. 18, 1927 in MAA, B-II, BB-4, env. 17.

32. Lambert Krahmer of Maria Laach to Maurus Snyder, Sept. 3, 1929: MAA, B-II-CC-5, env. 4. Maurus Snyder to Jerome Wespe, Dec. 5, 1928: MAA, B-II-BB, env. 13. Bonaventure Dressback to Jerome Wespe, Sept. 28, Oct. 10, and Oct. 18, 1928-29: MAA, B2-II-CC-2, s.n.

33. Romanos Rios (Barbastro) to Maurus Snyder, Feb. 23, 1932: MAA, vB-II-CC-5, env. 6.v

34. H. Schutten to Jerome Wespe, Oct. 5, 1926: MAA, B-II-DD, env. 1.

35. St. Matthias of Trier correspondence, 1935-37: MAA, B-II-BB-4, env. 18. Abbot Ignatius (St. Meinrad) to Mt. Angel, Oct. 30, 1941: MAA, B-II-BB-4, env. 21. For the prior's correspondence with Fr. Martin Pollard at Sant'Anselmo's, Rome, 1932-33 (8 letters), see MAA, B-II-15, env. 9.

36. MAA, Martin Pollard, "Recollections," s.n., 1 f.; Pollard to Lawrence McCrank, Sept. 24, 1975; and Fr. Luke Eberle, *Tagebuch für die Reise nach Rome* with trans., *My Trip to Rome in Detail*, pp. 17- , MAA typescript, s.n..

37. MAA, Luke Eberle, *Trip*, p. 1. The author thanks Fr. Luke for his review and corrections of this chapter in draft, especially details relating to the Aachen acquisitions.

38. Dr. H. M. Werhahn (Stadtbibliothek, Aachen) to Lawrence McCrank, Dec. 15, 1975. Dr. Werhahn spoke to Frau Hanny Cloth, Kreutzer's daughter, in behalf of the author and supplied some background information about the firm, plus photocopies from the *Aachener Adressbuch* (1932), 56, 200, 201.

39. MAA, Luke Eberle, *Trip*, f. 4.

40. *Ibid.*, f. 6.

41. Abbot Athanasius Polag (St. Matthias of Trier) to Lawrence McCrank, Dec. 29, 1973.

42. MAA, Luke Eberle, *Trip*, f. 10.

43. *Ibid.*.

44. *Ibid.*.

45. Johann Hau to Jerome Wespe, s.d. (1934?): MAA, B-II-CC-5, env. 4.

46. *Pacific Star* (Jan. 15, 1933), 1-2.

47. *Ibid.*, p. 2.

48. Jerome Wespe to Dunstant Juneman, May 30, 1936: MAA, B-II-CC-5, env. 4; see also MAA, "Appointments," B-7, env. 1, no. 4.

49. Letter of Aug. 14, 1936: MAA, B-II-CC-5, env. 4.

50. MAA, Mark Schmid, "The Mt. Angel College Library Museum," notes for a lecture before the Oregon State Library assembly, April 3, 1939, s.n., f. 1.

51. MAA, Mark Schmid, "Interesting Facts about Manuscripts and Cradle Books," typescript (1939), pt. 2, f. 1.

52. MAA, "Recent Press Notes" collected by Mark Schmid (1941), f. 1.

53. *Ibid.*.

54. E. O. Heinrich to Mark Schmid, Sept. 29, 1937; refers to Prof. Brüming's "Kunst in Laboratorium," *Kriminalistische Monagtshefte: Zeitschrift für die Gesamte Kriminaliste Wissenschaft und Praxis*, XI, no. 7 (July 1937), 154-55.

55. MA, Mark Schmid, "Library records," letters of Nov. 5, 15, and 25, 1937 and Sept. 17, 1938; MAA, B-II-4, env. 4, nos. 20-21.

56. "Abbey Builds Shelves for 15,000 Books," *Pacific Star* (Feb. 7, 1941), 6.

57. "Historical Volumes Displayed at Abbey," *Capital Journal* (Oct. 1941) from the MAA clipping file.

58. Beckman, *Kansas Monks*, 318.

59. Vatican Library. *Cataloging Rules*. See full citations for these generic references in the bibliography.

60. American Library Assn., *Anglo-American Cataloging Rules*, 2nd rev. ed., 1978.

61. *Ibid.*.

62. Oliver Kapsner, *Manual of Cataloging Practice for Catholic Author and Title Entries* (1953) and IFLA (International Federation of Library Associations), *List of Uniform Titles for Liturgical Works of the Latin Rites of the Catholic Church* (1975).

63. Oliver Kapsner, OSB, *Catholic Subject Headings* (1963).

64. Networking concerns have forced librarians to consider adopting the Library of Congress MARC (Machine-Readable Cataloging) format for tagging bibliographical data for the description of rare books and manuscripts. This led to the Independent Research Libraries Assn., *Proposals for Establishing Standards for the Cataloguing of Rare Books and Specialized Research Materials in Machine-readable Form* (1979), and the new guide under the auspices of the Library of Congress, *Bibliographic Description of Rare Books* (1981), both of which materialized too late to be of use in the design of the Mt. Angel project and its data base.

65. J. Lynn and G. Peterson, *An Alternative Classification for Catholic Books* (1965) with its supplement by Thomas G. Pater.

66. MAA, Barnabus Reasoner, *The Library*, typescript, s.n., 13 f..

67. MAA, Barnabus Reasoner, *Problem of the Library*, typescript (1956?), p. 1.

68. *Ibid.*.

69. *Ibid.*, p. 10.

70. *Ibid.*, p. 3.

71. *Ibid.*, p. 1.

72. Beck & Ass., *Self-Evaluation Study* (1969), 14. The figures herein do not correlate with those of Fr. Barnabus' library reports through 1958. For example, this study cites bookstock at 24,624 for 1959 vs. the library report, 24,101. The discrepancies, however, do not alter the general impressions about this small library.

73. Barnabus Reasoner, interviewed by Fritz Meagher, *Catholic Sentinel* (Jan. 26, 1968), 12-13.

74. *Catholic Seninel* (Feb. 10, 1978), 7.

75. Barnabus Reasoner to Erick Vartiainen, April 27, 1965: MA Library administrative files, "Aalto correspondence," s.n..

76. MA Development Office, Press release (1965), 3 p..

77. Note 73, *supra*.

78. Alvar Alto to Barnabus Reasoner, May 28, 1963: MA Library Admin. file, s.n..

79. MAA, Barnabus Reasoner, "Helsinki Report," MA *Library Bulletin* (Mar. 8-18, 1966), p. 2.

80. MA News Bureau (Fr. Albert Bauman), "Factsheet" for library dedication, May 28-30, 1976.

81. Barnabus Reasoner to Erik Vartiainen, July 18, 1965: MA Lib. Admin. file, s.n..

82. *Ibid.*.

83. Barnabus Reasoner, "Helsinki Report," p. 3.

84. *Ibid.*, p. 1.

85. MA Library, Administration files, *Library Bulletin* (April 9, 1967), p. 2.

86. *Ibid.*, p. 3.

87. MA News Bureau (Fr. Albert Bauman), "The Building that Moved," press release, n.d. (1968).

88. Beth Fagan, "Famed Architect to Arrive for Planning of Library at Mt. Angel Abbey," *Oregonian* (April 17, 1967), 21. See also "Focus on Finland," *New York Times* (Mar. 15, 1964), II, 10.

89. *Ibid.*. See secondary and critical accounts of Aalto's work in the bibliography.

90. MA Lib. Admin. files, *Library Bulletin* (April 9, 1967), 3 p..

91. *Catholic Sentinel* (Jan. 26, 1968), 12.

92. *Ibid.*.

93. See notes 88 & 90 *supra*.

94. See F. Debuyst, *Art d'Eglise* 39 no. 154 (1971), 146-153.

95. "Library gets motto," *Catholic Sentinel* (June 5, 1970), 1.

96. "Alvar Aalto Exhibit," *Mt. Angel Seminary Newsletter* (Winter, 1979-80), 3.

97. Barnabus Reasoner to Alvar Aalto, Mar. 16, 1965: MA Lib. Admin. file, s.n..

98. *Capital Journal* (May 30, 1970), 1.

99. Note 88 *supra*.

100. Fr. Boniface Lautz, interviewed by Fritz Meagher, *Catholic Sentinel* (Jan. 26, 1968), 13.

101. Fr. Bernard Sanders, interviewed by Fritz Meagher, *Catholic Sentinel* (Jan. 26, 1968), 13.

102. Abbot Damian Jentges, interviewed by Fritz Meagher, *Catholic Seninel* (Jan. 26, 1968), 13.

103. *Catholic Sentinel* (Feb. 10, 1971), 7.

104. Martin Pollard to Lawrence McCrank, Nov. 11, 1981.

105. MA Abbey Seminary, *Profile & Catalog, 1980-83* (St. Benedict OR, 1980), 73.

106. Sir Richard Southern's address was preserved on tape and in transcript in the MA Library archives, and was partially published in the *Mt. Angel Letter* (Dec. 1976). It was reprinted here with permission from the *Downside Review*.

BIBLIOGRAPHY

Aachen (city), Germany. *Aechener Adressbuch*. Aachen: Stadt druck., 1932.

"Aalto. Finland's Greatest Architect," *Architectual Forum*, 118 (Mar. 1963), 120-125.

"Aalto's Second American Building: An Abbey Library for a Hillside in Oregon: Mt. Angel Abbey Library, St. Benedict, Oregon," *Architectual Record* (May, 1971), 111-116.

"Abbey library attracts many architects and theologians," *Woodburn Independent Community Scene* (Jan. 14, 1976), 11.

Abercombie, Stanley. "Aalto, Alvar," ed. Muriel Emmanuel, *Contemporary Architects* (New York: St. Martins, 1980), 7-10.

Allen, T. J. *The Benedictine Fathers of the Swiss-American Congregation as a Factor in the Educational Life of the U.S*. Unpublished thesis, University of Notre Dame, 1935.

"Alvar Aalto," *Magazine of Art*, 32 (April 1939), 208-221.

"Alvar Aalto Today," *Architectural Record*, 133 (April 1963), 135-150.

Alston, R. C.; Jannetta, M. J.. *Bibliography, machine-readable cataloguing, and the ESTC*. London: British Library, 1978.

American Library Association. *Anglo-American Cataloguing Rules*. 2nd rev. ed., M. Gorman and Paul W. Winkler. Chicago: ALA, 1978.

Appelby, Aaron. "Anselm Wachter, OSB. Monks, Teacher, Missionary," *Mt. Angel Letter*, 33 no. 6 (Dec. 1981), 3-4.

Assenmacher, Hugh. *A Place Called Subiaco*. Little Rock, Arkansas: Rose Publishing Co., 1977.

Bachofen, Augustine, OSB. *Diary, 1894-1943*. Unpublished diary in ms., MAA, A-I-I, stack 5.

Bagley, Clarence B., ed. *Early Catholic Missions in Old Oregon*. Seattle WA: Lowman & Harford Co., 1932.

Barry, Colman, OSB. *The Catholic Church and German Americans*. Milwaukee WI: Bruce Pub. Co., 1952.

________________. *Worship and Work: St. John's Abbey and University, 1856-1956*. Collegevills MN: St. John's Abbey, 1956.

Bauman, Albert, OSB. "They called him 'Dominic' [Dominic Waedenschwyler]," *Mt. Angel Letter*, 34, no. 2 (1982), 3-5.

"Beautiful Mount Angel," radio broadcast for Station KOAC (Oct. 6, 1932). MAA, typescript (1932), ff. 34-45.

Beck, R. W., & Associates. Analytical & Consulting Engineers. *A Self-Evaluation Study of Mt. Angel Seminary*. Unpublished typescrript, MAA, s.n., 1969. Esp. sections I-III (ca. 40 pp.).

Beckman, Peter, OSB. *Kansas Monks: A History of St. Benedict's Abbey*. Atchison KS: St. Benedict's Abbey Student Press, 1957.

Behrendt, Roland, OSB. *The Bursfeld Union: A Benedictine Reform of the XVth Century*. Collegeville MN: St. John's Abbey, 1954.

Benedictus, st., abbot of Monte Cassino. *Benedicti Regula*. Ed. Rudolph Hanslik, vol. 75: *Corpus scriptorum ecclesiasticorum latinorum*. Vindobonae: Hölder-Pichter-Tempsky, 1977.

________________. *The Rule of St. Benedict*. Ed. & trans. Justin McCann. Westminster MD: Neuman Press, 1952.

________________. *The Holy Rule*. Trans. Boniface Verheyen, OSB. Atchison KS: St. Benedict's Abbey Student Press, 1949.

Benedictinische Lebensform: Satzungen der Schweiserischen Benediktinkongregation. [Engelberg:Abbey press, 1970].

Bernard, S.. "The Rape of Books from the Abbey of St. Gallen," *Downside Review*, 85 (1967), 35-38.

Bischoff, William N.. *The Jesuits in Old Oregon*. Caldwell ID: Caxton Press, 1945.

Blanchet, Francis Norbert, abp. of Oregon. *The Catholic Missionaries in Oregon*, interview by H. H. Bancroft. Portland OR: Oregon Historical Society, 1878.

______________. *Historical Sketch of the Catholic Church in Oregon*. Portland OR: Catholic Sentinel press, 1878.

______________. *Notices and Voyages of the Famed Quebec Mission to the Pacific Northwest... of Fathers Blanchet and Demers,... Bolduc and Langlois,... from related papers and documents in the Oregon Historical Society*, ed. & trans., Carl Landerholm. Portland OR: Oregon Historical Society, 1956.

Bowers, Fredson T.. *The Principles of Biobliographic Description*. Princeton NJ: Princeton University Press, 1949; 2nd ed., New York: Russell & Russell, 1962.

Butsch, Sister M. Agnes, OSB. *Reminiscences*. Unpublished ms., MAA, s.n., 1935. Appended letter of Feb. 13, 1935.

Braunfels, Wolfgang. *Monasteries of Western Europe*. Princeton NJ: Princeton University Press, 1973. Cf. London: Thames & Hudson, 1972.

Brown, Arthur. "Promotion of Emigration to the Washington Territory," s.n. *Pacific Northwest Quarterly* (1945).

Brunner, Sebastian, OSB. *Ein benediktinerbuch: geschichte und beschreibung der bestenden und aufführung der aufgehobenen benediktinerstifte in Oestereich, Ungarn, Deutschland und der Schweiz*. Würzburg, Germany: Leo Owerl, 1880.

Buchreis, Adam, OSB. *Die Benediktinerl ein Uberblick über die Geschichte des Ordens*. Regensburg, Germany: G. J. Manz, 1930.

Butler, Edward Cuthbert, OSB. *Benedictine Monasticism. Studies in Benedictine Life and Culture*. New York: Barnes & Noble [1961]. Cf. London & New York: Longmans, Green & Co., 1919.

Carey, Charles H.. *A General History of Oregon*. Portland OR, 1935.

Carthy, M. P.. "Oregon". *New Catholic Encyclopedia* (New York: McGraw Hill, Co., 1967), X, 737-38.

Catholic Library Association. *Catholic Subject Headings. A List Designed for Use with Library of Congress Subject Headings or Sears List of Subject Headings*. Ed. Oliver L. Kapsner, OSB. Collegeville MN: St. John's Abbey Press, 1963.

Catholic Truth Society of Oregon. *Catholic Sentinel*. Portland OR: Diocesan press, 1876-1980. See specific articles under title.

Chauvin, Paul, OSB. *L'Oblature dans l'Ordre de Saint-Benoit*. Paris: Ste-Marie, 1921.

Clark, Robert C.. *History of the Willamette Valley*. Chicago: University Press, 1927.

Clarke, S. A.. "The Oregon Central Railroad," *Oregon Historical Quarterly* (1915).

Conception Abbey (Immaculate Conception), Missouri, OSB. Archives. Correspondence files, as cited by E. Malone, 1875-1905.

______________. *Constitutionis & Sacrae Regulae declarationes Congregationis Helveto-Americanae OSB*. Conception MO: Abbey Press, 1901.

______________. *Statuta Congregationis Helveticae Ordinis S. Benedicti sub titulo Immaculatae Coneptionis B. M. V.*. Ed. Ignatius Staub, OSB. St. Benedict OR: Mt. Angel Abbey Press, 1932.

______________. *Declarations on the holy rule and constitutions of the Swiss-American Congregation, O.S.B.*. Conception MO: Abbey Press, 1938.

Congress of Abbots, Rome, 1967. *A Statement on Benedictine Life adopted by the Congress of Abbots held in Rome in September, 1967*. Trans. by the monks & nuns of the E.B.C. St. Benedict OR: Mt. Angel Abbey press, n.d. [1968].

Conrad, Frowin, abbot, OSB. *Tagebuch*. Unpublished diary to 1923, ms., Conception Abbey archives (*supra*), s.n..

Corning, Howard M.. *Dictionary of Oregon History*. Portland OR: Binfords & Mort, 1956.

Cowan, Ronald. "Dear, dear Abbey," *The Statesman Journal*, Salem OR (Aug. 15, 1976), sec. G.

______________. "Oh, what treasures it holds," *The Statesman Journal*, Salem OR (Aug. 15, 1976), sec. G.

Cross, Robert D.. "Origins of the Catholic Parochial Schools in America," *American Benedictine Review*, 16 (June, 1965), 194 ff..

Cummins, D.. *Catholics in the Early Platte Purchase and Nodaway County*. St. Joseph MO: for Conception Abbey, 1934.

Daly, Lourie & John. *Benedictine Monasticism: its formation and development through the 12th century*. New York: Sheed & Ward, 1965.

Dammertz, Vicktor, OSB. *Das Verfassungsrecht der benedicktinischen Monchskongregationem in Geschichte und Gegenwart*. Vol. 6: *Kirchengeschichte Quellen und Studien*. St. Ottilien: Verlag erzabtei, 1969.

Danzer, Beda, OSB. *Die benediktinerregel in der übersee; kurzer geschichte überblick über die ausbeitung des benediktinerordens und seiner zweige in den aussereuropäischen ländern*. St. Ottilien: Verlag der Erzabtei, 1929.

Davenport, T. W. "Mount Angel," *Shadows*, 5 no. 3 (1959), s.d. MAA typescript, excerpted from "Recollections of an Indian Agent" (1907).

David, Lucien, OSB. *Les grandes abbayes d'Occident*. Lille: Descleé, 1907.

Debuyst, Frédéric, OSB. "Benedictins pas Morts: La Bibliotheque de Mount Angel (Oregon)," trans. Vincent Ryan, "The Benedictines are not Dead: The Library of Mt. Angel," *Art d'Eglise*, 39 no. 154 (1971), 146-153

Deemer, Charles. "At Mt. Angel they want education where the action is," *The Oregonian Northwest Magazine* (March 15, 1970), 1-4.

Delaissé, L.M.J.; Marrow, James, & de Wit, John. *Illuminated Manuscripts: The James A. de Rothschild Collection at Waddeston Manor*. Fribourg: National Trust, 1977.

Desplanques, Marianus, OSB. *Spiritualité Bénédictine et liturgie Mission bénédictine*. Paris: Eds. Nouvelles, [1947].

Destrée, Bruno, OSB. *The Benedictines*. Trans. by the Benedictines of Princethorpe Priory. New York: Benziger Brothers, 1923.

Deutsch, Alcuin Heinrich, OSB. *Manual for Oblates of St. Benedict*. 3rd ed. Collegeville MN: St. John's Abbey Press, 1948.

Dieker, M. A.. "Mt. Angel College," *New Catholic Encyclopedia* (New York: McGraw Hill, 1967), X, 44-45.

Doppelfeld, Basilius, OSB. *Mönchtum und kirchlicher Heildienst; Enstehung und Entwicklung des nordamerikanischen Benediktinestums im 19. Jahrhundert*. Bd. 22, *Münster Schwarzach-Studien*. Münster: Vier-Türme Verlay, 1974.

Down, Robert H.. *A History of Silverton County*. Portland OR: Berncliff Press, 1926.

Dunkin, Paul S.. *How to Catalogue a Rare Book*. 2nd rev. ed. Chicago: ALA, 1973.

Duratschek, M. Claudia, OSB. *Crusading Along Sioux Trails*. St. Meinrad IN: Grail Press, 1947.

Durrer, R.. "Die Maler und Schreiberschule von Engelberg," *Anzeiger für schweizerische Altertumskunde*, 3 (1901).

Eschapasse, Maurice, OSB. *L'architecture bénédictine en Europe*. Paris: Editions de deux-mondes, 1963.

Eberle, Luke, OSB. *Account of my trip to Europe, Rome, etc.*. Unpublished ms., MAA typescript, n.d. Based on his *Tagebuch*, 1932.

______________. *Tagebuch*. Unpublished diary, MAA ms., n.d.

Einsiedeln Abbey, Switzerland, OSB. Archives. Correspondence files, as cited in the work of Malone, and MAA transcriptions by A. Zenner.

______________. *Directorium monasterii BVM Einsidlensis OSB*. Eremo: Typis Monasterii, n.d..

______________. *Millenium*. Einsiedeln: Abbey press, 1934.

______________. *Stiftsbibliothek Einsiedeln. Handschrift des schweizerischen Benediktinerblöstern, 8-18 Jahrhunderts*. Einsiedelm: n. p., 1971.

Eitel, Edward E.. *County Atlas of Oregon and Washington*. San Francisco: D. S. Stanley for Fireman Fund Insurance Co., [1894].

Eisenhart, Ruth C.. "Cataloguing of liturgies and other religious texts in the alphabetic catalogue," *ICCP [International Code of Catalaloging Principles] Report* (London: ICCP, 1963), 199-206.

Ellis, David. "The Oregon and California Land Grant," *Pacific Northwest Quarterly* (1948).

Engelberg Abbey, Switzerland, OSB. *Angelmontana: Blätter aus der Geschichte von Engelberg*. Jubilaumsgabe für Abt Leodegar II. Gossau: Engelberg Abbey, 1914.

______________. Archives. Correspondence files as cited by Malone, and in the transcriptions of A. Zenner, 1948-51. Selections from 552 letters (2,525 pages); microfilmed for MAA in 96 35 mm. rolls, s.n..

______________. *Benedictinische Lebensform: Satzungen der Schweiserischen Benediktinerkongregation*. Engelberg: Abbey press, [1970].

______________. *Catalogus codicum manu scriptorum qui asservantur in biblioteca monasterii O.S.B. Engelbergensis in Helvetia*. Ed. Benedikt Gottwald, OSB. Freiburg im Bresgau: Herde, 1891. Catalogs 914 mss..

______________. *Catalogus Religiosorum Monasteri de Monte Angelorum O.S.B. in Helvetia nec non Abbati de Neo-Monte Angelorum ac Prioratus Mount Angel per Monasterium Engelbergense in America Septentionali Fundatorum ac Sacerdoti Jubelaeum Reverendissimi DD*. Abatis Anselmi I. Sarnen: J. Müller, 1897.

Fabriel, Angelus, ESC. *The Christian Brothers in the U.S., 1848-1948: A Century of Catholic Education*. New York: Declan & McMullen Co., 1948.

Fagan, Beth. "Famed Architect to Arrive for Planning of Library at Mt. Angel Abbey," *Oregonian* (April 17, 1967), 21.

"Fall Construction Grows," *Mt. Angel Letter*, (Dec. 1968), 2-3.

Farmer, Judith A. and Karnes, Daniel B.. *An Historical Atlas of Early Oregon*, Portland OR: Oregon Historical Society, 1973.

Feldman, Basil, OSB. *Abt Anselm Villiger von Engelberg, Gedenkenblätter für de Freunde und Nöglinge der Stiftsschule*. Lucerne: Rober & Cie, 1901.

Feligonde, Jean de, OSB. *Pour une vie communautaire di clergé paroissal selon la spiritualité bénédictine: les Oblats de Saint-Benoit communautaires et paroissaux*. Paris: Eds. du Levain, [1953].

Fellner, P.. "Erzabt Bonifaz Wimmer, OSB, und die Anfänge der St. Benedicts Abtei, Atchison, Kansas," *Central Blatt und Social Justice*, 21 (May, 1928), 54 ff..

Fernsworth, Lawrence A.. *Mount Angel Parish and St. Benedict's Abbey. Foundation and Growth*. Unpublished typescript, MAA s.n., April 13, 1911.

Fitzgerald, John, OSB. *Union List of manuscript holdings in American Benedictine libraries*. Peru IL: St. Bede College Library, 1958. Supplement, for the American Benedictine Academy Library Science section; surveys 21 repositories, but not Mt. Angel.

Flanagan, James C.. "Abbey's New Library Can Help Heal World," *Capital Journal*, Salem OR (May 30, 1970), 1.

______________. "Mt. Angel Abbey Plans 3-Day Celebration," *Capital Journal*, Salem OR (Dec. 25, 1969), 1.

Frank, Barbara. *Das Erfurter Peterkloster im 15. Jahrhundert; Studien zur Geschichte der Klosterreform und der Bursfelder Union*. Göttingen: Vanderhoech & Ruprecht, 1973.

Frank, Karl S.. *Grundzüge der Geschichte des christlichen Mönchstums*. Darmstadt: Wissenschaftliche Buchgesellschaft, 1975.

Fuerst, A., OSB. "Benedictines, Swiss-American," *New Catholic Encyclopedia* (New York: McGraw-Hill, 1967), II, 301-2.

Fuller, George. *A History of the Pacific Northwest*. New York, 1931.

Ganoe, John. "The... Oregon and California Railroad," *Oregon Historical Quarterly* (1924).

Gaskell, Philip. *A New Introduction to Bibliography*. New York: Oxford University Press, 1972. Corrected repr., Oxford: Clarendon Press, 1974.

Gedert, C., OSB. *The Swiss-American Congregation of Benedictines and Its Contribution to the American Catholic Church*. Cincinnati OH: n.p., 1956.

Germania monastica. Klosterverzeichniz deutschen Benedicktiner und Cisterzienser. Augsburg: Verlag Winfried-Werk in Kommission, 1967.

Gill, J. K., Co.. *Map of Oregon*. Portland OR: J.K. Gill Co., 1878.

Gottwald, Benedikt, OSB. *Album Engelbergense seu Catalogus Religiosorum*. Lucerne, n.p., 1882. See Engelberg Abbey as corporate entry for other works.

Gruijs, Albert and Hollager, Per. "A Plan for computer assisted codicography of medieval manuscripts," *Quarendo*, 11 (1981), 94-127.

Guilmard, Jean. *Les oblats seculiers dans la famille de saint Benoit*. Sable: Solesmes, 1975.

Gravelle, Kim. "Mt. Angel Abbey Holds Rare Treasures," *Capital Journal* (Feb. 20, 1965), 5.

Güterbock, Ferdinand, OSB. *Engelbergs Gründung und erste Blüte, 1120-1223*. Zurich: n.p., 1948.

Gutheim, Frederick. "Master of World Architecture," *Architectual Forum*, 115 (1960).

Hartmann, Placidus, OSB. *Engelberg: Land und Leute*. Engelberg: Abbey Press, 1946.

Heer, Gallus, OSB. "Engelberg," ed. R. Aubert & E. van Cairvinberg, *Dictionnaire d'Histoire et de Geographie Ecclésiastique* (Paris: Letouzée et Ané, 1963), XV, 462-66.

Hemmen, Alcuin. "The Post-Vatican II Thrust of American Benedictines," *American Bendictine Review*, 24 no. 4 (1976), 379-99.

Hemmerle, Josef, OSB. *Die Benediktinerklöster in Bayern*. Munich: Verlag Bayerische Heimstforschung, 1951.

Henggeler, Rudolf, OSB. *Monasticon-benedictinum Helvetiae*. Zug: Eberhard Kalt-Zehnder, 1929.

Hess, Ignaz, OSB. *Anhang zur Geschichte der Klosterschule, Engelberg*. Lucerne: Buchdruckerei Raeber & Cie, 1905.

Heutger, Nicolaur C., OSB. *Bursfelde und seine Reformklöster*. Hildesheim: A. Lax, 1975.

Highsmith, Richard Morgan. *Altar of Oregon: Agriculture*. Corvallis OR: Agricu;ture Experiment Station, Oregon St. College [University], 1958.

_______________. *Altar of the Pacific Northwest*. Robert Bard, cart. Corvallis OR: Oregon State University, 1973.

Hilpisch, Stephanus, OSB. *Benedictinism through the Centuries*. Trans. Leonard J. Doyle. Collegeville MN: St. John's Abbey Press, 1958. Based on: *Das Benediktinertum im Wandell der Zeiten*. St. Ottilien: Verlag der Abtei, 1950.

_____________. *History of Benedictine Nuns*. Trans. M. Joanne Muggli, OSB. Collegeville MN: St. John's Abbey Press, 1958.

Hodes, M. Ursula, OSB. *History of Mt. Angel*. Unpublished typpescript, MAA, n.d..

Hogan, Gorman. "Mt. Angel Abbey," *Catholic Sentinel* (March 12, 19, 26, 1976), pt. 1, 14-15; pt. 2, 14-15; pt. 3, 8. Collected in MAA file "Mt. Angel Abbey-History-Newspaper/Magazine Materials" ff. 1-10.

___________. "Hidden Treasure Shines," *Catholic Sentinel*, 108 (Jan. 7, 1977), 1, 14.

Hogan, John Joseph, bp. of St. Joseph. *Fifty Years Ago—A Memoir*. Kansas City MO: Franklin Hudson Pub. Co., 1907.

______________. *On the Mission in Missouri*. Kansas City MO: Hellmann Pub. Co., 1892.

Holman, F. V.. *Dr. John McLaughlin, the Father of Oregon*. Cleveland OH: Case-Western Reserve University press, 1907.

Hostie, Raymond, OSB. *Vie et mort des ordres religieux: Approches psycho-sociologiques*. Paris: Desclée de Brouwer, 1972.

Hunkeler, Leodegar, OSB. *It Began with Benedict: The Benedictines, their background, founder, history, life, contributions to church and world.* Trans. Luke Eberle, OSB. St. Benedict OR: Mt. Angel Abbey Press, 1978. Based on: *Vom Mönchtum des heiligen Benedikt.* Basel: Hess Verlag, 1947.

Independent Research Libraries Association (IRLA). Committee on Standards. *Proposals for Establishing Standards for the Cataloging of Rare Books and Specialized Research Materials in Machine-readable Form.* Marcus A. McCorison, chm.. Worcester MA: IRLA, 1979.

International Federation of Library Associations (IFLA). Committee on Cataloging. *List of Uniform Titles for Liturgical Works of the Latin Rites of the Catholic Church.* London: IFLA, 1975.

Janssen, Werner, producer. *They Heard the Angels Sing.* Documentary film. Holywood CA: Clune Studios, [1954].

"Jewell Set on a Hill," *Oregon Statesman*, Salem OR (Mar. 1, 1970), 2.

Jackson, Sidney L.. *Libraries and Librarianship in the West.* New York: McGraw-Hill, 1974.

Johnson, Elmer D. & Harris, Michael H.. *History of Libraries in the Western World.* 3rd rev. ed. Metuchen NJ: Scarecrow Press, 1976.

Kapsner, Oliver Leonard, OSB. *A Benedictine Bibliography.* Collegeville MN: St. John's Abbey Press, 2nd ed., 1962.

______________. *A Manual of Cataloging Practice for Catholic Author and Title Entries; being Supplementary Aids to the ALA and Vatican Library Cataloging Rules.* Washington DC: Catholic University of America, 1953. See also his *Catholic Subject Headings* under Catholic Lib. Assn..

______________. *Catholic religious orders; listing conventional and full names in English, foreign languages, and Latin; also abbreviations....* 2nd ed. Collegeville MN: St. John's Abbey Press, 1957.

Kleber, Albert, OSB. *History of St. Meinrad Archabbey, 1854-1954.* St. Meinrad IN: Abbey Press, 1954.

Knowles, David, OSB. *The Benedictines.* New York:Macmillan Co., 1930.

______________. *Great Historical Enterprises.* London: Nelson, 1963.

Kominiak, Benedict, OSB. *Loci ubi Deus quaeritur: die Benediktinerabteien auf der hanzen Welt: The Benedictine Abbeys of the Entire World.* St. Ottilien: EOS, 1981.

Krebs, Engelbert, OSB. *Un die erde, eine pilgerfahrt.* Paderhorn: Bonifacius druckerei, 1928.

Lama, Karl von. *Bibliotheque des ecrevains de la Congrégation de Saint-Maur, ordre de Saint-Benedict en France.* Munich: C. de Lama, 1882.

Lartigus, Pius, OSB. *Benedictine Monastic Literature; A Selected, Evaluated, and Annotated Bibliography.* Unpublished thesis, Catholic University of America, 1956.

Lavender, David. *Land of Giants. The Drive to the Pacific Northwest, 1750-1950.* New York: Doubleday Co., Inc., 1958.

Leclercq, Henri, OSB. *L'ordre bénédictin.* Paris: Rieder, 1930.

Leclercq, Jean, OSB. *The Love of Learning and the Desire for God: A Study of Monastic Culture.* New York: Fordham University Press, 1974, repr., 1977.

Lehmann, Paul. *Mittelalterliche Bibliothekskataloge Deutschlands und der Schweiz.* Munich: Ver., 1918.

"Library Gets Motto," *Catholic Centinel*, 101 (June 5, 1970), 9.

Library of Congress. *Bibliographic Description of Rare Books.* Washington D.C.: L.C. Office for Descriptive Cataloging, 1980.

"Literary Treasures," *Mt. Angel Letter*, 28 (Dec. 1976), 2-3.

Lockley, Frederick. "Mt. Angel is a bit of the old world set down in the new," *Daily Journal* (Oct. 1, 1931), 1. *L'opera di Alvar Aalto.* Milan: Ed. di Communita, 1965.

Luetkemeyer, A. J., OSB. "Conception Abbey," *New Catholic Encyclopedia* (New York: McGraw Hill, 1967), IV, 108.

Lynn, Jeannette Murphy. *An Alternative Classification for Catholic Books: ecclesiastical literature, theology, canon law, church history.* 2nd ed., rev. Gilbert C. Peterson, SJ. Washiongton, DC: Catholic University of America, 1954. Supplement by Thomas G. Pater, 1965.

Malone, Edward Estrans, OSB. "A Long Lost Letter of Boniface Wimmer," *American Benedictine Historical Review*, 20 no. 3 (1969), 309-320.

______________. *Conception: A History of Conception Colony, 1858-1958; Conception Abbey, 1873-1973; New Engelberg College, Conception College, and the Immaculate Conception Seminary, 1886-1979*. Omaha NE: Interstate Pub. Co., 1971.

Maria Laach Abbey, Switzerland, OSB. *Benediktinerisches klosterleben in Deutschland, geschichte und gegenwart*. Berlin: Sankt Augustinus verlag, [1929].

Maria Rickenbach Abbey, Switzerland, OSB. *Hundert Jahre Benedicktinerinner kloster der ewigen Anbetung, Maria Rickenbach*. Stans: Von Matt & Cie., 1956.

Mathaiser, D., OSB. "Bonifaz Wimmer und König Ludwig I von Bayerns," *Jahrbuchfolge des Priester-Missionsbundes im Bayern*, (Munich, 1937).

Mayer, Hieronymous, OSB. *Das Benediktinerstift Engelberg*. Lucerne, 1891.

Maynard, Theodore. *St. Benedict and His Monks*. New York: P.J. Kennedy, 1954.

McArthur, Lewis Ankeny. *Oregon geographic names*. 4th ed. Portland OR: Oregon Historical SOciety, 1976.

McCrank, Lawrence J.. *Automating the Archives: Issues and Problems in Computer Applications*. White Plains, N.Y.: KIPI & ASIS, 1981.

______________. "Intellectual Access to Diplomatic, Codicological and Bibliographical Resources: A Review Essay and Case Study," forthcoming (1983).

______________. "Cost-effective Computer-assisted Rare Book Cataloging," forthcoming (1983).

______________. "The Manuscript and Rare Book Collection of Mt. Angel Abbey," *PNLA Quarterly*, 40 no. 3 (1976), 3-8.

______________ and C. David Batty. "Cataloging with FAMULUS: The Manuscripts and Rare Book Collection at Mt. Angel Abbey," *Computers and Humanities*, 12 (1978), 215-222.

McQuade, Walter. "A Man Standing in the Center [i.e. Aalto]," *The Forum*, (Jan/Feb. 1967), 109-112.

______________. "A Great Architect's Enduring Masterpieces," *Fortune*, 93 (Mar. 1976), 121-127.

Meagher, Fritz. "You Might Not Have Suspected It, but These Monks are Really With It," *Catholic Sentinel* (Jan. 26, 1968), 12-13.

Metkser, Charles Frederick, & Co.. *Metsker's Atlas of MArian Co., Oregon*. Tacoma WA/Metsker's Map Co., 1971.

______________. *Metsker's Marion Co. Atlans. State of Oregon*. Tacoma WA; Metsker's Map Co., 1929.

______________. *Metsker's State of Oregon Atlas*. Portland OR & Tacoma WA: Metsker's Map Co., 1932.

Miller, W. C.. "From Viipuri to Mount Angel: The Evolution of the Library in the work of Alvar Aalto," *Architectural Assn. Quarterly*, 10 (1978), 30-41.

Mizera, Peter F.. *Czech Benedictines in America, 1877-1961*. Lisle IL: Center for Slav Culture, St. Procopius College, [1970].

"Monastery Life," *Oregonian*, Portland OR (May 5, 1952), 2-4.

Moore, Fuller. *Perceptual Distortion of Space in Two Dimension Architectual Media*. Eugene OR: University of Oregon School of Architecture, 1971. US Office of Scholarly Research study of the Mt. Angel Abbey Library.

Moser, Werner M.. *Alvar Aalto, Symposia. Malerie, Architektur, Skulptur*. Basel: Ed. Birkhauser, 1970.

"Mount Angel Dedicates New Library," *Catholic Sentinel*, 101 (June 5, 1970), 9.

Mount Angel Abbey, St. Benedict OR, OSB. *The Benedictines Monks of Mount Angel*. St. Benedict OR: Mt. Angel Abbey Press, [1954].

______________. *Declarations on the Holy Rule and Constitutions of the Swiss-American Congregation of the Order of St. Benedict*. St. Benedict OR: Mt. Angel Abbey Press, 1955.

______________. *Golden Jubilee of Mount Angel Seminary, 1889-1939*. Text by Fr. Maurus Snyder, OSB. St. Benedict OR: Mt. Angel Abbey Press, 1939.

______________. *Monastic Life at Mount Angel*. Mt. Angel OR: Benedictine Press, [1933].

______________. *Mt. Angel Abbey*. St. Benedict OR: Mt. Angel Abbey Press, n.d.

______________. *Mt. Angel Abbey*. Ed. Gregory Duerr, OSB. Mt. Angel OR: Benedictine Press, 1973.

______________. *Mt. Angel ABbey*. St. Benedict OR: Abbey Press, [1981].

______________. *Mt. Angel Abbey, 1882-1982*. St. Benedict OR: Abbey Press, 1982.

______________. *Mount Angel Letter*. St. Benedict OR: Abbey Press, 1958-81. Vols. 1-23. See individual articles under author and title entries.

______________. *Mount Angel News*. St. Benedict OR: Abbey Press, 1888-90.

______________. *The New Order of Mass.... Institutio generalis missali romani translated by the monks of Mt. Angel Abbey*. Ed. Bruno Becker, OSB. Collegeville MN: St. John's Abbey Press, 1970.

______________. *Pacific Star*. St. Benedict OR: Mt. Angel Abbey Press, 1920-45.

______________. *St. Joseph's Blatt*. St. Benedict OR: Mt. Angel Abbey Press, 1937-53.

______________. *St. Joseph Magazine*. St. Benedict OR: Mt. Angel Abbey Press, 1935-53.

______________. *Silver Jubilee, 1887-1912*. [St. Benedict OR: Mt. Angel Abbey Press, 1912].

______________. *Souvenir of dedication, St. Mary's Church, Mt. Angel, Or., Sunday, June 30th, 1912*. Mt. Angel OR: Abbey Press, [1912].

______________. *TAP-A-LAM-A-HO*. [St. Benedict OR: Mt. Angel Abbey Press, 1922, 1941, 1942.

______________. *This is Mount Angel*. [St. Benedict OR]: Abbey Press, [195-].

______________. Archives. Mt. Angel College Alumnae Assn. records, 1894-96.

______________. Archives. Correspondence files, esp. of Prior Jerome Wespe, to 1950.

______________. Archives. College & Seminary records series, 1897-99, 1908-11, 1916-18, 1923-24, 1935-36, 1940-42, 1947, 1969-70.

______________. Archives. College. Administrative Council meeting minutes, 1980-81.

______________. Archives. Farm account series, 1922-30.

______________. Archives. History of Abbey Lands, binder IV, 1882-89.

______________. Archives. Index to Archive Contents, Vols. XI-XII [1954].

______________. Archives. Indian mission materials from Vancouver Island, pre-1930.

______________. Archives. Library shelf lists and inventories, 1933-54.

______________. Archives. Memoirs, journals, and diaries. See under the author entry, esp. those of Bachofen, Brabant, Eberle, etc. pre-1945.

______________. Archives. Reminiscences, 1950-55. Transcripts from interviews with Maurus Snyder, Jerome Wespe, Bernard Murphy, Martin Pollard, and Sister Agnes Butsch. Cited by author entries in notes.

______________. Archives. Transcripts, extracts, etc., esp. those compiled by Ambrose Zenner from Engelberg, 1948-51.

______________. Archives. Photographic files (Abbey and Abbey library archives, 1890-1980.

______________. College. *Mt. ANgel College*. St. Benedict OR: Abbey Press, [1926?].

______________. College. *Prospectus of Mt. Angel College*. Portland OR: Knox & Dore, 1887.

______________. Library. *A Guide to the Mt. Angel Abbey Library*. St. Benedict OR: Abbey Press, 1970.

______________. Library archives. Librarian administrative files, 1950-75.

______________. Library archives. Publications, 1898-1980.

______________. Seminary. *Mount Angel Seminary, 1889-1964*. Text by Fr. Blaise Turck, OSB. St. Benedict OR: Abbey Press, 1964.

______________. Seminary. *Mount Angel Seminary: Annual Report, 1976-77*. St. Benedict OR: Abbey Press, 1978.

______________. Seminary. *Newsletter*. St. Benedict OR: Abbey Press, 1970-81.

______________. Seminary. *Profiles & Catalog, 1978-80*. Ed. Jeremy Driscoll, OSB. St. Benedict OR; Abbey Press, 1978.

______________. Seminary. *Profiles & Catalog, 1980-83*. Ed. Gregory Duerr, OSB. St. Benedict OR: Abbey Press, 1980.

Mount Angel (city) OR. Incorporation of the City of Mt. Angel, 1905. MAA, A2-2-I env. 66.

Moosmüller, Oswald, OSB. *St. Vincenz in Pennsylvanien*. New York: F. Puslet Co., 1873.

Morton, Adelhelm, OSB. "The Fire of 1892," *Mt. Angel Letter*, [1967], 2.

Müller, Joannes, OSB. *Atlas OSB: Benedictines throughout the World*. n.d.

Müller, Theodore A.. *Liturgy and ritual: proposal for a revision of cataloguing rules (Latin and Orthodox liturgical books)*. Typescript. Washington DC: Library of Congress, 1965.

Murphy, Joseph, OSB. *Tenacious monks: the Oklahoma Benedictines, 1875-1975. Indian missionaries, Catholic founders, educations, agriculturalists*. Shawnee OK: Benedictine Press, 1974.

Necrologium Congregationis Americano-Cassinensis OSB, 1846-1946. Collegeville, MN: St. Johns Abbey press, 1948.

New York Times, Inc.. "Testing Ground for Great Architecture," *Focus on Finland* in *New York Times*, sect. 2 (March 5, 1964), 10.

Niguille, Jeanne. "Les bénédictines d'Engelberg," *Zeitschrift für Schweizerisch Kirchengeschichte*, 10 (19916).

Odermatt, Adelhelm, OSB. *Correspondence to Engelberg*. Extracts and Transcriptions, 1879-83. MAA typscript, s.n.

Ochs, Michael. *The Founding of Mount Angel Abbey*. Unpublished seminar paper, Portland State University, 1978. MAA, typescript, s.n.

Oer, Sebastian von, OSB. *Ora et labora; leben und sterben von laienbrüdern der Beuroner Benediktinerkongregation*. Beuron: Beuroner kunstschule, 1919.

Oetgen, Jerome. "Oswald Moosmuller: Monk and Missionary," *American Benedictine Review*, 27 (1976), 1-35.

O'Gorman, J. F.. *The Architecture of the Monastic Library in Italy, 1300-1600*. New York, 1972.

O'Hara, Edwin V.. *Pioneer Catholic History in Oregon*. Paterson, NY: St. Anthony Press, 1939.

Ouy, Gilbert. "Comment render les manuscripts médievaux accessibles aux chercheurs?" *Codicologica 4: Essais methodologiques*, ed. A. Gruijs and J.P. Gumbert (Leiden, 1978), 9-58.

Parshall, Peter W. *Illuminated Manuscripts from Portland Area Collections*. Portland OR: Portland Art Museum, 1978. Exhibit catalogue featuring 6 Mt. Angel mss..

Plas, John, OSB. *Memoirs from Holy Rosary Parish, Crooked Finger OR*. MAA, typescript, s.n., s.d.

Polag, Athanasius, abbot, OSB. Correspondence to Lawrence McCrank, Dec. 29, 1975. MAA, s.n.

Pollard, Martin, OSB. *Abbey History Materials*, to 1945. MAA, B-II-13, env. 7-9.

______________. "Mt. Angel Abbey Chronicle of 100 Years," *Mt. Angel Letter*, 33 (1981), cont'd..

______________. *Recollections: Purchase of the Aachen Books*. MAA, typescript, Sept. 24, 1975.

"Post-war reconstruction," *Magazine of Art*, 33 (June 1940), 363 ff.(on Alvar Aalto).

Preston, R. N.. *Historical Maps of Oregon*. Corvallis OR: Western Guide Pub., 1972.

Reasoner, Barnabus, OSB. *The Library*, report of Dec. 17, 1952. MAA, typsecript, s.n. 24 p.

______________. *The Library*, undated report. MAA, typsecript, s.n. 13 p.

______________. *The Problem of the Library*. MAA, typescript, [1953?].

Rees, Daniel, *et al.*. *Consider your call: a theology of monastic life*. London: SPCK, 1978.

Reiner, Cynthia. "Music on high," *Capital Journal*. Salem OR (Dec. 22, 1977).

Rengli, Maria Beatrice, OSB. "From Rickenbach to Maryville: An Account of a Journey (1874)," trans. Sister M. Agnes Roth, OSB, *American Benedictine Review*, 27 no. 3 (1976), 247-269.

______________. *Von Rickenbach nach Maryville, Reise Berecht der Schwester Maria Beatrix Rengli*. Stans: Buchdruckeri von Caspar, 1875.

"Rev. Adelhelm Odermatt, OSB," *Bibliographic Record* (Chicago IL: Chapman Pub. Co., 1903), 429-31. Note MAA typescript copy append. to *memoirs*.

Rimmele, Leo R., OSB. *Collins Foundation OR, correspondence*. Library administrative files, 1975-76.

Ringholz, Odilo. *Die kulturarbeit des stiftes Einsiedeln: eine kulturhistorische studie*. New York: Benziger Bros., 1913.

Rippinger, Joel. "American and European Benedictine Monasticism," *American Benedictine Review*, 27 no. 1 (1976), 63-84.

Rothsteiner, P.. *History of the Archdiocese of St. Louis*. St. Louis: Blackwell, 1928.

"St. Benedict's Abbey is a Mass of Ruins!" *Mt. Angel Magazine* (Sept. 30, 1926), 4.

St. John's Abbey, Collegeville MN, OSB. *Manual for Oblates of St. Benedict*. Collegeville MN: Abbey Press, 5th ed., 1955.

______________. *Oblate Directory, 1950*. Collegeville MN: Abbey Press, 1950.

St. Meinrad's Archabbey, IN, OSB. *Directory for the Swiss-American Federation of the Americas of the Benedictine Confederation*. St. Meinrad, IN: Abbey press, 1977.

St. Vincent's Archabbey, Latrobe PA, OSB. *Manual for Benedictine Oblates*. Latrobe PA; St. Vincent's press, 4th ed., 1962.

Sanborn Map Co.. *Mt. Angel, Marion Co., OR, Nov. 1913*. New York: Sanborn Map Co., 1913. Corrected update, 1945. Fire insurance maps.

Sander, Louis A.. "The Benedictines in Oregon," *The Acolyte* (Aug. 24, 1929), 11-12.

Sanjian, Avedis K.. *Catalogue of Medieval Armenian Manuscripts in the U.S.*. No. 16, *Near Eastern Studies*. Berkeley CA: University of California, 1976.

Schenker, Lukas, OSB. *Das Benedicktinerkloster Beinevil im 12. und 13. Jahrhundert*. Solothurn: Gassman, 1973.

Scherer, Leodegar, abbot, OSb. *Tagebuch*. Engelberg archives. MAA, transcriptions of A. Zenner, for 1901-04 (Sept. 1949), 21 ff..

Schieber, Joachim, OSB. *Fr. James Power and the Reading Colony from Reading, Pennsylvannia, to Conception, Missouri*. Unpublished dissertation. Washington DC: Catholic University of America, 1953.

Schiess, T.. "Die ältesten Urkunden des Klosters Engelberg," *Zeitschrift für schweizerische Kirchengeschichte*, 25 (1941), 81-97, 234-269.

Schmeitzky, René, OSB. *Beiträge zur Wirtschafts und Verfassingsgeschichte des Klosters Engelberg in Unterwalden (von 1100 bis Angang 15. Jahrhundert)*. Stans, 1952.

Schmid, Mark J., OSB. "Interesting Facts about Manuscripts and Cradle Books," MAA, typescript (1939), 9 ff..

______________. "The Mt. Angel College Library-Museum," address to the Oregon State librarians, April 3, 1939. MAA, typescript, 5 pp.

Schmid, Placidus, OSB. *Die benediktiner in Conception Mo., und ihre missionsthätigkeit; eine festgabe auf die rückkehr des Hochwürdigsten abten Frowin von siner Europe-reise*. St. Louis MO: Amerika, 1885.

Schmitt, Edmund John Peter, OSB. *Bibliographia benedictina: oder Verzeichnis der Schriftsteller des Benedictiner-Ordens in den Vereignigten Staaten Nord-Amerika*. Brün: Benedicktiner Buchdruckerei, 1893.

Schmitz, Philibert, OSB. *Histoire de l'Ordre de saint-Benoit*. 2nd ed. Maredsous: Abbey press, 1948-56. 7 vols.

Schneider, Edouard, OSB. *Cellules et convents bénédictins*. Paris: P. Amiot, 1958.

Schumacher, Johann Josef Hubert. *Deutsche Klöster mit besonder Berücksichtigung des Benediktiner und Zisterciensordens*. Bonn: Verlag der Buchgemeinde, 1928.

Schwegler, Theodor, OSB. *Geschichte der Katholischen Kirche der Schweiz, von den Anfängen bis auf Gegenwart*. Schlieren-Zurich: Verlag. Neune Brüche A.G., 1935.

Shad, Johann Baptist. *Ein Mönchsleben des 18. Jahrhunderts*. Berlin: Widuking Verlag, 1942.

Shannon, James P.. *Catholic Colonization on the Western Frontier*. New Haven: Yale University Press, 1957.

Siebenmorgen, H.. "Die Beuroner Kunstschule," *Münster*, 30 (1977), 20-36.

Skinner, Constance. *Adventurers of Oregon*. New Haven: Yale University Press, 1921.

Slemenda, Steven. "Holocaust engulfs Mt. Angel Abbey,...half century ago," *Appeal Tribune*, Silverton OR (Sept. 23, 1976), 2.

Snyder, Maurus, OSB. "Comments and Corrections of Fr. Ambrose's Letters," MAA, typsecript [1951], 8 f..

______________. *Historical Notes* in his transcriptions and abstracts of documents, 1881-1904. MAA, typescript, s.n. [1951?], 12 f..

______________. *Memorable Dates in Connection with the Founding of St. Benedict's Abbey*. MAA, typsecript, s.n., n.d., 10 ff..

______________. *Reminiscences*. MAA, typescript, June 6, 1950, 2 ff.

Southern, Sir Richard. "A Benedictine Library in a Disordered World," *Downside Review* (1978), 163-177; MAA, typsecript, 21 pp. See also excerpts in *Mt. Angel Letter* (Dec. 1976).

Stegmann, Basil Augustine, OSB. *The Benedictine Lay Brother*. Collegeville MN: St. John's Abbey press, 1924.

Straumeyer, Idefonsus, OSB. *Annales mon. Angels-montani*. Engelberg archives, 8 ms. vols. nos. 221-8. MAA excerpts by A. Zenner.

Swiss-American Federation of Benedictines. *Declaration on the Holy Rule and Constitutions of the Swiss-American Congregation, OSB*. Conception MO: Abbey press, 1938.

______________. *Directory of the Swiss-American Federation of the Benedictine Congregation*. St. Meinrad IN: Abbey press, 1982. See pp. 149-161 for Mt. Angel.

Tanselle, G. Thomas. "Descriptive Bibliography and Library Cataloging," *Studies in Bibliography*, 30 (1977), 1-56.

Tauber, Maurice & Feinberg, Hilda. *Book Catalogs*. Metuchen NJ: Scarecrow Press, 1971.

Time, Inc.. "Prickly Individualist" (i.e., Aalto), *Time*, 74 (Oct. 5, 1959), 74-9.

Tschudy, Julius Franz, OSB. *Der heilige Benedikt und das benedictinische Mönchtum*. St. Ottilien: Eos-Verlag, 1979.

Turley, Gladys. "From Alps to Oregon," *Northwest Magazine*, (Feb. 28, 1954), 6-8.

U.S. Department of Interior. "Silverton Quadrangle," *Geological Survey*. Denver CO: Dept. of Interior, 1956, 1970.

______________. *State of Oregon*. New York: Julius Brun, 1889.

"Valuable Shipment of Books from Europe Arrive at Abbey," *Pacific Star*, (Jan. 15, 1933), 1-2.

Vatican city. Biblioteca Vaticana. *Norme per il catalogue degli stampati*. 3rd ed. Vatican: Bib. Apostolica Vaticana, 1951. Trans. from 2nd ed., W. E. Wright as *Vatican Library Cataloging Rules*.

Vaughan, Thomas & Ferriday, Virginia Guest, eds. "Alvar Alto in Oregon," research by Nadine Skov Finch, *Space, Style and Structure: Building in Northwest America* (Portland OR: Oregon Historical Society, 1974), 656-660.

Villard, Oswald, ed. *The Early History of Transportation in Oregon*. Eugene OR: University of Oregon, 1944.

Villiger, Anselm, abbot, OSB. *Tagebuch*. Engelberg archives, s.n. MAA, excerpts and transcriptions by A. Zenner, Sept. 1949. 94 f. Translations by Fr. Luke Eberle [1974].

______________. *Letters*. Engelberg archives, 1866-1901. Transcriptions by the Swiss-Benedictine sisters [1935].

Volk, Paul, OSB. *Urkunden zur Geschichte der Bursfelden Kongregation*. Bd. 20, *Kanonistiche Studien und Texte*. Bonn: L. Röhrscheid, 1951.

Walcher, Bernhard, OSB. *Beiträge zur Geschichte der bayerischen Abtwahlen mit besonders Berüchsictigung der Benediktinerklöster*. Vol. 5, *Studien und Mitteilungen zur Geschichte des Benediktiner-Ordens und seiner Zweige*. Munich: Kommissionsverlag R. Oldenbourg, 1930.

Weiss, Albert, OSB. *Das Koster Engelberg unter Abt. Barnabus Burki, 1505-1546*. Frieburg am Bresgau, 1956.

Weissenberger, Paul, OSB. *Das benediktinische Mönchtum im 19./20. Johrhundert (1800-1950)*. Beuron: Beuroner Kunstverlag, 1952.

Werhahn, H. M.. (Aachen city librarian). Correspondence to L.J. McCrank, Dec. 15, 1975. 3 f.

Westminster Abbey, BC, OSB. *The Benedictines*. New Westminster BC: Priory press, 1947. 13 p.

Wespe, Jerome J., OSB. *Reminiscences*. MAA, typescript no. 96, n.d., 5 f.

Wilson, J. William. "Manuscript Cataloging," *Tradition*, 12 (1956), 456-555.

Winther, Oscar O.. *The Old Oregon Country*. Stanford CA: Stanford University Press, 1950.

Ziegler, Walter, OSB. *Die Bursfelder Kongregation in der Reformationzeit, dargestellt an Hand der Generalkaptielsrenesse der Bursfelder Kongregation*. Vol. 29, *Beiträge zur Geschichte des alten Mönchtum und des Benediktinersordens*. Munich: Aschendorf, 1968.

Zenner, Ambrose, OSB. *Pages from Mt. Angel's Early History. Written from Material collected at Engelberg Abbey, 1948-51, including letters of Frs. Adelhelm and Nicholaus to Engelberg*. MAA, typescript, s.n., 1952. 32 ff.

Zerr, Bonaventure, abbot, OSB. *The Psalms, by the monks of Mt. Angel*. St. Benedict OR: Mt. Angel Abbey press, 1975.

Index